CHARLES II

CHARLES II
The Man and the Statesman

MAURICE ASHLEY

What you read, I would have it history, and
the best chosen histories, that so you might
compare the dead with the living; for the
same humours is now as was then, there is no
alteration but in names.

The Earl of Newcastle to
Charles, Prince of Wales, c. 1640

WEIDENFELD AND NICOLSON
London

ISBN 0 297 17938 1

Printed in Great Britain by Redwood Press Limited,
Trowbridge, Wiltshire

Dedicated to my friends
in the Loughborough University of Technology

Contents

Illustrations

I

The Prince 'Unboyed'

The future King Charles II of England was born on the morning of 29 May 1630* in St James's palace, London. 'You are the son of our love,' his father, King Charles I, was to write when he was a prisoner in the Isle of Wight and soon to be put on trial for his life. Indeed Charles's father and mother had been married for five years when this, their first child to survive the hazards of birth, arrived to seal their newly found and hardly won devotion. The mother, the French princess Henrietta Maria, daughter of King Henri IV and sister of King Louis XIII, had been fifteen when she was married for reasons of state. At first she had met with antagonism and humiliation in her husband's court. The King had not welcomed the large group of Roman Catholic priests and women she had brought with her from Paris to sustain her in her wedded life in accordance with the terms of the marriage treaty. There had been quarrels and jealousies and once the angry King had used violence against her. But after his favourite, the first Duke of Buckingham, had been assassinated, their mutual love was realized and Charles, Prince of Wales and Earl of Chester, was its first fruit.

That spring day the Londoners greeted the birth of the heir to the throne with the burning of bonfires and the booming of cannon. All eyes were turned upon the planet Venus which happened, with singular appropriateness as it proved, to be the

* During the seventeenth century there was a difference of ten days between the English method of dating (Old Style) and that used in most other European countries (New Style). Occasionally in referring to events that took place on the European mainland I have given both styles; but where I give only one style, it is the Old Style.

morning star visible in clear daylight. Baptism followed in St James's on 27 June. In September the Queen wrote to a woman friend in France: 'If my son knew how to talk, I think he would send you his compliments; he is so fat and so tall, that he is taken for a year old, and he is only four months; his teeth are already beginning to come: I will send you his portrait as soon as he is a little fairer, for at present he is so dark that I am ashamed of him.'[1] But he never grew much fairer. He was always swarthy, and when in exile he was commonly known as the Black Boy. After the promised portrait arrived in Paris, it had to be explained away. 'He is so ugly that I am ashamed of him, but his size and features supply the want of beauty. I wish you could see the cavalier, for he has no ordinary mien, he is so serious that I cannot help fancying him far wiser than myself.'[2] He was not to remain too serious, but he was always to be charming. As to his looks, he himself was to exclaim as a man: 'Odd's fish, I am an ugly fellow!'

Seventeenth-century princes led precocious lives. When Charles was seven, it was proposed that he should marry the daughter of the Holy Roman Emperor; at eight he was installed at Windsor castle as a Knight of the Garter. At the same age he was taken out of the hands of the women; the wealthy magnifico, William Cavendish, Earl of Newcastle, was appointed Groom of the Stole to the Prince and his sole Gentleman of the Bedchamber. 'Though he shall not have the name of Governor', it was explained that he was to fulfil that task.[3] Charles's tutor was Brian Duppa, Bishop of Chichester. Newcastle was created a Privy Councillor by a patent of 4 June 1638 and his three years' governorship, though it was reckoned 'a great honour and trust', is said to have cost him £40,000 out of his own pocket.[4] At the same time Charles was provided with his own household to which four gentlemen were named. He was set up in his own court at Richmond, and here he received most of his education.

Newcastle, himself a cultivated man, fond of poetry and music, held strong views about the education of the Prince. He thought that he should study things rather than words. He was to read history, but he should 'take heed of too much book'. Also he should show reverence at prayers by way of princely example, but remember 'the greatest clerks are not the wisest men'. He must be courteous and civil to all – 'railing, scorn and jeering is fitter for porters, watermen, and carmen, than for gentlemen'. He must beware the common touch, for what preserves kings more than ceremony? To women he could not be too civil, 'especially to great ones'. Finally, he was to shun flattery, remember that he was mortal, but avoid divine melancholy as in a Capuchin or anchorite. 'Temper yourself so as to be brave, noble and just.'[5] Brian Duppa also, it appears, was not of too pedagogic a frame of mind. 'He hath no pedantry in him . . .' Newcastle observed; he 'reads men as well as books; the purity of his wit doth not spoil the serenity of his judgment.'

In May 1641 Newcastle resigned his position as Charles's governor and retired to the country. The Prince was now placed under the care of William Seymour, Marquis of Hertford. Hertford had no reason to love the Stuarts. Thirty years earlier he had been imprisoned in the Tower of London for daring to marry Arabella Stuart, the cousin of King James I, and then forced into exile. Hertford was rich, respected and loyal, but 'in many respects he wanted the qualities which might have been wished to be in a person to be trusted in the education of a great and hopeful prince'.[6] For one thing 'he loved his book above all exercise' and he took 'no delight in an open and liberal conversation and could not discuss and argue in those points which he understood very well only for the trouble of contending'; and though he was familiar with books both in Latin and Greek, 'yet he was so wholly given up to a country life, where he lived in splendour, that he had an aversion and even unaptness to business'. So he was remarkably philosophical, if not indifferent, about his duties. He accepted the government of the Prince of Wales purely out of obedience to the King; 'though for the performance of the office of governor he never thought himself fit nor meddled with it'. It was scarcely surprising therefore that he held the office for under two years, though when he gave it up, it was not because he wanted to retire to his quiet country life and his books, but in order that he might raise an army for his King in the west of England.

Charles's third governor, Thomas Howard, Earl of Berkshire, was rather different from his two predecessors. Unlike them, he was neither very wealthy nor cultured and, far from being pressed into undertaking the office, he obtained it 'for no other reason but because he had a mind to it'. In 1643 he had been imprisoned in the Tower of London by order of Parliament but then released as 'a man that could do no harm anywhere'. Hyde thought him a fool – 'a man who bore the name of a gentleman, the most unfit for that province or any other that required any proportion of wisdom and understanding for the discharge of it'.[7] Yet he was Charles's governor the longest of the three, from 1643 until the Prince himself departed from England in 1646.

In his childhood Charles dwelt in an atmosphere of peace, culture and family happiness. It was not until 1639, when his father went to war against his Scottish subjects because they signed a national covenant rather than accept a prayer book or service book from England, that clouds appeared on the political horizon. After the disloyal demonstration of 1629, when Members of Parliament held the Speaker of the House of Commons down in his chair while they passed resolutions against the Government, no Parliament had been summoned by the King; and with the aid of an expanding customs revenue he had been able to carry on the duties of his administration. The Queen does not appear to have been a fussy mother, while the King was absorbed in his public affairs and his hobbies. The Prince had his own household and his own friends, including the two sons of the murdered Duke of Buckingham and his brother James, who was four and a half years his junior. The Countess of Dorset had looked after the domestic side of the estate and she does not appear to have been restricted by lack of funds: a warrant for the payment of over £3,000 to her survives from the year 1639 for goods delivered for the services of the royal children. When Charles was ten years old the Earl of Newcastle instructed him how to 'ride leaping horses and such as would overthrow others' and 'to manage them with the greatest skill and dexterity to the admiration of all that beheld him'.[8] On occasion Charles would play a game of butts (archery) with Newcastle, though for low stakes

4

and only as a pastime. Broadly the picture is one of a boy more absorbed in outdoor sports than in his books, and learning the ceremonies and politenesses of court life without being unduly bothered about their social significance. It was perhaps unfortunate for him that during the crucial stages of adolescence he was under the care of the foolish Earl of Berkshire. Evidently Berkshire was fussy and Hertford not fussy enough. Newcastle, on the other hand, was a nobleman of much superior quality. Devoted to the monarchy, the personal friend both of Charles's father and grandfather, he was a magnificent horseman as well as a patron of literature. For the remainder of his life he followed Charles's career attentively and when at last he became the effective King of England Newcastle wrote him a long letter of advice reminding him of the values of ceremony and order. Alone of Charles's governors Newcastle must have made a strong and lasting impression on the character of a growing boy.

Three stories indicate the Prince's lightness of humour. First, when he was eleven, he refused to take some medicine which he was given. His mother, at Newcastle's request, wrote to reprimand him. His reply was to advise Newcastle that he himself would improve his health by not relying on too much physic. Secondly, when he and Newcastle played at butts together and his governor had the better of him, he remarked 'What, my lord, have you invited me to play the rook [sharper] with me?' Lastly, when Charles was in Oxford during the civil war the Earl of Berkshire was once incited to 'hit him on his head with his staff' because he observed the Prince to be laughing during service time in church and exchanging pleasantries with the ladies seated near him.

Contemporaries frequently reported the Prince having 'fevers' during his extreme youth – no doubt the usual childish diseases. The remedies, as was customary in those days, were fearful. First, he was given purgatives; then he was forced to vomit and was obliged to drink chicken broth accompanied by rhubarb and senna. Only his natural vigour enabled him to survive periods of nausea and diarrhoea produced by a strict course of purging. No wonder he refused to take his medicine. Religious as well as remedial practices may well have proved distasteful to him. His father was a fervid Anglican – the first Stuart ruler to be brought up in the Church of England – while his Roman Catholic mother had been allowed to have her own chapels and priests. Henrietta Maria, who had specially defined rights over her children up to the age of thirteen by the terms of the secret marriage treaty, attempted to stimulate Charles's interest in the outlook of her own Church by organizing games for which she gave prizes of holy relics and crucifixes. The King soon put a stop to that. William Laud, the Archbishop of Canterbury and future martyr, had baptised Charles and it was to men like Laud that the King looked for his son's religious upbringing. It is reasonable to assume that the religious differences between his father and mother made a permanent impression on the mind of the young Prince. It was the ceremonies rather than the teachings of the Church that attracted him. Laud laid store on outward good taste in the practice of religion rather than upon theology. Small boys then accepted the outward trappings of religion and were not much concerned over doctrine. But Charles was taught by his father that religion was a bulwark of the monarchy and that uniformity in religion (except for his mother) was important.

Before the Marquis of Hertford became Charles's governor, the Prince undertook his first public act. On 3 November 1640 the Long Parliament, as it was to be called, met at Westminster and King Charles I, twice humiliatingly defeated by the Scots, was compelled to listen to expositions of grievances by the House of Commons which objected in particular to taxes collected by the monarch to pay for his wars. Members also feared a *coup d'état* by Charles's ablest Minister, Thomas Wentworth, Earl of Strafford, who accused the parliamentary leaders of treacherous dealings with the Scots. The Commons tried to impeach Strafford for treason. The Earl put up a successful defence before the House of Lords, claiming that he was only loyally and constitutionally serving his King. It was of no avail, for the extremist elements in the Commons pushed through a bill of attainder against him, exacted the agreement of the House of Lords, and threatened the King with dire consequences if he did not give his assent to it.

Strafford, possibly because he hoped that once the King yielded his own life would in fact be spared, pressed Charles I to accept the bill. The leaders of the Commons were aided in their pressure by the London mob. In the spring of 1641 angry crowds, partly of well-dressed people and partly rabble, surged shouting at the gates of Whitehall palace. On 10 May the King bowed to these menaces in order to save the Queen and her children from the threatening mobs. In spite of the permission which he had given the King to endorse the bill of attainder, the Earl of Strafford was astonished. 'Put not your trust in princes nor in the sons of men, for in them there is no salvation', he exclaimed. Charles I, ashamed of what he had done, sent his son Prince Charles to the House of Lords on Tuesday, 11 May, with a letter containing an appeal for mercy towards his servant, 'by suffering that unfortunate man to fulfil the natural course of his life in close imprisonment'. A pathetic postscript added, 'If he must die, it were charity to reprieve him till Saturday'. The Prince himself – not yet eleven – 'made the strongest representations'. But he was dismissed 'with scant civility' and the letter was ignored.[9]

Such was Charles' introduction to the politics of revolution. Just as his cousin, Louis XIV of France, a few years later was to encounter the Paris mob bursting into the palace of the Louvre, Charles saw the London rabble besieging Whitehall until his father gave way to Parliament's demand for the life of his principal Minister. After the execution of Strafford, Charles I accepted all Parliament's other claims except to control the militia. In August the King visited Scotland in the hope of persuading his late enemies to assist him in his struggle with his English subjects. The mission to Scotland was abortive, and when the King returned to London he was confronted with a Grand Remonstrance outlining all the grievances of the kingdom against him. The remonstrance was presented to him on 1 December. Just over a month later the King retorted by trying to arrest and impeach five leading members of the House of Commons for attempting to subvert the fundamental laws and to deprive the monarchy of its rightful powers. But the King had not enough soldiers to enforce his aims and the City of London sided with Parliament, hiding the accused members. The King had shot his last bolt. Before leaving the south with a view to raising an army in the north of England, the King saw off his Queen from Dover to Holland, where she was accompanying her daughter Mary, who was betrothed to Prince William of Orange; but Henrietta Maria went chiefly with the intention of raising money and acquiring help for her husband against his rebellious subjects. After the King returned to Greenwich palace, he ordered the Marquis of Hertford to bring the Prince of Wales from Hampton Court to meet him there. The House of Commons objected and ordered Hertford not to go, but he preferred to obey the King. From Greenwich Charles was taken to the palace of Theobalds, whence he accompanied his father on his journey northwards through the midlands, arriving at York in April 1642. In May Charles was appointed captain of a troop of horse, known as the Prince of Wales's Own. He was at Nottingham in August when the King set up his standard and thus gave the signal for the outbreak of the first civil war.

Charles, with his brother James, was to be present at the first big battle of the civil war, Edgehill, which was fought on 23 October. The two princes were not expected to take part in the fighting and were first placed in the charge of William Harvey, the scientist who discovered the circulation of the blood. Harvey, satisfied that his charges were safe at the rear of the battle, possibly in a field dressing station, took a book out of his pocket and became forgetful of his surroundings. But they were not safe. Sir William Balfour, with his Parliamentarian cavalry, overran the Royalist left wing and penetrated towards the rear. A struggle took place and the royal standard was seized and rescued. Not only the boys but the King himself were at the risk of being taken prisoners. They had only a hundred cavalrymen to protect them and the enemy came within musket shot. Prince Charles realized how near the enemy horse were. 'I fear them not!' he exclaimed, and drawing a pistol out of his holster and cocking it he resolved to charge them. But his horse was pulled away and he escaped with the assistance of a doctor and of one of the King's Gentlemen Pensioners armed with a pole-axe.[10] After this inconclusive battle the King set up his headquarters at Oxford before his nephew, Prince Rupert of the Rhine, attempted an assault on London. Charles with his governor, the Earl of Berkshire, remained behind in Oxford and he stayed close to his father for much of the remainder of the civil war.

Prince Charles was twelve and a half at the time of the battle of Edgehill. During much of 1643 he was with his father and became friendly with his cousin, Prince Rupert, who was eleven years his senior and the most capable Royalist general. While Prince Rupert was taking Lichfield in April of that year and thus clearing the way for the welcome return of Charles's mother from Holland via Yorkshire, the Parliamentarian army besieged Reading on the road between Oxford and London. The King failed to relieve Reading and the acting governor, Sir Richard Feilding, surrendered. As often happened in the war, Feilding's brother was fighting on the other side, and Sir Richard came under suspicion for treachery and was condemned to death by a court martial at Oxford. Rupert, convinced that Feilding had done nothing dishonourable, persuaded the young Charles to plead his cause. Feilding obtained a pardon from the King. Later in the year Charles was with his father when the King vainly tried to raise the siege of Gloucester.

At the end of June 1644 Charles was at the battle of Cropredy bridge in Oxfordshire and in July, after his mother had fled from Oxford to give birth to a daughter in safety, he accompanied his father on a western campaign to exact revenge for Prince Rupert's defeat at Marston Moor on 2 July. The King addressed a large gathering on Dartmoor, where he promised his audience that should he not live to reward them if they chose to follow him, 'I hope this young man, my son and your fellow soldier, will.'[11] Though few responded to the appeal, the King pursued the Parliamentarian commander-in-chief, the third Earl of Essex, into Cornwall and cut off his army at Lostwithiel near Bodmin. The Parliamentarian infantry and artillery surrendered, though Essex himself escaped by sea. The King, accompanied by Prince Charles, returned triumphantly towards Oxford, but first attempted to relieve a Royalist garrison at Donnington castle in Berkshire. So

Charles was also present at the second battle of Newbury, which was something of a victory for the Royalists as they successfully relieved Donnington and returned safely to Oxford.

Thus during much of 1643 and the whole of 1644 Prince Charles followed the flag of war and listened to the sound of the guns. It is unlikely that he received much by way of education in Oxford from his complacent governor. Indeed, as Newcastle advised him, he was learning from things rather than books. He was given his reward by his father, who commissioned him, early in 1645, when he was not yet fifteen, as his captain-general in the west. While King Charles I himself remained in Oxford, the Prince was to take nominal command of an associated army of Somerset, Devon, Cornwall, Dorset, Bristol and Exeter with headquarters at Bristol. He was to be captain-general under his father, but was given the successful and experienced officer, Lord Hopton, as his lieutenant-general. The Prince was accompanied to the west by an able council which included Sir Edward Hyde, the King's Chancellor of the Exchequer, to whose memoirs we owe a detailed account of events, Sir John Culpeper, the Master of the Rolls, Lord Capel, the Earl of Berkshire, the Archbishop of Armagh and the Bishop of Salisbury. It was said by Hyde that the intention was to 'unboy' the Prince by conferring upon him this independent command. But the main object of his appointment was to try to cool the jealousies of the various semi-independent Royalist commanders in the west of England. Though nominally he was the Prince's deputy, Hopton acted as chief of staff for the Prince's council and as civil governor of Bristol, but had little to do with the army itself. In February Hopton sent to Bristol to provide a house there for his youthful master. On 4 March the Prince left Oxford. He wrote from Bath on 8 March to Lord Goring announcing his impending arrival and desiring immediate information on military matters. Undoubtedly the Prince was put up to this by his council, for Goring, a fine soldier but a man of licentious habits, was ambitious for the chief command and jealous of serving as an inferior. Indeed he formed an alliance with Lord Digby, the King's Secretary of State, to diminish the influence of Lord Hopton and Prince Rupert.

Prince Rupert, in effect the Royalist commander-in-chief although his reputation had been damaged by his defeat at the battle of Marston Moor, understandably resented the creation of a separate command and a separate royal court in the west of England. 'I expect nothing but ill from the west', he wrote on 20 March. Certainly Charles found everything there in a state of utter confusion. When he arrived at Bristol he had to borrow £300 from Lord Hopton to pay for his immediate needs. There were three Parliamentarian strongholds in the west, at Lyme, Plymouth and Taunton. Lord Goring, holding a somewhat vague commission, was desultorily besieging Taunton, which had long been defended for Parliament by Colonel Robert Blake. Sir Richard Grenville was besieging Plymouth. Sir John Berkeley sat at Exeter with a small armed force in reserve. Meanwhile Sir William Waller, the capable Parliamentarian general in the west, who had been nicknamed William the Conqueror, was on the war-path in Wiltshire. The Prince's council tried to bring some order out of the chaos by suggesting that Grenville should concentrate on the siege of Taunton, while Goring carried out a cavalry sweep in Wiltshire, thus covering the siege. This was at least a policy, but it was hardly helped when Prince Rupert demanded of the King whether the Prince's council had any right to give orders to Goring. Goring took umbrage and retired to Bath to enjoy himself. Though in the second week of April Rupert himself visited Prince Charles in Bristol in an attempt to straighten out the difficulties, little military progress was achieved. A fortnight later Charles and his council moved south to Bridgwater in an effort to rally the Somerset militia to the Royalist cause.[12]

The Governor of Bridgwater was named Wyndham and his wife had formerly been the Prince's governess. At Bridgwater Charles showed 'an extraordinary kindness' towards this lady and was 'diverted by her folly and petulancy from applying himself to a serious consideration of business'. She was allowed to 'speak negligently and scornfully of the Council' and 'upon all occasions in the company and when the concourse of people was the greatest, would use great boldness towards him and sometimes in dancing would run the length of the room and kiss him'.[13] Thus wrote Hyde, although he scratched out the last fourteen words from his manuscript. Charles was just fifteen. Is it possible that on this occasion Mrs Wyndham taught him the facts of life? One might read this between the lines. At any rate the Prince's council was in a turmoil. Its members took care that Charles should 'make no longer residence in that garrison' and later the Prince was to receive a letter of reproof from his father.

Charles returned to Bristol to learn no good news from the siege of Taunton. Sir Richard Grenville was wounded in an attack and Sir John Berkeley was appointed by the Prince's council to take over the conduct of the siege. But towards the end of April Sir Thomas Fairfax at the head of Parliament's 'New Model Army' marched westwards and relieved Taunton on 11 May. This setback enhanced the position of Goring, who had not been involved, and had gone to Oxford and done a deal with Prince Rupert. The Prince's council protested when it learned that Goring was returning to the west with supreme powers. Had not the Prince been given the chief command? New orders from Oxford to the forces in the west, it asserted, tended to diminish the powers granted to the Prince in his original commission and it was thought that to place the command in the hands of Goring would be 'very injurious'. King Charles I, who adopted the policy of dividing and ruling in military matters, hastened to send assurances that he did not intend to reduce the Prince's authority and gave Charles leave to reside, by the advice of his council, wherever he might judge to be the most expedient, thus by implication smoothing away the reproof over Bridgwater.

But now the New Model Army, having relieved Taunton, returned to the midlands and King Charles I changed his mind again by putting Lord Hopton, Prince Charles's military adviser, in command of the western army 'under the Prince of Wales' and recalling Goring to his own aid. Hopton, a dedicated man and no intriguer, did as he was ordered, though he was aware that Prince Rupert still disliked the whole idea of a separate command. 'I think it is my duty in all respects to desire from the Prince of Wales express commission for what I shall take in hand', he averred.[14] Thus the fifteen-year-old boy was his shield from the enemies on his own side.

Events were moving to their climax in the civil war. While Fairfax had been relieving Taunton, the King had left Oxford and three weeks later, on the prompting of Prince Rupert, the city of Leicester was laid to waste. Abandoning the siege of Oxford, to which he had returned from the west, and summoning Oliver Cromwell to be his second in command, Fairfax brought the King and Rupert to battle near the village of Naseby in Northamptonshire and there on 14 June 1645 won the most decisive victory of the civil war. The King's main army, unhelped by Goring, was crushed. Only in the west of England and in Wales was any organized Royalist resistance left. On 23 June the King wrote to his son telling him that he must never yield to dishonourable conditions to save his father's life. Charles stayed in Bristol, while Goring, again returning to the west, was defeated by Fairfax at the battle of Langport. But Hopton was the stalwart; he sent a cheerful letter to the court saying that he was rallying his Cornishmen and would 'make Fairfax as weary of the West as Essex was last year'. Yet the Royalists were forced to abandon Bristol, which surrendered on 11 September. Five weeks before that the King himself had begun to despair and ordered his son to retire to France if he was in danger in the west. The Prince's court moved to Exeter where they kept the King's orders a secret from the general public, but had a ship ready at Falmouth in case of emergencies. Hopton and the group of able men on the Prince's council struggled on. They hoped on the one hand to repel the advance of the enemy farther into the west and at the same time to negotiate for an agreed peace with the victorious Parliament at Westminster. Might not Cornwall and Devon become an irreducible royal bastion and a counter in the negotiations? From Exeter a safe conduct was requested from Fairfax for Hopton and Culpeper to pay a visit to the King in Oxford and press on him their point of view, which was 'to stop the issue of blood'. The request was forwarded to Parliament, which ignored it, and on 29 September the King wrote to Culpeper positively ordering the Prince to be sent to France. The council at Exeter deferred carrying out these orders for reasons of morale. Prince Charles put Hopton in command of what Hyde (who never thought much of the soldiers) described as 'a dissolute, undisciplined, wicked, beaten army'.[15] Sir Richard Grenville refused to accept orders from Hopton and was imprisoned by the Prince's command at Launceston. Hopton himself advanced with such forces as he had gathered together and on 15 February 1646 confronted Fairfax at the battle of Torrington.

This was virtually the last contest of the first civil war. Vainly Charles sent instructions from Pendennis castle in Cornwall, to which he had withdrawn from Exeter by way of Tavistock and Launceston, to make a stand at Stratton. This was 'a futile flourish', says Hopton's biographer. By now the Prince's own person was in peril. There is good evidence that various plans were concocted to kidnap him at this time. The Royalists were determined that at all costs the heir to the throne should not fall into the power of Parliament. On Christmas Day 1645 the Prince had received a letter from his father telling him to transport himself if not to France then to Denmark or any other country except Scotland or Ireland. 'If I mistake not the present position of the west', the King had written, 'you ought not to defer your journey one hour.'[16] Those words were written in November, three months before the battle of Torrington. Yet to the very last the Prince's advisers were reluctant for him to leave the soil of England. But their duty was clear. The orders from the King had thrice been reiterated. At the beginning of March the final resolution was taken. Their ship, the *Phoenix*, waited at Land's End. There the Prince embarked not for abroad but for the Scilly Islands at ten o'clock at night on Monday, 2 March 1646 and arrived at St Mary's on 4 March. On the journey the seamen pillaged the refugees; and when the royal party arrived they were destitute even of clothes, meat and fuel.

What lessons did Charles learn from his experiences in the west of England? In adolescence he had been forced to fend for himself. His mother had left England; his father was absorbed with his problems at Oxford and Charles was never to see him again. Though the Prince had capable and devoted counsellors, he could

see that it was in his name they were taking decisions. He attended
the meetings of his council and listened to what was being said.
Undoubtedly he came to play his own part there and to recognize
the genuineness of his own responsibilities. Secondly, he must
have become increasingly conscious of his own importance in
the scheme of things. His behaviour on the battlefield of Edgehill
testified that he was no physical coward, but he was not afterwards allowed to take any part in the fighting, even at Torrington
where the last Royalist stand was made. His father's letters to him
stressed the value of the safety of his own person, emphasizing
that the preservation of the Stuart dynasty depended on his
survival.

Charles's loyalty to his father was never in question. A sense of
family solidarity was taught to him by his nearest counsellors, and
this was to be fundamental to his character in the years to come.
But if he showed loyalty to others, it was not always given to
him. Hyde once exclaimed 'well, you generals are a strange kind
of people!'17 – and so they were with their personal vanities, local
concerns, and lack of public spirit. It seems that it was Prince
Charles himself who in the end decided to give the order for the
arrest of Sir Richard Grenville when he pointedly declined to
obey Lord Hopton; earlier Charles had witnessed Goring's blatant
refusal to accept his own orders as generalissimo. The Prince may
well have learned at this crucial stage in his youth that he dared
not trust any man, that it would become necessary for him to
make up his own mind and even to play off his servants one
against the other. Possibly Charles's attempt when in Exeter to
initiate peace negotiations with Parliament so as to save his father
from overwhelming defeat was his own determination: certainly
Hyde and other counsellors were opposed to the idea. Charles
had perceived his father's vacillations and hesitations both in
politics and in war. In later years both his mother and his brother
James were to tell him that his father had met his fate because he
failed to act strongly and preferred intrigue to resolution.

At the same time Charles was a fairly normal boy. Living in
time of war, seeing frustration on every side, watching the
struggles for personal power, and observing the constant need

for improvisation, it seemed necessary to take life as he found it and to preserve a sense of fun. His behaviour at Bridgwater disclosed how he sought some relief from his responsibilities when the opportunity presented itself. The very atmosphere offered temptation. In the west many of the Royalists, such as Goring, fiddled while Rome burned: 'the Cavaliers', it was said at the time, 'have the vices of men – the love of wine and women; but the Roundheads have the vices of devils – hypocrisy and spiritual pride.'[18] The incessant company of serious and sometimes censorious counsellors must often have become tedious. Hyde and Hopton were worthy men, whom Charles had reason to respect, but he could observe how the Gorings and Digbys got a lot more pleasure out of their adventurous existence. Though Charles saw little of him in the west, he must have leant on Prince Rupert who, despite his dedication to the profession of arms, was a connoisseur of the arts and himself a painter and scientific experimenter; his daring on the field of battle and strong personality could not but have influenced the Prince his cousin. Hyde Charles respected; Rupert he admired; Goring he may have envied. These were the men among whom he spent his youth. In the west he had indeed been 'unboyed', and as he now left England he was already in the process of becoming a man.

2

The Second Civil War

Life in the Isles of Scilly during the early spring of 1646 proved a disappointment to Prince Charles and his court. The gales and rain depressed their spirits; 'truly,' wrote one who was there, 'we begged our daily bread of God, for we thought every meal our last.'[1] Lord Culpeper managed to send a message to Charles's mother asking for provisions from France, but the exiles were immediately dependent on two days' supplies from Cornwall plus what could be scrounged on the spot. The inhabitants of the islands showed no enthusiasm for the sudden descent made upon them; and the military situation was precarious. General Fairfax evidently thought that he had the Prince cornered, for he forwarded to him a letter from Parliament inviting him to come to London 'to reside in such a place and have such attendants and counsellors ... as should be approved by both Houses'.[2] To reinforce this invitation a Parliamentarian fleet, consisting reputedly of twenty-seven or twenty-eight ships, surrounded the island on Sunday, 13 April and it must have seemed as if Charles would soon, like his father, become a prisoner. However the ships were dispersed by a tempest; but the incident made plain the defensive weakness of St Mary's. A meeting of the Prince's council was promptly held at which, to the general surprise, Charles produced a letter written to him by his father after the battle of Naseby commanding him under no circumstances to put his own life at risk. After that it was at once agreed that the Scillies must be evacuated (only the Earl of Berkshire dissented), and on 16 April the royal party moved on to the isle of Jersey where a prosperous breeze enabled them to land the following day.

Jersey proved altogether more agreeable and satisfactory to the exiles than the Scillies had been. Here Charles was welcomed by the governor, Sir George Carteret, 'a man formerly born a sea-boy and born in that island' who, according to Lady Fanshawe, a member of the Prince's entourage, 'endeavoured with all his power to entertain his Highness and court with all the plenty and kindness possible, both which the island afforded, and which was wanting he sent for out of France'.[3] The whole place consisted of grass except for some small parcels of land where corn was grown. The chief employment of the islanders, who were a cheerful and good-natured people, was knitting. The Prince was lodged in Elizabeth castle and on the Sunday after his arrival he gave immense delight by attending the church in St Helier, the capital of the island. Sir Edward Hyde considered it was a 'most pleasant island and truly, I think, the strongest in the world'.[4] There seemed no reason why the Prince's stay should not be prolonged indefinitely or at any rate until information about the situation in England, Scotland and Ireland should determine the next move.

The position was soon clarified. A letter was received from King Charles I in Oxford, written under the impression that his eldest son had already joined his mother in France, and exhorting him to be 'totally directed' by her as well as by his council. Meanwhile Culpeper had gone to St Germain, seen the Queen, and brought back a message from her which appeared to express her satisfaction with Charles's presence in Jersey. It was now decided that Culpeper, accompanied by Lord Capel, should go back from Jersey to tell her that they believed the island defensible and did not think it would be wise for Charles himself to leave it and put himself in the hands of the French. Surely, it was suggested, he should remain in an English dominion from which, in any case, he could easily remove himself to France if any danger arose. Oxford had not yet fallen to the rebels and the Royalist Marquis of Montrose had been victorious in Scotland. The Queen, how-ever, was reluctant that the Prince should stay any longer in Jersey. She had been under the impression that he was going to Scotland or Ireland. The Prince's counsellors were bitterly divided over the question whether Charles should continue into France. But when on 20 June Culpeper and Capel came back from their mission, reinforced by Lord Jermyn, Lord Digby and others, it was difficult for Charles to resist his mother's orders. It now became known that the King (who had left Oxford on 27 April before its surrender to the Parliamentarians) was a prisoner in the hands of the Scots at Newcastle. The Prince's council met together with the Queen's emissaries from France. The arguments for staying in Jersey or moving were put on both sides, Culpeper upholding the point of view of the Queen, Hyde opposing it. The Prince himself finally took the decision. 'He declared himself', wrote Hyde, '[ready] to comply with the commands of the Queen, and forthwith remove into France; which being resolved, he wished that there might be no more debate upon that point, but that they would all resolve to go with him. . . . This so positive declaration of the Prince made all farther arguments against it not only useless but indecent. . . . '5 Nevertheless the majority of the King's council refused to accompany him. They regarded the sudden departure of the Prince out of the King's dominions as damaging to Royalist morale, while Oxford and much of the English midlands still remained (as they believed) in Royalist hands. They considered that the appearance of the heir to the throne as a suppliant at a foreign (and Roman Catholic) court was a matter of 'very ill consequences'. It is doubtful if Charles himself thought in those terms. After all, he had received positive orders both from his father and his mother to go to France. Paris was likely to be much more amusing than Elizabeth castle. Once he was in Paris he could consult with his mother what was best to be done for his father; indeed it might even be possible to persuade the French to intervene on the Royalist side.

Charles arrived in France on 26 June 1646 and lived with his mother at St Germain. He had been accompanied by Digby, Jermyn and Culpeper, but Hyde remained in Jersey and there continued work on what was to become his famous *History of the Rebellion*, which he had begun to write while in the Scillies. According to this history, the Prince had been with his mother for two months 'before any notice was taken of his being in France by the least message sent from the court to congratulate his arrival there'.[6] Protocol had to be consulted. What should his position be, as heir to the English throne, in the ceremonies at the French court? Where should he sit and when take off his hat? Should he rank above the King's uncle, the Duke of Orleans? All these questions merited serious consideration. Hyde noted sourly that they ought to have been settled before Charles even arrived.

At any rate by October Charles had been invited to the royal palace of Fontainebleau. He paid his respects to the eight-year-old King Louis XIV and to the Queen Mother, Anne of Austria, and was regaled with balls, comedies and promenades in the forest and by the waters of the Seine. Madame de Motteville, who noted this, thought that his appearance had improved since he had arrived in France. His misfortunes excited pity among the courtiers. But he was reckoned to be shy. His displayed no wit and was even inclined to stammer. However he was not so dumb as to be unmoved by the beauties at the French court, notably by the Duchess de Châtillon, an attractive widow. Cardinal Mazarin, the principal French Minister, welcomed the arrival of the young Prince; at the same time he was aware that the English Parliament had been victorious in the first civil war and regarded Charles rather as a pawn in the diplomatic game than as a celebrity actively to be supported. The French Treasury granted him an allowance. But Henrietta Maria was proud. She treated this allowance as supplementary to her own, which was fully justified as she was the French King's aunt; but a tight fist was held on the purse-strings by the Queen and her closest adviser, Lord Jermyn, so that the Prince and his servants were placed in a highly embarrassing situation. Henrietta Maria's own idea was to get her son married to a rich heiress and she aimed her sights high, having in mind for him Anne-Marie-Louise d'Orleans, the granddaughter of Henri IV of France and first cousin to the boy king. But the Grande Mademoiselle, as she was called, was not much attracted by a penniless prince. She hoped to marry the Holy Roman Emperor or at least the King of Spain. Charles did his best to please his mother. When the court returned from Fontainebleau to Paris in the winter of 1646–7 the Prince appeared at all the plays that were given at the Palais Royal and, as the Grande Mademoiselle remarked in her memoirs, 'he never failed to place himself beside me'. 'When I visited the Queen', she continued, 'he conducted me in his coach; and whatever the weather might be, he held his hat in his hand until he had left me. His courtesy to me was apparent in the smallest things.'[7]

One day at an aristocratic party the Prince held a *flambeau* so as to light the Princess clearly, and wore her colours of red, white and black in his hat, gloves, stockings and sword-knot. But he suffered from one insuperable handicap: he could not or would not speak French. It has been suggested that Prince Charles really did not much care for the formidable subject of his courtship and therefore feigned ignorance of the language. The large princess was no beauty; she was self-conscious about her own importance and must have taken pleasure in humiliating the young exile, who was three years her junior. No doubt he was nervous; but that does not mean that he could speak French fluently all the time. He does not appear to have been well educated in the language in the days of the Earl of Newcastle's somewhat lackadaisical governorship. The speaking of French had not been encouraged at his father's court and he had not seen a great deal of his mother, who in any case spoke English. According to the Grande Mademoiselle, he told Prince Rupert, who served him as an interpreter, that 'he understood everything I said to him', although he was not supposed to know one word of French. Even if he had been able to pay compliments in French, it is doubtful if he would have got any further with the lady. 'The thought of the Empire so occupied my mind', she wrote, 'that I thought no longer of the Prince of Wales except as an object of pity.' When her father ventured to draw attention to the age of the Emperor, who was a widower with children, and suggested that she would be happiest in England, she told him haughtily, 'it is for me to decide'.[8] In any case neither her father nor Cardinal Mazarin really wanted her huge fortune to leave the country; and in the event it did not.

It was during the summer of 1646 that Charles for a short time enjoyed the services of the political philosopher, Thomas Hobbes, as a tutor. Hobbes had wanted to move away from Paris, but was persuaded to stay behind to teach the young Prince some mathematics, a subject on which Hobbes prided himself. At the same time George Villiers, the second Duke of Buckingham, Charles's boyhood friend, stayed for a while in Paris on his way back home to London. The clerical historian, Gilbert Burnet, whose authority on the subject is poor – he even gets the year wrong – tried later to make out that Buckingham was responsible for 'corrupting' his friend, 'being seconded in that wicked design by the Lord Percy'. And Burnet alleges that Hobbes then 'laid before him his schemes, both with relation to religion and politics, which made deep and lasting impressions on the King's mind'.[9] But neither Buckingham nor Hobbes was in Paris for long; it is true that Charles was always a good friend to Hobbes, whose intellect he admired, and that he always found Buckingham amusing. But Paris itself was a source of gaiety to a young prince escaped from the civil wars; and the blood of his grandfather, Henri of Navarre, was more likely to have led him to seek amusement in the company of women than the example of the young Buckingham.

Amid such distractions Charles now grew up rapidly, his dark looks, tall figure, and black eyes giving him a distinction to which the ladies were not insensible. He was joined at St Germain by his two-year-old sister, Henriette Anne, who had been left behind in Exeter by her mother but had been brought over by her governess in a party disguised as French beggars. Charles gave her the nickname of 'Minette' or 'little puss'. He asked permission to serve with the French army against Spain, but was told that his life was too precious to be risked. But both he and his mother felt frustrated that they could do nothing to help Charles I, who by now had become a prisoner, first of Parliament and then of the New Model Army.

While Charles lived in France, his father was trying from his position of honourable captivity to negotiate terms on which he could be restored to his throne. His highest hopes rested on the Scots: the Stuarts had, after all, been kings in Scotland for over 200 years, whereas in England they were newcomers. But, after long discussions in Newcastle, the Scottish army had handed over the King to the care of the English Parliament and at the end of

1646 had withdrawn home. Meanwhile antagonisms had arisen between the victorious New Model Army and the parliamentary leaders. The disputes had related to the future employment of the army and its arrears of pay. In 1646, to please the Scots, an ordinance had been passed establishing Presbyterianism in England; some of the army's leaders, notably Oliver Cromwell, demanded toleration for all Christian sects. The dissensions grew so hot that eventually a party of soldiers went and forcibly removed the King from the power of Parliament, placing him still in honourable captivity at Hampton Court. The King now appeared to have the choice between negotiating with Parliament, whose terms for his restoration as a strictly controlled constitutional monarch were the most far-reaching, with the army leaders, who in 1647 drew up heads of proposals for a settlement of the kingdom, and with the Scots, who were anxious to bring the two kingdoms into a closer religious and political union. The Scots dispatched commissioners to England to represent their point of view both to Parliament and to the King. One of these commissioners, the elderly Earl of Dunfermline, was sent across the Channel by his fellow commissioners and by some of the English Presbyterians to discover whether Queen Henrietta Maria would allow her son to go to Scotland ready to head an army to confront the New Model Army and thus give security to the majority in Parliament. The difficulty from the Scots' point of view was whether Prince Charles would be willing to uphold Presbyterianism. After all, his father had fought the civil war partly at least in defence of the Church of England. The Marquis of Argyll, the most influential of the Scottish nobility, insisted that Charles must give satisfaction over religion before he was invited to lead a Scottish army into England.

Scotland was not the only country from which offers for Charles's services reached St Germain. In Ireland the Marquis of Ormonde, representing the King, had more than held his own, but he left Ireland temporarily and, after seeing Charles I at Hampton Court, came to Paris to consult the Queen and her son about future policy. The Irish General Assembly sent three commissioners to France to invite the Prince of Wales to sail to

Ireland in order to head an army there. But the Scottish negotiations seemed more promising. The Duke of Hamilton, the second most influential figure in Scotland after Argyll, was ready to conclude a treaty with the King. In order to obtain greater freedom of action Charles I had in November 1647 escaped from Hampton Court to the Isle of Wight. Here in Carisbrooke castle he remained a prisoner of the English army, but was allowed free access to the Scottish commissioners who visited him there. These commissioners continued to press for the Prince to be sent to Scotland. But, as Hyde wrote, 'the King would by no means consent that the Prince should go into Scotland, being too well acquainted with the manners and fidelity of that people; but he was contented that when they should have entered England with their army the Prince of Wales should put himself at the head of them.'[10] On 26 December 1647 King Charles signed a secret agreement with the Scottish commissioners. By this he promised to establish the Presbyterian system in England for three years at which time an assembly of divines would be called to arrange a final settlement of Church questions; in any case the King agreed to suppress the sects. In return the Scots undertook to send an army into England in effect to enforce the King's restoration to his throne. This engagement was accepted by Hamilton, but not by Argyll.

At the same time that these secret negotiations were being pursued in the Isle of Wight, the English army and Parliament were at loggerheads. The army had marched on London in August and had begun debating the future of the kingdom among themselves. The failure to reach a constitutional settlement had brought about a Royalist reaction, especially among numbers of Presbyterians who had fought against their King in the first civil war. Political discontent was rife in Kent and Essex. Part of the navy was on the verge of revolt. By January 1648 everything was boiling up towards a renewal of the civil war. Queen Henrietta Maria sent an emissary, Sir William Fleming, to Amsterdam to pawn her remaining jewels for the good of the cause. The Prince of Wales was to move from Paris to Calais so as to be ready for any eventuality. At the beginning of March 1648 Hamilton secured a majority in the Scottish Parliament which enabled him to take whatever steps he thought necessary. Three weeks later Sir William Fleming arrived in Scotland and told Hamilton that Prince Charles was prepared to come to Scotland only if the Scots would take up arms on the King's behalf. Hamilton, who was not a strong man, still hesitated to plunge into war. But on 1 May he sent back a letter by Fleming formally inviting Charles to come to Scotland. Charles was not anxious to put himself in the power of the Scots without any conditions. The reply – dispatched in mid-July – was that Charles would only go to Scotland if the conditions were right, for example that he be allowed to use the English prayer book at his public devotions. He was thus loyal to his father's view that on no account must he betray his Church. His mother did not quite see it that way. She had written to her husband to point out that if he were willing to hand over the kingdom to the Presbyterians for three years, he might as well do so for all time as the price of his regaining his freedom.

It was not until 25 June 1648 that Prince Charles at last left St Germain for Calais. Before then the second civil war had broken out in south-eastern England and in Wales. The risings were not co-ordinated with the planned Scottish invasion, and General Fairfax had almost succeeded in suppressing the risings in Kent and Essex by the time Hamilton and his army of 'Engagers' had crossed the frontier at the beginning of July. But the best news from the Royalist point of view was of the growing discontent in the Parliamentarian fleet. It was because of this that Prince Charles himself did not go to Scotland.

A more glorious opportunity appeared to have presented itself for him to give help to his father. It was known by midsummer that discontent in the fleet had flared into action and that not only had a number of vessels, formerly stationed in the Downs, come over to Holland but William Batten, until lately the Parliamentarian vice-admiral, was coming with them. At the beginning of the war the fleet had been commanded by the able and much-respected Earl of Warwick. But in 1645 he had been forced to resign his post by the 'self-denying' ordinance, and Batten had in effect taken his place. Batten was a Presbytarian who in 1647 became discontented with the conduct of the Parliamentarian army.

He also sympathized with the King, who was now in the army's power, and was afraid, he said, that it 'would in the end take off his head'. Hearing the rumours of his dissatisfaction, the Committee of the Two Houses of Parliament sent for him – ordering him to come by land and not even in his own ship – and subjected him to close examination. Nothing could be proved against him, but he was suspended from his duties as vice-admiral and Colonel Thomas Rainsborough, a notorious republican extremist, was appointed in his place. Batten was furious and determined to change sides. He was aided in his treachery by the fact that Rainsborough soon made himself unpopular among the sailors, who resented his being foisted upon them. Batten played on the naval unrest during the winter of 1647 and a former chaplain of his organized Royalist propaganda at Deal, near the Downs. In May an impostor, pretending to be the Prince of Wales, came to the Downs and was enthusiastically received by the sailors. That was the spark which set off the revolt. On 25 May ten or more ships sailed away from the Downs headed for Holland while Rainsborough 'defiantly waved his sword at them from the roof of Deal castle'.[11] The mutineers found at Helvoetsluys at the mouth of the Meuse no less a person than the King's Lord High Admiral, his second son, the fifteen-year old James, Duke of York. The Duke had been a prisoner in London but had just managed to escape disguised as a girl. James did not remain in command of the revolted fleet for long. On 9 July a Dutch ship fetched his elder brother from Calais to Helvoetsluys. By 14 July Batten himself had arrived in the thirty-gun *Constant Warwick*. And while the Parliamentarians, dismayed by the new situation, recalled the Earl of Warwick to replace Rainsborough as their naval commander-in-chief, Prince Charles himself took charge at Helvoetsluys, appointed Batten his rear-admiral and knighted him.

On 17 July 1648 the fleet sailed for the Downs. What could it do to help the Royalist cause? Warwick still had an equally powerful fleet at his disposal collected near the mouth of the Thames, while another ten warships were available at Portsmouth. Charles's men were agog for action. Could they rescue the King from the Isle of Wight? Might they be able to inflict a defeat on Warwick before the Portsmouth ships could reinforce him? Could they even sail up the Thames and oblige the city of London to surrender? Warwick was slow to move. The opinion aboard the revolted ships was divided. Batten himself wanted to take the fleet to Scotland. The majority of the seamen, however, were all for entering the Thames and capturing rich prizes. They might even be able to block the river and prevent Warwick from attacking them. But Prince Charles had many difficulties. The winds had originally blown his fleet as far as Yarmouth and although he had collected some supplies there, he was painfully short of both food and drink. The sailors were obstreperous because merchantmen captured at the mouth of the Thames had been ransomed with a view to soothing the Londoners and their officers were suspected of pocketing the proceeds. On 28 August Charles ordered the ships to return to Holland and refuel. The sailors refused to obey him – 'a very arrant mutiny' – and four of his leading ships steered for the Thames.

But by now the enemy under Warwick had been sighted. The fleet cleared for action. Charles was begged to go below but refused, took hold of a gun and said: 'I am confident with this piece today to shoot Warwick through the head, if he dares in person to appear in the fight.'[12] At eight in the evening of 29 August Prince Charles summoned Warwick to surrender under promise of a general pardon. It was a gallant gesture but no more; for by now, though the Prince commanded eleven ships, Warwick was his equal in numbers and in quantity of gunpowder and the Portsmouth fleet was on its way to join him. 'Next morning, on the 30th, for the first time in English history two fleets of Englishmen stood ready to battle with each other.'[13] But Warwick refused action and a change in the wind forced both fleets to anchor. Then dwindling supplies compelled the Royalists to withdraw. As they sailed back across the North sea in the dark there was a rumour that the Portsmouth squadron was passing them, but it proved to be only a fleet of colliers. In any case the risk of a sea fight in darkness was too severe. The Prince's life was valuable to the royal cause. So the revolted ships were brought back in safety to Helvoetsluys where they anchored on 1 September.

Soon Warwick, having been reinforced by the Portsmouth squadron, followed them across. On the night of 19 September Warwick summoned the Prince to surrender. On the twenty-fourth a reply was sent demanding the surrender of Warwick's ships. In fact Charles himself was no longer at Helvoetsluys, for he had gone to The Hague where he was taken ill. Next day the Dutch intervened to protect their own neutrality. Admiral Tromp anchored between the rival fleets. Tromp dipped his sails to the Royalist admiral, showing which way his sympathies lay, for he ignored Warwick. For his failure to defeat the Royalists Warwick was again dismissed from his post. But by now Oliver Cromwell had crushed the Scots at a series of battles in Lancashire; the south-eastern counties had been subdued; the Parliamentarian soldiers were beginning to agitate for King Charles to be put on trial; and Prince Charles, though he kept his new-found fleet in being, if with some losses, was to become the helpless spectator of his father's fate.

It appears to have been during the week he spent in Holland before he led his fleet across the North Sea to menace London that Charles met his first love, Lucy Walter, described by John Evelyn who met her as 'a brown, beautiful, bold but insipid creature', and by Hyde as 'a private Welsh woman of no good fame but handsome'. Nothing is really known about how she came to Holland at this time. On 9 April she gave birth to James Scott, the future Duke of Monmouth, who was acknowledged as his eldest son by Charles; in the years to come Monmouth was to be the Protestant rival of James, Duke of York, Charles's brother, as his successor to the throne of England. For this reason James's opprobrious stories about the character of Monmouth's mother are hard to credit and must be ignored by the impartial historian. Not only Charles's prompt acknowledgement of the paternity but a comparison of the portraits of Monmouth with portraits of Prince Charles as a boy give very little reason to doubt that Charles was in fact Monmouth's father.[14]

Lucy Walter must have been about the same age as Charles when the affair began. She was of respectable lineage, though her father deserted her mother. It is likely enough that the Welsh girl and the young Prince, released from his mother's apron strings and freed from the ceremonial restraints of the French court, where he had been forced into his dumb courtship of the Grande Mademoiselle, fell passionately in love in an entirely natural way. But immediately they saw little of each other; after his father's death Charles was soon to be absorbed in travel and adventure and Lucy was not faithful. Yet Charles's correspondents were frequently to refer to her as his 'wife' in a jocular kind of way, which shows that when he was in Holland again he renewed the connection, though a daughter to whom Lucy later gave birth was not acknowledged by him. Marriage was clearly out of the question. Lucy took other lovers and so did Charles. She became a termagant. The King's advisers were to be embarrassed by her outrageous behaviour when the court moved to Brussels, as she was involved in several scandals and threatened blackmail. Ultimately her son was taken away from her with the warning that otherwise he would be disowned. Lucy died in Paris when she was twenty-eight. Hers was a not uncommon tragedy. But it can hardly be said that Charles had behaved badly. He was never to be cruel or ungenerous to his mistresses; and he seems to have put up with Lucy long after her conduct became intolerable. Monmouth was always to be his favourite son.

Meanwhile a deeper tragedy had occurred on the public stage. When Charles returned to Holland he was received by the States respectfully and lodged in the town hall at The Hague where he was entertained by his brother-in-law, the Prince of Orange. But many recriminations were exchanged over the failure at sea. Courtiers were accused of having profited from the sale of captured merchant ships and 'there was a general murmur that the fleet had lain so long idle at the mouth of the river [Thames] when it had been proposed that it might go to the Isle of Wight' and rescue the King.[15] Messengers came from the Parliament in Scotland again demanding Charles's presence there in spite of the defeat of Hamilton's army in England. The fleet was mutinying from lack of pay; some ships deserted and rejoined the Parliamentarian side. The Prince's council was far from unanimous and intrigues were put on foot against him in which his brother was involved. On top of this Charles had been taken ill. Hyde says 'he appeared to have the small-pox' though it is more likely to have been measles or chicken-pox because 'he recovered in a few days the peril of that distemper and within a month was restored to perfect health'. At this time he received a long letter from his father in the Isle of Wight telling him that if God gave him success he should 'use it humbly and far from revenge. If he restore you to your right upon hard conditions, whatever you promise, keep.'[16]

This letter was written in late November 1648 just before King Charles I was removed by order of the army from the Isle of Wight, first to the grim discomfort of Hurst castle in Hampshire and then Windsor, whence he was brought up to London as a prisoner on trial for his life on 19 January 1649. Six days earlier Prince Charles wrote a letter to General Fairfax asking him to 'testify his fidelity by reinstating your lawful King' and 'to defend him, whereto you are by oath obliged'.[17] Charles also wrote letters to European rulers begging them to intercede on his father's behalf with the authorities in England. On 23 January he appeared personally before the Dutch States-General to seek their help and they agreed to send the Pensionary of Holland, the highest official in the province, as an ambassador extraordinary to London. Two Dutch ambassadors actually pleaded with the Commons for the King's life on the day before his execution. The Queen also sent her appeal for her husband's life through the French representative in London. It was all in vain. The extremists in the House of Commons and in the New Model Army had made up their minds that King Charles I must pay the supreme penalty for bringing the two civil wars upon his kingdom. On 27 January he was condemned to death and on 30 January was executed in Whitehall. The tidings reached Holland in the first week of February. One of the Prince's chaplains broke the news to him, addressing him as 'Your Majesty'. Charles, seizing the meaning of the words, withdrew to his bedchamber to indulge in a passionate outburst of grief. He found the awful news hard to credit. He had fought since he was little more than a child on both land and sea to sustain his father's cause. Now he had acquired what seemed a hopeless heritage.

3

In the Arms of the Scots

Charles was not yet nineteen when his father was executed. But he had been in command of an army and a navy and he had been obliged to take some critical decisions. He was prepared to undergo the strains of a monarch in exile from his kingdom. Although he could see that the republican government in England, as it had now declared itself to be, was too strongly entrenched for foreign countries willingly to come to his aid, he had high hopes both of Ireland and Scotland. In Ireland the Marquis of Ormonde had on 17 January 1649 concluded a treaty with the native Irish at Kilkenny so that all the Irish Roman Catholics and Irish Royalists were united in his cause. Prince Rupert and his ships (survivors of the Royalist fleet of 1648) were off the coast of Ireland and it was envisaged as a base from which England might be invaded on the King's behalf. Ormonde promptly invited Charles to come to Ireland and Queen Henrietta Maria wrote him a letter invoking him to declare himself a Roman Catholic: 'only so can you win Ireland'.[1] On 7 February he was proclaimed King in Edinburgh but he was told he must 'give satisfaction' about his religion, the union of the two kingdoms, and the good and peace of Scotland according to the National Covenant and the Solemn League and Covenant. The Covenanters, led by Argyll, were now in full control of the lowlands after the defeat of the Engagers by Cromwell, but the Marquis of Montrose was travelling around Europe seeking funds to support a revival of the Royalist cause in the highlands.*

* The Covenanters had allied with the English Parliamentarians in 1643 and fought against Charles I; the Engagers had fought for Charles I against Parliament in 1648.

It was obvious that the last thing Charles could afford to do was to change his religion. The Irish wanted him to become a Roman Catholic, the Scots required him to be a Presbyterian, while his supporters in England expected him to be loyal to the religion for which his father had died a martyr. Charles and his advisers decided to wait and see which way the winds blew both in Scotland and Ireland. On 20 February the Marquis of Argyll, the effective ruler of Scotland, sent him an invitation to come there, but two days later the King created James Graham, Marquis of Montrose, his lieutenant-general in Scotland and captain-general of all his forces there. Just over a month later commissioners, dressed in deep mourning, arrived in Holland from Scotland to ask Charles to take the two covenants. He said that he would accept the covenants for Scotland only; and obviously he hoped that when Montrose got back to Scotland the Covenanters would be less demanding. The commissioners, on the other hand, thought that as soon as Charles's hopes from Ireland went unrealized he would concede the full stringency of their terms.

Some of the older members of Charles's council were firmly opposed to his coming to any compromise with the Scots at the expense of the Church of England. Meanwhile he continued to press his claims on all foreign courts for money and aid. He sent Hyde and Lord Cottington to try to raise a loan in Madrid and he himself left Holland for Brussels, capital of the Spanish Netherlands, in order to back the appeals of his envoys. In July he visited his mother at St Germain. The Queen had now recovered from the shock of her husband's death and had emerged in full widow's weeds from the convent where she had learned the news of her bereavement. She still hoped for her son's marriage to the Grande Mademoiselle, who had been disappointed of her other suitors. But the lady was not willing. 'I considered', she wrote in her memoirs, 'that if I married him I might be called upon to risk my entire possessions for the chance of reconquering his kingdom. I confess that this reflection caused me some dismay. Having been brought up in opulence and comfort, I was alarmed at the prospect of reverses.'[2] The King himself seems to have preferred the company of his pretty young cousin Sophia, the sister of

Prince Rupert. She had some money but not enough and it does not appear that marriage was seriously contemplated: it was odd that this chance should have presented itself, for this Sophia was to be the mother of another English king, the first of the Hanoverians. Charles put his foot in it when he told his cousin that she was handsomer than his mistress, Lucy Walter.

After this somewhat unsatisfactory visit to France – during which he made it clear to his mother, much to her annoyance, that she was no longer going to rule him – he left in the early autumn for Jersey to await news from Ireland. He carried away with him his younger brother James, whom his mother had been trying to convert to her faith. The news from Ireland when it came just after Christmas was as bad as it could be; for it told of the defeat of Ormonde's forces near Dublin and Cromwell's subsequent victorious campaign in the south of Ireland. So perforce Charles turned his attention back to Scotland. A fresh commissioner of the Scots arrived in Jersey in George Winram, Laird of Libberton, a moderate Presbyterian. Winram was optimistic that Charles would be compelled to accept the Covenanters' terms: 'Now is the time to pray that God the Lord will prevent [protect] the King with his tender mercies, for indeed he is brought very low. He has not bread both for himself and his servants and betwixt him and his brother not one English shilling. . . . '³ From his counsellors Charles received the advice to return to Holland and there wait until Montrose or some one else achieved a miracle for him. But the King himself refused to be depressed; he determined to explore every way forward. So he offered to meet representatives of the Covenanters at Breda in March 1650. At the same time he wrote to Montrose assuring him that he would not in any treaty with the Covenanters do anything contrary to the power and authority he had conferred on him as captain-general. In spite of the intransigence of the Covenanters, Charles hoped to unite all the Scottish factions in his cause and, when he himself reached Scotland, to be the effective king of all the Scots and prepare there to fight for his other kingdom of England. Indeed in writing to Montrose in January 1650 he suggested that the Marquis's very preparations had been responsible for the Covenanters' approaches; he added that his own aim was 'a present union of the whole nation in our service'.[4] He also sent him the Order of the Garter. Whether with the King's consent or not, his letter to Montrose was published in Paris by one of Montrose's agents there. The letter made plain to the Covenanters what Charles's policy really was. But they had no intention of allying themselves with Montrose, whom they regarded as an enemy to their own supremacy. Charles's position in relation to the Scots became increasingly difficult and subject to justifiable criticism.

In the middle of February 1650 Charles left Jersey. After seeing his mother at Beauvais, where she had advised him to come to an understanding with the Scots but not to take the covenants, he arrived in Breda in mid-March to await the coming of the Scottish commissioners. While he was there he appointed Lord Eythin as Montrose's second in command. Soon after, Montrose landed in the Orkney Islands, preparatory to raising a new force in the King's name in the highlands. Meanwhile Charles desperately sought other means to his restoration by trying to hire foreign troops of mercenaries to invade England, offering the dubious pledge of the Scilly Islands as a guarantee for loans. But nothing, as might have been expected, came of these plans.

The terms that the Scottish commissioners brought to Breda were extremely stiff. Charles was once more asked to take the covenants, to establish Presbyterianism in England, Scotland and Ireland, to recognize the loyalty of the existing Scottish Parliament (which was under the influence of Argyll) and to enforce the penal laws against the Roman Catholics in all his kingdoms. So far as the government of Scotland was concerned, he was to leave it to the Parliament and Committee of Estates, while religious affairs were to be handled by the Kirk. In effect he was required to abandon both Ormonde and Montrose and to place himself entirely in the hands of the Covenanters. For a month the two parties haggled over terms, but the Scots were not inclined to give way an inch. Those of Charles's advisers who were insistent that he should remain loyal to his Church and his conscience were overruled. Hyde was in Madrid whence he wrote warning letters. Other counsellors, such as Hopton, the heroic commander of the Cornish, and Edward Nicholas, the friend of Hyde, were removed from the King's Privy Council and replaced by men like Newcastle, Charles's old governor, and the second Duke of Buckingham. It was asserted that Charles's brother-in-law, Prince William of Orange, and Queen Christina of Sweden both pressed him to come to terms with the Covenanters. So it was that on 1 May 1650 he reluctantly signed the so-called treaty of Breda.

Charles's acceptance of the Covenanters' terms meant the abandonment of Montrose who had crossed the Pentland Forth from the Orkneys and landed at John o'Groats on 12 April. He had fewer than a thousand men, and hoped to recruit among the highland clans, particularly the Mackenzies. Charles immediately summoned an emissary, Sir William Fleming, to go to Scotland and tell Montrose that he must lay down his arms. In a letter he then wrote he said: 'We hope upon good grounds that we shall be able in a little time to make his [Montrose's] peace in Scotland' and to restore him to his honour and estate and that 'we shall shortly have an honourable employment for him in our service against the rebels in England'.[5] In two more private letters he gave to Fleming he insisted that Montrose must lay down his arms and refrain from all acts of hostility. He assumed that Montrose would readily comply with these instructions, but promised him that he would look after his interests and obtain restitution for his losses; and he added a personal assurance of his constant affection for him. He also sent Montrose a sum of money. Sir Robert Long, who was Charles's secretary at this time, noted that Sir William Fleming was 'sent with orders, all his officers and soldiers indemnified, M. to stay in safety for a competent time in Scotland and ship to lie provided for transporting where he pleased'.[6] Montrose never received any of these messages from his master. On 27 April he was defeated at the battle of Carbisdale; the Mackenzies had failed to come to his aid, and the Covenanting troops outnumbered his. A week after the battle Montrose was handed over to his enemies by a laird with whom he had sought asylum. And although Charles wrote to the Estates asking that Montrose and his forces should be allowed to leave the country in safety, Montrose was sent a prisoner to Edinburgh, was degraded in every conceivable way, and was finally hanged as a traitor. After his death on 21 May his head was cut off and his limbs scattered in other Scottish towns as a warning to all traitors. But Montrose himself said before he died: 'I could wish that I had flesh and limbs enough to have a piece sent to every city in Christendom, as proofs and tokens of my unshaken love and loyalty to King and country.'

Charles was already on his way to Scotland when he heard the news of Montrose's defeat and horrible death. The first thing he did was to write a letter of condolence to the new Marquis assuring him of his care and affection. This letter has been described as 'singularly inadequate to the occasion'. Four days earlier the letters that Charles had dispatched to Scotland by Sir William Fleming at last reached Scotland. They were too late to help the dead Montrose; but they served to show the Covenanters that Charles was 'heartily sorry that Montrose had invaded this kingdom'. Argyll also informed the Scottish Parliament that the King was 'no ways sorry that James Graham was defeated, in respect he had made the invasion without, and contrary to his command'.[7]

It was understandable in the conditions of the time that Charles should repudiate Montrose and should be reticent in the letter of condolence that he wrote to his son. Charles's behaviour on this occasion has been deemed a blot on his honour. But it is hard to measure the pressures to which he was subjected. Defeated in England and Ireland, the only hope of restoration to his throne was for Charles to yield to the Covenanters' extreme demands and that involved the repudiation of Montrose. Yet it is clear from all the correspondence that Charles had honestly hoped, as the price of his concessions to the Covenanters, that he would not only be able to preserve Montrose's life, but to use his services during what he counted upon as being an imminent invasion of England.

Charles arrived in Scotland on 24 June 1650. Before he was allowed to land he was required to swear a solemn oath to uphold the covenants. Neither of the two parties to the so-called treaty of Breda trusted one another. A reporter who was there wrote: 'It is easy to see that the Scots' edge is much taken off him

[Charles]. They say they find nothing but vanity and lightness in him, and that he will never prove a strenuous defender of their faith'; while one of the commissioners who accompanied the King later wrote that they compelled him to 'sign and swear a Covenant, which we knew from clear and demonstrable reasons that he hated in his heart'.[8] When during the journey across the North sea the Scottish Covenanters insisted on making the terms of the commitment more stringent by forcing him to swear to both the Covenants and to renounce Ormonde's treaty with the Irish, he rebelled and said he would prefer to throw himself on the mercy of the King of Denmark than be so humiliated. But the winds had driven the ships off course from Denmark and he again gave way.

At first his welcome in Scotland caused the world to look a trifle brighter. On the Spey ordinary people acclaimed their King with singing, bell-ringing, trumpeting, dancing in the streets and bonfires. The poor market women sacrificed their baskets and stools to augment the bonfires. Two days after he landed he was compelled to part with most of the Scottish and English advisers who had accompanied him. Hamilton and Lauderdale, the two Engagers, were dismissed and it was made clear to Charles that the saturnine Marquis of Argyll, the destroyer of Montrose, with his squinting eyes and pious demeanour, was 'in absolute credit' in the lowlands.

The King continued his journey through Aberdeen and Kinnaird to Falkland palace where he was greeted with respect by Argyll. By the palace was a deer park, and hunting and golf (which Charles did not much care for) were available. But the King was in effect the prisoner of the Covenanters. The Engagers were kept away from him; and only nine Englishmen including Buckingham were allowed to remain with him in his palace. It was probably never intended that he should be more than the figurehead of Scottish nationalism; there seems to have been no immediate plan to invade England on his behalf. For that reason General Thomas Fairfax had refused the request of the English Council of State that he should head a preventive invasion of Scotland. But the English Parliamentarians were not prepared to risk the north being again overrun by Scots and on 22 July Oliver Cromwell, replacing Lord Fairfax as captain-general of the New Model Army, crossed the border and the Covenanters were compelled to fight.

The day after Cromwell invaded Scotland King Charles left Falkland palace for Perth; thence he travelled via Dunfermline to Stirling where he was invited to join the Scottish army. He visited Leith on the left of the Scottish defensive line where he was clamorously received by the soldiers. But then he was obliged to return to Dunfermline while the leaders of the Scottish Kirk proceeded to purge the army of all officers and men who were suspected of being Engagers or too enthusiastic Royalists.

In Dunfermline the Covenanters imposed on their King the utmost humiliation. He was obliged on 16 August to sign a long declaration in which he did 'ingenuously acknowledge all his own sins and the sins of his father's house, craving pardon and hoping for mercy and reconciliation through the blood of Jesus Christ'.[9] He desired to be 'deeply humbled and afflicted in spirit before God because of his father's hearkening unto and following evil councils . . . by which so much of the blood of the Lord's people hath been shed in these kingdoms'. He also apologized for 'the idolatry of his mother' and promised to do what was necessary 'to promote the ends of the Solemn League and Covenant, especially in those things which concern the reformation of the Church of England'; and he condemned Ormonde's treaty 'with the bloody Irish rebels'. Above all, he promised to help fight those who had now invaded Scotland. He declared that he would have no enemies but the enemies of the Covenant and promised an act of oblivion (with certain exceptions) for those who had fought against his father. That same evening the crown and sceptre of the kingdom of Scotland were brought from Stirling to Dunfermline, but there was 'no word of coronation'.

What Charles himself thought of this treatment was revealed in a conversation which he had four days later with Dr King, the Dean of Tuam in Ireland, who had been a member of his entourage brought over from Holland. 'Mr King,' he said, 'the Scots have dealt very ill with me, very ill.' 'You have heard how a declaration was extorted from me, and how I should have been dealt with, if I had not signed it . . . yet what concerns Ireland is no ways binding.'[10] Dr King was about to go to Ireland with messages for Ormonde, and Charles realized that the declaration he had made for the benefit of the Scots would be injurious to him. Charles felt that he could not be bound by oaths with regard to the future of England or of Ireland where, he asserted, he could do nothing without the advice of his Privy Council and parliaments. At the same time he recognized that the Scottish Covenanters would not fight for him and might even hand him over as a prisoner to the English republicans (as they had handed over his father) unless he pretended to obey their wishes. As has been seen, even then they did not trust him, but only felt that if he humbled himself sufficiently in public he would assuage the wrath of God. When on 3 September Cromwell and his generals inflicted an overwhelming defeat on the Scottish army at the battle of Dunbar, although the English had been cut off and had been outnumbered, the Scots hastened to blame themselves for fighting in the cause of a malignant king. Furthermore they declared that Charles was a hypocrite because he had complied with their demands not for conscience's sake but 'for the love of a crown'.

According to Sir Edward Hyde, who was not in Scotland at the time, the King and Cromwell were 'equally delighted' about the defeat of the Covenanters at Dunbar. The truth would appear to have been that Charles learned the news with mixed feelings. On the very day of the battle Charles had been writing to his former Secretary, Sir Edward Nicholas, about the hypocrisy of the Covenanters, and had asked him to arrange for the dispatch of a small Dutch fishing vessel to Scotland so that if things became too desperate he could effect his escape back to Holland. He realized, however, after the battle had been lost and the Scottish commander-in-chief, David Leslie, had resigned because of the criticisms made of him, how profoundly Argyll and his adherents were weakened by the defeat. Could not he himself as King therefore rally the Engagers and the Royalists to his side and, invoking the aid of Leslie, create a genuinely national Scottish army to resume the fight with Cromwell? It was known that many of the highlanders who had sympathized with Montrose had withdrawn to their fastnesses and might respond to the King's patriotic appeal.

In early October 1650 Charles, after preliminary inquiries undertaken on his behalf by a former doctor of his named Frazer, prepared to leave Perth for the highlands. When the King set out, he pretended he was going hunting. But the plot was ill prepared. Information about it was betrayed to the Covenanters. Some of Charles's closest advisers, including the Duke of Buckingham, were against the attempt. Colonel Montgomery with six hundred horsemen was sent after him and the King was easily persuaded to return to Perth. This episode, known as 'the Start', did not however redound to Charles's disadvantage. It made plain to Argyll, who was already inclined to come to terms with some of the less extreme of Hamilton's faction, that the King had ceased to be a puppet and that his name was required to rally a united Scotland to fight against the English. It is true that some of the Covenanters – and this is one of the complications of Scottish history at the time – were prepared to conclude peace with Cromwell and even hand over the King to him. These discontented 'Remonstrants', as they were called, blamed Charles's very presence among them for the disaster at Dunbar. Their leaders were sent off westwards of Glasgow to recruit fresh forces there, and Leslie was restored to his command. While Leslie took up an impregnable position at Stirling with the Firth of Forth protecting him from the English, who now occupied the whole of Edinburgh except for the castle, Cromwell himself moved west to deal with the Remonstrants. Though they were covered by the swollen waters of the Clyde, Cromwell's able second in command, John Lambert, overwhelmed them on 1 December.

Meanwhile the Scottish Parliament meeting at Perth voted in favour of the restitution of the Engagers. Charles was now invited to take part in the councils of the kingdom and to address the Parliament. He was a superb actor who played his part well. On 27 November he expressed his confidence in the continuance of God's favour because He had moved him 'to enter into a covenant with His people, a favour no other king could claim'. Thus reconciled, superficially at any rate, to all his Scottish subjects,

Charles once more swore to uphold the covenants and was invited to be crowned at Scone. After two days of fasting all the necessary preparations had been completed. The Moderator of the General Assembly preached from a text taken from 2 Kings, but explained that the anointing was now to be carried out not by priests but by the Lord Himself. In fact the Marquis of Argyll placed the crown on the King's head. The King recognized the solemnity of the occasion and also its significance. Argyll might be a king-maker but Charles could henceforward appeal to all the Scottish people – not merely to the Covenanters – as their publicly ack-nowledged monarch.

Gradually during the spring of 1651 Charles II's influence in Scotland increased and he bent all his efforts towards unity. At first, under the impact of the defeat at Dunbar, his counsellors were pessimistic. Two of them actually suggested that he would be well advised to try to compound with Cromwell for a kingdom north of the Firth of Forth. Argyll, whose policy had inspired the defeat, was shaken by the course of events. When his old rival, the second Duke of Hamilton, was invited to court, Argyll retired in dudgeon to his home in the highlands. And it was about this time that Argyll in a desperate effort to strengthen his position proposed to Charles that he should marry his eldest daughter, Lady Anne Campbell. This lady was described as 'a gentlewoman of rare parts and education' and, more to the point, as 'very handsome, extremely obliging and her behaviour and dress equal to any seen in the Court of England'.[11] Some sources have in-dicated that the offer came from Charles himself to 'raise an imagination' in the powerful Marquis. This might well have been the case when the proposal was first rumoured and Charles was still an outcast in Holland. But now that he had been crowned King of the Scots and Argyll had been discredited by defeat, it is more likely that it was the father who was the advocate for his daughter's betrothal. Charles evaded the issue by saying that his mother must be consulted, and on 21 January 1651 he sent an envoy to France to seek her counsel. That was conveniently to postpone the answer for three months. In due course it arrived. The Queen observed carefully that both father and daughter must be considered eligible parties. But would not such a marriage arouse jealousies in Scotland, let alone in England, which was Charles's ultimate goal? So the proposal was dropped. If indeed she were handsome, Charles may have conjured up in her hopes of becoming the Queen of Scots. But by now he was far too shrewd a politician to give his hand in marriage without fore-thought.

That was not the only setback to Argyll and his Covenanters in 1651. Charles threw his energy into reversing the former decision against having a united army: he aimed to build up a strong and devoted force to withstand any further advance by Cromwell and the English across the Forth and indeed to defeat him. He inspected the defences along the river; in February he went to Aberdeen to persuade the ministers there to assist a recruiting campaign organized by General Middleton, a former supporter of Montrose. Meanwhile the Scottish Engagers, headed by Hamilton, were ready to acknowledge their earlier faults so that they might be admitted again to the public service. Hamilton himself was exonerated, though his followers were made to sit in sackcloth on stools of repentance. When in the middle of March the Scottish Parliament again assembled, Charles set about persuading it to give approval to the levying of troops in the highlands. His aim was to constitute a fresh army which would include the Engagers and the former adherents of Montrose. Finally, at the beginning of July, the act known as the Act of Classes, which had been passed two and half years earlier banning the Engagers from office or service in Parliament, was repealed; and everything was ready for a new Scottish army to fight for its King. Although the King had renounced a marriage to his daughter, Argyll was neither dishonoured nor dismissed. Charles's policy, as it emerged after the self-abasements preceding his coronation, had consistently been one of an astute if unscrupulous statesman.

Before the Scottish Parliament adjourned at the end of March it had invited Charles II himself to become the commander-in-chief of the new united army. On 8 June the Dean of Tuam reported that 'the King's power is absolute, all interests are received, all factions composed, the ambitious defeated, the army cheerful, accomplished, numerous'.[12] The Scots had taken up what appeared to be an unassailable position south of the Firth of Forth, a position which Cromwell had been unable to attack successfully even immediately after the Scots had been shattered at Dunbar. A bad winter had provided further assistance to the Scots and in the spring Cromwell himself had been taken ill. Encouraged by the strength of his position at Stirling, which guarded the only bridge across the river Forth, Charles at the end of June 1651 marched his army south to take up an advanced position at Torwood in the hills south of Stirling. For a fortnight Cromwell manœuvred in an attempt to bring the Scots to battle. His objective was another victory as complete as that of Dunbar; but Charles hoped that with their communications stretched the English would be compelled to withdraw across the border. Then he might be able to follow up a demoralized army. But Cromwell was by no means completely frustrated. He decided to try to draw off the Scots from Stirling by sending a force across the river well to the east of the city. By 20 July 4,500 English were ferried over the Firth of Forth by boat. David Leslie, the professional soldier who, under Charles, was in effective command at Stirling, could not ignore the threat to his flank. But he detached too small a force to deal with it and Major-General Lambert won a considerable victory at Inverkeithing. Cromwell now reinforced Lambert's success. Sending four more regiments to assist Lambert, he himself feinted at Stirling and then rapidly counter-marched to join Lambert with his main force, leaving only eight regiments south of the river. Then Cromwell calmly marched behind his enemy's back to Perth on the Firth of Tay, thus cutting the Scots' communications. Perth surrendered on 2 August.

Three courses were open to Charles II. He could move his army north and do battle with Cromwell; he could withdraw his army into the western highlands; or, taking advantage of the smallness of the enemy in front of him, he could lead his army south into England, hoping to pick up Royalist recruits on the way. There was little doubt which of these courses would most appeal to Charles himself. He had now spent more than a year in Scotland, where he had been acknowledged as an absolute king, having cleverly thrown off the abject restraints to which he had at first submitted. But what he wanted was to be restored to the throne of England. There had been stirrings in his favour as far afield as Norfolk and London. Lancashire was considered to be largely Royalist: indeed, according to Hyde, 'all the northern parts of England had given him cause to believe that they were very well affected to his service'.[13] Therefore Charles II resolved to lead his army into England. The second Duke of Hamilton approved this decision, though he knew that it savoured of desperation. Argyll and Leslie (it seems) were opposed to it. But Charles himself was in supreme command. So on 31 July Charles led his army out of Stirling, making for the English town of Carlisle; Argyll and his friends retired resentfully to the western highlands. 'All the rogues have left us,' declared Hamilton, 'I shall not say whether from fear or disloyalty; but all now with His Majesty are such as will not dispute his commands.'[14] It was in this spirit that the Scots marched across the border.

Cromwell was not in the least taken by surprise at Charles's move; in fact, he had tempted him to make it. Since there were two main routes into England, General Harrison had been stationed at Newcastle and General Fleetwood was ordered to concentrate his forces, called up from southern England, to the west. Twenty-four hours after Charles began his march from Stirling Cromwell learned of his departure, and four days later Lambert with three or four thousand cavalry rode out in pursuit of the Scots. Cromwell himself followed next day with the bulk of the infantry. Thus four armies had been gathered to cut off Charles's advance towards London.

The King had high hopes of recruiting Royalists on his way and had formed the nuclei of a cavalry and an infantry regiment under the command of the Duke of Buckingham ready to receive them. He also sent General Massey, a Scottish Presbyterian and former Governor of Gloucester in charge of the advance guard, who, he hoped, might rally his fellow religionists in the west midlands. But Massey was subjected to contradictory orders and the leaderless Royalists in the northern counties did not show themselves eager to join the invading Scots. One who was there wrote: 'I am

sure the King omitted nothing that might encourage the country
to rise with him or at least to lie still as neuters, but they, on
the contrary, rose against us. . . .'[15] On 9 August Charles's army
reached Carlisle, having crossed the border with some 16,000 men
three days earlier. By mid-August Lambert's and Harrison's
forces, largely consisting of cavalry, had met at Preston and on
16 August they tried to intercept the invaders at Warrington
bridge. But the country was not suited to cavalry action and
Charles's army brushed them aside after a skirmish and successfully negotiated the bridge. This victory rejoiced the hearts of
true Royalists, but David Leslie throughout the whole march
was 'sad and melancholic' and when Charles rode up to him
and asked how he could look sad when he was at the head of
so brave an army, answered that 'however well it looked, it would
not fight'.[16] Next day the Earl of Derby, whom Charles had
summoned from the Isle of Man, met the King with 250 foot and
60 horse, a disappointing number to those who had expected the
whole of Lancashire to rise for him. The Lancashire Presbyterians
refused to unite with the Scots, and indeed many local militiamen
joined Cromwell's subordinate, Colonel Robert Lilburne. Equally
the Governor of Shrewsbury rejected an appeal from Charles to
surrender to his forces. Having marched from Warrington by way
of Wolverhampton and Kidderminster, on Friday, 22 August
Charles's army entered Worcester, whence the Parliamentarian
garrison had withdrawn. 'The city', wrote a Royalist soldier, 'was
neither fortified nor victualled; His Majesty thought he could not
in honour leave them to be plundered by the enemy who had so
willingly received him.' But in any case the halt was enforced.

The King's 'happy progress' through England to within 100
miles of London was learned with joy by the Royalists abroad.
Indeed the advance had been no mean feat of generalship. The
Scots had marched over 300 miles in just over three weeks – an
average rate of ten miles a day, which was similar to the rate of
Cromwell's much praised march from Wales to Preston in
1648. Though some complaints were heard about plundering,
on the whole the army had been admirably disciplined and had
broken past the cavalry of Lambert and Harrison with considerable

aplomb. But it was now essential that the troops should be rested and where better than near the borders of Wales whence Royalist reinforcements might arrive? On Saturday, 23 August the Mayor and Sheriff of Worcester greeted Charles with deference; in the Guildhall he was proclaimed King of Great Britain, France and Ireland. In return the Mayor was knighted. Next day, Sunday, King Charles attended service in the cathedral where an effusively Anglican sermon gave offence to the Scots.

But meanwhile overwhelming forces were gathering to head the Royalists off from a farther advance towards London. On that very Sunday Cromwell met his second in command, Charles Fleetwood, at Warwick. Lambert had arrived at Coventry, 35 miles north-east of Worcester; and on 25 August Colonel Lilburne defeated the Earl of Derby away in Wigan. Cromwell proceeded methodically to surround the city of Worcester. 'During the enemy's lying there the King was very active and sent often very strong parties,' it was reported, 'but the enemy was so watchful and lay so strong that though our men behaved themselves courageously, they could get no advantage of them.'[17] Thus the Royalists. Fleetwood was now joined by a new army at Evesham south-east of Worcester. Lambert was dispatched to Upton on the Severn, ten miles south of Worcester, with instructions to get across the river. As soon as that had been achieved, Fleetwood was sent to Upton to make it his headquarters for an advance on Worcester from the south, while Lambert and Harrison joined Cromwell's army at the village of Spetchley, two miles east of the city, whither he had advanced from Evesham.

The Royalist army had to make ready to meet the attack. Worcester was a walled city that might be defended, and the bulk of Charles's army was concentrated in the city itself; though three fine Scottish infantry regiments were deployed amid the hedgerows south of the city to try to prevent the crossing of the river Teme which flowed eastward into the Severn on which Worcester itself lay. The right-hand regiment under Sir William Keith was stationed at the village of Powick, south of the Teme, guarding the only bridge across the river and this was partly broken down. The left-hand regiment under Colonel Pitscottie was posted near the confluence of the Teme and the Severn, while the third regiment under Colonel Dalziel was in reserve.

The battle did not develop until the afternoon, for Fleetwood had to await the arrival of a bridge of boats which was towed up the Severn in order to force the Teme. At about two o'clock Fleetwood ordered a general assault on the line of the Teme. As soon as the firing began Charles and his staff climbed the cathedral tower to watch what was happening. The King perceived that the city was being attacked by Fleetwood from the south and rode off at high speed to encourage the Scots at Powick in their defence and to reinforce them with a brigade of 2,000 men. He also visited Colonel Dalziel's regiment, which was in immediate support, but was unable to reach the third regiment in the fighting line, that of Colonel Pitscottie, who was hard pressed by Fleetwood's men. All these three regiments put up so gallant a fight that Cromwell himself had to throw in his reserves in support of Fleetwood, the Parliamentarian commander-in-chief himself leading his infantry across a second bridge of boats that spanned the Severn just above where it joined the Teme.

Resuming his watch from the tower of the cathedral, Charles observed the struggle swaying to and fro along the line of the Teme; the young King himself then made up his mind to lead a sally against Cromwell's army to the east of the city where his main artillery was posted. Whose advice he took is not known. It was not Leslie's who, with much of the Scottish cavalry, was standing idle in the meadow known as Pitchcroft to the north-west of the city. Under the King's own command therefore Royalist horse poured out of St Martin's gate and Sidbury gate (to the east and south-east of the city) and under cover of their own artillery attacked uphill. The contest lasted for three hours, the Royalists continuing the battle at push of pike and butt of musket after their ammunition was exhausted. The second Duke of Hamilton fell mortally wounded. Finally Charles and his men were forced back into the city. Meanwhile Fleetwood had at last crossed the Teme and was nearing the city from the south. Thus two sets of fugitives mingled with one another by the city's gates and the chaos was complete. Leslie appeared 'dispirited and confounded', and 'rode up and down as one amazed or seeking to fly he knew not whither'. A Royalist officer, who was at the battle, recounted:

the King being closely pursued by the enemy and our men stopping the passage, he was forced to quit his horse and climb up our half-raised mount and there so encouraged our foot that the enemy retired with loss. The King, perceiving the enemy too numerous and our men worsted, drew them within the walls where it was long disputed. Then the King, taking a fresh horse, rides to the cavalry with an intention to rally them and secure the foot from the walls but it was in vain . . . for they were so confused that neither threats nor entreaty would persuade them to charge with His Majesty.[18]

Then the King ordered that the gates should be shut, but as Hyde related, 'all was confusion: there were few to command and none to obey':[19] the King himself remained till many of the enemy's horse had forced their way into the city and not till then was he persuaded to withdraw himself.

Though the fighting had been fierce, Cromwell had lost few men. Nine thousand prisoners, including Leslie, were taken – some cut off in flight at Bewdley bridge – and of the rest of Charles's army nearly half were slain. Many were killed when the two groups of fugitives were crushed together inside the city. Major-General Harrison reported: 'What with the dead bodies of men and the dead horses of the enemy filling the streets there was such a nastiness that a man could hardly abide the town.' Cromwell himself wrote it was 'as stiff a contest for four or five hours as ever I have seen'. Outnumbered by more than two to one, Charles II had little cause to be ashamed of himself or his men.

4

In the Arms of France

The Queen Mother received a satisfactory report of her son's conduct at the battle of Worcester from a Scottish officer who was there:

Certainly a braver prince never lived, having in the day of the fight hazarded his person much more than any officer of his army, riding from regiment to regiment, and leading them into service with all the encouragement (calling every officer by his name) which the example and exhortation of a magnanimous general could afford, showing so much steadiness of mind and undaunted courage, in such continual danger, that had not God covered his head and wonderfully preserved his sacred person, he must, in all human reason, needs have perished that day.[1]

Charles's escape from Worcester and ultimately safe return to France after seven weeks' wandering was a tribute alike to his own adventurous spirit and to the number of good friends he had scattered throughout England. He often used to regale, and sometimes to bore, his courtiers with the story of this escapade and in 1680 at Newmarket race course, of all places, he dictated a full account to Samuel Pepys, his Secretary to the Admiralty, who possessed the rare gift of shorthand in which he kept a diary destined to become famous. Though this account was given nearly thirty years after the event, Charles had been twenty-one at the time, an impressionable age, and it is therefore likely to have been the most authentic of all the many stories that have been preserved.[2]

After the battle Charles and a number of companions, including Lord Wilmot, rode up the Lancashire road via Kidderminster and

Stourbridge presumably with the intention of regaining Scotland. But Charles saw that a conspicuous group of fleeing Royalists was soon likely to be cut off and decided (though he confided this only to Wilmot) that as soon as the opportunity presented itself he would relieve himself of his embarrassing entourage and try to find his way to London. But there were difficulties: 'though I could not get them to stand by me against the enemy, I could not get rid of them now I had a mind to'. After riding through the night Charles obtained shelter at Whiteladies, a house tenanted by five brothers named Penderell on the Boscobel estate north of Stourbridge. Here he was pressed to continue on the road to Scotland, but thought this was impossible 'knowing very well that the country would rise upon us, and that men who had deserted me when they were in good order would never stand by me when they have been beaten'. So he stuck to his plan of finding his way on foot to London in disguise.

At Whiteladies he put on a countryman's clothes, consisting of a pair of grey cloth breeches, a leather doublet and a green jerkin, and he wore a greasy grey soft hat without ribbon or lining. He also had his black hair lopped off, a fact which soon became known to his enemies. Being over six-foot tall and extremely dark he was a detectable figure even in disguise. He had to be closely looked after by enterprising friends all the time lest he should give himself away. Casting his own clothes into a privy, he set out with one of the Penderell brothers, Richard, but soon realized the obstacles to reaching London safely without having places of refuge prepared for him all the way there. In any case his consistent objective was to arrive at the sea and hire a ship that would take him to France. So he now thought of getting across the river Severn into Wales and making for Swansea. But in preparing to ferry over the river they were spotted by an inquisitive miller and forced to spend the night in a barn belonging to an old and nervous Royalist sympathizer before returning next day to Boscobel. It was at Boscobel that Charles spent a day (6 September) hiding in an oak tree, consuming bread and cheese and beer, while down below in the woods the Roundhead soldiers were searching for him and other escapees.

Next day Charles left Boscobel for Moseley hall, belonging to a Roman Catholic family and complete with priests' holes in which he could hide. Here he met a Roman Catholic priest named Father Huddlestone and read through a manuscript of his entitled *A Short and Plain Way to the Christian Faith*. After he read it, he said: 'I have never seen anything more plain and clear upon this subject. The arguments here drawn from succession are so conclusive I do not see how they can be denied.' Whether that was mere politeness to his hosts or not is unknown, but, thus fortified, he set out for another country house, this one belonging to Anglicans, the Lane family. Jane Lane, the daughter of the house, offered to take the King, disguised as her servant, in the direction of Bristol in the hope that he might find a ship there. Dressed as a poor tenant's son in a grey cloth suit, he had an adventurous journey, once running into a troop of enemy horse. But no ships were immediately available at Bristol and so Charles next made for Somerset and by 22 September was at an inn in Charmouth in Dorset and inquiring about a possible ship at Lyme (now Lyme Regis). Though a ship was engaged it failed to be at the rendezvous, and Charles was compelled to spend the next night (23 September) at an inn in Bridport. He had ridden boldly to the best inn in the town where he found the yard full of soldiers about to embark for Jersey. 'I alighted', he related, 'and taking the horses thought the best way to go blundering among them, and lead them through the middle of the soldiers into a stable. Which I did and they were very angry with me for my rudeness.' At Bridport the faithful Wilmot turned up with the bad news that the sea captain at Lyme had lost his nerve. Once more Charles retreated inland and found a safe refuge again with hiding holes at Trent house belonging to Sir Francis and Lady Wyndham; here he stayed in concealment for twelve days. Inquiries were made on his behalf for a ship from Southampton. He had attempted in turn to find ships at Swansea, Bristol, Lyme and Southampton and all in vain. But on 6 October good news at last reached him: there was a promise of a ship at Shoreham near Brighton. So once again he set out for the south and the sea.

Charles spent a week with a discreet widow at Heale house,

five miles away from Salisbury. On Monday, 13 October he was again on his way, once more accompanied by Lord Wilmot. The party broke the night in another friendly house seven miles from Portsmouth and next day reached the George inn at Brighton. Here he had a fright.

For as I was standing after supper by the fireside [he related] leaning my hand upon a chair (the rest of the company being gone into another room) the master of the inn came in and fell a-talking with me, and just as he was going about and saw there was nobody in the room, he upon a sudden kissed my hand that was upon the back of the chair, and said to me 'God bless you wheresoever you go; I do not doubt before I die to be a lord and my wife a lady'.

Charles laughed and went into the next room. At Shoreham, which he reached on 15 October, a loyal ship's captain awaited him. He said he knew the King very well and would venture his life and all he had in the world to conduct him safely to France. And so he did. At seven in the morning at high tide with the wind blowing north they sailed past the Isle of Wight and reached Fécamp on the ebb tide. Charles and Wilmot thought they were espied by an Ostend privateer just as they were within sight of land. They hastened ashore in 'a little cock boat'. Next day they spent in an inn at the fish market in Rouen, 'where they made difficulty to receive us, taking us by our clothes to be some thieves'. An English merchant vouched for them. They bought new clothes there and, after setting out in a hired coach, were met by the Queen Mother with coaches near Paris. 'By her,' Charles concluded his narrative, [we] were 'conducted thither [to Paris] where I safely arrived.' It was 18 October, forty-five days after the battle of Worcester.

When Charles returned to France he was lean, tall and dark and his looks betrayed to those who saw him a disappointed man with a mind deeply affected by defeat. He was described as sombre and silent, though cheerfulness had a way of breaking through. He made the most of his adventures, for his reappearance, after he had been missing for so long following the battle of Worcester, caused something of a sensation at his mother's court. The Grande

Mademoiselle, whom he began to woo again, found him 'much better looking' and she noted that he had learned to speak French very well, although how he found the time to master the language during his stay in Scotland is obscure.[3] He related his exploits with an extreme lack of veracity, saying, for example, that during his attempt to escape from his enemies he had visited both Scotland and London, though he had been in neither, for he was anxious that those who had helped him on his way should not be detected (English republican spies were everywhere) and survive ultimately to be royally rewarded. He wrote, for instance, to Jane Lane, who had followed him abroad, that 'it was impossible I can ever forget the great debt I owe you, which I hope I shall live to pay in a degree that is worthy of me'.[4]

For the time being Henrietta Maria's court in the Louvre was the only suitable refuge for Charles. Scotland, though many high-landers remained loyal to him, was under the 'iron rule' of General George Monck. The Marquis of Ormonde had been forced by the Roman Catholic clergy to leave Ireland and had handed over his responsibilities there to the Marquis of Clanricard who was of their faith. Thenceforward the Irish relied for victory over the English republicans entirely on God. Charles summoned Ormonde to join his council, which also included Edward Hyde, the Chancellor of the Exchequer, Lord Jermyn, the faithful friend of his mother, Lord Norwich, father of the drunken and daring George Goring of the civil wars, and Lord Wilmot, the companion of Charles's travels. Lord Inchiquin, formerly Ormonde's lieutenant-general, also joined the council later. But financial stringencies prevented Charles from summoning either Sir Robert Long or Sir Edward Nicholas, both of whom had at one time been his Secretaries of State. Every week Hyde wrote to Nicholas, who lived at The Hague, and their correspondence throws a flood of light on the new court.

Queen Henrietta Maria welcomed her son with surprise and enthusiasm. Her second son, James, was already with her and her youngest daughter, Henriette Anne, was to be joined in March 1653 by her youngest son, Henry, Duke of Gloucester, who was released by the English republicans. She was surrounded by her

family and held an assured position as the aunt of the King of
France. But she was now in her forties and, as her biographer
notes, was at that season of her life a very difficult person constantly engaged in quarrels. She had been shy at meeting the
returned King whom she feared she would find 'very ridiculous'
with his shorn hair (on which he hastened to put a wig that he
bought or borrowed) and she vainly tried to rule him, as she had
ruled her dead husband.[5] Charles was obliged later to warn his
mother that he did not necessarily intend to take her advice or
reveal to her all his secrets. She, for her part, let him know as
soon as he sat down at her table that he must pay his share of all
the household expenses including the food eaten by his brother
James. The position of these English royal exiles was far from
serene, for France itself was in turmoil and money promised by
way of pensions was generally not paid.

France was absorbed in civil war. When Charles returned from
England the second Fronde (or Fronde of the Princes) was in full
swing. This was in essence not a conflict arising from the constitutional grievances of the bourgeoisie, as the first Fronde had been
in 1649, but a blatant struggle for power between the princes of
the blood, headed by the successful General Condé, and Cardinal
Mazarin, the successor of Richelieu and the trusted chief Minister
of the Regent, the Queen Mother, Anne of Austria. Louis XIV
was in 1651 to attain his majority on his thirteenth birthday and
both sides claimed to be fighting in his cause. In February of that
year Mazarin had been forced to release Condé from prison and
then departed abroad. To sustain his claims to supremacy Condé,
more skilful as a soldier than as a politician, allied himself to
Spain, with which France had long been at war. Though Mazarin
returned to France in January 1652, he was soon obliged to leave
again, while the Queen Mother and the boy King abandoned
Paris, leaving Marshal Turenne to fight their battles for them.
Thus Charles was caught up in a maelstrom that was none of his
business. One of the first things he and his council had to decide
was whether or not they would allow James, Duke of York, to
serve as a volunteer with Turenne's army: with some hesitation
they resolved to let him do so on the understanding that they

merely accorded with his personal wishes. James therefore went each year to the field of battle: it was not long before he acquired the rank of general and 'got the reputation of a prince of very signal courage ... universally beloved of the whole army by his affable behaviour'.[6]

As to King Charles himself, it was not unnatural that he should be employed as a mediator. By the spring of 1652 he had assisted in procuring a treaty between the opposing parties and Nicholas optimistically wrote from The Hague to Hyde saying that he hoped this would mean an end to the intestine troubles of France and even bring about a peace with Spain. But the treaty fell through and soon the civil wars reached the gates of Paris. Fighting took place in the suburbs while Turenne was occupied in besieging Etampes, south of the capital. A further complication was that the Spaniards dispatched the Duke of Lorraine, a military adventurer with an army but without a duchy, to support Condé against Turenne. In Paris Condé and Gaston, Duke of Orleans (Henrietta Maria's ineffable brother) treated Charles II to compliments and assurances, and he received a message from Louis XIV asking him to conduct the Duke of Lorraine to visit him at Melun. The Duke was an evasive customer, rich in promises but poor in performances. Before the Duke's arrival in Paris Charles sent two of his council, Wilmot and Jermyn, to interview him and they returned with 'a general answer'. 'I think nothing is left undone on our parts to unite the King of France and the Duke of Lorraine,' wrote Hyde on 24 May 1652, 'but all the business hath been so often baffled on either side that neither dares to believe each other's promises'.[7] After seeing Charles, Lorraine eventually withdrew, but Condé was for the moment in control of Paris. He ordered Charles, his mother and their entourage to leave the capital for St Germain. There the English King had no alternative but 'to sit still until he found some good occasion to move'.[8] He had no money, not having received a penny of his French pension for eight months, while, according to Hyde, the French people were 'as mad as their enemies can wish them' and he saw no hope of peace.[9]

The war of the Fronde put an end to Charles's courtship of the

Grande Mademoiselle. She had thrown in her lot with the Prince de Condé; thrusting her hesitating father aside, she had turned the guns of the Bastille on the French King's forces when Condé was in difficulties during the fighting round Paris that summer. Now she came to say goodbye to the English party as she left for Orleans, which earlier in the year she had defended heroically against the royal troops. Queen Henrietta Maria compared the Grande Mademoiselle to Joan of Arc, the Maid of Orleans, who had likewise repulsed the English. Whatever the ins-and-outs of Charles's wooing of this amazon may have amounted to, it became impossible for him to pursue her once she had declared war on the French King and his mother. Condé's triumph proved a mere flash in the pan. Turenne was loyal and victorious, but the leaders of the Fronde quarrelled and intrigued interminably against one another. By October 1652 the French King was back in Paris, himself taking up residence in the Louvre. In February of the following year Mazarin also returned to the capital and the second Fronde was over.

While France was torn asunder by civil war the English Commonwealth was somewhat fortuitously involved in a naval war with the Dutch. The two nations were, as a leading English republican was to declare, 'rivals for the fairest mistress in all Christendom – trade'. The Dutch had built up a world-wide commerce and a busy mercantile marine, so that the English republic had thought it necessary to encourage its own seamen with a protective navigation act in 1651. Thus clashes at sea, caused in part by the English claim of the right to search Dutch ships for French goods – since a sort of undeclared war existed with France – created enmity which was enhanced by national pride. Must the Dutch navy strike its flag whenever the English navy hove into view? A minor incident, when two Dutch frigates, protecting seven Dutch merchantmen, ran into a superior English force in the Channel in May 1652, projected a major battle. The veteran Dutch admiral Martin Tromp saw red when one of his sailors was killed by a cannonade ordered by the English admiral Robert Blake after Tromp refused to strike his flag in the Channel, and in the engagement that followed two Dutch warships were sunk. Four Dutch ambassadors were at work in London during June and each side vainly sought compensation from the other. War was declared at the end of the month. The Dutch were at a disadvantage. The break-up of the Stadholderate following the death of Charles II's brother-in-law, William II of Orange, in 1650, had in effect decentralized the Dutch naval administration and led to confusion; while the English had a powerful navy, originally built up by Charles II's father. Soon English warships were everywhere wreaking havoc on the Dutch merchant ships and herring fishermen.

Charles naturally and reasonably hoped 'to reap some benefit from this war, so briskly entered upon by both sides'. His first idea was to send an ambassador to the United Netherlands to draw the attention of the Dutch to the value of his friendship. But he waited until the Dutch envoys returned from England and asked for permission to come to Holland himself. The Dutch authorities were not enthusiastic about this proposal. After all, what had Charles to offer them apart from a handful of ships under the command of Prince Rupert which were occupied in piracy off the West Indies? Except for the highlands of Scotland there was no area where the King could command any considerable measure of support. Moreover since the death of William II, whose last act had been a *coup d'état* against leading Dutch republicans, the Orange faction had been in disrepute among the Dutch ruling class. In waging war with the English republicans, the Dutch republicans had no wish to undermine their own internal position by reviving the Orangist party. So it was pointed out to Charles that it would be a prejudice to his widowed sister and his baby nephew, the third William of Orange, if he arrived in Holland to promote his cause.

This was a disappointment. Charles tried another tack. He invoked the help of the Dutch ambassador in Paris, who had formerly been ambassador in England and was on friendly terms with the King. Charles asked him to pass on a message that 'if the States will assign me some ships, no more than they think may fitly serve under my standard, I will engage my own person with them in the company of their fleet, and either by God's blessing prevail with them, or perish in the attempt'. This informal, if heroic, offer was not accepted for precisely the same reason that had caused the King's request to visit Holland to be refused. Indeed the Pensionary of Holland, John de Witt, thought that the King's presence with the Dutch fleet would be more likely to prolong the war, by exacerbating the English republicans, than to help to bring it to a victorious end;[10] and de Witt had no wish permanently to alienate the powerful Commonwealth. A final scheme adumbrated was that Sir George Carteret, the former Governor of Jersey, should raise a squadron of four or five English ships to be commissioned by the King, which would be received and assisted in the Dutch ports and might be used to recapture Guernsey and put it in the hands of the Dutch. But even if the Dutch had agreed to this there were really no funds for such an adventure.

As the war developed and spread, more political consequences flowed from it. Not only did defeats at sea and the destruction of their foreign trade break the hearts of the Dutch, but the English had no scruple in attacking French interests as well. The war between France and Spain continued and the French tried to defend Dunkirk, which they had captured in the Spanish Netherlands, against a close Spanish siege. Robert Blake received orders to attack a relieving fleet accompanied by supply ships, which had been dispatched from Calais in September 1652, and he completely destroyed it. Dunkirk at once surrendered and the French protested against an act of aggression carried out without any declaration of war by the English Commonwealth. At the same time the Danes, who were friendly to the Dutch, entered the war on the Dutch side by interfering with British commerce in the Baltic.

Charles II watched all these developments with close attention. Blake's action against Dunkirk had made the French government more amenable to the idea of stirring up trouble for the English; Cardinal Mazarin now pressed the King to go to Holland. Charles attempted to persuade the Dutch that if his cause were embraced by them Jersey, Guernsey, the Scilly Islands and the Orkneys might be recovered and could be placed at their disposal for an assault on England. Many of Charles's courtiers also thought that he should continue to insist upon visiting Holland, but this still proved hopeless. Charles sent Lord Wentworth as his ambassador to Denmark; and when he heard that twenty Danish warships were being put to sea he asked if he might be allowed to command the squadron. Though that was not conceded, the King was satisfied with Wentworth's progress in promoting an alliance between the Danes and the Dutch, and hoped that he might be 'comprehended in any treaty'. The King also sent Sir William Bellenden on an informal embassy to Queen Christina of Sweden to urge her also to join in an alliance with the Danes and the Dutch against the English Commonwealth. But during the summer of 1653 Charles was taken ill with a fever and five times let blood so that he became weak and melancholy. It was not until the autumn that he recovered and went to recuperate at Chantilly. No diplomatic avenue was left unexplored. Lord Wilmot, now promoted to be Earl of Rochester, had been sent to Germany in the spring to attend as an observer at a meeting of the Diet at Ratisbon, called to elect the King of the Romans, so that he might put Charles's case for the commiseration and assistance of the German princes. Spain, it was thought, ought also for her own interest to support the King. Hyde, however, remained doubtful about acquiring help for Charles from anywhere abroad and declared that he was 'still so mad as to expect some good turn from England rather than foreign princes'.[11]

As the war with England went increasingly badly for the Dutch, Charles's hopes faded. He did what he could. He suggested that the Dutch should provide arms and ammunition for 24,000 men to refurbish the Royalist highlands of Scotland as the highlanders had only bows, arrows and spears. Some Dutch provinces showed a willingness to furnish help but Holland remained adamant. It is also true that some English Presbyterians in exile in the United Netherlands believed that both the Dutch and the English would help with money if the King himself went to the highlands, but in fact Charles's closest advisers were rightly of the opinion that once the Dutch had been reduced to seeking peace with the English republicans, they would not contemplate sending any underhand assistance to the Scottish highlands. The main obstacle to any constructive moves on the King's part remained lack of money. He had to withdraw Lord Wentworth from the court of Denmark because he could no longer afford to pay him. His hopes of raising capital by the sale of prizes captured by Prince Rupert in the West Indies proved abortive, though Rupert had returned to France in 1653. Cardinal Mazarin deliberately kept Charles short of money because so long as his relations with the English Commonwealth stayed unsettled (the Cardinal had sent an ambassador there after the Dunkirk episode) he did not want the King to leave Paris where he might prove at least a useful pawn in the negotiations.

Nobody knew what Oliver Cromwell, Lord Protector of England, Scotland and Ireland from December 1653, might decide to do with his navy and army once the Dutch war ended. No doubt, observed Hyde on 10 April 1654, if the French 'did once enough see Cromwell's purpose to invade them', they would 'enable the King to kindle such a fire in England, Ireland and Scotland that Cromwell would have enough work at home'.[12] But the French were not to be trusted to be loyal to their guest. The English Commonwealth's victories at sea had put the fear of God into all the European powers. Mazarin's representative in London was promoted to the rank of ambassador and sought a treaty of amity and commerce. In April 1654 the Dutch concluded a humiliating peace, and the French and Spaniards vied with each other for the favours of the government in London.

Thus the only place where Charles could hope to revive the Stuart cause was in Scotland. The Scots had resented the military occupation of their country by the English republicans and were far from delighted at the idea, announced in February 1652, that their ancient kingdom was to be incorporated into England. In June Charles received a message from the highland chieftains that they were prepared to resume the war on his behalf; for this reason the King issued a commission to John Middleton, who had distinguished himself in earlier fighting and had escaped from London where he had been taken a prisoner after the battle of Worcester, to be his lieutenant-general in Scotland. But it was thought wise that Middleton should first go to Holland in order to raise money, collect supplies and hire ships. In the meantime the Scottish nobility, so the King told Middleton, could elect a temporary commander among themselves. But the King's commission enabling them to do this was not immediately sent, and since the Scottish leaders were jealous of one another it was by no means a satisfactory solution.

Charles was disappointed that progress was not at once achieved in the campaign in the highlands. In March 1653 he wrote to Middleton saying: 'Who would have thought after so much discourse of an army in the highlands that had taken Inverness and would quickly drive the English out of the kingdom that there should indeed be no men there but such as lodge in their own beds, and only project what they will do when they are able?'[13] That was scarcely fair, for the highlanders had no leader and very limited resources. But in the summer of 1653 the royal cause brightened. William Cunningham, Earl of Glencairn, a Hamiltonian from the south, now assumed, at Charles's request, the temporary command. The powerful Lord Balcarres threw in his lot with the Royalists. At the end of the previous year General George Monck, the republican commander-in-chief, had left Scotland to assume the role of a general-at-sea during the Dutch war. His successor, Colonel Robert Lilburne, was an Anabaptist, and far from welcome to the prickly Scottish Presbyterians. Indeed Lilburne showed himself nervous of the Scottish Presbyterians in the lowlands who, before the execution of King Charles I, had been the allies of the English Royalists. When the General Assembly of the Kirk met in Edinburgh in July Lilburne decided on his own responsibility to dissolve it on the ground that he suspected that the ministers were about to enter into treasonable communications with the Royalists in the highlands. Such an action was bound to turn the lowlands against the English Commonwealth: for, according to the Scottish Presbyterians, 'the glory and strength of our Church upon earth' was 'crushed and trod under foot' by the English soldiery. In August 1652 Lord Lorne, son of the Covenanter chief, the Marquis of Argyll, joined up with the rebellious highlanders. Virtually the whole of

Scotland showed itself opposed to the military rule of Lilburne.

Lilburne was in a position of genuine difficulty. He had not enough troops to establish order among an alien population. As the resources of the English Commonwealth were at the time fully deployed in the naval war with the Dutch, he could get no support from the sea. Though the experienced English soldiers could contend with the Scottish rebels on open ground, the highlanders were able to retreat into the hills and carry on guerrilla warfare. Lilburne was also understandably afraid that the highlanders in their eastern lochs would receive sustenance from the Dutch fleets. In the summer of 1653 the Scottish Royalists appeared to have a unique opportunity. The skill of Monck was missing, and Lilburne was neglected by the London government occupied with the Dutch war. But the Scots did not engage in more than harassing operations. Glencairn and Angus Macdonald of Glengarry were 'busy up and down', and as winter drew on many small parties came down into the lowlands by night to steal horses. But the Scottish chieftains quarrelled among themselves, the Campbells distrusted the Macdonalds and Balcarres disliked Glencairn. Duels were even fought. Mixed reports reached Charles II of the progress of events. Vainly he tried to pour oil on the troubled waters, expressing his discomfort at 'the falling out, difference and unkindness amongst those whom I love the most'.[14]

The decision had deliberately been taken to act on the defensive and not to risk a battle before Middleton arrived. But Middleton had achieved little progress in Holland. He was taken ill when he was there. Some of the Dutch Provinces promised help but did not provide it. Money came in only in dribs and drabs. Though he was pressed from Paris to get a move on, he still delayed; and it was not until he received positive orders to linger no longer that he sailed from Holland for Scotland in February 1654.

Ought Charles himself to have returned to Scotland at this time and personally assumed the command there, aiming to reconcile by his presence the fierce differences among his followers? Some of his advisers urged him to steal into Scotland with two or three chosen companions. There can be no doubt that when good news arrived, as it did in the autumn of 1653, he was desperately longing to do so. As early as June of that year Hyde was writing from Paris that 'the King is resolved very shortly to go from hence, and I am verily persuaded that if no more probable adventure offer itself he will go for Scotland. . . .'[15] In October Hyde wrote again, this time to Rochester, that 'if nothing else occurs the King will go to the highlands, from which no one will dissuade him'.[16] But two obvious difficulties stood in the way. The first was that as long as the Dutch war lasted and the French government had not come to terms with the English, Mazarin wanted the King to remain in Paris and had potent means of obliging him to do so. The English Royalist court could not be sure that events might not take a favourable turn for them elsewhere. The Dutch might, after all, seek to make use of Charles's services; the French might furnish him with means for resuscitating the civil war in England itself. The Dutch navy might occupy one of the outlying islands or sponsor a properly organized invasion of Scotland. The second consideration was that Charles himself had only recently had devastating experiences of the un-reliability of the Scots as allies and feared that if he returned there he would be 'betrayed and given up'. Though Lorne had come over to his side, Argyll, still the most important figure in Scotland, had failed to pledge his support, while the lowlanders, whose alliance was essential for the reconquest of Scotland by the Royalists, were likely to stipulate the same frustrating restraints upon his freedom as they had done in 1650. Glencairn, it was clear, was no Montrose. In the conditions of the winter of 1653 a Montrose might have debouched from the glens and spread terror into the hearts of the English republican soldiers under the uncertain leadership of Lilburne. The sensible thing to do was to await a report from Middleton, who might perhaps be able to unite the Scots in the royal service. The King, Hyde reported in March 1654, intended to leave France as soon as he could and 'will rest somewhere till from Lieutenant-General Middleton he know the true state of Scotland and so proceed accordingly'.[17] It might not have been a heroic decision but it was a statesmanlike one.

A great deal of criticism has been made, and has been repeated by biographers, about Charles II's behaviour during those years in Paris. Much of it derives from the correspondence between Hyde and Nicholas, who deplored the King's inattention to business and accused him of indulging in undesirable pleasures. Hyde, now in his forties, had been a critic of the Stuart monarchy in the Long Parliament and was an admirer of Oliver Cromwell as a statesman if not as a man. Something of the austerity which is associated with seventeenth-century Puritanism flowed through his mind. Nicholas, melancholic and hypochondriac, was nearing his sixties and tended to live in the past, in the world of Charles the Martyr. Both of them detested Queen Henrietta Maria and her adviser, Lord Jermyn, and thought that they were a bad influence on Charles. They disliked the French and distrusted Mazarin. They resented it when their advice was not accepted by the King and muttered about the underhand inspiration of others than themselves. Nicholas asserted in May 1652 that 'the King suffers himself to be persuaded against his own judgments and conscience in affairs of importance'.[18]

The dominant fact about the years in Paris was Charles's lack of money. In view of that it was remarkable that he was able to organize a not ineffective diplomatic service for himself in the attempt to build up alliances and recruit assistance. In addition to the embassies sent out during the Dutch war and the essential mission of Rochester to Ratisbon Charles had in 1652 dispatched missions to Spain, Moscow, Persia and Morocco and he kept a permanent resident in Brussels in Sir Henry de Vic. He also had a representative in Vienna and on French advice he wrote to the Pope promising good treatment for his Roman Catholic subjects when he was restored to his throne, though he promised nothing more. In most cases the foreign potentates contented themselves with sending presents (the Tsar sent furs) or small sums of money, but these rarely did more than cover the costs of the missions, while promises of cash frequently vanished into thin air. Prince Rupert, after twenty months' absence, maintained that the prizes he had captured and the ancient ship in which he returned were insufficient to cover the debts which he had incurred and that in fact Charles owed him money. After this episode the King was alienated from his cousin, but the friendship was to be restored later. Still it was no wonder that the King wanted money to get away from Paris, where even his mother demanded payment from him and the French Government, because of the Fronde, failed to make good his promised pension. In June 1653 the King was said to owe for all he had eaten since April. In October he 'had not money to keep him for twenty days'. In December he was said to be awaiting the arrival of Rupert with money that would enable him to leave France.[19] It was not until 1654 that a promise of 100,000 rixdollars from the Emperor and other sums from German princes gave him some hope of solvency. It was hardly surprising that he felt there was little that he could do to regain his thrones.

Hyde complained that the King did not like writing personal letters: 'when anything is to be done by the King's own hand we must sometimes be content to wait, he being very unwilling to work, which vexes me exceedingly'.[20] He took his pleasures where he could find them, no doubt often on the cheap, and was contrasted by the censorious with his brother James who went punctually on campaign every year and was said to be a gallant prince who enjoyed 'an extraordinary esteem with the army' and 'will really come to great matters'. But James was not much more than a stupid soldier, and he too was fond of the ladies when he could find them. A republican spy reported in 1653 that 'the King is so whelmed in pleasures, specially women (so that the whole town rings of him) that the Queen and Council urged him to move'. That was untrue, and Hyde indeed told Nicholas that 'all the counsel of the world cannot reform the King while he is with the Queen'.[21] It is plain however that during that year the King's reputation had fallen. He was deeply upset by the rejection of all his offers to take part in the Dutch war, as his brother did in the Spanish war, and he was taken ill. Hyde was then writing that Charles was so given over to pleasure that 'if he stay here he will be undone'. At one time Hyde's assistance was invoked to remove a lady from the Louvre who should not have been there. But even Hyde perceived that Charles was, after all, a young man with all the natural instincts of his age: 'it is true,' he wrote, 'there are and always will be some actions of appetite and affection which cannot be separated from the age of twenty-one, and which we must all labour by good consent to prevent and divert and when we have done our duty we must make the best of what we cannot help.'[22]

The truth was that, apart from these foibles, the King played his part to the best of his ability. He would much have preferred to put to sea or adventure into Scotland than to dally in Paris. Outwardly he remained faithful to his father's religion and refused to attend the services either of the Huguenots or the Roman Catholics, though he was pressed to do both. Taking a firm line with his mother, he frustrated her attempts to convert his younger brother, Henry, to her religion. He tried to maintain peace between the warring bodies at his court. Hyde himself had reason to value his personal loyalty at this time. For the King's former secretary, Robert Long, accused the Chancellor of the Exchequer of intriguing with Cromwell and of receiving a large pension for his intelligence work. The Chancellor was able to prove that he had never been in London since the civil wars began, but it was rather awkward for him when, to back up Long, Lord Gerard recalled a conversation with Hyde when the latter had complained about the King's 'inactivity and habitual neglect of business'.[23] This was unpleasantly near the bone in view of the tenor of some of Hyde's letters to Nicholas, but the King took no notice. Charles remained consistently trustful towards his most energetic Minister, though no doubt he well knew that he was the subject of his adverse criticisms; and it did not make for harmony that Hyde was not on speaking terms with the Queen Mother. In view of these divisions and rumblings at his court the King did not manage too badly.

It was not only his personal conduct that was the theme of dis-approval. Lord Gerard had asserted that 'rather than sit still in France, his Majesty ought to go to every Court in Christendom' and, in particular, should have attended the German Diet himself instead of sending Rochester. Alderman John Bunce, a Pres-byterian exile in Holland, observed that 'many people were dis-satisfied with the King's proceedings in France', and that he should have gone to Scotland.[24] Did the King in fact stay in France too long? He certainly did not want to remain there. He searched for every means of escape. He carried out a sensible policy of seeking help in every direction. He offered a variety of suggestions about how he might be allowed to participate in the Dutch war without insisting on the Dutch committing themselves to his restoration. He pressed Middleton to go to Scotland quickly and immediately to send his report. He entered into correspondence with his leading supporters in England but gave them no encouragement to engage in a premature rising or to try to assassinate Cromwell. 'Many light foolish persons propose wild things to the King,' noted Hyde, 'which he civilly discountenances . . . the truth is the King thinks there are some honest men who will do what is possible and stir when it is fit'. In spite of all the compulsions to which he was subjected and all the criticisms which were made of him, the young King maintained his personal control. Charles refused to be bullied by his mother. He made it clear that Middleton went to Scotland as his personal representative. He announced that 'there will be no other General in England but himself nor Lieutenant-General but the Duke of York'.[25] He brushed aside the accusations against Hyde and expressed his willingness to be reconciled to Prince Rupert even if he thought that Rupert had treated him badly. Whatever Hyde may have said, Charles was clearly the master in his own house and, apart from his original handling of the rising in Scotland, he committed no serious political errors. Before he left Paris in the summer of 1654 Hyde wrote to Nicholas: 'If you knew the miserable life the King leads, and how he is used, you would believe that he acts his part not amiss; nor is it enough to say that it is his own fault.'[26] That was a fair summing up of Charles's conduct in France.

5

Towards the Restoration

Once Cardinal Mazarin had decided to conclude a treaty of friendship and commerce with the English Commonwealth (although the treaty was not in fact signed until October 1655) it became inevitable that Charles II must leave France. He had long been impatient to do so; his mother had kept him on a tight financial leash and Louis XIV's court had grown cold towards him. But now he was helped on his way out. As Hyde remarked, the only good reason for the King's going was the willingness of the French that he should be gone. Suddenly Charles was told that the arrears of his pension would be paid as well as a six-month advance if he would be out of the country in ten days. Where could he go to? The United Netherlands were closed to him and the Spaniards, who were also seeking an alliance with the English Commonwealth, did not want him in their part of the Netherlands. But the Germans seemed friendly, and as a first move Charles decided to meet his devoted sister Mary at Spa. Under the stress of his mother's importunities he left behind his younger brother Henry but instructed him to obey the Queen in all things except religion. His other brother, James, still serving with the French army, also remained in France. Charles gave him a list of strict instructions about what he should or should not do and told the Duke to see that their mother did not violate the promises which she had given about not attempting to convert Prince Henry to Roman Catholicism. Charles also paid a secret farewell visit to the beautiful Duchess de Châtillon, whom he had at one time thought of making his wife. Then on 14 July he started by way of Cambrai and Mons to Spa. 'The King's resolution to go into Germany', Hyde wrote in his *History*, 'was very grateful to everybody, more from the weariness they had of France than from the foresight of any benefit and advantage that was like to accrue from the move.'[1]

Hyde gives the impression that Charles's intention was to settle down and amuse himself for six months, forgetting his duty of labouring for the restoration of his thrones. For once the King was in a position of comparative affluence. There was the French pension, and some money had been collected from the princes of Germany. The future Sir Stephen Fox (grandfather of Charles James Fox), a highly competent young man, was selected to take charge of the household finances. It was believed that by careful management the King's court could be supported for a whole year out of the existing revenues, while any other money that became available could be used for assisting the Royalists in Scotland or for enterprises elsewhere. The King and his sister indeed had a pleasant time together first in Spa and then at Aachen, where they were driven by an outbreak of smallpox; but Charles constantly kept in mind the possibilities of risings in Scotland and England and was ready to go to either country if his presence was likely to be needed.

A spy reported in August 1654 that 'some about him [Charles] tell him that it were better to hasten to Scotland than stay at the Spa and dance, which is his daily and nightly practice'.[2] Hyde, who accompanied Charles to Aachen, had a serious interview with him and pressed him to go to the Scottish highlands where General Middleton was reported to be having some success. Charles, recalling his earlier adventures with the Scots, expressed a doubt that he could live there in health and security and was sceptical of the Scottish ability to maintain the fight for long. In this he proved absolutely right, for even before he arrived at Aachen Middleton had been defeated at the battle of Dalnaspedal, and after that neither Middleton nor any other Scottish commander was able to collect more than a few hundred men; it was only small and isolated bands that managed to keep the field in different parts of Scotland for another year. On his return General Monck had taken effective control for the Commonwealth and laid waste part of the highlands, while the Royalist leaders had quarrelled among themselves and had nothing but poorly equipped and ill-disciplined levies with which to confront Monck's organized forces. The intelligence received from Scotland was always out of date and usually far too optimistic and Charles, drawing on his experiences, had a more realistic view of the possibilities than had Hyde who had never been there.

Nevertheless Charles stood ready to go back to Scotland should his gloomy forecasts prove wrong. He had indicated as much to his brother James before he left Paris, for he had informed him that *when* he himself went to Scotland he would leave the transaction of the business of England in his brother's hands.[3] In answer to Hyde's pressures Charles said that if his friends positively advised him, 'he would transport himself into the highlands, though he knew what would come of it'; and spies, reporting to John Thurloe, Oliver Cromwell's Secretary of State, from Spa and Aachen, said that the King's Council was considering when the King should go and 'you may be assured Charles Stewart stands absolutely for Scotland'.[4] As late as December Monck was concerned with rumours that the King was on his way there, while boasting 'I doubt not we shall (through the blessing of God) keep him in such a country, where he cannot ride or travel but in trousers and plaid, if you continue the forces now afoot here'.[5] It is clear that had Charles ventured into the highlands in the summer of 1654 he would only have suffered another defeat and the likelihood of capture by his enemies. Sir Edward Nicholas, Charles's Secretary of State, was as opposed to the King going there as Hyde was in favour of it. But Hyde was unwilling to admit that he had ever been in the wrong.

Another reason which made Charles hesitate to risk his life in Scotland was that a Royalist organization had now been established in England to promote a rising there. Charles had been asked to give his approval to the constitution of a group of old Royalists who would have the secret management of his affairs in England. A committee of six men, known as the Sealed Knot, was formed about the time that Oliver Cromwell became Lord Protector in December 1653. The members were mostly younger sons of the aristocracy – only Sir Richard Willys, who had been one of King Charles I's guardsmen, was not. They were wealthy, influential and cautious men and highly regarded at Charles II's court. The King gave the committee the full stamp of his approval, though he empowered them in May 1654 to 'admit such persons into their number whom they think and at such times as they think necessary'.[6] They appointed a secretary and communicated regularly with Hyde and Ormonde, and represented the side of the Royalist movement that was opposed to the King seeking his restoration through concessions to the Scots and the English Presbyterians. It was naturally hoped that Cromwell's appointment by the army as Lord Protector would antagonize many English republicans, and that once dissensions came into the open a successful revolution might be engineered on the King's behalf. Charles himself appears to have felt optimistic, and was even convinced (in July 1654) that if all his supporters in England would cooperate 'the work would be done without difficulty'. But his counsellors were divided. In September it was reported that there were three factions at Charles's court, one for Scotland, one for Ireland and one for England. Until the news of Middleton's defeat was confirmed, the King's council was unable to agree on a specific line of policy. But in December 1654 Middleton himself opened negotiations with Monck, and in April 1655 he left Scotland where the other Royalist leaders capitulated.

In October Charles settled his court in Cologne. Cologne was an imperial electorate, but the Elector was an archbishop who did not live in the city; and the governing body or senate welcomed Charles's presence there and treated him with civility and respect. After a short visit with his sister to Düsseldorf, where they were magnificently entertained by the Duke of Newburg, Charles settled in Cologne for the winter. Part of his days was spent reading and studying French and Italian; he walked much on the walls of the city and sometimes rode and hunted. But all the time he closely followed the news from England where Cromwell's first Protectorate Parliament was now in session and was proving obstreperous. The captious conduct of the House of Commons aroused the hopes of the more active Royalists. In January 1655 the King was writing to the Marquis of Ormonde, who was living in Antwerp, to discuss whether Ormonde himself should venture into England to see how the land lay, and saying that he was ready to go there himself 'at an hour's notice'.[7] To the Duke of York he wrote in February saying that his brother must not despise the reports of plots in England, but keep himself in readiness to move.[8]

In fact the Royalists in England were divided and so were Oliver Cromwell's other enemies. In September 1654 when the Protectorate parliament met, Major-General Thomas Harrison, formerly one of Oliver's most trusted subordinates, was put under arrest for agitating against the Protector. There was dissatisfaction in the army over Cromwell's religious policies tending towards genuine toleration, but at the same time such extreme sects as the Anabaptists, Fifth Monarchy Men and Quakers were all expressing fears of tyranny. Outside the House of Commons the Levellers, led by John Wildman (their former leader, John Lilburne, was languishing in prison), conspired with some extremist colonels and published a petition demanding 'a free parliament'. Finally the republicans inside the House were trying to tear to pieces the Protectorate constitution known as 'the Instrument of Government'. Cromwell, finding that unrest was spreading from the army to the navy and that the fierce critical debates in the Commons provided a focus for discontent, decided to dissolve the House at the earliest opportunity and to arrest conspirators and nip rebellion in the bud. The mutinous colonels were discovered and placed under arrest. Major-General Robert Overton who, after some conspiratorial conversations with Wildman, had endeavoured to stir up trouble in the army in Scotland was arrested by Monck and sent to London. Finally on 10 February 1655 Wildman himself was arrested.

It was no wonder if under these circumstances some of Charles's supporters in England grew optimistic and thought the time was ripe to overthrow the Protectorate and bring back the King. For more than six months Charles himself had been nursing hopes. On 16 July 1654, when he was on his way to Spa, he had written a letter to a member of the Action party in England saying that though he had been 'so tender of my friends that I have deferred to call upon them to appear till I could find myself able to give them good encouragement from abroad ... since I find that comes on so slowly I will no longer restrain those affections which I most desire to be beholden to', and expressed his belief that 'if there was any handsome appearance in any one place, the rest would not sit still'. It was at this date too that he had assured Colonel Edward Grey (half-brother to Lord Grey of Wark) that he believed that 'the work could be done without difficulty'.[9] But Charles's supporters in England were divided between the wealthy and influential leaders of the Sealed Knot and men like Grey who were impoverished gentry and the more adventurous perhaps because they had the less to lose.

Both the Action party and the Sealed Knot sent messengers to Charles at Cologne during January 1655, the former asking for his approval for a rising to take place on 13 February, the latter insisting that a revolt would be dangerous and self-destructive. Ormonde, who was watching the developments in England from Antwerp, informed Hyde that while the Sealed Knot was 'dissuading all from a rising now as being precipitate and unreasonable, the Knot will appear if commanded by the King, although desirous to remain quiet: he must therefore either forbid the enterprise or direct them to help it'. Charles, confronted with contradictory advice supplied by the two messengers from England, was in an awkward situation. His intelligence was not sufficiently good for him to be able to measure what the chances really were. As a frustrated young prince his instincts were all in favour of immediate action. But instead of making up his mind and giving positive instructions he compromised, as statesmen do. He decided to send to England a member of his staff, Daniel O'Neill, to try to unite the two parties. His message was to the effect that he could not look for any great success if whilst the Action party stirred, the Sealed Knot stood still. Yet he felt that it would be 'unreasonable to give any positive command against their judgment and inclinations'.[10] The same advice was sent to the Action party: 'It cannot', he said, 'be reasonable for him to hinder those who are ready to move ... nor yet unreasonable to command the latter to join against his judgment.' He also told

Lord Willoughby of Parham, a Presbyterian who had formerly fought alongside Cromwell in the first civil war, that he could not 'direct him what to do' but that he hoped that 'if any of his friends appear in any engagement, the rest will join, which will be the best security of all'.[11]

Besides O'Neill Charles sent his friend Henry Wilmot, Earl of Rochester, to England to assume the supreme command of his forces there. Rochester got into England safely, but O'Neill was arrested at Dover, although after a week he managed to escape. So he arrived later than was intended with his ambiguous messages. But Charles's refusal to follow the advice of Ormonde, one of the sagest of his counsellors, either to forbid the enterprise or to order all the Royalists in England to join it, was most unhelpful to his cause. Admittedly he was in considerable difficulty. For he himself had set up the Sealed Knot as his own representatives on the spot to direct his affairs in England and had virtually given them a free hand. At the same time his heart was with the Action party and most of the news from England suggested that then and there was the time to strike. So he hesitated and compromised and no doubt felt sure that when the agreed date for action arrived the Sealed Knot would join in. There was no lack of courage on his part. He immediately left the comforts of Cologne and went secretly to Middleburg in Holland (where he was forbidden to be) so that he might be ready to embark for England as soon as he was summoned over by Rochester or any other successful Royalist leader.

In the event the Royalist rising of 1655 was a fiasco. Cromwell's government was forewarned. Thurloe had spies in Germany, one of whom actually followed Charles to Middleburg, who informed Thurloe of the Royalists' plans. Moreover the precautions that Cromwell had taken against his other enemies, which included the rounding up of all the horses in London, were applicable to any insurrectionary movement. In his farewell speech to Parliament which he had dissolved on 22 January Cromwell had observed: 'I say unto you whilst you have been in the midst of these transactions that party, the Cavalier party ... has been designing and preparing to put this nation into blood.' On 13 February he had read to the Lord Mayor, Aldermen and Common Council of the city of London Charles's letter of the previous July. The original date for the Royalist rising had been fixed for 13 February, but owing to the controversy between the Royalists in England it had been abandoned, while O'Neill's arrest at Dover had delayed the arrival of Charles's instructions. Thus the date was postponed until 8 March. Except in Wiltshire sufficient troops failed to appear. The Action party had leaders but few followers. When Rochester arrived for a rendezvous on Marston Moor ready to head a revolt in Yorkshire only 150 horsemen turned up. Sir Marmaduke Langdale, who might have rallied the Lancastrians, was forbidden to come over from the continental mainland on the ground that he was a Roman Catholic. At Newcastle a few conspirators gathered only to melt away; in Nottinghamshire a cartload of arms was driven up in the night by a Royalist sympathiser but nobody knew what to do with it. Only at Salisbury did Colonel John Penruddock and some four hundred of the Action party actually make any progress; but when they tried to march into Hampshire and seize Winchester they were soon overcome and their leaders executed.

The reasons for the failure of the rising were not hard to find. First, the move was too late. Cromwell was alerted and took every precaution. A Royalist insurrection would have stood a better chance of success if it had taken place during the winter when Cromwell's hands were full because of the discontent with the Protectorate among the republicans, Levellers, and some sections of the armed forces. Secondly, insufficient effort was made to enlist the cooperation of Cromwell's other enemies. Though the rising followed the collapse of the Wildman plot, there is no evidence of any understanding between the Royalists and the Levellers. Finally the Royalists themselves failed either to plan or to work together. Few or none of the most influential Royalists in England took part at all and, in spite of the King's promptings, the Sealed Knot refused to act. Thus even if the King's own policy was defective in that he neither cancelled the rising nor ordered the Sealed Knot to join it whole-heartedly, it is doubtful if there was much hope of success in 1655. Charles himself was depressed and contrite, and mourned for his dead followers. 'His heart was almost broken,' wrote Hyde, 'and the fact that the King had authorized the rebellion after much consideration and against his better judgment was no consolation.'[12]

It is doubtful if Hyde was correct in writing that Charles's support of the Action party in England was given against his better judgement. The King was consistently impatient for action, but the summer of 1655 marked a low point in his hopes and fortunes. 'Charles Stuart's friends are wonderfully disheartened', reported one of Thurloe's spies on 11 May, 'their chief business now is to relieve the handful in Scotland.' But neither in Scotland nor in England did the state of affairs look promising. Perhaps it was more sensible to wait for better times. Hyde was writing to Nicholas: 'If it be once evident that we are not for the present to expect any notable revolutions in England, we must endeavour to draw money from thence to the King'.[13] One gleam of light was seen in assurances from the Levellers. Colonel Edward Sexby, who had been mixed up in the abortive Wildman plot, had escaped from prison and presented himself to the Royalists in Amsterdam with all sorts of offers to stir up mutiny in Cromwell's army and to assassinate the Protector. A champion liar, who spoke fluent Spanish and drank the King's health with gusto, Sexby now proceeded to make some impression in the Spanish Netherlands. The wiser counsellors of the King urged caution. But others grasped at straws. 'Now all expectation is from the Levellers,' reported another of Thurloe's spies on 21 May from Cologne. 'Many are for assassinating the Protector, but Charles Stewart is not forward in having it done.'[14]

A more concrete hope offered itself as the summer drew on. Cromwell with a large army and navy at his disposal had been hesitating whether to accept a military alliance with France or Spain, the two great warring powers of western Europe. Refusing to recognize Spain's huge claims in the New World, Cromwell had dispatched an expeditionary force from England at the end of 1654 with instructions to seize territory in the West Indies. The Spaniards, saddled with a war against France and a revolution in Portugal, were prepared to tolerate a good deal from the

English Commonwealth. But Cromwell opened his mouth widely, demanding a free hand in the West Indies and the exemption of British merchants from the operations of the Inquisition. By June 1655 negotiations had broken down and British troops had conquered Jamaica. Moreover another fleet under Robert Blake, who had been carrying on an aggressive policy in the Mediterranean, was stationed off Cadiz with orders to intercept the Spanish treasure fleet if it could. This series of provocations ended in October with the Spanish ambassador being recalled from London and an embargo being imposed on British shipping in Spanish ports. War could not be far distant.

Charles II and his advisers were quick to embrace this new opportunity to acquire foreign aid. At the end of June 1655 Hyde was instructing Charles's representative in Brussels, Sir Henry de Vic, not to go on leave because of the prospects of Royalist negotiations with Spain. The King sought an invitation to leave Cologne and go to Flanders to argue the value of his alliance. He believed that he had many supporters in the English republican navy who would transfer their allegiance to him if such ports as Ostend and Dunkirk were opened to him by the Spaniards. One other remote source of assistance to Charles at this time was the Pope, but the King could see his chances there were poor unless he declared himself to be a Roman Catholic. On 8 September he wrote to his friend the Duke of Newburg that while he found he had nothing to hope for from Rome, he was doing all he could to make the Spaniards see he could provide them with some service.

The Spaniards responded slowly to these overtures. But Charles became increasingly optimistic. On 17 September Hyde informed de Vic that the King could 'see some dawning of a cheerful countenance from the Spaniard towards him'.[15] While he did not want de Vic yet to press the business of the ports any further, he felt sure that if he himself received an invitation to come to the Spanish Netherlands he would be able to present a forcible case. He was convinced that he could prove that he would be in a position to 'interrupt Cromwell's designs more than can be imagined'. As usual, Charles was offered contradictory advice. The Earl of Norwich told him that he should not await an invitation at all, but should make all haste to Flanders incognito 'with a light train'.[16] The Spaniards remained reluctant to believe that an official war with the English Commonwealth was unavoidable. But Charles with his eyes on England, where Cromwell had been compelled to institute an unpopular system of local government by Major-Generals in an effort to overcome his internal enemies, tried to persuade the Spaniards that with a little help from them a big rising on his behalf could be organized. In February 1656 he instructed Henry de Vic that although the oppression and tyranny of Cromwell were so great that he had forbidden his friends to stir, 'if they knew he had the support of Spain their spirits would be raised'.[17] Again he was sure that warships would join him once he himself arrived in Flanders.

Eventually Charles decided not to wait any longer for an official invitation but banked on not having received a downright refusal to venture from Cologne to the Flemish frontier with a couple of servants. He stayed at the Sun inn at Louvain where he met the two principal Spanish Ministers. At first, he told Ormonde, who soon came to Flanders too, 'I found them dry . . . yet at last they began to be very free with me'.[18] On 12 April 1656 two treaties were signed. By one treaty the King of Spain offered to lend Charles 6,000 soldiers as the nucleus of an invasion force. In return Charles promised that if he were restored to his throne he would help the Spaniards against Portugal and return any West Indian islands seized by Cromwell. By another treaty Charles undertook to suspend the penal laws against Roman Catholics in all parts of his dominions. Charles was later granted a pension from Spain to help him over his financial difficulties. The main trouble about the first treaty was that the Spaniards would not allow it to come into force until Charles's supporters in England had captured a port at which the expeditionary army could land. Nor was it likely that as long as Cromwell's fleets held the seas such an army could be carried across the English Channel. Thus the treaty could hardly become effective until the lavish promises made by Charles and his advisers of wholesale desertions from the Commonwealth navy awoke into the realm of reality.

But positive gains had been achieved. Though the documents

remained secret, Charles had been treated as the King of England by a Great Power and had been given promises, admittedly subject to conditions, of assistance both in men and money. 'That which we have gotten already,' wrote Charles to Hyde from Brussels on 17 April 1656, 'is more than I hoped for when I left Cologne and which if anybody could have assured us of two months since would have made you caper in spite of your gout.'[19] Charles settled in Bruges to await developments. He summoned his brother James to join him there: he could obviously serve no longer in the French army with which the Spaniards were at war. In early May Charles told Hyde to wind up his court in Cologne, where he hoped to pay all the debts he owed, and to 'make such haste as your gouty feet will give you leave to me'.[20] In July the treaties were ratified by the King of Spain and Charles looked forward to the ending of his incognito and the opening of Flemish ports to Royalist ships. Gradually Charles's court reassembled around him in Bruges, but elaborate negotiations had still to be completed before Charles's wish to have a small army and navy of his own could be realized.

Prospects began to brighten for King Charles at the opening of 1657. As usual, he was impatient for action and disappointed by the slowness of the Spaniards to fulfil their promises. Money on which he had counted did not arrive; Madrid put the blame on Brussels and Brussels on Madrid. In March 1657 Hyde was telling Ormonde, who was negotiating on the Royalist behalf in Brussels, that he had never seen the King more troubled between anger and shame and that he was weary of his treatment; two months later Charles himself was writing to Hyde from Brussels that he had received no money from Don Juan, the illegitimate son of the Spanish King, who had now taken over the command of the Spanish army in Flanders, and said 'the truth is this scurvy usage puts me beyond patience, and if I were with Don Juan I should follow your counsel and swear two or three round oaths'.[21]

Charles's principal difficulty was that he now had an army of his own to provide for. The Spaniards had allowed him to enlist mercenaries largely out of Irish troops who had previously been fighting with the French. As early as October 1656 he had 800 men, and quarters for four regiments had been assigned to him. By January four or five regiments were in the process of being formed (under the commands of the Duke of York, Rochester, Middleton, Ormonde and the Duke of Gloucester). By May 4,000 men were reported to have been collected, though Thurloe was informed that they were 'all ragged miserable creatures'. Charles's hope was that they would be allowed to co-operate with the expeditionary force assigned to him in the Spanish treaty in an invasion of England to take place during the winter when bad weather obliged the republican navy to lift its blockade. Don Juan told Charles that permission would have to be obtained from Madrid for him to possess a separate army, but meanwhile he could appoint a commander-in-chief while he himself stayed in Bruges attending to the correspondence with the Royalists in England.

But Charles had no intention of being pushed into the background. He himself wanted to lead the invasion of England as soon as the summer campaign in Flanders was over, and to be his own commander-in-chief. In July the King wrote to the Earl of Bristol that every week brought letters from England inquiring when they should make ready and what they might expect: 'if this winter pass without any attempt on my part,' he continued, 'I shall take very little pleasure in living till the next.'[22] It began to look as if the Spaniards were at last in earnest about assisting him. The campaign in Flanders had begun with the capture of St Ghislain, in which they were helped by the fact that Charles had ordered the Irish in the garrison to surrender. A military alliance signed between Cromwell's government and the French in March had provided for a republican expeditionary force to land in Flanders; it was therefore wholly in the interest of the Spaniards to cause the maximum confusion in England by lending support to Charles. Don Juan treated the King with ceremony, and towards the end of the campaign invited him to join the Spanish army in the field where he gallantly led a charge at the siege of Mardyke. By September Don Juan was 'professing all imaginable alacrity towards the business of England'. And though in the late summer the royal funds had sunk so low that there was talk of the King having to manage with a single dish for his meals, now Don Juan offered 100,000 crowns for the expenses of Charles and his brother, which was said to be sufficient 'to make a beginning' if the King were sure of a port where the soldiers could land.

But, after all, nothing happened. The Spaniards had consistently taken the view that they were not going to risk their troops unless the Royalists in England rose against the Government and captured a port for disembarkation. At one time indeed they were of the opinion that they were more likely to obtain a port through the exertions of the Levellers than of the Royalists. The enigmatic Wildman had talked about having several ports at his disposal; it was just a question of his being given enough money and he would arrange for their seizure and also for the assassination of Cromwell. Wildman had been released from prison in July 1656, apparently having promised to act as one of Thurloe's spies, and he paid several visits to Flanders during 1657, though he avoided seeing the King. The exiled court never entirely trusted him and Charles refused to advance him the money he demanded. If Wildman was boastful about what the Levellers were competent to do, the Royalists in England were less sanguine about their capabilities. Since the disaster of 1655 a new Action party had been formed, but it was amorphous and unorganized. The Sealed Knot not only remained wary but actually had a traitor in its midst, Sir Richard Willys, the most impecunious of its members, having also sold his services to Thurloe in the summer of 1656. How far the treacheries of Willys extended has been hotly debated, but that they existed seems to be well proved. So in England Charles's supporters waited for him to land; while in Flanders the expeditionary force waited for a rising in England. As Charles's ambassador in Spain, Henry Bennet, wrote in November, it looked as if the King was likely to fall between two stools.

In December 1657 Don Juan proposed a compromise. Let the King send the Marquis of Ormonde to England to report on the new Action party's plans. If he found that good prospects existed of obtaining a port, then it would not be too late to invade England before the winter ended. Ormonde was delighted to embark on this risky adventure and Charles overruled objections from Hyde. Cromwell was in the middle of a quarrel with his second Protectorate parliament, and plenty of dissatisfaction with the regime prevailed. But although the rule of the Major-Generals was now at an end, the internal security arrangements were tightly organized and the army remained loyal to the Lord Protector, especially since he had soothed its republican susceptibilities by refusing the title of king offered him by Parliament in the previous year. Ormonde was told that even the Action party would not move until the King arrived in England and he found that regional plots were mostly of little substance and uncoordinated. The Levellers were useless and nobody trusted Wildman.

Surprisingly Ormonde's report was far more optimistic than the facts warranted. When he returned to the Spanish Netherlands he asserted that the King should be able to land without difficulty at or near Yarmouth. But the military realities were all against a successful invasion. Before the end of February 1658 the blockade of the Spanish Netherlands by the Commonwealth navy had been re-established and Cromwell, who had been fully informed about Ormonde's mission (the Marquis had only by a hair's breadth escaped arrest when he was in England), strengthened his precautions, gave further warning to the authorities of the city of London, and placed a number of Royalists under arrest. In spite of pressure from Charles and his Ministers the Spaniards refused to take action. When the spring came and John Mordaunt (a younger brother of the second Earl of Peterborough), the self-appointed leader of the Action party, complained because Charles had failed to come to England, Hyde retorted that 'the King would venture his person tomorrow on satisfactory assurances, but the Action party had given no information of any particular design'.[23] He added that the Duke of York stood ready with an army in Flanders and would embark instantly if Cromwell should die or if the republican army in England mutinied against him.

So during the summer of 1658 Charles was demoralized and frustrated. He hated Bruges where his court was stationed, and envied his brother James who was now allowed to serve with the Spanish army. In May a Royalist plot for a rising in London went off half-cock and the leading conspirators were arrested and executed except for Mordaunt himself who was unexpectedly acquitted. In Flanders the Spaniards suffered defeat by French and English forces at the battle of the Dunes in June, and Dunkirk was surrendered and handed over to Cromwell. Charles's only scheme was to visit Madrid and put his case directly to the King of Spain. But he was told he would not be welcome there and in August he retired to the village of Hoogstraeten to hawk and hunt. But 'the standing corn impeded sport and few partridges were found for the hawks'.[24]

After the campaign of 1658 ended the long war between Spain and France petered out and negotiations were opened for a peace treaty which was to be concluded in the Pyrenees during the following year. Immediate Royalist hopes from Spain receded, but Charles believed that once the peace was signed the two western powers would join together since Oliver Cromwell had died on 3 September and they had less reason to fear republican England. But the death of the Lord Protector, who was succeeded by his mild son Richard, did not as might have been expected arouse immediate optimism in Charles's mind. It is true that he issued a declaration requiring all his subjects to find means to restore his royal authority and 'resist the usurper Richard Cromwell', but at the same time he announced that he did 'not expect his friends' to do 'any rash thing for him' and indeed thought that they should not stir till they had some advantage given them by 'other parties rising'.[25] What Charles expected was that the Presbyterians who had never loved Cromwell might attempt to overthrow the Protectorate; he did not mind if they did not move under his banner so long as they destroyed the Cromwellian government. In retrospect Hyde wrote of Oliver that 'never monarch, after he had inherited a crown by many descents, died with more silence nor with less alteration; the same or a greater calm in the kingdom than had been before. . . . So that the King's condition never appeared so hopeless, so desperate.' More than four months after Oliver's death Hyde was writing: 'We have not yet found that advantage by Cromwell's death as we reasonably hoped, nay, rather we are the worse for it, and the less esteemed, people imagining by the great calm that hath followed that the nation is united and that in truth the King hath very few friends.'[26]

However in January 1659 a Parliament was summoned and this contained a number of concealed Royalists – Charles had prompted them to stand for the House of Commons – and they proceeded to cooperate with the vociferous republican leaders in Parliament and the commanders of the Commonwealth army. The Royalist Action party, again led by John Mordaunt, urged Charles to profit by these dissensions. On 1 March Charles showed his confidence in Mordaunt by creating him a viscount and establishing a 'plenipotentiary or Great Trust and commission' to represent him in England. This Trust did not so much supersede the Sealed Knot as add Mordaunt to its members and give them more positive instructions how to deal with 'the rebels' – Charles was particularly thinking of the Presbyterians. In fact the Sealed Knot was reluctant to accept its new commission and it was left to the enthusiastic Mordaunt to negotiate with the Presbyterians and try to organize a fresh rising.[27]

Meanwhile the divisions between the republican leaders in the House of Commons and the army commanders were coming to a head. Richard Cromwell was unable to mediate between them. The army chiefs forced him to dissolve Parliament; but then they realized that they had no constitution ready to replace the Protectorate and they were driven to recall the remnants of the Long Parliament of 1640, known as the Rump, which the republican leaders considered to be the legal government, despotically destroyed by Oliver Cromwell. A Council of State and a group of committees became rulers of England, and John Thurloe, who had for so long held the threads of the administration in his hands, was dismissed from his office of Secretary of State. The Rump showed itself even more critical of the army leaders than had Richard Cromwell's Parliament so that the new alliance of Cromwell's former generals and his former republican critics was an uneasy one. The Speaker of the House of Commons became the nominal head of the army. In Scotland General George Monck promised his support for the new regime, but did not take kindly to its attempts to interfere with the organization of his army.

In May, while this revolution was taking place in England,

Charles was still feeling his way cautiously. If he was disappointed that the Sealed Knot was still being 'unprofitably wary', he nevertheless repeated his orders that his friends should 'lie still and be quiet till a good opportunity offered'.[28] As in 1655, he was in two minds. He felt reluctant to undertake preparations for an expedition unless he had evidence that he now enjoyed the general good wishes of the English people and that the republican army was seriously divided; yet he announced himself ready to come over at the first summons. In the third week of June Mordaunt paid a flying visit to Brussels where he saw the King and his advisers, making as good an impression upon them in person as he had previously done by his letters. The King was persuaded that his own presence in England was necessary. He planned that in mid-July he would arrive in one part of England and his brother James in another. He told his brother that he would issue a declaration offering a pardon to all except those who had voted for the murder of their father, and expected that they would link up in England. But, as in 1655, the date for the rising was postponed and, also as in 1655, the members of the Sealed Knot were resolutely opposed to action. It is true that the new Trust had enlisted a number of Presbyterians, but an effective concerted movement throughout England demanded activity by Royalists everywhere. The Earl of Northampton warned the King that he must not repeat the mistake he had made on the previous occasion but give firm orders that all of his supporters should move together at the same time.

But the republican Council of State proved as efficient as Oliver Cromwell had been in frustrating Royalist plans. Neither in the west nor in the east, where Charles himself had first proposed to land (his objective was Lynn in Norfolk) did anything much happen except the arrest by the authorities of a few local sympathizers with the King. The date finally fixed for the rising was 1 August. On 3 August Charles left Brussels for Dieppe and made ready to sail across from Brittany, but bad news reached him and he never left France. The only success for the rebels was in the north-west of England where Sir George Booth, a Presbyterian who had fought against Charles I and now declared not for his son but for 'a free Parliament', captured Chester; but his untrained troops were easily defeated by John Lambert, whom the Rump dispatched to deal with him. It was to Chester that Charles had finally intended to sail. After Booth's defeat Charles abandoned the hopes that had been raised by Mordaunt and were embodied in the activities of the Trust, and began again to look for foreign help to restore him to his throne.

Mordaunt blamed the failure of this rising on the pusillanimity of the leaders of the Sealed Knot and in particular on the treachery of Sir Richard Willys. Though the King had been warned in June about Willys he hesitated to credit the accusations. It is doubtful if Willys played a significant part in the failure of the rising. The Sealed Knot had taken the consistent view that the whole scheme had been unduly hurried, inadequately prepared, and fixed for a bad time when most of the population was more concerned with getting in the harvest than creating political upheaval. These 'wary gentlemen' thought that violence would merely close the ranks of the King's enemies.

How far was Charles himself to blame for this second fiasco? Certainly he seems to have been unduly swayed by Mordaunt, a daring not to say rash young man far from popular with the older Royalists whom he had supplanted in the King's favours. But Hyde too had been infected by Mordaunt's persuasiveness. It does not appear to be true, as has been suggested, that on this occasion the King hesitated and compromised. He made it perfectly clear in his messages to England that he wanted the attempt to be undertaken, even though Mordaunt had warned him that the Sealed Knot was virtually boycotting it. To his mother he conveyed the strength of his confidence. As always, he had been reluctant to neglect any conceivable opportunity that presented itself for his restoration.

Impatience was indeed the keynote of Charles's character during the years of exile. During these years he had grown from a youth cast into the cauldron of civil war into a prince who lived by adventure, and his spirit was tempered by struggles and disappointments. Consistently, resolutely and impatiently he sought any means to regain for himself the throne of his ancestors.

Sometimes he was depressed, but when opportunities appeared, his hopes rapidly revived. Understandably he wearied of his lot when events became bogged down and he had little money to spend: in succession he grew tired of his life in Paris, Cologne and Bruges. Ormonde once wrote of his 'unseasonable impatience'; but the months passed so often in frustration or obstruction, and eleven years was a long time to wait.

Many accusations have been made about Charles's conduct during those years. It was said that he was extravagant and that his Royalist supporters in England objected to paying for the upkeep of his supper table. Not only was Lucy Walter an expense – she tried to blackmail him by holding on to his son, the future Duke of Monmouth, as long as she could – but there were other women, such as Catherine Pegge, by whom he also had a son, who cost him money.[29] For a brief time in 1658 he was engaged to Princess Henriette of Orange, but her mother revoked her consent, possibly because of Charles's notorious reputation with women. He complained of gossip circulated by 'blind harpers, they have done me too much honour in assigning me so many fair ladies as if I were able to satisfy the half'. In his make-up were a light-heartedness and sense of humour that gave him a charm which comes through some of his surviving letters. As Osmund Airy wrote, 'the insouciance which developed later into a fixed cynicism never failed him; while the mixture of familiarity and affectionate banter with which he wrote to Hyde and Ormonde reminds us of the child's letter to Newcastle [about his medicine], and shows that he felt absolutely safe in their patient loyalty.'[30] He joked about Hyde's gout, over playing cards with Henry Bennet, or having a good meal of wine and mutton, and no doubt at times he omitted the dignity of a king. A letter of Ormonde's to Hyde has often been quoted in which he wrote: 'I fear his immoderate delight in empty, effeminate and vulgar conversation is becoming an irresistible part of his nature and will never suffer him to animate his own designs and others' actions with that spirit which is requisite for his quality and much more to his future.'[31] But then no man is a hero to his own valet.

What was more to the point and has been little remarked by

his biographers was Charles's propensity to sudden and rather unaccountable dislikes. One case was that of Lord Balcarres, who had fought for the King in Scotland and then come over to Holland where his wife obtained employment in the service of the widowed Princess Mary of Orange. Since his adventures among the Scottish Covenanters Charles had acquired a dislike of Presbyterians which he sometimes forgot to conceal. He seems to have suspected Balcarres of intriguing at the French court and he severely reproved his sister for patronizing those who had earned his disfavour. Equally he quarrelled with Mary for showing kindness to Henry Jermyn, the son of his mother's devoted chamberlain, Lord Jermyn, though in view of Charles's own love affairs to censure his sister for being human on the ground that she was 'reflecting on his honour' was the pot calling the kettle black. Similarly he took a dislike to Sir John Berkeley, who served his brother James. Again Charles appears to have thought that Berkeley was on too friendly terms with the French court and was using his influence to prevent his brother from joining him after Charles himself had left France. James was so annoyed by Charles's treatment that he threatened to return to France from the Spanish Netherlands and actually vanished from the court at Bruges. This quarrel had to be patched up and eventually Charles created Berkeley a baron.

Charles's disagreements with his mother were more justifiable. She was by no means easy to get along with. Her treatment of her son on money matters when he returned a fugitive from Worcester was scarcely conducive to a happy relationship, while her refusal to be on speaking terms with Charles's chief adviser made the running of his court in Paris distinctly uncomfortable. After Charles left Paris Henrietta Maria broke her promise to him that she would not try to procure the conversion of his fourteen-year old brother Henry to her religion. Charles did not feel very strongly about religion – the cruel behaviour of the pious Scottish Presbyterians had made an indelible impression on his mind – but he could see plainly enough that the conversion of another member of his family (his youngest sister had already been converted by her mother) would damage his image with English Protestants. For the same reason he resisted pressure to declare himself a Roman Catholic in order to buy assistance from the Pope. Yet he did not mind committing himself secretly to removing the disabilities on Roman Catholics by his power to suspend the penal laws, as he did in the Spanish treaty, if he regained his dominions. Indeed at one stage in the summer of 1658, having suffered disappointments from the Spaniards, Charles actually entered into negotiations with that elusive figure in French history, the exiled Cardinal de Retz, who boasted of his value as an intermediary with the Vatican. Retz thought that Charles was 'very naturally disposed to favour the Catholics of his kingdom' and that in time 'these affections which the King hath for their persons might even pass to their religion'.[32] Charles owed a debt to English Roman Catholics for their help during his escape after the Worcester campaign, while the nucleus of the army that he formed in Flanders was Irish Catholics.

Our knowledge of Charles in exile derives largely from the letters written by Hyde, Ormonde and Nicholas, the staider members of his council and those on whom, to do him credit, he chiefly relied. These letters are supplemented by the reports of Thurloe's spies which are always highly coloured and by no means trustworthy. To Hyde and his colleagues it appeared reprehensible that the King should not always be on his dignity and not always hard at work. But he rarely failed them, for he depended upon them. He employed Ormonde on his most delicate missions, for example on the reconciliation with his brother James and on the secret visit to the Royalist leaders in England in 1659. In 1658 he insisted on promoting Edward Hyde from the office of Chancellor of the Exchequer to that of Lord Chancellor, thus showing the world the respect in which he held him. He had a will of his own, but only in the affair of the 1655 rising could he have been said to have acted unwisely and in disregard of sensible counsel.

Historians, basing themselves on Hyde's later writings, have sometimes maintained that there was a fundamental difference in policy between Hyde and his master, that Hyde had consistently declared that the King could only be restored by a call from England, while Charles himself depended on the aid of foreign arms. But a close study of the voluminous correspondence hardly bears this out. All of the King's council had hopes at different times that Charles's restoration could be assisted by French, Dutch, Spanish or even papal help. After all, other kings of England – Henry IV and Henry VII for example – had gained their thrones by invasion from abroad. The idea was neither novel nor entirely unrealistic. Only the loyalty of Oliver Cromwell's army and navy to the Protector prevented it. After the fall of Richard Cromwell England relapsed into a state of anarchy and so in the end Charles was invited by almost universal acclaim to return to England. But neither Charles nor anyone else could have foreseen that this was going to happen.

6

The Restoration

When at the beginning of August 1659 King Charles left Brussels his original intention had been to sail for the south of England. But within a week he learned that the general Royalist rising planned for 1 August had failed except in Cheshire, where Sir George Booth had moved into action, and in North Wales and Lancashire. Charles then went to Rouen with the idea of getting a ship from St Malo which would carry him to join his adherents in north-west England. From Rouen he wrote to Hyde on 28 August:

We do not doubt but by the help of God to get to our friends [in England] with less hazard than is imaginable on such a voyage, for upon the whole matter I am very cheerful, and though I am not altogether so plump, I begin to grow as sanguine as Mr Skinner [Ormonde] himself.[1]

But though they went on to St Malo, Charles and Ormonde were to hear the news that Booth had been defeated and, after ignominiously trying to escape from the battlefield dressed as a woman, had been lodged in the Tower of London. Hyde, still in Brussels, thought that the King should have gone on to Calais as messages were being received from England that people were still disaffected and would welcome his presence there. Charles himself saw no point in taking the risk of landing in southern England, and turned to another plan that he had been considering for some time: to go to Fuenterrabia on the borders of France and Spain where the delegates of the two kingdoms were engaged in negotiating a peace treaty – to be known as the treaty of the Pyrenees – and see if he could persuade the leading statesmen there to grant him positive military aid.

Charles had some reason for optimism, for Condé's army, which had been fighting for the Spaniards, was now free, while Turenne, the French marshal, was personally willing to put part of his forces at the disposal of James, Duke of York, who had formerly served in his army. The Spaniards had indicated that they would have no objection at all to Charles coming to Fuenterrabia, but Cardinal Mazarin – although hard pressed by Queen Henrietta Maria – had not only objected but had put obstacles in the way of the King's journey across France. King Charles, whose sanguine outlook had not worn off, nevertheless determined to cross France incognito, and for a time he disappeared from the map. Among those accompanying him were George Digby, the second Earl of Bristol, whose Spanish was fluent and who was reputed to know his way about France; and Daniel O'Neill, who was an expert in conjuring up good meals and good company in the most unlikely places. Ormonde was sent ahead to Fuenterrabia by another route. The royal party waited at La Rochelle for eight days in a vain effort to secure a passage to Spain by ship, and it was not until the middle of October that Charles reached his destination. During the three months that he had spent travelling Charles enjoyed himself immensely and was not at all contrite. O'Neill wrote to Hyde from Fuenterrabia that he blamed nobody for the circuit they had made 'since it is the common opinion that we are come here very seasonably'.[2] The main treaty negotiations had just been completed and the document was ready to be signed. In no case would it have been possible for Charles himself to be included within the scope of the treaty: for this carried a secret article binding the King of France to give neither direct nor indirect assistance to the English Republic or any other regime in England so long as the Anglo-Spanish war continued. 'Spain,' wrote Lord Culpeper, who was at Fuenterrabia, 'neither will nor can help us except France join in the work, which it never will do until Mazarin is fully satisfied and that as well in his hopes as in his fears.'[3] The point was that Mazarin was ready to promise his neutrality to the existing Government in England and show his willingness to act as mediator between it and the Spanish monarchy. Still the news from England was confusing. On 13

October General John Lambert had overthrown the Rump Parliament at Westminster and no one knew what was going to replace it. Hence Mazarin's extreme caution. He refused to see Charles at Fuenterrabia or to give any promises, though he was affable to Ormonde whom he met there. Not even an offer from Charles II to marry Mazarin's twelve-year-old niece, Hortense Mancini, could shake him from his neutral policy. On the other hand, the Spaniards were quite prepared to enlist Charles on their side in their prolonged war against the English Commonwealth. They also hoped that if Charles were restored he would reciprocate by aiding them in their war against Portugal. Charles was therefore officially welcomed by the leading Spanish Minister, Luis de Haro, who offered him his own quarters and afterwards accompanied him back to Hendaye.

Charles's position was therefore a delicate one. But universal testimony was to the effect that he conducted himself admirably. Bristol told Hyde that the King's journey into Spain was 'the happiest that ever he made in his life'.[4] O'Neill wrote that the King had 'behaved himself as if he had been bred more years in Spain than France'.[5] On 25 November Hyde himself wrote to Ormonde:

> I hope the King's dexterity and composedness (of which there is very good mention in many letters hither) hath removed the fatal misfortune, which you say follows us, of not being believed. For till the King be thought to understand our business, and to be able to conduct it, all our striving is against the stream, and towards that good reputation, an opinion of his industry is as necessary as of his conception.[6]

Thus Hyde and Ormonde continued to be critical of their master. Ormonde, who had hung about for him in Toulouse, was annoyed with the time he took over his journey; and Hyde evidently did not trust him to behave himself properly when out of his own reach. What Charles of course wanted to do was to obtain the joint help of the two powers towards his restoration. But the French and the Spaniards were suspicious of each other and still remembered fearfully the military strength of Cromwell's England. But Charles had undoubtedly done good work for his cause. Doubts had been thrown upon the stability of the new republican government in England which had replaced that of the Protectorate. And although Mazarin was not willing at this stage to allow either Turenne or Condé to place his troops at Charles's service for an invasion of England, and the Spaniards were reluctant to act without French cooperation, neither government excluded the possibility that it might soon be in its own interest to help the King. In January 1660 Hyde wrote that 'the King has done all in his power' and that if only Mazarin would declare his resolution the growing feeling in England that the time was ripe for the King's restoration might be utilized.[7]

For now events were beginning to move in his direction in England. Charles did not return straight to Brussels but visited his mother at Colombes on the way back. He realized that she was his best ambassador to Mazarin. When he was at Colombes Charles was fully reconciled to his mother and met his pretty young sister, Henriette Anne, who was now sixteen, and whom he did not at first recognize. He gratified his mother by creating the elder Jermyn, her confident, an earl. He got back to Brussels soon after Christmas. This was the time when General George Monck in Scotland was preparing for his march into England. Monck had disapproved of Lambert's overthrow of the Rump, and though he had negotiated with Lambert he made it clear that he refused to acknowledge a government of England by the sword. He said that what he had tolerated in Oliver he would not stomach in a lesser man. Monck had behind him a well-paid and well-equipped army which he had carefully purged of all officers not completely loyal to himself. Lambert on the other hand found that his soldiers, largely unpaid, were deserting him. When the garrison of Portsmouth identified themselves with the dismissed Rump Parliament and General Fleetwood, the late Protector's son-in-law and nominally commander-in-chief of the southern army, proved himself incapable of any decided action, the Rump met once again on 26 December 1659; and Monck declared his intention of leading his army from Scotland to London to give the Parliament his protection.

The King and his advisers had for some time been hopeful that

Monck would favour the restoration of the Stuart monarchy. They had their eyes both on him and on John Lambert, the two protagonists in the last of the mid-seventeenth-century English civil wars, as possible agents of a restoration. Monck, a thoroughly professional officer, had actually fought for King Charles I until he was taken prisoner by the Parliamentarians in 1644 and been put in the Tower of London, and might therefore be described as an ex-Royalist. Lambert, for his part, had consistently opposed the Royalists, but had finally been dismissed from his command by Oliver Cromwell because he objected to the Lord Protector's assumption of far-reaching powers. Both Lambert and Monck were extremely ambitious and fond of money; neither of them had been concerned with the execution of Charles I. It therefore seemed to the exiled Royalists that they might well be bribed. Hyde expressed the opinion, even after Lambert's defeat of Booth, that while he might be worth gaining, he would be of less value than Monck.

Immediately after Oliver Cromwell's death King Charles II had put out feelers towards Monck. He sent a message to Sir John Grenville, who was a wealthy Devonshire landowner, a Royalist and a cousin of Monck, saying, 'I am confident that George Monck can have no malice in his heart against me nor hath he done anything against me, which I cannot very easily pardon'.[8] Charles therefore authorized Grenville and two other Royalists to 'treat with' Monck. Monck also had a brother, Nicholas, who was a clergyman and occupied a Devonshire benefice in the gift of Grenville and was of a Royalist frame of mind. It was in the middle of August 1659 that Nicholas paid a visit to Scotland carrying a letter from the King to Monck. George Monck refused to receive this letter, although its contents were made known to him. Presumably this was of the same nature as a letter written by Charles on 4 July 1659 to General Edward Mountagu, the commander-in-chief of the Commonwealth navy, in which he offered Mountagu an earldom or any office he would care to name if he would bring over the navy to the Royalist side. Mountagu succumbed to these blandishments and made a premature attempt to bring over the navy in 1659, which resulted in his being superseded by Vice-Admiral John Lawson, a former Leveller. Monck was far more cautious. But the evidence of John Price, one of Monck's chaplains with Royalist sympathies, indicates that Monck was fully aware that if he moved his army into England (as he contemplated doing this same August) he would be suspected of 'carrying the King in his belly'.

When Monck eventually marched into England in January 1660 he was besieged *en route* with a number of petitions from different parts of the country asking him to call a free Parliament at Westminster. But he insisted that he was coming to London, which he reached on 3 February, merely to uphold the authority of the existing Rump Parliament. Pressure was exerted upon him as an alternative to calling a free Parliament to allow the Presbyterian members who had been expelled from the Rump in Pride's purge of 1648 to resume their seats – the Rump, as a Royalist put it, 'being enlarged to a Gigot'. As most of these so-called Presbyterians were now in fact secret monarchists, this step would have been in the direction of a restoration. The Common Council of the city of London went so far as to announce that it would pay no more taxes until the House of Commons filled its vacancies. Thereupon the Council of State ordered Monck to arrest the leading citizens and pull down the city gates. Monck resented these orders and it was at this stage that, abandoning the views of a lifetime about the necessary subordination of the army to the civil power, he finally decided to exert military pressure upon the government and insist upon the enlargement of Parliament that the City demanded.

Up to this time neither King Charles nor any of his advisers was sure of Monck's intentions. 'He is a black Monk and I cannot see through him,' John Mordaunt wrote as late as 16 January.[9] A week later Charles was still aware that Monck had refused to receive his letters. Mordaunt had wanted the King to come over and intervene even before Monck's arrival in London. Charles drafted a proclamation on 12 January saying that 'if the present distractions continue to the wideness they are at, I will make all haste that is possible to make two descents, one from these parts [that is, the Spanish Netherlands] the other from France, in one of which I will be myself and in the other my brother the Duke of York'.[10] But events in London moved rapidly after Monck's arrival there and on 17 March, under pressure from Monck, the Rump dissolved itself and elections for a free parliament were called. A week later Mordaunt, now Charles II's leading representative in England, wrote to tell him that Monck was ready to receive his letters through his cousin Grenville, while the fleet now seemed to be at his service. Lord Fairfax, the former Parliamentarian commander-in-chief, had some weeks before thrown in his lot with the King. No stone was left unturned to induce Cromwell's old generals to renew their allegiance to the monarchy. Charles II's hand in marriage, having been rejected by Cardinal Mazarin's niece Hortense, was even put on offer by Hyde to Lambert's daughter Mary in return for Charles's restoration to all his kingdoms. Grenville was bombarded with missives for Monck. But it was not until after the Rump was dissolved that the mists began to clear.

It is plain that Charles had no firm information about Monck's purposes until the end of March 1660. It is true that early in the previous December Hyde had received a report from England that Monck's intentions were even then really for the King, but contradictory reports were also received. At the beginning of January 1660 they were wondering at Charles's court whether Monck meant to put himself in Oliver Cromwell's position or whether he had decided to give his unqualified support to the Rump, either of which courses was believed likely to make him odious. But once Monck had forced the Rump to admit its secluded members Charles became optimistic and prepared to leave the dominions of the King of Spain ready for recall home. It was thought improper that Charles should return to England from a Roman Catholic kingdom if he were invited to come back by the newly elected Parliament. On 27 March Charles had again written to Monck telling him how much he relied on his assistance and promising him that he would 'take all ways he can to let the world see his entire trust in him'.[11] Monck replied by advising Charles, among other things, to leave Brussels for Breda in Holland. The King had already realized the importance of doing so and sought the permission of the States-General of the United Netherlands to come to Holland. Mazarin, scenting the way the wind was blowing, had now enthusiastically invited the King to return to France and the Spaniards became increasingly affable. But on learning that the Dutch had no objection to his coming, Charles had at once gone to stay with his sister, the Princess of Orange, at Breda on 4 April and it was there that he drew up letters to Monck and the new Convention Parliament, as it was called, which was in the process of being elected. These documents were drafted on the basis of suggestions offered by Monck and approved by Hyde.[12]

Accompanying the Declaration of Breda and delivered in England by Lord Mordaunt and by Monck's cousin, Sir John Grenville, now a Gentleman of the King's Bedchamber, were five other letters, one addressed to Monck as commander-in-chief of the army, one addressed jointly to Monck and Mountagu as commanders of the navy, one to each of the two Houses of Parliament, and one to the authorities of the city of London. The time of dispatch was propitious, for the Rump had been dissolved and the so-called Convention had not yet met. John Lambert, who escaped from imprisonment in the Tower and rallied a few adherents to him, had been rounded up by Monck's troops and the King had now come to a secret understanding with Monck. In his declaration Charles dealt with three problems: the question of an amnesty, that of religion, and that of the disposal of landed estates which had changed hands during the Interregnum. Each of these questions was referred to the coming parliament. Parliament was to make exceptions to the act of oblivion; it was to handle religion on the King's recommendations; and it was to determine the land settlement. But the King did specifically promise 'a liberty to tender consciences'. The Speaker of the House of Commons was told that 'in a word, there is nothing you can propose that may make the kingdom happy, which we will not contend with you to compass' and he was also assured by the King that 'our opinion of parliaments' is 'that their authority is most necessary for the government of the kingdom'. In his letter to Monck he wrote: 'We have more endeavoured to prepare and to improve the affections of our subjects at home for our restoration than to procure assistance from abroad to invade either of our kingdoms as is manifest to the world"[13] That was, to say the least, an ingenuous way of covering up his recent endeavours to obtain troops both from Spain and France to support a landing. However with regard to Charles's promises that were in fact to be broken – for liberty of conscience and for the regular summonsing of parliaments – the historian can only say that circumstances alter cases and no doubt it was Charles's genuine intention at the time he was writing to keep his word.

Ever since Christmas, Monck's march south, and the overthrow of Lambert, the King had been in excellent humour. He had tried to prevent his extremist supporters from pushing their luck too hard. At the end of January he had written to Mordaunt to say that he was agreeable to holders of Crown, Church and Royalists' lands being compensated if they specially merited it.[14] But he had pointed out that previous failures had been owing to persons promising what they afterwards could not perform. Three weeks later he had 'desired his friends to consult and communicate but to make no rash attempt'.[15] He was then still waiting to see which way Monck would move. And he was still ready to seek military aid from abroad if he could be assured of ports where troops could be landed. He had been showered with advice from England, it even being suggested that he ought to give away the Crown, Church and sequestered lands to buy his passage home. But the King had naturally refused to be pushed into issuing too early a declaration of his intentions. As soon as he saw the way things were going he instructed his friends in England to stand for membership of the new House of Commons and expressed the hope that 'it would do his business'. Oliver Cromwell's former Secretary of State, John Thurloe, had sent him a message in March to the effect that it would damage his reputation if he were to marry Mazarin's niece, Hortense Mancini. That was at the same time as Monck sent the message that he was at last ready to receive a letter from the King. At the same time again Hyde had received a letter from Alderman Robinson, who had been the leader of the exiled Presbyterian Royalists, expressing his fear that the King 'would slip in without conditions'. On 31 March, four days before the King's letters were dispatched from Breda, Hyde noted two points in his correspondence with England. The first was that whatever conditions might be imposed, the surviving commissioners at Charles I's trial would not be spared from punishment; and the second was that the King should not buy his Crown on conditions which would make him ashamed of wearing it. On the other hand, Hyde was able to assure his correspondents that there was no truth in the Mancini affair.

The Declaration of Breda and the King's other letters were presented to the new Parliament on 1 May. It has been estimated that about ninety per cent of the members of the new House of Commons (which first met on 25 April) consisted of Cavaliers or Royalist Presbyterians and that only sixteen or eighteen persons who had sat in the Rump Parliament were elected. Thus it can be seen how necessary it was for the King to conciliate the Presbyterians and not to be committal about what was going to happen to landed properties that had changed hands since the first civil war began. The King, pressed by Monck, did however give it to be understood that the officers and soldiers of the army would be treated generously, and his promise of liberty of conscience appeared on the face of it to be positive. One thing may be said: that throughout his exile Charles had been ready to make any promises – including the taking of the two Covenants when he was in Scotland in 1650 – as the price of winning back his throne. The only exception was that he always demanded revenge on those whom he deemed his father's murderers. On that he remained adamant throughout. How far the verbal ingenuities of the Declaration of Breda were owing to Hyde cannot be conclusively established. Hyde himself did not boast about it. And it looks as if a natural caution had crept into the King's attitude of mind during the months that extended from Christmas 1659 to May 1660. As soon as Monck had quarrelled with the Rump and insisted on allowing the excluded members to take their seats in the House of Commons, it had become plain to Charles that playing a waiting game and exercising restraint from giving rash promises were the wisest courses. The Declaration of Breda was received with enthusiasm in England and Alderman Robinson's fear that the King might 'slip in without conditions' was realized.

As soon as the King's declaration and letters were received by the Houses of Parliament on 1 May he was unanimously invited to return to England and be crowned. The Commons voted £50,000 for his immediate needs and the City of London chipped in with £10,000. Bonfires were lit, bells were rung, and the guns were fired from the Tower of London and by ships in the Thames. There were cries of 'long live King Charles' as his health was drunk in the streets. Soon the heralds proclaimed him in London and Westminster and thanks were given to God in the churches, while Monck hastened to tell the House of Commons that it must not think of subjecting the King's return to any conditions. At Breda the King and his court awaited news of this great day with anxiety. Hyde wrote to Sir John Grenville saying that 'His Majesty is full of expectations of the success of that day which he hopes hath put an end to all those devices and inventions which some of the Presbyterians had designed, contrary to their professions to the King and which they would fain persuade the world were not forsooth their own desire but infused into them by the General'.[16] Bernard Grenville, Sir John's brother, was the first to reach the King with the good news and General Mountagu did not stay for Parliament's decisions but brought over the English navy to the coast of Holland ready to escort his master home. On 15 May Charles accepted an invitation to go to The Hague where parties and dances were given in his honour. He had the pleasure of refusing invitations from France and Spain to return to Paris or Brussels to await the delegation which Parliament was sending over to beg him to return to England.

On 14 May the delegation from the Lords and Commons had duly arrived at The Hague; the City of London, which had some-what guilty feelings about the way it had treated him and his father, sent a separate delegation and there also arrived a group of Presbyterian ministers who spent some time advising Charles not to use or reintroduce the Book of Common Prayer. The King was courteous to all and after spending eight days at The Hague he embarked on the fleet, he himself travelling on the warship *Naseby*, which was appropriately renamed the *Royal Charles*. Samuel Pepys, who had accompanied Edward Mountagu, his master at that time, recorded in his diary how the King kissed Mountagu and spent the evening of 23 May renaming other ships in the fleet. 'All the afternoon,' Pepys noted, 'the King walked here and there, up and down . . . very active and stirring.'[17] Charles related with gusto to the company on the quarterdeck his adventures in escaping from the battle of Worcester. One can recapture the nervous excitement of the moment. The fleet was under sail all night and the weather was glorious. By the next evening the King was in sight of England. The following morning Charles and James, Duke of York, breakfasted on pease, pork and boiled beef, the usual rations of the seamen. Upon his landing at Dover on 25 May the King was received by General Monck 'with all imaginable love and respect'. The Mayor of Dover presented him with a very rich Bible 'which he took and said was the thing he loved above all other things in the world'. Then he got into a coach and made straight for Canterbury.

At Canterbury many of the notables from London had already gathered to greet him as well as many suitors demanding offices and rewards for their faithful services. For example, the Venetian envoy, Giavarina, was introduced to Charles there and was delighted when the King replied in Italian to his compliments.[18] At Canterbury too, where he spent the weekend, the King held a meeting of his Privy Council, gave the Order of the Garter to General Monck and knighted William Morice, Monck's land agent in Devon, whom on Monck's advice the King appointed as one of his two Secretaries of State (in place of the Earl of Bristol who had become a Roman Catholic). The King had proceeded from Dover to Canterbury by coach but from Rochester he rode into London. He stopped first at Blackheath where Monck's army was drawn up to welcome him. He entered the borough of Southwark on horseback between his two brothers at three o'clock on Monday afternoon, 29 May, his thirtieth birthday, and reached Whitehall accompanied by a procession of soldiers at seven in the evening. The way was 'strewed with flowers', wrote John Evelyn who was there, 'the bells ringing, the streets hung with tapestry, fountains running with wine'. The Mayor and Aldermen had greeted him at Deptford. The streets were crowded, but the King had no fear of showing himself to his people. That evening the streets of London flowed with wine: the Venetian envoy kept a fountain of wine going outside the doors of his house, much to the delight of the populace. In Whitehall palace the King took all his meals in public and by his royal presence afforded the people 'the utmost consolation and enjoyment'. As Evelyn stood in the Strand and perceived the King's reception, he blessed God, because all this had been achieved without one drop of blood being spilt 'and by the very army which rebelled against him: but it was the Lord's doing and marvellous in our eyes'.[19]

7

The Settlement

What was the King like who at the age of thirty thus entered into his heritage? He was tall and dark but not handsome. 'His face', wrote Sir Samuel Tuke at this time, 'is rather grave than severe, which is very much softened whensoever he speaks; his complexion is somewhat dark, but much enlightened by his eyes, which are quick and sparkling.'[1] During his exile he had lost weight; he had often been short of food, as can be told by the appreciation he expressed in his letters when he had enjoyed a good meal. In general, Tuke records, he was sober in his diet. He also rarely drank to excess and he tolerated tobacco. Although his education had been interrupted, he took advantage of his long stay abroad to master languages. He understood Spanish and Italian and wrote French correctly. It was noticed how when he first went to France he had to struggle with the language, but now he spoke it fluently. He had enough Spanish to manage when he was in Fuenterrabia and he greeted the Venetian envoy in Italian.

According to Tuke, Charles was 'well versed in ancient and modern history'. He had benefited from lessons in mathematics from Thomas Hobbes. He was also said to have been 'a true friend to literature and learned men'. His chief delight, however, was in navigation, for which he may have acquired a taste when in command of the fleet during the second civil war. Gilbert Burnet wrote that 'he had a great compass of knowledge, though he was never capable of much application or study. . . . He understood navigation well; but above all he knew the architecture of ships so perfectly that in that respect he was exact rather more than became a prince.'[2] He interested himself in the early experiments carried out by members of the Royal Society, whose origin dated back before his restoration, but of which he became the patron; and he had his own private laboratory. 'His apprehension was quick,' adds Burnet, 'and his memory good. He was an everlasting talker. He told his stories with a good grace: but they came in his way too often.'

Much has been written about Charles II's religion. There seems very little doubt that his experiences with the Scottish Covenanters had a searing effect on his mind, for he detected cruelty and hypocrisy in their make-up and could never forgive the way they bullied him when he was in their power. He once said that Presbyterianism was no religion for a gentleman. Writing after his death, the Marquis of Halifax observed that 'when he came into England he was as certainly a Roman Catholic as that he was a man of pleasure ...'[3] but this view has hitherto not been generally accepted. It is clear that he was much more sympathetic to the Roman Catholics even than his father had been, and was grateful for the help that they had given both to him and his father. He was too astute not to realize that his restoration to the throne and his maintenance upon it depended on his giving at least outward deference to the Church of England and its Book of Common Prayer. 'It will be said that he had not religion enough to have convictions,' wrote Halifax; 'that is a vulgar error; and he goes on to suggest that it was emotion rather than reason that attracted him to the Church of Rome.[4] Burnet was more positive. 'He seemed to have no religion: both at prayers and sacrament, he, as it were, took care to satisfy people that he was in no sort concerned in that about which he was employed. So he was very far from being a hypocrite. ... He disguised his popery to the last.'[5] It is indeed clear, as subsequent events proved, that Roman Catholicism appealed both to his reason and to his belief in the political order of things: 'I find he is well aware', wrote a French ambassador, 'that no other creed matches so well with the absolute authority of kings.'[5] He never disguised his sympathy for it and if the posthumous writings that he left are genuine – and there is no solid reason to doubt them – he accepted the argument of the apostolic succession. In fact he put this argument to Sir Robert Moray as early as 1672 when he said: 'Our Saviour would certainly leave some body or power to whom the Church might have recourse for solution of difficulties, and he very well knew where that power must be lodged.'[6]

Tuke drew attention to Charles's easiness of access – so different from the habit of his father – his patience in giving his attention even during the most boring interviews, such as those with the Presbyterian ministers who badgered him in Breda, and his gentleness in speech. Hyde thought that he 'expressed himself with more condescension than was necessary to persons in all conditions, heard all they had to say to him, and gave them such answers as for the present seemed full of grace'.[7] Among his intimates he was frank and good-humoured. An amusing instance of this occurred just about a year after he was restored to the throne. John Evelyn, who had access to the court, insisted on presenting Charles with a panegyric he had written on the occasion of the coronation. The King was pleased 'most graciously to accept this' when he was in his privy chamber. But after Evelyn had departed, he asked the bystanders if it were in Latin and expressed the hope that it would not prove very long.[8]

Tuke wrote that Charles's clemency was as natural as his courage. About his courage there can be little doubt. It has been observed how at various times during his exile he was ready to risk his life by venturing into England with virtually no armed support, and he had fought gallantly both at sea and at the battle of Worcester. As to his clemency, that is much more of a question. He was not prepared to spare his political enemies and later, at the time of the Popish plot, he allowed those whom he suspected to be innocent men to suffer execution. But fundamentally he was easy-going and would put up with most things that did not interfere with his pleasures. Edward Hyde indeed thought the King too easy-going. This emerged when the question of the Duke of York's marriage to Hyde's daughter Anne was under discussion in 1660. 'You are of too easy and gentle a nature,' Hyde then said, 'to contend with those rough affronts which the iniquity and licence of the late times is like to put upon you before it be subdued and re-formed. The presumption all kind of men have upon your temper is too notorious to all men, and lamented by all who wish you well.'[9]

That was not the only reprimand that Hyde had given the

King in the course of their long association. It has been noted how both Hyde and Ormonde deplored the King's laziness and neglect of his duties during exile. Complaint was again made at the outset of his reign that he gave too much time to self-amusement. The trip through France to Spain and the eight-day stay at The Hague were also thought to have been wasted opportunities. Historians have differed over the question of Charles's degree of application to his duties, but it is generally agreed that though he was capable of strenuous work in an emergency, he was not by nature a hard worker. That did not mean that he had no mind of his own on political affairs. On the contrary, he was quick and intelligent; he had, said Tuke, 'understanding and sagacity'. As Burnet wrote, 'his apprehension was quick'. Halifax observed that 'his wit consisted chiefly of his quickness of apprehension'. Finally, he was a good mixer; his long stay abroad – quite apart from his adventures in Scotland and England in 1650–1 – had brought him into the company of all sorts and conditions of men and women. He was never aloof. He learned to suffer fools, if not gladly, at least without betraying his feelings. But to compensate for that he always had a preference for amusing company, even if it were the company of rogues. But he rarely allowed second-raters or irresponsible courtiers to sway his decisions. On the whole, the Ministers he chose to serve him were men of real ability. Like his mistresses, it was said that he used them but did not love them.

It was natural that the King should select his Ministers first from those who had served him loyally during his exile abroad and had shared his penury. Of these the chief was Edward Hyde, who had been appointed Lord Chancellor in 1658, as well as holding the position of Chancellor of the Exchequer when there was virtually no exchequer to manage. Writing in 1660, Hyde himself said that 'the Chancellor was generally thought to have the most credit with his master, and most power in his counsels, because the King referred all matters of what kind soever to him'.[10] There is the evidence too of notes passed by the King to Hyde during meetings of the Privy Council that the King consulted Hyde about most of the appointments he made. Hyde relinquished the post of Chancellor of the Exchequer at the

Restoration. He was created Earl of Clarendon, but refused to become a Knight of the Garter. His long association with Charles since the King's boyhood tended to make him somewhat avuncular, but though the King gave him a free hand in many things, Charles expected to be consulted on everything of importance and required to be obeyed.

For the Lord Treasurership, the most important Ministry, the King chose the Earl of Southampton, who had remained in England during the Interregnum but had refused to have any dealings with Cromwell. Anthony Ashley Cooper, an exceptionally able Dorsetshire man, who had twice changed sides during the civil war and was Southampton's nephew by marriage, took over from Hyde as Chancellor of the Exchequer. Ormonde was made Lord Steward of the Household. He could not retain his position as Lord Lieutenant of Ireland because Parliament had conferred this title on General Monck. But Monck, though he enjoyed the large salary, had no wish to go to Ireland nor had his deputy, Lord Robartes; Ormonde, who knew Ireland better than any other dignitary, was restored to his post late in 1661. Sir Edward Nicholas, who was now sixty-seven, was retained as Secretary of State for the South, the other Secretary (for the North) being William Morrice, Monck's protégé. Culpeper, who belonged to the inner circle of royal advisers during the exile, died soon after the Restoration. Thus the King's principal counsellors were the Chancellor, the Treasurer, the Marquis of Ormonde, General Monck, and the two Secretaries of State. These formed a 'secret committee' which (wrote Clarendon) 'under the notion of foreign affairs was appointed by the King to consult all his affairs before they came to the public debate; and in which they could not be a more united concurrence of judgments and affections'.[11]

The Privy Council, which also met regularly and covered many subjects, ranging from important questions of state to minutiae, was an unwieldy body consisting of some forty to fifty members including men like Mountagu, Lord Anglesey, Lord Holles, the Earl of Manchester, Lord Robartes and many others. The King had perforce not only drawn for his counsellors upon his friends during exile and General Monck's group, but also on those Presbyterian Royalists who had acted in his favour in the Convention parliament. There was also a fourth group of men who attracted the King by their wit, conversation, and knowledge of the society world and were more agreeable to him personally than the older generation represented by Clarendon, Ormonde, Southampton and Nicholas. These included Sir Henry Bennet, who had functioned as the King's ambassador in Madrid, the Earl of Bristol, Sir Charles Berkeley and the second Duke of Buckingham. As early as the summer of 1661 Pepys had heard the rumour that 'my Lord Chancellor much envied that very great men such as Buckingham and Bristol do endeavour to undermine him, and that he [his informant] believes it will not be done; for that the King yet cannot be without him for his policy and service', though he was of course 'no companion like the young gallants'.[12] Many offices and perquisites were, as always, in the King's gift and from the very beginning of the Restoration he had been embarrassed by the pressure of suitors. Monck also had been committed by promises or half-promises made by him. It was understood, however, that not all the promises could possibly be honoured. Yet there seemed to be few who did not obtain a share in the loaves and fishes.

For his representatives in Scotland Charles selected men who had fought for him there, such as the Earl of Glencairn and John Middleton, now first Earl of Middleton. John Maitland, Earl of Lauderdale, who had been imprisoned after the battle of Worcester, was appointed secretary of the Council. Lauderdale was an extraordinary character, a strange mixture of roughness and culture and of what the Duke of Buckingham called 'a blundering understanding'. Charles was to take much notice of his opinions. Both Scotland and Ireland were placed under the direct absolute authority of the King, who rejected the idea of having any form of parliamentary union with England such as had existed under the Protectorate. Episcopacy was re-established in both countries and, although Charles himself was favourable to the Roman Catholic interest in Ireland and antagonistic to the Presbyterians of Scotland, this was not of immediate consequence.

Finally Charles appointed judges who held office during good behaviour. While loyalty to the Stuart cause was considered the most important qualification, Charles and Clarendon took care to select experienced lawyers and did not necessarily exclude men who had officiated during the Interregnum. In fact Sir Matthew Hale, the most eminent lawyer in the Cromwellian period, was soon appointed Chief Baron of the Exchequer Court in place of Sir Orlando Bridgeman, who became Chief Justice of the Common Pleas.

One problem that immediately presented itself to the King was the marriage of his brother James. James, who was Lord High Admiral and the heir presumptive to the throne, had while in exile in Holland promised to marry Anne, the daughter of Edward Hyde. This was most embarrassing for all concerned since, in spite of the Lord Chancellor's high position in the state, he was a commoner and princes were not expected in those days to marry commoners. In his memoirs James admitted that he had been 'overmastered by his passion' and gave a formal promise of marriage in November 1659.[13] When it was discovered in the summer of 1660 that Anne was with child, the affair became of public importance. Sir Charles Berkeley, King Charles's friend, tried to help out by claiming that Anne Hyde had also been his mistress and that he was now ready to marry her. The Lord Chancellor was dreadfully upset and asserted that he would rather his daughter should be the Prince's mistress than his wife and threatened to send her to the Tower. When the Queen Mother arrived on a visit to England, she said that if Anne came in at one door of Whitehall palace, she would go out of the other. Charles's other brother, Henry, said that he could not bear her because she always carried about with her the smell of her father's green bag. Although he pretended otherwise in his memoirs, James himself appears to have been not unwilling to get rid of the lady, who proved a formidable character. However Charles himself insisted that the promise of marriage should be honoured by his brother. The other parties thereupon toed the line. The couple were married on 3/4 September at Worcester house according to the Book of Common Prayer; and at a meeting of the Privy Council on 18 February 1661, when forty-four members were present, the marriage was approved and upheld. This episode showed conclusively that the King had a mind of his own and that at this stage he was not going to give offence to his chief Minister.

This was not the only question that required settlement. First it was necessary to disband the army. Monck's army was by no means happy at the way events had worked out; it had not realized when it followed him from Scotland that it was destined to help restore the King and abandon 'the Good Old Cause'. The traditions of the army were republican and when it greeted the King on Blackheath it had showed subdued enthusiasm. Monck had insisted that his soldiers must be generously treated. The soldiers and sailors had been owed large arrears of pay. Many of the officers had invested in lands that had been thrown on the market during the Interregnum. The King had taken a brave resolve. He decided to ask Parliament to vote him money to pay off the forces. Soldiers were given their arrears plus one extra week's pay and their entry into civilian life was facilitated by waiving the requirements of the apprenticeship acts. The main fear of unrest came from extremist sects like the Fifth Monarchy Men or Fighting Quakers. A rising took place in the city of London by the Fifth Monarchy Men in January 1661. In a manifesto entitled *The Door of Hope* it was stated that 'they would rise up against the carnal, to possess the Gate, or the world, to bind their Kings in chains and their nobles in fetters of iron'.[14] Only fifty persons took up arms, but they managed to kill several people in the City before they were rounded up by Monck's soldiers at Ken Wood. The episode was sufficient to cause consternation and Monck was then allowed to retain a regiment of infantry, which was to be known as the Coldstream Guards. But otherwise Charles relied on the loyalty of his subjects for the maintenance of order in his kingdom.

A severe example was made of the surviving leaders of the rebellion against the monarchy. In accordance with the King's wishes the act of indemnity, passed on 21 August 1660, had exempted all the regicides 'for their execrable treason in sentencing to death or signing the instrument for the horrid murder or being instrumental in taking away the precious life of the late sovereign Lord Charles'. Forty-nine persons were named plus the two unknown executioners of Charles I (clause XXXIV). But nineteen of these regicides who had given themselves up were by another clause (XXXV) in effect allowed to escape with their lives: there was a proviso that in the event of their being attainted for high treason their fate should be suspended until the King, by advice and consent of both Houses, should order their execution. Two regicides escaped to die in Massachusetts. The remaining twenty-eight of the original forty-nine plus one supposed executioner, who had been completely exempted from the act, were put on trial in October 1660, but only ten were sentenced to death. The House of Lords had wanted to extend the list of exceptions to the death penalty to include members of Oliver Cromwell's High Court of Justice which had sentenced four peers to death. But Charles II was insistent that the death penalties should be confined to actual regicides and his father's executioners. In fact there were two other victims of the King's revenge, one the Marquis of Argyll and the other Sir Henry Vane. Neither of them had in fact been regicides, but Argyll had used his influence in Scotland against Charles I and had been responsible for the execution of the heroic Montrose; while Vane had been one of the most outspoken of the English republicans. Vane was accused of treason not against Charles I but against Charles II. The Lord Chief Justice reprimanded him for his 'very ill deportment' and Charles too was annoyed by the courageous manner in which Vane had conducted himself at his trial, justifying all he had done and acknowledging no power in England except Parliament. In June 1662 Charles wrote to Clarendon to say 'if he [Vane] had given new occasion to be hanged, certainly he is too dangerous to live, if we can honestly put him out of the way'.[15] Charles himself watched some of the executions, but when in July 1661 it had been been proposed to the Privy Council that the nineteen regicides named in clause XXXV should also be brought to trial for their lives Charles passed a note to Clarendon in which he wrote: 'I must confess that I am weary of hanging except on new offences; let it sleep. You know that I cannot pardon them.'[16] On the whole, it may be said that Charles was relatively lenient. Several of the regicides in fact owed their lives to Charles's mercy. John Lambert, Oliver Cromwell's second in command, also, like Vane, excluded from the Act, was allowed to make his submission and spent the rest of his life a prisoner in some comfort in the Channel Islands.

Apart from the dangers presented by an unpaid army and the emotions aroused by the execution of the regicides a principal problem that faced the King after his restoration was a religious settlement. Charles II, whatever his innermost feelings might have been, remained publicly loyal to the Church of England. Even during his frustrating experiences in Scotland he had stood out for his right to use the Book of Common Prayer and to employ Anglican chaplains. And while it is true that he had been made to swear to the Covenants and to forswear his father and mother in fact he never committed himself to imposing Scottish Presbyterianism on England; when he returned to France it was with a rooted dislike of Presbyterianism, which he thought should be subjected to episcopacy. Outwardly during the period between 1651 and 1660 he had remained loyal to the Church of England; and even if at heart he preferred Roman Catholicism he was aware that if he was to regain his throne, he must not appear to be other than loyal to the old establishment. Two episodes show this. The first was that the King had moved swiftly and dramatically to prevent his mother from forcibly converting his young brother Henry to her religion while he was with her in France. This episode, in which the Marquis of Ormonde had snatched the intended victim from the jaws of spiritual death, had been a *cause célèbre* in the Europe of the time. Secondly when in 1657 a Roman Catholic peer, Lord D'Aubigny, had urged him to come down more definitely on the Roman Catholic side Charles said:

As I very well know the person [D'Aubigny] is very much mistaken in the temper of England as to its indifference to religion of which I may reasonably be thought to understand somewhat, by having opportunities for many weeks during my last being there [that is, during his flight from Worcester] to discover the humours of the people without dissimulation, myself being unknown amongst them.

That was a striking testimony to his view. The Ministers upon whom he relied for advice in exile had all been unanimously in favour of maintaining the Church of England and laboured to persuade its remaining bishops to consecrate others so that the succession should not be threatened. Lord Mordaunt, Charles's favourite in England at the time, had averred that 'Nothing can secure the Crown that destroys the Mitre'.[17]

Thus both for reasons of state and by personal inclination Charles resisted the pressures of his Presbyterian supporters to commit himself in advance to their cause. They were anxious that he should not be restored without conditions and they frequently referred to the so-called treaty of Newport by which Charles's father had agreed to accept Presbyterianism as the national religion in England with toleration for sectaries. Charles II of course appreciated that Presbyterian support was necessary for his restoration, and never for one moment suggested that it should be repressed. On the other hand, he had been so careful to avoid giving countenance to the Presbyterians that he had refused to attend services in Huguenot churches in France. Charles's mother had ingeniously hoped that if he attended such services the Anglicans would be alienated and thus he would be induced to favour Roman Catholicism. A central figure in this question had been Monck. Monck himself does not appear to have been a Presbyterian but his wife was and he had been affected by the Presbyterian atmosphere of Edinburgh. He had tried to persuade Charles to uphold the confiscation of the wealth of the Church of England during the Interregnum and asked that he should agree to religious toleration for all his subjects. Charles had already perceived during Booth's rising* that the Presbyterians were among his best friends in England and, if he were to receive the invitation he sought from the Convention Parliament in un-animous terms, he must persuade the Presbyterians that they had no cause to fear the consequences of his return. It was largely because of the need to please Monck and to assuage the temper of the English Presbyterians that in his declaration of Breda Charles

*See pages 85–86.

committed himself to this statement: 'We do declare a liberty to tender consciences, and that no man shall be disquieted or called in question for differences of opinion in matter of religion which do not disturb the peace of the kingdom.'[18]

In promulgating his declaration at Breda did Charles have in mind the comprehension of all sorts of Christians in a reconstituted Church of England, or did he think mainly in terms of toleration for dissenters? It seems plain that in spite of his dislike of un-adulterated Presbyterianism, Charles's debt to the Presbyterians for his restoration had, in his initial opinion at any rate, to be repaid by a system of comprehension. Charles accepted the services of no fewer than ten Presbyterian chaplains at the outset of his reign. In June 1660 he had expressed his aim of finding an 'accommodation' between the Presbyterians and Anglicans. In October 1660 he offered bishoprics to three leading Presbyterians – Baxter, Calamy and Manton. This offer was followed by a meeting called by the King at Hyde's residence, Worcester house, of representatives both of the bishops and of the Presbyterians to discuss a declaration, drafted by Hyde and to be issued by the King, on religious affairs. It was proposed that no bishop should ordain or exercise jurisdiction without the advice of presbyters forming the cathedral chapters; that no one was to be denied the Lord's Supper because he refused to kneel; that no one was to be obliged to bow at the name of Jesus or to use the cross in baptism; and that clergy were not to be compelled to wear the surplice. And it was promised that obsolete words and expressions used in the Book of Common Prayer would be reviewed, and in general that future rules about Church ceremonies would be left to the determination of a national synod to be summoned later. The Presbyterians wanted the terms of the declaration to be altered still more in their favour. In the matter of confirmation they gained the point that the consent of the local minister should be required and that no one should be admitted to communion until he had offered a credible confession of faith and that scandalous offenders should be excluded from communion altogether; at the same time provision was made for appeals against the in-dividual minister's decisions. Thus in terms of the declaration presbyters were to officiate both at the level of the bishops and at the level of the parishes. The representatives of the Anglicans thought that the declaration conceded too much, while the Presbyterians thought it gave them too little. But it was a notable compromise and was duly published by the King as a royal declaration on 25 October.

When the subject of this declaration was brought before the Convention Parliament, which met after a recess in November 1660, the Presbyterians naturally attempted to give it the force of law. The issue was bitterly debated and the House was divided between the Presbyterians who supported the declaration and the Anglicans who thought it gave far too much away. Some Independents – enemies to the Presbyterians – voted against the bill. Charles II, according to the French ambassador in London, exerted his own influence against it and at the end it was narrowly defeated.

Some historians have argued that Charles II and Hyde were insincere when they promulgated the Worcester house declaration; that it was never intended as a permanent ecclesiastical settlement; and that Charles's intervention against the Bill showed where his real feelings lay.[19] But there is no concrete evidence for these assumptions. It was a practical attempt to comprehend the Presbyterians – who at that time constituted a substantial number of the members of the House of Commons – inside the Church of England. The reason for Charles's reported intervention against the proposed bill may well have been because he upheld the view, expressed by his father and dating back to King Henry VIII, that ecclesiastical affairs formed a part of his prerogative; that he was the Supreme Governor of the Church; and that it was not a matter for Parliament at all. Indeed it was fairly obvious that if the Bill had been passed in the Commons it would have been strangled by the bishops and Anglicans in the Lords.

The Convention Parliament was dissolved at the end of the year, and before the new Parliament met in the following May invitations were issued to the national synod which had been promised both in the declaration of Breda and the Worcester house declaration. This conference sat for the best part of ten weeks at the Savoy. As a background to the conference came the meeting of the so-called Royalist or Pensionary Parliament, from which the formerly big group of Presbyterians had been swept away, and which was representative of the right-wing elements in the Church of England who hated the puritans. The main question under discussion was the revision of the Book of Common Prayer. For a time it seemed as if another compromise solution might be found between the twelve Anglican bishops and the twelve Presbyterian divines who attended the conference. But Richard Baxter, who led the puritans and took most of their case on his shoulders, was extremely stiff and impatient and eventually the conference completely broke down. It is doubtful if in any case agreement could have been reached over ceremonial matters. The two Houses of Convocation now proceeded to meet and draw up a revised liturgy; this was approved by the King and was accepted by the new Parliament in April 1662. It was followed by a Bill of Uniformity which required all the clergy not only to subscribe to the new prayer book but also to accept the whole of the thirty-nine articles, to declare themselves against the Covenant, and to swear to the doctrine of non-resistance to the King.

Particular interest [writes Anne Whiteman] attaches to the . . . proviso which would have given the King authority to allow any incumbent in possession of a living on 29 May 1660 to refrain from the use of the surplice or the sign of the cross in baptism, as long as he arranged for another to baptise for him when the full Anglican rite was wanted, and did not write or speak against the liturgy, rites or ceremonies of the Church of England.[20]

This proviso was introduced into the House of Lords at the King's own request, but was thrown out by the House of Commons. As a consequence of this unamended Act of Uniformity some 1,000 clergy – about an eighth of those who held benefices – were expelled from the Church of England on St Bartholomew's day, 24 August 1662. (Nearly 700 were also ejected under the Act for Confirming and Restoring Ministers of September 1660.) It is likely enough, however, that of those who remained many were men who described themselves as Presbyterians during the Interregnum. It was only the more rigid of the puritan incumbents who gave up their livelihood as clergy to wander out into the wilderness.

Charles made one last effort to fulfil the promises he had given in the declaration of Breda. On 26 December 1662 he published a declaration in which he said he would try to induce Parliament to allow him to exercise in favour of the puritans his prerogative right to dispense with the law. The Speaker of the House of Commons at once informed the King that it could not agree to this and a bill that was introduced into the House of Lords, which would have permitted the King to use his prerogative to dispense with the Act of Uniformity, was defeated. The Earl of Clarendon himself spoke against the Bill in the House of Lords. In publishing his Declaration of Indulgence it is said that Charles also had the Roman Catholics in mind.

What is at any rate certain is that Charles II during the years 1660–2 consistently stood for toleration. In the Worcester house declaration he had attempted to comprehend most Christians within the established Church by reducing the old powers of the bishops and giving the individual clergyman an opportunity to exercise his own authority in the parishes. When that failed he had sought to bring the two main parties to an agreement at the Savoy conference; and finally, when the conference broke down, he had tried his best to induce Parliament to allow him to modify the severity of the Act of Uniformity. The fact that his chief Minister, had in the last resort contended against him shows that the policy of toleration was the King's own. It was a measure of the passions of the times that, in spite of its exuberant royalism, Parliament, led by the bishops, had resisted the King's wishes and fastened an unbending and old-fashioned Anglicanism on the Church.

A matter of even greater practical importance to Charles at the outset of his reign was his finances. Lavish promises had been given and in fact the Convention Parliament voted sufficient money by way of land assessments and poll tax to pay off the army and navy. But Charles had both his own and some of his father's debts to honour and no special provision was made for them. A committee of the Commons estimated that the King's peacetime expenses would amount to £1,200,000 a year and a recent re-examination of the figures makes out that this was quite adequate.[21] On the other hand, the principal sources of revenue – customs and excise duties – were liable to fluctuate; the yield was often over-estimated and it was sure to be reduced as it flowed through the hands of many officials who had pickings from it. The King's unpaid debts, an overestimate of the yield from taxes, and delay in establishing effective methods of collection meant that within a few years of his accession the King was in financial difficulties. Two remarks in general may be offered about the King's revenue. The first is that a Parliament largely consisting of landowners was entirely unwilling to retain the assessments, which had proved a fruitful source of revenue during the Protectorate, as a regular tax. Secondly, the peacetime revenue of the Crown was rarely sufficient because the services of an army and a navy frequently had to be called upon, the navy for the protection of commerce, the army for internal security measures (such as those necessitated by the Fifth Monarchy rising of January 1661). Southampton, the Lord Treasurer, was an old man who did not hold office for long, while his assistant, Anthony Ashley Cooper, was accused of lining his own pockets. So, whoever's fault it may have been, the King's revenue at first regularly fell short of his income.

One of the trickiest problems of the Restoration government was the land settlement. The Interregnum governments had sold off all the Crown and Church properties to pay for the wars; they had passed three acts confiscating the properties of certain eminent Royalists, including Hyde; they had also levied duties on the values of the lands of other Royalists known as 'sequestrations' or 'compositions', and in order to pay these duties many Royalists had been obliged to sell part of their lands. One reason why there had been resistance to the recall of the King after the death of Oliver Cromwell had been that the purchasers of these confiscated or sold lands did not want to lose them. Some of Charles's advisers in England had written to him as late as February 1660 saying that he ought to 'give away' the Crown, the Church and the sequestrated lands as the price of his restoration.[22] General Monck had also been insistent that his soldiers who had purchased Royalist lands should not suffer, and had asked the King to confirm the sale of the confiscated lands including those of the Church. But in his declaration of Breda Charles had been extremely cautious, saying that all differences over grants and purchases of estates 'shall be determined in parliament which can best provide for the justification of all men who are concerned'. In private Charles had assured Lord Mordaunt four months before the declaration of Breda that compensation would be paid to holders of Crown, Church and Royalists' lands if they specially merited it. In fact no compensation was granted to purchasers of Crown lands. Some of those who bought Church lands were allowed to stay on as tenants. Private acts secured for Royalists, whose lands had been confiscated, their due return. But few of those who had to sell land to pay their compositions were compensated. One modern historian says correctly that this was the first great example of Charles's ingratitude to his supporters at the Restoration. But recent research tends to prove that very few landed families appeared in the reign of Charles II whose rise can be attributed to the purchase of Royalist lands during the Interregnum, while few disappeared because they had been obliged to sell their estates.[23]

The King was crowned on St George's day, 23 April 1661. Before it certain preliminary ceremonies took place. On 19 April sixty-eight Knights of the Bath were created with a bathing ceremony in the Painted Chamber at Westminster. This was the last occasion when such a ceremony was performed in connection with a coronation. Then on 22 April the King went in a splendid cavalcade from the Tower of London to Whitehall, where he created a number of peers, including Hyde, who became the first Earl of Clarendon, and Anthony Ashley Cooper, who became the first Baron Ashley. Hyde relates in his memoirs how he had accepted the title with reluctance after he had refused the Garter. Charles was accompanied to Whitehall by all his nobility and various officers of state. 'The magnificent train on horseback', wrote Evelyn, who was there, 'proceeded through the streets, strewed with flowers, houses hung with rich tapestry, windows and balconies full of ladies, the London militia lining the ways and several companies with their banners and loud music in their orders: the fountains running wine, with speeches made at several triumphal arches.'[24] Before entering his palace the King was greeted at Temple Bar by the Lord Mayor and Bailiff of Westminster. Next morning Charles rode from Whitehall in his crown and robes to Westminster hall and then walked on foot upon blue cloth from Westminster hall to the Abbey where his throne was erected. The Bishop of London presented the King to the people who cried out 'God save King Charles II!' After a sermon by the Bishop of Worcester the King took his oath before the altar and swore to maintain religion, Magna Carta, and the laws of the land. Then he was anointed and the ailing Archbishop of Canterbury, William Juxon, placed the crown on his head. More shouts of 'God save the King' and the booming of cannon from the Tower completed the ceremonies. A coronation feast was held in Westminster Hall and the King then returned by water on a triumphal barge along the Thames to his palace.

A year after the coronation came Charles's marriage. This was partly decided by personal considerations but mainly by foreign policy. Charles II's foreign policy was determined in its turn partly by Charles's own predilections but chiefly by what had happened under the Commonwealth. When he was in exile Charles had some reason to be grateful to Spain, though Spain's friendship had been influenced by the fact that it was then at war with the English republic. The first thing that Charles did when he had regained power was to conclude peace with Spain. He had less reason to be grateful to France because, although his mother as a French princess had enjoyed Parisian hospitality, Charles himself had been shunned and almost insulted by Cardinal Mazarin. On the other hand, Mazarin was soon to die and Charles admired the absolutism enjoyed by the French monarch, Louis XIV. The Spaniards, for their part, were anxious to regain Dunkirk and Jamaica, which had been conquered by Oliver Cromwell's forces. The United Netherlands were still the rivals of England for commerce and shipping and Charles had no reason to love the

Dutch republicans, who had repudiated his relatives of the House of Orange.

Such was the general foreign situation immediately after the Restoration. Charles had at once demonstrated his own independence not merely by concluding peace with Spain but also by expelling the French ambassador, Bordeaux, who had notoriously intrigued with his enemies. As to marriage, Charles, at the age of thirty, was anxious to marry into one of the royal houses of Europe so as to obtain a legitimate heir to his throne. On the face of it he should have married a Protestant princess so as to please the majority of his subjects and to avoid associating himself too closely with one of the great Catholic powers. But where was there a suitable candidate? 'I hate Germans,' the King had announced, 'or princesses of cold countries.'[25] That really settled the matter so far as Protestants were concerned. The Spaniards had no suitable princesses available. Of the minor Roman Catholic candidates on offer Mazarin's beautiful young niece, Hortense Mancini, had already rejected him and was now disregarded; another was the daughter of the King of Portugal, while the Duke of Parma had two daughters on offer. The Duke came to England to push his wares, but the Earl of Bristol, who had examined the princesses on the King's behalf, reported that one was too ugly and the other too fat. On the other hand, the Portuguese princess, Catherine of Braganza, was not only stated to be young, innocent, and reasonably good-looking but she had a generous dowry to bestow. The Spaniards, who strongly disliked the idea of such a marriage, correctly, if vainly, warned that she was incapable of bearing children.

Even before the Restoration General Monck had been attracted by the idea of a Portuguese alliance. First of all Tangier was offered as a means of strengthening English naval power in the Mediterranean. Then the town of Bombay in India was added, together with the sum of two million crusados, said to be worth about £300,000. Finally British merchants were to have free access to trading facilities throughout the Portuguese overseas empire, including Brazil. This was well calculated to spike the guns of the Dutch who had previously been engaged in warfare with the Portuguese and at one time controlled Brazil. In return, all that the Portuguese demanded was the right to recruit troops in England (which they would pay for) and enjoy benevolent British neutrality in their continuing war against Spain. As early as November 1660 Charles had entered into correspondence with Lisbon and sent Hyde a letter 'that is for the Queen of Portugal in the worst Spanish that ever was writ'.[26] The alliance was in line with traditional foreign policy. Cromwell had concluded a treaty with Portugal which had proved profitable to British commerce. Early in May 1661 the King's council opted in favour of the Portuguese marriage and the King announced this to the new Parliament in a speech in which he also condemned the amount of drinking at election time. In the background the French Government pushed the marriage because although France was precluded by the treaty of the Pyrenees from helping the Portuguese against the Spaniards, the French were only too delighted to annoy their old Habsburg enemies. A treaty of marriage had already been concluded between England and France, Charles's Roman Catholic sister Henriette having been betrothed in August 1660 to Louis XIV's brother, the homosexual Duke of Orleans. During September 1661 there had been a public quarrel in London between the French and Spanish ambassadors, as a result of which the Spanish ambassador was asked by Charles to leave the country. Thus in fact Charles renewed Cromwell's friendship with France and indirectly, through the Portuguese marriage, sustained the conflict with Spain.

In order to get round any difficulties with the Papacy there was no formal marriage by proxy in Portugal but Catherine of Braganza sailed to England (Tangier having first been taken over by a British expeditionary force) in May 1662. On 28 May Charles wrote to Clarendon from Portsmouth, where he had travelled to meet his bride, telling him he was glad he was not called upon to consummate the marriage the previous night for he was sleepy 'and matters would have gone very sleepily'.[27]

I can now give you an account of what I have seen abed [he added], which in short is, her face is not so exact as to be called a beauty though her eyes are excellent good, and not anything in her face that can in the least shock one, on the contrary she hath as much agreeableness in her looks altogether as ever I saw, and if I have any skill in physiognomy, which I think I have, she must be as good a woman as ever was born; her conversation as much as I can perceive is very good for she has wit enough and a most agreeable voice . . . in a word I think myself very happy.

How Charles discovered the quality of her conversation is obscure since the Queen spoke neither French nor English: perhaps they conversed in broken Spanish. Catherine had been brought up in a nunnery; her ladies were unprepossessing and their heavy native skirts or farthingales made them a laughing stock at the sophisticated English court. Nor did the announcement that there was nothing in his wife's face 'to shock one' sound exactly promising. Charles was also rather careful in a letter that he wrote to his sister Henriette. He thought himself 'the happiest man in the world' or so he told his mother-in-law. But in private he is supposed to have remarked that he thought they had brought him a bat instead of a woman.

Things became no easier for the Queen when jokes were made about her Portuguese attendants and their farthingales. She was given pretty English women as her Maids of Honour. The King insisted that his mistress, Barbara Palmer, Countess of Castlemaine, should be appointed a Lady of the Bedchamber to the Queen and Frances Stuart, another girl much admired by Charles, became a Maid of Honour. Barbara Palmer had attracted Charles in Holland before his return from exile and her husband Roger had been created a peer as a price for being a cuckold. Samuel Pepys thought her the most beautiful woman he had ever seen. Charles had warned Clarendon that he must not resist his wishes so far as Barbara was concerned. 'I wish', he wrote to him in 1662, 'I may be unhappy in this world and in the world to come if I fail in the least degree of what I have resolved . . . whosoever I find to be my Lady Castlemaine's enemy in this matter, I do promise upon my word to be his enemy as long as I live.'[28] 'Thus early in his reign', in the late David Ogg's words, 'was Charles, like Solomon, advised by strange women'.[29]

8

Charles and Clarendon

In the spring of 1665 Charles II once explained to the French ambassadors who had come to England on a diplomatic mission: 'I am not so absolute in my state as the King my brother is in his. I have to humour my people and my parliament.'[1] From the beginning of his reign Charles had recognized the need to handle Parliament delicately. He may not have cared for its existence – indeed in the light of what the Long Parliament had done to his father it would have been surprising if he had – but he saw the necessity for carrying Parliament along with him in everything he did. In his declaration of Breda he had referred all difficult questions to Parliament. It was a Parliament, although not summoned by royal writ, that had called him home from exile. And he had good reason to hope that, in view of the enthusiastic manner in which he had been received back into London, he would be able to have a Parliament congenial to his purposes.

The Parliament that met on 8 May 1661 seemed to be full of exultant Cavaliers. In addressing them Charles said:

> I think there are not many of you who are not particularly known to me; there are few of you of whom I have not heard so much good that I am as sure as I can be of anything that is to come that you will concur with me, and that I shall concur with you, in all things which may advance the peace, plenty and prosperity of the nation. I shall be exceedingly deceived else.[2]

In the same speech he informed the two Houses of his forthcoming marriage. Subsequently the Commons settled down to work on a series of messages which are said to have been 'of such a character as to create a second Restoration settlement far more uncompromising than the first'.[3] These included a high treason bill, a bill to restore the temporal powers of the bishops, a bill against tumultuous petitioning, a militia bill vesting the control of all armed forces in the Crown, and a bill for regulating corporations. At the end of the session on 30 July 1661 the King thanked the Parliament for 'the many good Bills you have presented me with this day', and the King and Parliament parted in mutual harmony until the following November.[4]

The King's attitude to Parliament hardened somewhat as he recognized that it was not going to provide him with all the revenue for which he hoped. It was also made clear to him that the House of Commons was far less tolerant than he was himself over religious questions and would not allow him to use his dispensing power in accordance with his declaration of indulgence. This despite a speech in which Charles said he did not doubt that they would concur in his declaration. 'The truth is,' he said, 'I am in my nature an enemy to all severity for religion and conscience, how mistaken soever it be, when it extends to capital and sanguinary punishments which I am told were begun in Popish times.'[5] The next measure he recommended to Parliament was even more significant. When Parliament met in March 1664 he was reminded of the Triennial Act or 'act for the preventing of inconveniences happening by the long intermission of parliaments' to which his father had given his consent in February 1641. According to the terms of that act a new Parliament had to be called every three years and if the King did not himself call it, the Lord Chancellor might do so or, failing the Lord Chancellor, the House of Lords could assemble and issue writs for a House of Commons to be elected. Charles regarded this act as having been forced upon his father in derogation of the royal prerogative, and having opened a way for 'desperate men' to carry out their 'wicked resolutions'. In asking Parliament to repeal it Charles said: 'I need not tell you how much I love Parliaments. Never King was so much beholden to Parliaments as I have been; nor do I think the Crown can ever be happy without frequent Parliaments.'[6] Nevertheless Charles's eagerness for the repeal of the act disclosed his true attitude. Though a new act declared that the sitting and holding of parliaments 'should not be intermitted or discontinued above three years at the most', it contained no provisions for enforcing this if the King chose to ignore it. And in the event during the last four years of his reign Charles was able to dispense with calling a Parliament. On 5 April the King thanked the Houses warmly for passing the new Triennial Act and gave his assent to it. Samuel Pepys noted that this speech was the worst that he had ever heard in his life.

Charles was not in fact a ready speaker, at any rate when he was addressing Parliament. He read out what he had to say and often did so haltingly. That was perhaps not surprising as his speeches were generally punctuated by requests for money. The Convention Parliament had voted him a revenue of £1,200,000 a year, and later a hearth tax was added which was expected to yield £300,000 a year (in fact in its first year it yielded only £80,000).[7] The Convention had also given him a grant sufficient to pay off the armed forces, but most of his debts had to be paid out of his own total allowance. As usually happened in those days, the actual yield from taxation was insufficient to meet the promises made. According to a manuscript found among the Clarendon papers, the King's actual expenditure between Michaelmas 1661 and Michaelmas 1662 was £1,588,234 whereas taxes (excluding the hearth tax) amounted to £1,218,500 of which the customs and excise accounted for £670,000.[8] Although the King made four speeches to Parliament drawing its attention to this shortfall, it refused to grant him more than four subsidies – an unsatisfactory medieval tax (which yielded a mere £137,000) as distinct from the efficient modern assessments which had been granted to Oliver Cromwell. It was not until the Anglo-Dutch war broke out in 1665 that Parliament showed itself more generous. By then rumours of the King's personal extravagances, such as his payments out of his privy purse to his mistresses, in particular to the Countess of Castlemaine, were common knowledge and in November 1664 Charles had to assure Parliament that if he were voted a large sum he would not 'make a sudden peace and get all that money for private occasions'.[9]

By this time Charles's relations with his principal Minister had deteriorated. The Earl of Clarendon did not care for Charles's dependence upon the Countess of Castlemaine and resented the influences that were brought to bear on the King in her chambers and at her parties. It had been with the deepest reluctance that he had forced 'the lady', as Clarendon always called her, into the Queen's service after Charles's marriage and neither the Chancellor nor his wife ever paid a social call on the Countess. It was the general gossip in Whitehall that a number of courtiers, including the Duke of Buckingham and the Earl of Bristol, were gunning for Clarendon; and though it was thought that Charles could not do without him, his enemies had access to the King's ears outside the council and mocked at the old man as His Majesty's schoolmaster.

The first setback to Clarendon's influence occurred when Sir Henry Bennet, Charles's representative in Spain, returned to England at the beginning of 1661. Bennet was forty-three. 'He had not the distinguished beauty of the Earl of Bristol,' wrote his biographer, 'nor the grace and sparkle of the Duke of Buckingham, but he was a man of stately ministerial presence.'[10] He was recognizable by the strip of black plaster across his nose covering a wound he had received in a skirmish in the civil wars. Clarendon was asked by Charles to find Bennet a seat in the House of Commons. This he did, but he resisted the King's wish to appoint Bennet as his ambassador in Paris on the ground that he was pro-Spanish. But the King was determined on Bennet's promotion. He therefore offered Sir Edward Nicholas a large sum to lay down his office as first Secretary of State and promoted Bennet in his stead. Bennet already held the office of Keeper of the Privy Purse, but this was now bestowed on another of the King's younger friends, Charles Berkeley, afterwards Lord Falmouth. Describing Bennet in his memoirs Clarendon wrote of a man unversed in any business, who 'never had nor ever was like to speak in the House, except in his ear who sat next him to the disadvantage of some who had spoken'.[11] But Nicholas was over seventy and was glad to have the money, while Bennet was a hard worker, adaptable and affable in all he did for the King. Henceforward Clarendon had to put up with Bennet as a member of the inner royal councils. He missed Nicholas and also his former colleague, Ormonde, who had gone to Ireland. Writing in October 1662, however, Clarendon assured Ormonde that his own credit with the King was not diminished. But, Clarendon added, 'that which breaks my heart is that the same affections continue still, the same laziness and unconcernedness in business and a proportional abatement of reputation'.[12]

Clarendon, it has been observed, came into the open in opposition to the King in resisting Charles's declaration of indulgence in the House of Lords. But on the question of war with the Dutch they were agreed. Both were reluctant to embark upon it: partly because they were afraid that the French, with whom they both wanted to remain on good terms, would be dragged into the war against them. The causes of the Anglo-Dutch war were deep and wide. First came economic grievances, such as the huge haul of fish that the Dutch took every year off the British coasts, and the prohibition imposed on the export of raw wool from England to which the Dutch replied with a ban on the import of dressed wool. Secondly there were disputes over naval rights, particularly the right to search neutral vessels for enemy goods. The Convention Parliament had passed a Navigation Act even more stringent than that of the Commonwealth era forbidding the Dutch to carry into England goods other than those of their own manufacture or to take British or colonial goods away. The East India Company had many grievances against the Dutch company and resented the fact that one of the spice islands, Pulo Run, promised to it by the treaty that concluded the first war, had not been handed over. The newly formed Royal Africa Company, of which James, Duke of York, was president and in which Charles had invested £5,000, also had its complaints against the Dutch who, it claimed, tried to enforce a monopoly on the Guinea coast. Lastly quarrels developed over the damage done to various British vessels; neither side would trust the impartiality of each other's admiralty courts.

Although an Anglo-Dutch commercial treaty had been signed in 1662, this scarcely papered over the cracks between the two sides. Dutch possessions and Dutch shipping were a huge and tempting target, so much so that Sir George Downing, the English ambassador at The Hague, assured the government that the Dutch would do everything in their power to avoid war. In so far as any one man was the protagonist of war it was the Duke of York. He had set up the Africa Company with the aid of the merchants trading there deliberately to hinder the Dutch from becoming masters of it. Towards the end of 1663 he sent a friend of his, Sir Robert Holmes, in a warship borrowed from the King and other merchant ships to seize the fort at Cape Verde on the Guinea coast and occupy the castle of Cormantin on the Gold Coast. Much to Dutch indignation, he was successful in his mission. The Duke of York also borrowed two warships and sent them out under Colonel Richard Nicolls to take part in an attack on the New Netherlands (the site of modern New York State) lying adjacent to the English colonies of Virginia and New Jersey. Nicolls successfully occupied New Amsterdam, the capital of the New Netherlands, which was renamed New York in deference to the heir presumptive to the English throne. These two actions provoked the Dutch when they heard of them, and a sizable fleet was dispatched under de Ruyter from Holland to the Guinea coast. But the Dutch were still not anxious for war in Europe.

On 2 June 1664 Charles wrote to his sister, Henriette: 'The States keep a great bragging and noise but I believe that when it comes to it, they will look twice before they leap.'[13] Meanwhile a joint resolution of the two Houses of Parliament had demanded that the King provide protection for English trade against the Dutch. There is 'a great appetite for war in Parliament', Charles noted in the same letter, but said that all this would not govern him; he would be 'very steady in what he resolved, but if forced to war, he would be prepared for it'. James noted in his memoirs that Van Gogh, the Dutch ambassador in London, 'perceived that the King himself was not too much inclined to war and that the Chancellor was wholly averse to it', which gave Van Gogh a wrong view since he thought that nothing could be carried out against the wishes of the King and the first Minister. During the summer tempers on both sides continued to flare. The Dutch sent twelve warships to Africa, and the English equipped a fresh force under Prince Rupert in August. Charles did his utmost to pour oil on the troubled waters. Sir George Downing was sent back to

Holland to try to obtain peaceful satisfaction of English grievances against the Dutch. Charles wrote to his sister in France (who was also the sister-in-law of Louis XIV) telling her that he very much desired a strict friendship with the French King, who had earlier concluded a defensive alliance with the Dutch, and on 19 September Charles declared that he was the only man in England who was against war with the United Netherlands. On 24 November he disavowed Sir Robert Holmes's action in Guinea and actually sent him to the Tower of London. In rejoicing over the capture of New Amsterdam, he averred that 'it did belong to England heretofore but the Dutch by degrees drove our people out of it'. And he assured the Dutch ambassador that Cape Verde was 'a stinking place' and not worth a war.[14]

It is thus clear that Charles was reluctant to be forced into war, for he saw that the grievances between the two countries might be compromised by treaty. Also he wanted to come to terms with France before such a war should break out since he had no wish to be confronted simultaneously by both countries. In December 1664 he was writing to his sister: 'I believe my friendship to France is and will be more considerable than that of the Hollanders in many respects, and you may have it if you will.'[15] Furthermore he tried to persuade her that the Dutch were the aggressors, for whereas he had put Sir Robert Holmes in the Tower for a month or two because of his unauthorized actions in Africa, the Dutch had provocatively sent de Ruyter there to interfere with British trade. After an English admiral had attacked a Dutch merchant fleet coming home from Smyrna, however the peace could no longer be kept. On 14 January 1665 the Dutch declared war. Meanwhile the House of Commons, which had during the previous session voted the unprecedented sum of £2,500,000 specifically for the war (though the Bill was not passed ultimately until the following Easter), was insistent on war and this was eventually declared by the King on 4 March. Charles still had hopes of averting war with France, for at the same time that Anglo-Dutch hostilities were declared King Louis XIV had sent over to London a powerful embassy known as the *célèbre ambassade extraordinaire* dedicated to mediating a treaty between the contending nations and thus preventing the need for France to honour her earlier promises of aid to the Dutch in war.

In the spring of 1665 England was devastated by a great plague, the last of the nation-wide epidemics to hit this country. The court was moved from Whitehall to Hampton Court, then to Salisbury and finally to Oxford; and the French ambassadors who followed the court round had a most uncomfortable time. In any case their mission was hopeless. England was united in the war and, after the Dutch had been severely defeated at the battle of Lowestoft on 3 June and England had obtained an ally in the warlike Bishop of Münster, nothing could restrain their military enthusiasm or prevent them from wishing to teach the Dutch a resounding lesson. In any case the French ambassadors had instructions to bring about an end to the war, while Charles's own aim was to keep the French out of it. Consistently maintaining that the Dutch were the aggressors, he therefore failed to perceive any obstacle to an Anglo-French alliance. But before the end of the summer – and the end of the plague – King Louis had announced that if the English government refused to accept his terms for mediation, he would be obliged to declare war.

The battle of Lowestoft had an extraordinary aftermath. Proud in his victory, the Duke of York retired to sleep in his cabin. Whereupon his secretary, concerned for the safety of his master, persuaded the captain of the flagship that he had orders from the Duke to shorten sail and so abandon the pursuit of the Dutch. Thus the defeated Dutch fleet received no further damage and in escaping even claimed to have achieved victory in the battle. Charles now decided that the precious life of his brother must be risked no more and gave the command of the fleet to the Earl of Sandwich. Sandwich decided to launch an attack on Dutch merchant ships sheltering in the harbour of Bergen whilst awaiting escort by de Ruyter. Believing that the Danes had acquiesced in this attack in return for a share of the booty, Sandwich sent in fourteen warships, but they were met by a blistering fire from the shore batteries and had to retire. De Ruyter himself succeeded in evading the English naval cordon and returned home safely. Although later that summer Sandwich managed to capture nine

Dutch ships coming from the East Indies in convoy, he blotted his copybook by arranging to sell part of the proceeds to be distributed among his own officers. From the beginning of the war Charles had been sensitive about prizes and had put Anthony Ashley Cooper, now Lord Ashley, the Chancellor of the Exchequer, in charge of prize money. As Treasurer of Prize Money Ashley was responsible to the King alone for receiving and paying out the money. The King allotted some of it to 'secret service' payments and a portion was spent on his own amusements, including the Countess of Castlemaine, but the bulk of the takings in fact went to the Treasurer for the Navy.

In October 1665 the House of Commons voted, while meeting at Oxford owing to the plague, a further £1,250,000 for the war. Sir George Downing, who was a member of the House and had returned from his unsuccessful negotiations in Holland, proposed the addition of a proviso to the Bill whereby it was enacted that all the money raised should be applied only for a definite purpose, that is for urgent use in the war. This was the earliest instance of appropriation for supply in British history, and might well have been thought to be a derogation from the royal prerogative. Clarendon at least considered that it was, so he and Southampton were strongly opposed to the novel idea. They were overruled by Charles who was understandably sensitive at the notion that he was not to be trusted with money.

This Parliament also passed a bill against the embezzlement of prize goods, thus striking against the Earl of Sandwich who was deprived of his command and sent on an embassy to Spain. A third bill introduced in this session dealt with the prohibition of the importation of Irish cattle into England. 'The country gentry who sat in the Commons,' writes Professor Haley, 'and particularly those from the south-west, believed that the disastrous decline in rents, probably due in fact to a combination of slump, war and plague, was the result of competition between English cattle and fat cattle imported from Ireland' and it was assumed that English interests counted for more than Irish.[16] This then was an illogical bill, but it was favoured by Henry Bennet, now Lord Arlington, and by Lord Ashley. The House of Lords vainly attempted to modify its provisions. Though Clarendon was opposed to it, Charles himself decided in its favour and ultimately it became law.

In January 1666 both France and Denmark declared war on England in support of the Dutch and in the following April the Bishop of Münster, England's sole ally, concluded a separate peace. Nevertheless the English retained their superiority at sea. The Four Days battle, which opened on 1 June, may have been a draw because, owing to false intelligence during the first three days of the battle, two parts of the English fleet got separated; but the English had the better of another conflict in the North Sea, known as St James's Fight, which took place on 25 July, and in consequence of this defeat the Dutch feared invasion.

In March 1666 the King returned to Whitehall from Hampton Court and 'members flocked thither from all parts upon the fame of the King being at Whitehall, all men being ashamed of their fear of the plague when the King ventured his person'.[17] The King and Duke followed the war closely; in August they were inquiring into how the victuals for the fleet stood and Samuel Pepys, as the most able servant of the Navy Commissioners, was delighted with the King's concern. But on 2 September the Great Fire of London broke out and blazed throughout the entire city stretching as far west as Temple Bar. On Pepys's suggestion the King commanded the Lord Mayor to spare no houses but to pull them down before the fire everywhere. The Lord Mayor was struck dumb by the disaster and exclaimed: 'What am I to do? I am spent: people will not obey me,' but Charles himself was of sterner stuff and laboured to stop the spread of the flames.[18]

The pains the King had taken day and night during the fire [recounted Clarendon], and the dangers he had exposed himself to, even for the saving of the citizens' goods had been very notorious. He spoke with piety. But some rejoiced in the burning of the City and tried to persuade the King it was God's vengeance on his enemies. This kind of discourse did not please the King.[19]

It was the force of Charles's own personality that prevented the fire reaching Whitehall and Westminster; and he also gave orders that members of his Privy Council should go into the several quarters of the City so that by their authority they might prevent the inevitable looting and other crimes that accompanied the fire.

The fire lasted for four days and destroyed over 13,000 houses as well as many churches and public buildings. Charles hoped that the city would rise again rather 'purged with fire . . . to a wonderful beauty and comeliness than consumed by it'. Charles was offered plans for a new London by Dr Christopher Wren and Robert Hooke, both geometricians, and by John Evelyn, who loved to design gardens. But private property rights and lack of resources prevented any grandiose scheme from being undertaken. The King therefore devoted himself to hurrying on the reconstruction and ensuring that the new city should be built of brick and stone. Charles volunteered to pay for a new Customs House at a cost of £10,000 out of his own pocket. It was designed by Wren but was burnt down within half a century. Wren also supervised the designs of all the new churches. But it was not until the end of the reign that the desolation was erased.

The damage was very considerable and the burning of London had demoralizing consequences. When Parliament met immediately afterwards, it could be seen that the initiative had passed from the hands of the court. The King gave way reluctantly over the Irish cattle act and Charles's Ministers had to plead desperately for more money. Eventually £1,800,000 was voted and thus the King was given a total of £5,500,000 or the equivalent of four and a half years ordinary revenue to spend on the war. When Charles addressed Parliament on 18 January 1667 he spoke quite harshly to its members. He said that he had been forced to anticipate the revenue to pay off last year's fleet and added that he had little time to make preparations for the coming campaign against three foreign enemies. He said it was high time that the Commons fulfilled their promises of supply, and he showed his resentment over the Downing proviso. He insisted that the war must go on and concluded:

> I do not pretend to be without infirmities: but I have never broken my word with you; and, if I do not flatter myself, the nation never had less cause to complain of grievances, or the least injustice or oppression, than it hath had in these seven years it hath pleased God to restore me to you. I would be used accordingly.[20]

Later, before he prorogued the Parliament in February, he thanked them for the supply but added, 'the season of the year is very far spent, in which our enemies have got very great advantages over us; but by the grace of God I will make all the preparations I can, and as fast as I can'.

But whatever pose the King may have taken up before Parliament, he was fully conscious of the difficulties of renewing the war; and in his own private councils he relied less on his ability to exert force and more on being able to attain peace by diplomacy. A number of elaborate schemes had been tried. On the one hand, an attempt had been made to come to a separate peace with France. On the other, envoys had been sent to Denmark and Sweden to try to induce the Scandinavian countries to join with Holland and England in a quadruple alliance to resist French aggression in northern Europe. But these Scandinavian negotiations ended in fiasco and the French refused to conclude peace without Dutch concurrence. As early as the winter of 1665–6 Charles's Ministers had tried to negotiate with the enemies of the Dutch Pensionary, John de Witt, but this also had come to nothing. So the facts had to be looked in the face. The peace negotiations had broken down. The Great Fire, in which the Customs House and its records had been destroyed, added to the King's financial difficulties and made the City of London unwilling or unable to lend him money. A bad winter during which the Thames froze over had damaged trade. There were disturbances in Scotland and Ireland, and abroad the French fleet had been engaged in attacking the British West Indies and assaulting New York. Peace was the universal cry at home, where the government was becoming increasingly unpopular because of its incompetence.

Under these circumstances Charles had a twofold policy: first to induce the French, who wanted this war brought to an end, to persuade the Dutch to come to terms; and secondly to go on to the defensive in the naval war. 'The King in those straits', recorded Clarendon, 'called that council together with whom he used to consult his most secret affairs; and the chief officers at sea and the commissioners of the navy attended to give such information as was necessary before any resolution was taken.'[21] After prolonged conferences it was decided to lay up the greatest ships at Chatham, Portsmouth and elsewhere and to maintain a squadron of frigates based on Scotland, Plymouth and the Downs 'to intercept the trade of Holland both outward and inward'. The surplus seamen, released by the laying up of the big ships, would, it was thought, join privateers which would also prey on French or Dutch shipping. At the end of the summer when the enemies' ships were 'weary and foul' and when more money became available to Charles, it was proposed that the great ships, having been got ready in harbour, could be sent out again to the full attack. But before that of course it was hoped that peace would be concluded.

This policy, known as commerce-destroying, was one which weaker nations at sea invariably employed, but it was in fact a confession of failure by a once great naval power. Even more an admission of failure was the suggestion that British merchant ships should be restrained from going to sea lest lack of escorts should put them at the mercy of the enemy; the seamen, finding no employment, would be available when the King required their services. This last suggestion was understandably rejected, for it was pointed out that if British seamen were thus prevented from going about their normal business, what was the point of being at war with the United Netherlands at all? However the policy of laying up the big ships and concentrating on commerce-destroying was accepted.

The King [wrote Clarendon], had not himself thought of this defensive way but approved of it very much when he heard it so fully discussed . . . and it may be he liked it the better because at that time he was heartily weary of the war so that he was not without reasonable hope of peace which he resolved to cherish, as he told the Parliament at parting that he would do.[22]

Samuel Pepys, who was by now an expert in naval matters, did not put it so kindly. On 14 February 1667 he noted in his diary how the King was in treaty with the Dutch and added: 'The Court mightily for peace while the King has money he may save something and thus need the help of no more parliaments.'[23]

Clarendon himself washed his hands of the whole question, leaving it to the experts. He confessed that he did not even know where Sheerness was and that when he was on the river Thames his sole thought was how to get on shore again as soon as possible. The Duke of York as Lord High Admiral alone appears to have expressed misgivings about the policy of laying up the fleet and relying on commerce-destroying. The King did what he could to help the new policy and, knowing where Sheerness was, twice visited it to ensure that it and Chatham were adequately defended. Meanwhile two ambassadors were sent to the agreed conference centre of Breda to open negotiations.

Most of the other Ministers accepted the royal policy. When in the spring of 1667 many of the seamen were being paid off and their ships laid up for repair, Lord Arlington as Secretary of State instructed the Lords Lieutenant to undertake defensive measures with the local militia, 'horse being the force that most discourage the enemy from landing'.[24] But John de Witt and his elder brother Cornelius determined to take advantage of Great Britain's defencelessness. They sent a squadron into the Firth of Forth at the end of April; and at the end of May they planned an attack on the Thames and its tributary, the Medway, Cornelius himself accompanying the expedition which was under the command of Admiral Michael de Ruyter. Surprise was complete. On 10 June Sheerness fort was captured and a force raided the Isle of Sheppey. Although Chatham docks were defended by a chain stretched across the Medway and by sunken ships and guardships, the Dutch broke through, set on fire six warships and towed away two others including the *Royal Charles* on which the King had first arrived in England. Panic was terrific and the blame was laid squarely on the King and his Ministers. Trees outside Clarendon's new house in Piccadilly were uprooted by a London mob which also broke the windows and erected a gibbet and painted on his gate the words: 'Three sights to be seen: Dunkirk, Tangier and a barren Queen.'[25] Charles and James repudiated responsibility for the policy of laying up the fleet and proceeded to raise twelve regiments. Parliament was recalled on 25 July. But the principal reaction of the House of Commons was to object to the new regiments being raised since they might be employed as a standing army in peace time. Clarendon lost his nerve and opposed the recall of Parliament altogether. He was said to have spoken caustically of 'four hundred country gentlemen ... only fit to give money'[26] and actually to have advocated the raising of taxes by prerogative, one of the causes of the civil war. Charles himself kept his nerve and assured the Parliament that he had no intention of governing with a standing army. He then promptly prorogued the two Houses.

Peace with France and the United Netherlands had been concluded four days before Parliament met. The treaty was based on the principle *uti possidetis*, that is to say each country retained the conquests it had made during the war. Thus England failed to obtain Pulo Run, which was still occupied by the Dutch, and lost the West Indian islands captured by the French; on the other hand, England retained New York and New Jersey. But she lost almost everything in West Africa and received no compensation for her shipping losses. Although in view of the humiliation at Chatham the peace of Breda was better than might have been expected, the English gained none of the benefits for which they had entered the war in the first place. Thus the treaty was little more than an armistice and Charles awaited his revenge.

The poor results of the war demanded a scapegoat and the obvious victim was the Earl of Clarendon. Clarendon was regarded as the chief Minister and as such was held responsible for the disasters. He was known to have opposed the 'unseasonable' summoning of Parliament in July, to which the news of the peace was announced, and was believed to have encouraged the King to raise a standing army. It was said further that 'it was the Chancellor only who had hindered their [the Parliament's] continuing together and that he had advised the King to dissolve them'.[27] The authority of the group of elder statesmen who had been so loyal to Charles in his exile had been weakened not only by Ormonde's departure for Ireland but also by the death in May 1667 of Southampton, the Lord Treasurer. Southampton had not been adept at handling the King's finances and Charles had quite reasonably insisted, to Clarendon's displeasure, that Southampton should be replaced by a group of commissioners who included Ashley and Sir William Coventry, the secretary to the Duke of York. Coventry and Arlington as Secretary of State were both convinced that Clarendon was past his prime and urged his dismissal on the King. Clarendon's failure either to assert his authority during the winter of 1666-7 or to negotiate a favourable peace through the mediation of France counted against him. He was also made vulnerable by the recent death of his wife. Charles was painfully aware that when Parliament met again, as it was due to do in the autumn, a movement to impeach the Chancellor and possibly other Ministers would follow. 'I could not retain the Chancellor', he wrote to the Duke of Ormonde, 'and do those things in parliament that I desired.'[28] Moreover he ran the danger of losing his most capable Ministers. After all, Coventry and Arlington themselves were equally culpable of the failure to send out a fleet that summer or to achieve a better peace. The King feared, so Clarendon was informed, that his innocence would no more secure him against the power of Parliament than it had the Earl of Strafford who had brilliantly defended himself for his loyalty to Charles I's service a generation before. Moreover the King was not unnaturally to fear that blame for the calamities might be extended to himself and his Ministry in general; and he was to tell Parliament when it met that he would 'protect no man' and would leave to Parliament the investigation of the responsibility for the success of the fatal Dutch attack on the Thames that had compelled the peace. Thus from the King's point of view it was convenient if the parliamentary assaults concentrated on one target – Clarendon.

But Charles had his own reasons for having tired of his faithful Minister. There were personal reasons. Clarendon had constantly reproached Charles for his slackness in government, for speaking foolishly at the council table, and for his devotion to his debauches and his mistresses. When during the Court's visit to Oxford the Queen had been *enceinte* but had suffered a miscarriage Clarendon had prayed that the King might mend his ways. Not only had Clarendon been opposed to the appointment of the Countess of Castlemaine as a Lady of the Bedchamber to the Queen, and to her husband being ennobled, but he had been blamed unjustly for the marriage of Frances Stuart, who had also engaged the King's generous affections. More important, it has been observed how the Chancellor had openly opposed Charles's policy of religious toleration and he also differed from his master over other questions such as the embargo on Irish cattle. Clarendon was blamed too for the King's not having secured a larger revenue after the Restoration. In public he was held responsible for the sale to the French government of Dunkirk, the trophy of Cromwell's red-coats, his house in Piccadilly being nicknamed Dunkirk house. He was also criticised in some quarters for the series of harsh measures passed against nonconformists including the Con-venticle Act of 1664 and the Five Mile Act of 1665. These various acts were known as 'the Clarendon Code', although in fact it was the Anglican majority in the House of Commons that pushed them through. They went against the grain with Charles, who was nothing if not tolerant. Both Clarendon's public policies and private behaviour proved uncongenial to the King. Certainly he was mocked at Charles's parties by the Countess of Castlemaine, by the second Duke of Buckingham (Charles's boyhood friend who had recently, on Clarendon's instigation, been imprisoned on a false charge of disloyalty to the Crown and then restored to favour), and by Coventry who genuinely thought that the time was over-ripe for a change of Ministry.

Clarendon was conscious of his own rectitude. 'He doubted very much', he said, 'that the throwing off of an old servant, who had served the Crown in some trust for thirty years . . . should on a sudden without any suggestion of a crime, nay with a declara-tion of innocence, would call His Majesty's justice and good nature into question.' But he did not improve his case when in the course of his apology to the King 'he found a seasonable opportunity to mention the lady with some reflections and cautions, which he might [he admitted] more advisedly have declined'.[29] Charles was thoroughly displeased and on 30 August 1667 he sent William Morice, as Secretary of State, to demand the surrender of the Chancellor's seals of office.

Coventry and Arlington were entirely content with Clarendon's dismissal by the King and they had no wish for dirty linen to be washed in public through an impeachment of the Chancellor when Parliament met. The Duke of Buckingham, who had been released from the Tower of London in July and was high in the King's favour again, was anxious to convert himself into a popular hero, unlike his father who had once been a public scapegoat. It was Buckingham who organized a movement in Parliament completely to destroy the Chancellor. Charles himself hesitated between the two parties, one of which was against impeachment proceedings, the other for them. It was not until 20 October that he agreed to an impeachment for high treason being brought forward. Earlier he had ordered the Lord Keeper to draw up articles condemning the conduct of the ex-Chancellor that fell short of treason. But now he not only acquiesced in a full-scale assault but warmly contributed to it. Clarendon and his friends (who included his son-in-law, the Duke of York) were able to rebut all but one of the charges levelled against him. When, for example, on 26 October Sir Edward Seymour claimed that Clarendon had advised the King to govern by means of a standing army, the law officers assured the Commons that this was not a treasonable offence. In any case the accusation was rejected by a large majority. Eventually the imperial ambassador in London sent a message to the anti-Clarendonians to the effect that the former Chancellor had been betraying secrets to the French. Although there was no substance for this – and the ambassador failed to provide any evidence – it was sufficient to induce the Commons to believe that he was guilty of crimes more reprehensible than mere mistakes, negligence or unwise advice. But when in November Seymour carried the accusations before the Lords, the Upper House would have nothing to do with them. The Lords refused to commit Clarendon to the Tower, and Buckingham, his main enemy, was able to rally only twenty-six peers on his side. However at the end of the month, to the general surprise, Clarendon fled abroad to France, where he ate out his heart and completed his famous memoirs. It is said that a threat by the King to establish a special commission to try him induced Clarendon to flee, but there is little firm evidence for that. The King was unquestionably pleased to be rid of his imperious and hectoring chief Minister.

Historians have usually blamed Charles for his behaviour to Clarendon. 'Strong in the gratified hate of a harlot and unshamed by the congratulations of a pimp', wrote Osmund Airy, 'Charles abandoned the wise old man to whom he owed his throne.'[30] It is said that he treated him worse than Charles I had treated Strafford. But the facts must be considered in the light of politics rather than of emotion. Charles had certainly had real differences with his Minister during the seven years Clarendon had been in office, yet the King had acquiesced in his criticisms and his open opposition, for example, over the question of religious toleration, and had put up with being treated like a naughty schoolboy. Moreover Clarendon was no longer the effective director of policies, and was said to have fallen asleep during the discussions of vital naval questions. Charles saw himself at this stage to some extent as a constitutional ruler dependent for supplies upon the House of Commons, whose nursing he had entrusted to Clarendon. If the House now turned against Clarendon, what could he do? When things go wrong someone has to take the blame. That is the price of political life. It was perfectly clear that after Parliament met in July 1667 it was going to demand the punishment of evil counsellors for the failure of the war and the humiliation of the peace; and that Clarendon, as the self-avowed head of the King's government, was sure to be selected as the culprit. By dismissing Clarendon that August Charles had shown that he wanted to find new counsellors and a new policy. By offering up a victim he had no wish to risk the ex-Minister's life. Charles realized that the House of Lords was not going to find Clarendon guilty of treason. But the agitation in the Commons and the public clamour against Clarendon were such that some action to punish him had to be taken. The King promised Clarendon that his honours and estates would not be touched if he left the country. By spurring him to go into banishment abroad Charles saved Clarendon's life. It was more than the King's father had been able to do for Strafford.

9

The Private Life of Charles II

After the fall of Clarendon, Bab May, the Keeper of the Privy
Seal, sycophantically fell on his knees before Charles II and said
it was the first time he could truly call him King of England.
Personal resentment was certainly among the factors in Charles's
treatment of his Minister. The Chancellor had become domineer-
ing and almost insulting. In September 1667 Sir George Downing
said that the King had called Clarendon 'the insolent man' and
added that 'he would not let speak himself in Council'.[1] When
Lord Gerard told the King that the Chancellor said openly that
Charles was a lazy person and not fit to govern, 'Why!' says the
King, 'that is no news, for he hath told me so twenty times and
but the other day told me so.'[2] The fact that the King was courteous
and good-humoured most of the time and was indolent over
matters of routine did not mean that he was devoid of character
or strength of feeling. Nor did his easy condescension to his
inferiors imply that he expected them to treat him as an equal.

When the Count de Gramont came to London, having been
exiled from the French court because he made love to one of
Louis XIV's mistresses, he was pleasantly surprised at the elegance
and good manners of the English court.

The King [wrote Anthony Hamilton, Gramont's biographer] knew
no equal in his grace and dignity; he had an agreeable wit, he was
affable and easy by temperament and mind. Capable of varying re-
actions, he was in turn compassionate towards the unhappy, inflexible
towards the wicked, and tender almost to excess. To matters of
importance he could devote infinitely hard work, but he was incapable
of concentrating when dealing with trifles. His heart was often the fool
and more often still the slave to his flirtations.[3]

To this thumbnail sketch may be compared the testimony ot Gilbert Burnet, the Scottish cleric who was in close touch with the doings of the English court. He too thought Charles 'the best bred man in the world', who was civil rather to excess. He was condescending in private as well as in public, 'only he talks too much and runs out too long and too far'. He thought that the King's love of pleasure gave too much power to women. Although Charles was very kind to those he loved, he never put himself out to help them. He was mercifully inclined, but could be severe to those who opposed him, as Clarendon had done. Of his religion Burnet said that the King thought all appetites were free and that God would never damn a man for allowing himself a little pleasure. He was no atheist, but he had 'rather an odd idea of the goodness of God'. Charles thought that to be wicked or to design mischief was the only thing that God hated, and he once told Burnet that he was sure that he was not guilty of that.[4]

Sir William Temple, the diplomatist and a voluminous writer of essays, memoirs and history, also left a fascinating portrait of Charles's temper and character. It was his belief that the King's easiness of manner and desire to be liked by everybody made him give way too often to the last person with whom he had spoken. Concealed behind his familiarity and pleasant wit Temple detected 'a great variety of knowledge and true judgment of men'.

From his own temper [Temple added] he desired nothing but to be easy himself and that everybody else should be so; and would have been glad to see the least of his subjects pleased, and to refuse no man what he asked. But this softness of temper made him apt to fall into the persuasions of whoever had his confidence and kindness for a time, however different soever from the opinions he was of before; and he was very easy to change hands, when those he employed seemed to have engaged him in any difficulties: so that nothing looked steady in his conduct of affairs nor aimed at any certain end.

That therefore was the source of a weakness of character, but it also caused him to be widely loved. For he was neither proud nor vain and he detested flattery. Yet, Temple concluded this humour of his 'made him lose many great occasions of glory to himself, and greatness to his Crown, which the conjunctures of his reign conspired to put into his hand'.[5] Indeed he was not at all like his more famous contemporary, Louis XIV, who never demeaned himself and, after consulting his Ministers, always made up his own mind.

Charles was a good family man. It has been seen how carefully he looked after his youngest brother Henry when they were both in exile, and how devoted he was to his youngest sister. In February 1660 he wrote to Henriette, his 'dear dear sister': 'I will never give up the friendship that I have for you, and you give me so many marks of yours that we shall never have another quarrel but as to which of us shall love the other most.'[6] In September 1660 Henry died and this event cast a shadow over a family reunion after the Restoration. A banquet was held at Dover where the Queen Mother had come together with her daughter Henriette and they were joined by James, Duke of York, and Princess Mary of Orange, bringing together the four surviving children of the martyred Charles I. But on Christmas Eve Princess Mary, like her brother Henry, died suddenly of smallpox; and in January 1661 Charles's mother and his sole surviving sister left London to live in France. Although in writing to Henriette, which he did constantly, Charles referred to Queen Henrietta Maria as 'the best of mothers', it is doubtful if they usually saw eye to eye. Henrietta Maria visited London to collect her pension, and Somerset House was prepared for her to live in, but she preferred to return to Paris. Her main activity while she was in England was to disapprove of her son James's marriage. Charles was intensely loyal to James, but the latter was a very different character from the King – except for his obsessive love of women – and Charles must at times have found his haughtiness and lack of humour trying.

Charles was a lover of outdoors, but he did not have that passion for hunting which consumed most of the other Stuarts. Nor was he as keen on golf as his brother James. On the other hand, he was an enthusiastic player of tennis, croquet and bowls. On one occasion in 1661, John Evelyn relates, he sailed with the King in a yacht race on the Thames from Greenwich to Gravesend in which they raced against the Duke of York for a wager of £100.[7] When he stayed in Winchester at the end of his reign

Charles enjoyed the access to yachting round the Isle of Wight. Although much gambling took place at court, the King was not a big betting man, but he loved attending the horse races at Newmarket and sometimes took part in them himself. He was accustomed to rise early in the morning and go for long walks in St James's Park and elsewhere. He regularly visited the fleet and on one occasion took off his wig and pourpoint (a quilted waistcoat) to be more at his ease because of the heat of the sun. On the whole, he made a practice of informality and, according to Pepys, spoke contemptuously of the King of Spain who would 'do nothing but under some ridiculous form or other and would not piss but another must hold the chamber pot'.[8]

For much of his life Charles's year was governed by an almost fixed routine. He visited Newmarket in the spring and autumn; and spent the summer at Windsor and the winter in Whitehall. At Windsor he walked and fished and supervised improvements in the castle. In Newmarket he attended the races, but he loved the country for its own sake. Sir John Reresby, who visited him there one spring, noted that:

the King was so much pleased in the country, and so great a lover of the diversions which that place did afford, that he let himself down from Majesty to the very degree of a country gentleman. He mixed himself among the crowd, allowed every man to speak to him that pleased, went a-hawking in the mornings, to cock matches in the afternoons (if there were no horse races), and to plays in the evenings, acted in a barn and by very ordinary Bartholomew-fair comedians.[9]

For indoor amusements the King liked plays and dancing. Cominges, the French ambassador in London from 1661 to 1665, reported that there was a ball and a comedy every other day. The rest of the week was spent at play either at the Queen's or Lady Castlemaine's. Charles was a patron of music and employed both French and Italian artists. He had a French orchestra, which he lent on one occasion to the ambassador. Artists were welcome at his court and he took pride in his Raphaels, Titians and Holbeins. Dutchmen were often employed to paint London scenes and seascapes. As to science, Charles was the official founder of the Royal

Society and, even after he lost interest in its experiments, he sent venison for its anniversary dinners. He was also the founder of the Mathematical School at Christ's Hospital and the Royal Observatory at Greenwich, both aimed at the improvement of navigation. Towards the end of his reign Chelsea College, which had formerly been occupied by the Royal Society, became the site of a famous home for army pensioners. Finally he was a lover of animals: he had a pet monkey and the breed of spaniel that is named after him. Dogs roamed freely about his bedroom.

At the beginning of his reign the King attended the services of the Church of England with assiduity, but found the sermons trying. On 28 February 1664 he wrote to his sister: 'We have the same disease of sermons that you complain of there but I hope you have the same convenience that the rest of the family has of sleeping most of the time, which is a great ease to those who are bound to hear them.'[10]

The atmosphere of the court was condemned by outsiders – 'no faith, no truth, no love, nor any agreement between man and wife, nor friends': so said Thomas Povey, who could recall the more austere court of Oliver Cromwell.[11] How far did this atmosphere tend to corrupt? The King's laziness was often spoken of both in exile and in office. During July 1666 Pepys complained that 'the King and Duke of York play bowls in the Park while the guns could be plainly heard'.[12] Later he told the famous story how on the night that the Dutch burned the English warships in the Thames 'the King did sup with my Lady Castlemaine at the Duchess of Monmouth's and they were all mad in the hunting of a poor moth'.[13] It could be recalled that Sir Francis Drake played at bowls before the coming of the Spanish armada, and the court might have been merely trying to relieve its anxieties when it chased moths at a supper party. Still the condemnation of the King's insouciance was widespread. Sir Hugh Cholmley thought that nothing could save them but the King's giving up all to a Parliament,[14] and a month later (in July 1667) Clarendon declared apropos the Dutch invasion: 'Treachery! I could wish we could prove there was something in that; for that would imply some wit and thoughtfulness; but we are ruined by folly and neglect.'[15]

Charles II delighted in the company of ladies, but it is necessary to distinguish between his treatment of those of whom he was really fond like his Queen Catherine, his sister Henriette, and perhaps the young Frances Stuart, and those who were his mistresses including Lady Castlemaine, Miss Middleton and Miss Wells. 'The Queen', wrote Hamilton, 'was a sensible woman and devoted all her energies to pleasing the King by those services which were least painful to her tender feelings. She was attentive in providing the kind of pleasures and amusements which she could arrange – above all when she could be included herself.'[16] Charles respected her and admired her feelings and when she was thought to be dying in 1663 he showed himself distraught and wrote to his sister for Roman Catholic 'images' to be put into Catherine's books. He never seems seriously to have contemplated a divorce in spite of Catherine's inability to bear him children. It is often said that he treated her badly by forcing her to take the Countess of Castlemaine as her Lady of the Bedchamber after the Queen first arrived in London. But it appears as though at that time Charles was genuinely determined to turn over a new leaf, and imagined that the mere possession of this post would mollify his angry mistress. He also thought that he owed her the obligation since her husband had left her. In fact the Queen had been warned by her mother about the Countess. She had struck her name off the list of ladies in waiting put before her and at first had resisted all blandishments and pressures to change her mind. However Charles cunningly introduced the Countess to the Queen before Catherine realized who she was. Later the Queen gave way. Had she stood out longer, she might indeed have won her case. As it was, she came to a way of living with the Countess and although the King continued to sup with her, he returned each night to his wife.

No one appears to have had a good word for Barbara, Countess of Castlemaine, apart from her beauty. 'The crudeness of her manners,' wrote Anthony Hamilton, 'her ridiculous haughtiness and her perpetual suspicions and petty passions made Lady Castlemaine a disagreeable companion.'[17] Born in 1641, daughter of a Royalist killed in the civil war, she was a nymphomaniac greedy for love and money. Before she married her complaisant husband in 1659 she had been the mistress of the second Earl of Chesterfield and told him 'my life is never pleasant to me but when I am with you or talking of you'. Later she had love affairs with Henry Jermyn, the son of Queen Henrietta Maria's major-domo, now Earl of St Albans, and with Jacob Hall, a handsome tight-rope walker. Her first child by the King, a daughter, was born in February 1661 and her second, a son, in 1662. Described by Gramont as 'a lively and demanding woman', she took under her charge when she first came over from France to England in 1662 the very pretty young Frances Stuart who was appointed a Maid of Honour to the Queen on the recommendation of Princess Henriette. Frances, though coming from a distinguished family, had little means and was willing to take advantage of the position she rapidly attained at King Charles's court. The King himself was soon attracted by this fascinating teenager. Tall and slim, possessing a sense of humour, she aroused the most romantic feelings in a man nearly twenty years her senior. Charles often saw her at the Countess of Castlemaine's apartments and overwhelmed Frances with his presents, promises and attentions. It is suggested that the Countess, who sometimes shared her bed with Frances, was not averse from providing this innocent young rival to herself for Charles's affections to offset her own affair with Henry Jermyn. If so, her motives were complicated, but no doubt she genuinely felt that she had no reason to fear the seriousness of a young girl's rivalry.

But the King's assiduity grew with the years. When the court was at Oxford in 1666 and Lady Castlemaine was about to give birth to another of his children, he visited her and Frances every morning before he took his breakfast. Growing more and more infatuated, he did not even mind when the Countess, to make her absence felt, retired from Whitehall to Richmond. In 1663 when Frances was only fifteen the King was reported to be 'besotted' with her. Yet he continued to visit the Countess, who at this time became a convert to the Church of Rome, whether or not to please the King is obscure. Charles said that he did not interfere with the souls of women, only with their bodies. But his hankering after Frances continued. Frances was not entirely unresponsive. 'Miss Stewart do do everything with the King that a mistress should do', wrote Pepys.[18] But although stories went the rounds including one of a 'mock wedding' and another of Frances offering to pay any price for a drive in a new coach, it is evident that she never became the King's mistress. At one time she said that she would marry any gentleman with £1,500 a year to get away from the King. Eventually in March 1667 she married the twice-widowed Duke of Richmond, much to the fury of Charles, whose permission had not been asked. Frances eloped, and returned the King's presents. Princess Henriette had to intercede with the King to obtain forgiveness for her protégée and at first she did not succeed. 'I do assure you', he wrote to his sister on 26 August 1667,

> I am very much troubled that I cannot in everything give you that satisfaction I could wish, especially in this business of the Duchess of Richmond wherein you may think me ill natured. But if you consider how hard a thing it is to swallow an injury done by a person I have so much tenderness for [he had started to write 'love'] you will in some degree excuse the resentment I use towards her.[19]

However eventually he forgave her; she and her husband were allowed back to Court and she became a Lady of the Bedchamber to the Queen, who was always fonder of her than of Lady Castlemaine.

How far did Lady Castlemaine's hold on the King detract from Charles's responsibility as a statesman? Burnet wrote that 'his passion for her and her strange behaviour toward him did so disorder him that he was not master of himself or his business'.[20] Thomas Povey, not a very well informed witness, said that 'the King hath taken ten times more care and pains in making friends between my Lady Castlemaine and Mrs Stewart, when they have fallen out, than ever he did to save his kingdom'.[21] Habitually he visited the pair of them at or before breakfast and he supped with Lady Castlemaine even when she was big with child. This dependence or sense of obligation endured for at least the first seven years of his reign. In January 1666 when the court was at Oxford it was reported that Charles could not leave until Lady Castlemaine was ready to come along with him, 'she being lately put to bed'. John Evelyn thought that the King's and his brother's sexual conduct undermined their authority. He observed to Pepys in the autumn of 1666 that 'none of the nobility come out of the country to help the King after the Great Fire or comfort him or prevent commotion at this fire; but do as if the King were nobody'.[22]

There can be little doubt that the three women required much of the King's attention. The Queen probably took up the least of his time, although he once told his sister: 'I have been all this afternoon playing the good husband ... and I am very sleepy.'[23] But Lady Castlemaine was a termagant. Charles was little concerned over her infidelities but mocked at them. When she took up with the handsome John Churchill, the future Duke of Marlborough, and Charles found them together in Barbara's apartments, he said to Churchill: 'Go; you are a rascal, but I forgive you because you do it to get a living.' Lady Castlemaine could not stand the King's sarcasm.

She told him once [related Hamilton] that it very ill became him to reproach the one woman in England who least deserved it; that he had never ceased to pick quarrels with her since his low tastes had first declared themselves; that to gratify his base desires he needed only stupid geese like Stuart and Wells and that little slut of an actress [Nell Gwyn] he had recently taken up with.

Floods of angry tears accompanied these storms; after which, taking on the part of Medea 'she would close the scene by threatening to massacre her children and burn the palace over his head'.[24] As for Frances Stuart, she constantly provoked the King by increasing his ardour 'without diminishing her virtue by making the final sacrifice'.

Much time was occupied in providing entertainment for these demanding ladies. Hawking was pursued because it was convenient for them. When the weather was very warm in London and 'the heat and dust made it impossible to walk in the park' the river Thames offered an agreeable site for amusement. It was then filled with 'an infinite number of open boats, carrying all the charmers of the Court and City, accompanied by barges in which all the Royal family sat'. Light suppers, music and fireworks were all part of the diversions. But the court did not always remain in London. Tunbridge Wells was a favourite resort, the court overflowing into the neighbouring parts of Kent. It was compared to Fontainebleau. Charles hoped that the waters there might prove helpful to the Queen's health and he also tried the waters of Bath spa for that purpose.

It is said that it was when the King was at Tunbridge Wells in the summer of 1668 that he first met two actresses both of whom were to become his mistresses, 'Moll' Davis and Nell Gwyn. Moll Davis was a singer and dancer who appeared at the Duke's theatre. There when she took the part of Celania in *The Rivals* she sang a ballad 'My lodging is on the cold ground' which greatly impressed the King. The ballad 'raised the fair songstress from her bed on the cold ground to the royal bed'. She was provided with a house in Suffolk street and in 1673 bore the King a daughter, Mary, who was later married to the Earl of Derwentwater. Pepys thought her 'the most impertinent slut' but he admired Nell Gwyn, a comedienne who appeared at the Theatre Royal, Drury Lane. Nell was generally popular. She is reputed to have said 'I was but one man's whore, though I was brought up in a bawdy house to fill strong waters for the guests.' She had two sons by the King; her first Charles Beauclerk (later Duke of St Albans) was born in May 1670. But Charles did not confine these passing affairs to the stage. Another of his mistresses, Winifred Wells, was a Maid of Honour to the Queen. Gramont said she had the 'carriage of a goddess and the physiognomy of a dreamy sheep'. Charles treated all his mistresses generously. He arranged for the upkeep and ennoblement of their children. He does not appear to have practised birth control. In all he was to have thirteen illegitimate children, eight sons and five daughters.*25

On the whole one may picture Charles as living a full life from his early morning walks before breakfast, his visits to the 'two goddesses' at breakfast time, his dining in public, his afternoons at the theatre, his supping in private and his return to the Queen's bed at night. The general opinion was not so much that he neglected business for his pleasures, as that he was only ready to arouse himself in times of political crisis. The fall of the Lord Chancellor and the defeat in the Dutch war constituted such a crisis. Thenceforward – whatever his other proclivities may have been – Charles became his own first Minister.

* See Appendix for list of his mistresses and children.

10

The Foreign Policy of Charles II
1667–72

When they had been in exile both Charles II and the Earl of
Clarendon had been impressed by the greatness of France. After
the death of Cardinal Mazarin, Charles had admired the way in
which the young French King, Louis XIV, had become his own
Prime Minister and had taken personal charge of foreign policy.
But Charles realized that it was not at all easy for him to imitate
the *Grand Monarque*. In the first place, he did not possess Louis's
infinite capacity for hard work and attention to detail. Secondly,
Charles had to pay regard to public opinion as expressed in
Parliament; for although the conduct of foreign policy was accepted as a royal prerogative, diplomacy could not be effectively
pursued without the ability in the last resort to go to war; and the
House of Commons alone possessed the power to provide the
money needed for the maintenance of armies and fleets. Lastly,
Charles had to take into account the advice of his Ministers, who
met regularly in the committee of foreign affairs and handled the
correspondence with English ambassadors abroad and many of the
interviews with foreign ambassadors in London. Charles had his
own ideas about foreign policy, but he recognized the limitations
within which he had to work.

The Dutch war had been a disaster. Neither Charles nor Clarendon had been enthusiastic about it in the first place. Before his fall
Clarendon had virtually washed his hands of it, though the blame
had been placed squarely on his shoulders. But the fact was that
Parliament had wanted the war, as had been witnessed by the
large sums that had been voted for it, while in spite of all Charles's

efforts to prevent it the French had lent moral and material support to the Dutch in accordance with the treaty of 1662. One lesson that Charles had learned was that he was never again going to allow himself to be involved simultaneously in a war with the strongest naval and commercial power in Europe and with the greatest military power in Europe. A principal object of British foreign policy became to separate the United Netherlands from their alliance with France.

This was easier said than done. It is true that Charles had close personal relations with the French court. His mother was the King's aunt and his favourite sister was the King's sister-in-law. But the policy of Louis XIV since the death of his father-in-law, Philip IV of Spain, in September 1665, who had been succeeded by his five-year-old son, Carlos II, was to lay claim in the name of his wife, Maria Theresa, to a part or the whole of the Spanish Netherlands on the ground that the local law of Brabant provided that a daughter by a first marriage had superior claims to inherit over a son by a second marriage. If, in order to enforce that claim, the French army overran the Spanish Netherlands and laid hold of ports facing the straits of Dover, this would be a threat to British security; and a British government would have to demonstrate that there were very definite advantages in a French alliance to offset such a threat. Again, it had been the life work of John de Witt, the Grand Pensionary of Holland and the most influential single statesman in the United Netherlands, to maintain the friendship of France. And though the Dutch were equally sensitive to a French advance into the Spanish Netherlands, they had reason to be grateful to the French King for his support in the war they had just won against England.

Even before the fall of Clarendon and in spite of his lack of success during the Dutch war, Henry Bennet, created Baron Arlington in 1665, had emerged as Charles II's principal adviser on foreign affairs. He was an ardent worker and eager to please the King. But in so far as he had any sympathies, they lay rather with Spain than with France; that was why Charles had been persuaded not to appoint him ambassador in Paris before he became Secretary of State. It was a curious example of the crossed wires that often existed in the conduct of British foreign policy that in May 1667, just at the time when Louis XIV launched his attack on the Spanish Netherlands, the British government had concluded a commercial treaty with Spain which contained a secret clause that neither party would aid each other's enemies. Yet a month earlier Charles II in an interchange of letters conducted through his mother had privately assured Louis XIV in writing that what was being negotiated with Spain was 'only a simple treaty of commerce which could in no circumstances be prejudicial to France' and that he would make no agreement directed against France for a year, while during that year he would negotiate a close agreement (*une liaison étroite*) with France.[1] It might be said therefore that – secretly at any rate and on the word of a king – Charles was committed to absolute neutrality in the Franco-Spanish war. But when the French armies overran the Spanish Netherlands in the summer of 1667, and when the treaty of Breda brought an end to his war against the United Netherlands and France, Charles felt that a more positive policy must be found.

In August 1667 Louis XIV announced the terms on which he would end the war and conclude peace with Spain. Either he would keep the conquests his armies had made in the Spanish Netherlands or he would accept some lesser towns plus the Spanish possessions of either Franche-Comté or Luxembourg. These were called 'the alternatives' and their advantage from the French point of view was that, whichever alternative was accepted by the Spanish Regency, it would imply the recognition of the French Queen's right to share in the inheritance of the Spanish empire should the new Spanish King die without leaving an heir. In theory Maria Theresa had renounced all her rights to any Spanish inheritance when she married Louis XIV, but the validity of the renunciation had been challenged by the French on the ground that her marriage dowry had never been paid. Now if the Spaniards accepted these peace terms, they would in effect acquiesce in the French contention.

The French generals, who had found the campaign in the Spanish Netherlands so gratifyingly simple, wanted to persuade their master to push on and conquer the entire country. But Louis XIV, who had seen for the first time what war meant, was not so enthusiastic and tended to listen to his diplomatic advisers, who argued that he had made his point and could now rest on his laurels. So, instead of further alarming Europe, Louis decided to enlist the support of other countries to achieve his ends. He entered into negotiations with the Holy Roman Emperor, Leopold I, who was an interested party since he also had a Spanish wife with claims to share in the inheritance if the Spanish empire should break up; he invoked the friendship of the Dutch, whom he wished to reassure as to the extent of his ambitions in the Netherlands; and he sent a special ambassador to England, a French Protestant, the Marquis of Ruvigny, who he thought would be agreeable to the tastes of London society.

Ruvigny arrived in London in September 1667, just after Louis XIV had announced his peace terms and after Clarendon's dismissal. Charles was delighted. Ruvigny's proposal for an offensive and defensive alliance between France and England was in accordance with the wishes that the English King had privately expressed through his mother to Louis XIV in April. Charles felt obliged to warn Ruvigny however that both Parliament and the majority of his council were hostile to the French King, whose power they feared, and that only the offer of substantial advantages from such an alliance would enable him to secure public consent to it. He hoped for support, money and territorial acquisitions.[2]

George Villiers, the second Duke of Buckingham, who held no ministerial post but was an ambitious politician and a member of the committee on foreign affairs, also favoured a French alliance on suitable terms, and it was apparently on Buckingham's advice that Charles told Ruvigny in October that he wanted a subsidy from France, a share in the French conquests in Spanish Flanders (such as a Channel port) and commercial privileges in return for continued British neutrality.[3] Arlington went even further and suggested that the French should commit themselves to join with England in a war of revenge against the Dutch.

The French had no intention at this stage of acceding to such terms. They did not place a high value on English neutrality or mediation in a war they had already won. They knew that the States of Holland had just passed a resolution that the Spaniards should be forced to accept the French peace conditions, while active negotiations with Vienna were on the point of conclusion for an agreed partition of the whole of the Spanish empire in what seemed the likely event of the young Spanish King's early death. Thus the reply to the English proposals was devious and non-committal in the extreme, and at a meeting of the committee of foreign affairs on 1 January 1668, presided over by the King himself, it was decided, instead of trying to come to direct terms with France, to propose to England's recent enemies, the Dutch, that they should jointly mediate between France and Spain.

The objects of the two governments were the same: both wanted, for the sake of their own security, to stop the war in the Spanish Netherlands; neither wanted to offend the French. The treaty therefore provided for armed mediation, for the use of force against Spain if it refused to accept one of Louis xiv's alternatives, for a defensive alliance if either country should be attacked as a result of their joint intervention, and for a guarantee of the peace when it was made. There was a secret clause, however, which stated that if the French obstructed the peace the allies would join with Spain and push back the frontiers of France to the limits laid down in the peace of the Pyrenees. The treaty was concluded surprisingly quickly, although complicated arrangements were planned to induce Sweden to accede to the treaty, on the payment of subsidies by Spain, thus making it a triple alliance.

The two signatories hastened to assure the French that all they were doing was to help obtain a peace treaty on the terms that Louis xiv had already laid down. Charles ii wrote to Henriette on 23 January:

I believe you will be a little surprised at the treaty I have concluded with the States. The effect of it is to bring Spain to consent to the peace upon the terms the King of France hath avowed he will be content with, so I have done nothing to prejudice France in the agreement. ... And finding my propositions to France received so cold an answer, which in effect was as good as a refusal, I thought that I had no other way to secure myself.[4]

In other words, the treaty was 'to serve as a demonstration to Louis that the English alliance was valuable and must be bought at a decent price'.[5] Writing to Henriette again in March, Charles was still pleased with himself: he told her that not only had he arranged a defensive league with the United Netherlands, but he had secured peace between Spain and Portugal.

Louis XIV's plans were not immediately affected by the Triple Alliance. In January 1668 he had come to his agreement with the Emperor; in February, at a time when fighting did not usually take place, he launched the Prince de Condé into Franche-Comté, which was occupied with virtually no opposition. Three days before the Triple Alliance was completed, a peace treaty was signed with Spain from which the French King gained a line of fortresses in the Spanish Netherlands, but he returned Franche-Comté and most of his other conquests, being satisfied, it appeared, with this recognition of his Queen's rights. But through some leakage he soon got to hear of the important secret clause in the Anglo-Dutch treaty and he was much more angry with the Dutch, who were his allies and had an army on the continental mainland, for attempting to lay down the law to him than with the English, with whom he had not made an alliance and who had no army at all.[6]

It is sometimes said, on the basis of statements by Samuel Pepys and Gilbert Burnet, that the Triple Alliance was popular in England on the ground that it was anti-French. But there is no evidence that the House of Commons, to which Charles II announced the agreement with the United Netherlands in a short speech on 10 February, was particularly impressed. Indeed it was much more concerned with an appeal made by Charles in this same speech for 'a better union and composure in the minds of my Protestant subjects in matters of religion',[7] and with trying to find more culprits for the loss of the Dutch war. Charles also asked for money to build more ships to give teeth to the treaty, but although the House agreed to provide £300,000, a very small sum compared with the one voted for the Dutch war, it took a long time to decide how the money was to be raised. On 10 March Charles had to admit to his sister that 'the Parliament goes on very slowly in their money, but they advance something [a little] every day'. He added that he was preparing his ships to go to sea for the summer guard.[8] But a month later the Commons defied the King by giving a second reading to a bill against conventicles providing for the distrainment of the goods of dissenters who attended them.[9] It was not until 1 May that the money bill was agreed to; the source for raising the £300,000 was to be mainly a tax on French wine and brandy.

Charles was disappointed with the behaviour of the Parliament which he had welcomed so effusively seven years earlier. He disliked the policy of intolerance towards the nonconformists and Roman Catholics, and he was disappointed – however much he tried to conceal this from his sister – that the formation of the Triple Alliance had not resulted in a more generous provision for the navy. He also resented the supposition that because he had agreed to the new alliance he was under Arlington's thumb, though Arlington, remembering the fate of Clarendon, was most anxious to disclaim his being a Prime Minister.[10] The King reacted in three ways. First, he tried to reopen negotiations with Ruvigny for a French alliance; secondly, he asked his sister to take as much as she could out of the French King's head the idea 'that my Ministers are anything but what I will have them, and that they have no partiality but my interest and the good of England'.[11] Lastly he acquiesced in his brother James secretly joining the Roman Catholic communion (though the Duke continued for four years to take the sacrament according to the rites of the Church of England) and on 25 January 1669, according to James's memoirs, Charles himself announced with tears in his eyes to a select gathering in James's apartments his own adherence in principle to the Roman Church.

Historians have questioned how far the circumstantial account of the meeting held on 25 January, which was appropriately the day on which the Church celebrated the conversion of St Paul, is to be relied on, as it is dependent on a single not very trustworthy source. This account recorded not only how uneasy Charles found it 'not to profess the faith in which he believed' but that he asked advice 'about the ways and methods fittest to be taken for the settling of the Catholic religion in his kingdoms and to consider of the time most proper to declare himself'. The conclusion that was reached was 'that there was no better way for doing the great work than to do it in conjunction with France and with the assistance of his Most Christian Majesty'.[12] One reason that has been given for doubting the story is that three months later, in a letter to his sister, Charles implied that his brother James had only just been let into the secret of the negotiations with France.[13]

However, whether the story of the meeting on 25 January is entirely accurate or not, there is no question about the events that followed during 1669 and 1670. Charles II was personally responsible for pursuing a 'Grand Design' of publicly announcing his conversion to Roman Catholicism and relying on French support if his action should lead to a rebellion against him in England. Yet in fact that announcement was never to be made, and it was not until he lay on his death-bed that Charles was received into the arms of the Roman Catholic Church. The important question to be decided is why he confided his intention to be converted to a select group of advisers at this particular time.

Various explanations have been offered. The first is the simple one that his conversion was genuine. He could have been influenced by his brother and his brother's wife, who were both Roman Catholics. Indeed he was surrounded by Catholics or crypto-Catholics, including not only his brother, but his own wife, the Queen, his former chief mistress, the Countess of Castlemaine, who had lately entered the Roman Catholic Church, and also by his favourite sister with whom he was a constant correspondent. His mother too had always been an active Roman Catholic proselytizer, and there were many Roman Catholic priests about his court. Yet Charles was an astute statesman, entirely conscious that the parliamentary opposition to his father had been strongly influenced by the Roman Catholic atmosphere of his Court, and that the existing Parliament was violently anti-Catholic. As Sir Keith Feiling observed, 'the tears he shed in January 1669 on confiding to York his religious fears had died by June 1670 when he told Madame [his sister] he was not yet satisfied of Catholic truth and had disappeared when in 1675 he complained to Barrillon [the then French ambassador] that York's Popery had endangered the throne.'[14]

A second explanation that has been put forward is that Charles was jealous of the absolute power of Louis XIV, which he attributed to his ruling over a Catholic instead of a Protestant realm, and that he believed that if he could induce enough of his own subjects to follow him into the Roman Catholic Church his own political position would be immensely strengthened. But that explanation again does not square with Charles's realism. For he must have known that there were relatively few Roman Catholics in England and that the wholesale conversion of Protestants was unlikely.

A third suggestion is that his plan was an excuse to extract money from the French King. He had been disappointed with the amount of money that he had been voted by the House of Commons after the signature of the Triple Alliance; he knew that he could achieve nothing of importance for his kingdom without the aid of a navy, of which he was immensely proud, but which had failed to win a final victory over the Dutch. It is true that a sum of money equivalent to about £140,000 was in the end granted to him by the French King because of his promise that he would ultimately announce his conversion, but this was negligible and Charles could scarcely have imagined that millions would be coming from the French Treasury for the purpose.

Another more recent and more plausible explanation is that Charles wanted to wean Lord Arlington, who was in effect his Foreign Minister, from his attachment to the Spaniards and Dutch. After the signature of the Triple Alliance Arlington had concentrated on obtaining an agreement with the Dutch guaranteeing to uphold the treaty of Aix-la-Chapelle, which had been concluded between France and Spain, and a 'concert' binding the two countries to help Spain if it were again attacked by France. Thus Arlington's political alignment was with the United Netherlands and Spain and all he wanted from the French was a commercial treaty which would reduce the duties that the French Minister, Colbert, had imposed on British goods. It is argued that

Charles aimed to persuade Arlington to change the whole direction of his foreign policy and work for a close alliance with France, the strongest power in Europe. So long as he believed that the King could be subjected to purely realistic arguments, Arlington would not change his course. But if Arlington were persuaded that the King's own personal position was involved on account of his new religion, 'Royalist and courtier that he was', he 'would bow and acquiesce'.[15] The difficulty about this theory is that it involves the belief that Arlington was indispensable to his master. But no Ministers are ever indispensable. Charles could have dismissed Arlington as he had dismissed Nicholas and Clarendon and was later to dismiss William Coventry. Arlington could certainly have been replaced by some other politician – Sir Thomas Clifford, for example – who was known to be in favour of an alliance with France and sympathetic to Roman Catholicism.

There is, however, another and not too complicated explanation of Charles's conversion: that he wanted to persuade the French King, despite the Triple Alliance and despite Arlington's continuing negotiations in support of Spain, that he, Charles, as ruler of his kingdom and master of his Ministers, was genuinely anxious for a close political alliance with France. Louis XIV, he knew, was angry that the three 'heretical' Protestant powers, England, the United Netherlands and Sweden, had been defying him. As Professor Wolf has written, 'Louis persuaded himself that religious hostility had united "heretical potentates" in the Triple Alliance against him.'[16] Now he was to learn that Charles II was no 'heretical potentate' and that as there was no likelihood that rulers of the United Netherlands would change their religion, the French King could be induced to offer England an alliance not on the vague and unsatisfactory terms put forward in the autumn of 1667 but in accordance with the political and economic desires of Charles.

During 1669 therefore elaborate negotiations were pursued by Charles for a close alliance with France. Neither the English ambassador in Paris nor the French ambassador in London was informed about them; they were concealed from Charles's anti-Catholic advisers, such as the Duke of Buckingham; and

Arlington was permitted to carry on his diplomatic negotiations with the Dutch in order to dupe them about the King's real intentions. Even before the announcement of his conversion Charles had begun to pave the way for a French alliance in his correspondence with his sister. He told her that he must begin with a treaty of commerce in order to 'make the rest more plausible here'.[17] On 14 December 1668 he promised that he would send her a cipher in order that 'she shall know the way I think most proper to proceed in the whole matter'. In January 1669 he told her that he had written to Louis XIV seeking his personal friendship and assuring him that 'the only possible impediment was the matter of the sea', that is to say Colbert's attempt to build up a French fleet which would dispute British supremacy. On 7 March 1669 he informed her that he was sending over Lord Arundel of Wardour, who was a Roman Catholic and, because he was Master of the Horse to Charles's mother, would not be suspected of visiting Paris to open diplomatic negotiations. His instructions were to stress the Catholicizing policy and to ask the French to suspend their construction of warships for a year.

The negotiations were long and complicated. Louis XIV's aim was to prepare for a war against the United Netherlands: this was partly to be a preventive war because he feared that the Dutch would interfere with his ultimate purpose of securing the whole of the Spanish Netherlands, Franche-Comté and Luxembourg for the French Crown; it was also partly intended to destroy Dutch commerce and shipping because Colbert believed that this would be beneficial to the prosperity of France. Thus Louis was less than enthusiastic about the conditions that Charles had first laid down for a treaty, namely that it must not conflict with the terms of the Triple Alliance and that the French should stop building warships. But Charles soon made it clear that he did not regard the Triple Alliance as an obstacle to going to war with the Dutch. In a letter to Henriette of 7 June Charles said that he would 'fain know . . . how ready France is to break with Holland. That is the game that would, as I conceive, most accommodate the interests of England and France.'[18] He ceased to press his demands about the French suspending the construction of warships. But he did insist that his public declaration that he had become a Roman Catholic should precede the declaration of war on the Dutch. By this means he seems to have hoped that he would be able to influence the timing of the outbreak of war. Louis xiv, however, who feared that Charles's declaration as a Roman Catholic might cause a rebellion in England, wanted the war to begin first. It was argued that Charles was much more likely to succeed with a Catholicizing policy if he had this time been victorious over the Dutch. But in any case Louis offered to contribute money and soldiers if necessary to help Charles with his declaration of Catholicism. By the end of August the Kings were agreed on two principal points: that Louis would help Charles when he chose to make his declaration that he had become a Roman Catholic and that Charles would join with Louis in attacking the Dutch. But in fact Charles had been diplomatically outmanœuvred. He had abandoned the conditions he first put forward for the alliance; and he did not even obtain a commercial treaty with France, for he allowed himself to be persuaded that he could 'extend the confines of his kingdom beyond the sea and become supreme in commerce' once the Dutch republic was destroyed.[19]

In December 1669 the English government made one more effort to screw better terms out of the French. The negotiations had now been shifted from Paris to London. The French ambassador, Colbert de Croissy, who was the brother of the famous Colbert, was let into the great secret; and Arlington and his colleague and former protégé Sir Thomas Clifford joined in the negotiations. One may attribute to them the terms of the draft treaty which made the French gasp. The draft proposed that the time when Charles (supported by French money and men) should declare himself a Roman Catholic was to be left to his own discretion but must precede the declaration of war on the Dutch. The French King must keep to the terms of the treaty of Aix-la-Chapelle (that is to say he must not make war again on Spain) and if the Spanish King should die childless, the English were to be given Ostend, Minorca and Spanish America. France was to pay Charles £200,000 in advance of the declaration of Catholicity and £800,000 a year (with an advance of £400,000) during the war with the Dutch. When the war was won, England was to obtain Walcheren, Sluys and Cadsand and territory was to be allotted to Charles II's nephew, Prince William of Orange, over which he could reign as sovereign. It was also intimated – Charles himself was very insistent on this point – that England must have complete control over the war at sea, the Duke of York or some other Englishman being appointed the supreme commander. For 'English sailors could never take orders from a French admiral'.[20]

During the first four months of 1670 a compromise was reached. Specific stipulations about the division of the Spanish empire were omitted and the amount of money to be paid by the French to subsidize Charles II was reduced. It was decided that the actual signature of the secret treaty should take place at Dover in May under the cover of a State visit by Charles's sister Henriette, who had been at the heart of the negotiations, she having with difficulty obtained short leave of absence from her husband, the Duke of Orleans.

Charles was so anxious to meet his sister, whom he had not seen for nine years, that he arrived far too early at Dover. Then he returned to London and embarked on a ship with the intention of meeting her in mid-ocean. But the winds were unfavourable. Instead he went by road to Dover and greeted the French fleet from his royal barge. Dover itself was little more than a village; as the King was accompanied by a train of diplomatic staff and musicians and as the Duchess of Orleans had with her courtiers and members of her own household numbering 250 persons, the available accommodation was overstrained. However there were ample balls, concerts, plays and other festivities sufficient to camouflage the signing of the secret treaty, which was also to be known as the treaty of Madame. The terms of the treaty had been virtually settled before Henriette arrived; all that she was now required to do was to try to persuade her brother to postpone his declaration of Catholicity until after the Dutch war had begun. As it was unlikely that Charles had any serious intention of taking this dangerous step in the near future, the matter was soon agreed. On 22 May 1670 the treaty was signed by Arlington and Clifford

– who, like their master, were both to declare themselves Roman Catholics at the end of their lives – and by Lord Arundel of Wardour and Sir Richard Bellings (he had acted as secretary during the negotiations) who were already Roman Catholics. The French ambassador, Colbert de Croissy signed the treaty on behalf of France. It was to be ratified by the two Kings themselves at the beginning of June.

The treaty provided for an alliance between Great Britain and France.[21] The second clause stated that 'the lord king of Great Britain, being convinced of the truth of the Catholic religion and resolved to declare it and reconcile himself with the Church of Rome as soon as the welfare of his kingdom will permit' had every reason to hope and expect that his subjects, even those of a different religion, would continue to obey him. But if by any chance trouble should arise, the King of France undertook, in case of need, to supply him with 6,000 foot-soldiers at his own expense to assist Charles in the execution of his design. A sum of £140,000 (two million *livres tournois*) was also to be paid by the French King, half in advance, as a proof of his friendship. The timing of the declaration was left to Charles.

By the third clause the French King promised never to break or infringe the peace he had made with Spain at Aix-la-Chapelle. Thus Charles would be able to remain faithful to the objectives of the Triple Alliance. The fourth clause laid down that if the French King acquired any new titles or rights to the Spanish monarchy – that is to say in the event of the death of the Spanish King without heirs – Charles should assist him with land and sea forces to facilitate the acquisition of those rights. The fifth clause provided that the two Kings should declare war on the States-General of the United Provinces 'to reduce the power of a nation which has so often rendered itself odious by extreme ingratitude to its own founders and the creators of its republic'. The next three clauses outlined the military, naval and diplomatic arrangements necessary to carry on this war. The timing of the declaration of war was left to Louis XIV, but it was not to be made until after Charles had announced his belief in the truth of the Catholic religion. However the Duchess was convinced that her brother would not insist on fulfilling this clause. A total payment of three million *livres tournois* was to be paid to the King of Great Britain during the war of which the first instalment – one quarter – was to be paid three months in advance of the declaration of war.

Henriette believed that she had achieved a triumph in thus uniting her brother and her brother-in-law. After the treaty was signed the Queen and the Duchess of York came to Dover and joined in the festivities. There were ballets and comedies and fireworks over the sea. Then presents were exchanged and Charles three times embraced his sister as he reluctantly bade her farewell. But for Henriette these hectic days of excitement concealed a tragic heart. Before she arrived she had been living only on milk and easily tired. Her husband had at the last moment tried to stop her visit and had to be overruled by the French King. On her return she wrote one more letter to her brother, for the first time in English, asking him to reward Lord Arlington as the principal architect of the alliance.[22] But she was worn out by her exertions and was taken violently ill on a visit to Versailles. Before the end of June she died in fearful agony. Her last thoughts were of her brother Charles.

Charles now hoped, with the active assistance and support of Louis XIV, to become the true master of his kingdom. But before he could embark on the new war he must let his other Ministers and advisers know that the war was intended so that they could help him to prepare for it. Secondly, he had to raise more money for his navy, since the subsidies promised him in the treaty of Dover were quite inadequate for that purpose; thirdly, he had to take some action which would at least lend colour to the personal sympathy he had shown for the Roman Catholic Church: the least he could do was to relax the penalties which were imposed by statute on the Roman Catholics in his dominions.

Since the banishment of Clarendon Charles had taken a more positive part in government himself, but he was of course still dependent on the assistance of others who had their own skills and points of view. Clarendon himself had been succeeded by Sir Orlando Bridgeman but with the title of Lord Keeper, not Lord Chancellor, and William Morice, General Monck's nominee, had been replaced by Sir John Trevor as Secretary of State for the North. Neither of them was a significant figure. Arlington and Buckingham were still prominent in the King's councils, though a temporary cloud had fallen on Buckingham when he killed the husband of his current mistress, the Countess of Shrewsbury, in a duel.

In addition to these two, Charles valued the services of John Maitland, second Earl of Lauderdale, as Secretary of State for Scotland. Lauderdale was an ex-Covenanter who, after fighting for the King at the battle of Worcester, had been for nearly nine years a political prisoner. A fellow Scotsman described Lauderdale as a 'man very national and truly the honour of our Scots nation for wit and parts'.[23] He was a scholar with a mastery of Latin, Hebrew and Greek. He made himself all-powerful in Scotland and although he worked unsuccessfully for a political union with England, he won for Charles the control of a Scottish army and supremacy over the Scottish Kirk. Another useful royal Minister was Sir Thomas Clifford, a Devonshire squire who proved himself a capable administrator during the first Dutch war and, with the patronage of Arlington, had been appointed a Treasury commissioner after the death of Southampton. Later he was to hold the office of Lord Treasurer for seven months, but he died when he was forty-three. He was pro-French and anti-Dutch and during the last years of his life had become more and more attracted to the Roman Church. Thus he had been entrusted with the signature of the Treaty of Dover. Lastly, there was Anthony Ashley Cooper, who had married Southampton's niece as his third wife, and in spite of having at one time served in Oliver Cromwell's Council of State, was created Lord Ashley in 1660, Chancellor of the Exchequer in May 1661, and a Commissioner of the Treasury in May 1667. For economic reasons he had been anti-Dutch. He was a consistent believer in liberty of conscience for all Protestants.

Charles wanted to bring Buckingham, Lauderdale and Ashley into the preparations for the Dutch war. It was therefore decided, with the connivance of Louis XIV, that they should be invited to negotiate a treaty with France, which was to be identical with the treaty of Dover except that, out of deference to their Protestant susceptibilities, the second clause of the treaty of Dover was to be concealed from them and omitted. This second treaty – known as the bogus treaty or treaty *simulé* – was worked on during the second half of 1670 and was signed by Clifford, Arlington, Buckingham, Ashley and Lauderdale on 21 December. Their initials spelt the word Cabal, and this was the nickname given to Charles's administration before the second Dutch war. But the name had no constitutional significance; the five men did not necessarily agree with one another, though all at the time were faithful servants of the King. Charles did not particularly want a united Ministry. 'When rogues fall out', he said, 'the master is like then to know the truth.'[24]

When the bogus treaty was signed, it was found that two more Dutch possessions, Goeree and Woorne, had been added to the promised English part of the spoils; the payment on behalf of Catholicity was added to the French subsidy during the first year of the war; and the date of the outbreak of hostilities was fixed for the spring of 1672. Louis wanted Charles and the negotiators of the Dover treaty to sign a declaration annulling the so-called bogus treaty. But Charles insisted that this was the only treaty he could acknowledge publicly. Indeed the new treaty was more to his taste. But at Dover the French had acquired a useful instrument of blackmail to be placed in the diplomatic archives.

The question of money was more difficult to solve and proved as puzzling to Charles as it has been to later historians. A distinction has to be drawn between Charles's ordinary revenue, needed to cover his household expenses and the day-to-day work of government, and the extraordinary revenue required to sustain the armed forces, that is to say chiefly the navy. The House of Commons suspected that extraordinary revenues were not always used for the purposes for which they were voted, while officers of the Crown, such as Sir George Carteret, the former Treasurer of the Navy, were accused of incompetence or worse. It has recently been stated that up till 1669 Charles might have been justified in wondering whether he could ever expect an adequate parliamentary supply, but that after the Parliament which met at the beginning of 1670 had voted him £400,000 for seven years, he ought to have been able to manage with his ordinary revenue.[25] Charles was disappointed with the meagre £300,000 that had been voted him for the navy after the conclusion of the Triple Alliance, and his advisers were in general agreement that much more would be needed if a second Dutch war was to be waged successfully.

When Parliament reassembled on 24 October 1670, five months after the signature of the secret treaty of Dover, Sir Orlando Bridgeman informed the House of Commons that the King was £1,300,000 in debt on his ordinary revenue and that he needed £800,000 for the navy. These figures were confirmed later by Sir Thomas Clifford and Sir George Downing. On 10 December Charles took the unprecedented step of sending for the House of Commons to meet him in Whitehall and, by implying that there was possible danger from the French, supported his Ministers' plea for more money for defence. The Commons proceeded to examine at length how more money could be raised. All sorts of expedients were considered, from a land tax to a tax on playhouses. The latter gave rise to a furore. For when the courtiers said that a tax on playhouses would be a tax on the King's pleasures, Sir John Coventry asked whether the King's pleasures lay among the men or women who acted – a palpable reference to Nell Gwyn and Moll Davis, the King's mistresses. Later Sir John was found one evening in the street with his nose slit. Eventually various supply bills were passed, but one of them, a proposed import duty on sugar and tobacco, led to divisions among the King's own advisers. The net result was that taxes were voted which would increase Charles's ordinary revenue by £160,000 a year, while a new 'subsidy', a kind of tax on income and profits, was estimated to yield a lump sum of £350,000 for the navy. As Charles adjourned Parliament on 22 April 1671 the import duties bill was lost. Some blamed Arlington for advising the adjournment and claimed that the King had thereby lost a million pounds; but the real figure appears to have been £160,000.

The truth is that Charles himself had tired of the inquisitiveness of Parliament. He was determined not to summon it to meet again until the Dutch war had been launched. So a drastic decision, made on the advice of Sir Thomas Clifford, was taken, known as the Stop of the Exchequer. The government was heavily in debt to the bankers because it had borrowed from them at an exorbitant rate of interest on the security of forthcoming taxes, the money being automatically repaid as the revenues flowed into the Exchequer by what were known as 'orders in course', a system begun when it had been decided in 1665 that revenues were to be appropriated to specific purposes ('the Downing proviso'). If these orders in course were stopped, the money would become available for current expenditure. The government was not thereby declaring its bankruptcy, but postponing for the time being the repayments of its debts with interest to the bankers. Although an outcry was raised that this would ruin women and children because the bankers in turn would refuse money to their creditors, this does not appear to have happened nor was any banker immediately ruined.

One reason why Charles had prorogued Parliament when he did in April 1671 was because it was showing anti-Popish tendencies quite out of tune with Charles's scheme to set an example to his subjects by joining the Roman Church as embodied in the treaty of Dover. On 10 March Charles had been petitioned to halt the growth of popery in the country, and he had felt himself obliged to give orders that all Jesuits and Romish priests should leave the kingdom by 1 May. It was only by proroguing Parliament that Charles had been able to prevent the passing of another conventicle bill aimed at the dissenters as well as a bill against Roman Catholics. Less than a year later, with the enthusiastic support of all the members of the Cabal, who were either Roman Catholics or tolerationists, Charles issued a second Declaration of Indulgence which suspended all the penal laws, permitted the dissenters to hold public worship conducted by licensed ministers in places approved by the authorities, and allowed Roman Catholics to worship in private houses. But so far as London was concerned, it has been pointed out that Charles's Queen and several of the Roman Catholic ambassadors had their own chapels which Roman Catholics attended. It was also common knowledge that the Duke of York had become a Roman Catholic. So the declaration was widely regarded as 'a deep popish design' that might easily prepare the way for the toleration of popery. However, the King might claim that he had now fulfilled the spirit of the bond. Two days after the Declaration of Indulgence was published, war was declared on the Dutch republic.

Thus it can be seen that all the purposes that Charles had in mind since 1669 – religious toleration, the war to crush the upstart Dutch, and the raising of sufficient money to put the fleet to sea in the first year of the war – were achieved not with the approval of Parliament (even though the Commons had shown themselves on the whole friendly to the court) but by the exercise of the royal prerogative. If victory was achieved, Parliament could be invited to pay for its cost and to confirm the Declaration of Indulgence; or perhaps parliaments could be dispensed with altogether. But first of all the war had to be won and here was an irresistible obstacle: the stubbornness of the Dutch people.

The Break-up of 'the Cabal'

At the opening of 1672 King Charles II appeared to be at the peak of power and success. It is true that the Stop of the Exchequer had invited a setback to public confidence. But the bankers had done excellently out of the government and out of the growing prosperity of the kingdom, especially in the export trade. After the Restoration commerce with the Americas had flourished. England was ceasing to be so dependent on the export of woollen textiles as it had been in the past, for the re-exports of such commodities as sugar, tobacco and calicoes had diversified foreign trade. Business conducted around the world, in the West and East Indies, in the Levant and in New England, had stimulated ship-building for distant voyages and it has been estimated that 48,000 men, a substantial part of the working population of England, were directly employed in shipping.[1] Charles and James had shown a deep interest in the navy and in commerce and colonies. In the course of 1672 a Council of Trade and Plantations was established and became the effective administrative body under the presidency of the able Earl of Shaftesbury (formerly Lord Ashley).

Now Charles had high hopes from his alliance with France. If all went according to plan, there would be a short and decisive war against Great Britain's principal rivals in shipping and trade; a partition of the United Netherlands would bring enormous profits to British trade and industry, while leaving the rump of the Dutch republic to be ruled by Prince William of Orange, the King's nephew, who, it was assumed, would show gratitude to his uncle. In April, after the war began, Charles had hastened to write to William to tell him that though he feared their correspondence must cease for some time 'upon this misunderstanding between the States and me', yet he could assure him that his kindness 'shall never change to you in my heart'.[2] Not only would England gain trade and territory from the destruction of the Dutch, but, if the King of Spain died, Charles's close alliance with the French King would enable him to obtain material benefits in the Spanish empire. In spite of restrictions British merchants customarily did good business with Spain and this could then be profitably expanded.

Charles was also satisfied with his own personal position. Since he had got rid of the hectoring Earl of Clarendon, he had been able to assert himself more effectively and to carry out his own policies with less opposition. In Arlington he had found a capable and hard-working Minister who, whatever his personal predilections might have been, in the end always accepted his master's wishes. He had, for example, unscrupulously carried on the diplomatic negotiations with the Dutch and Spaniards while the scheme for a secret alliance with France, which culminated in the treaty of Dover, was being completed. As late as January 1670 a concert between England and the United Netherlands was signed by him at The Hague binding England to help Spain, if it were attacked, with 6,000 soldiers and forty warships. In Sir Thomas Clifford, Charles had discovered a congenial Minister to take care of his finances, from whose brain had sprung the idea of the Stop of the Exchequer to give him funds immediately needed for the war. In March 1672 the King had signified his pleasure with the members of his 'Cabal' by creating Arlington an earl, Lauderdale a duke, Clifford a baron and Ashley an earl. Only the Duke of Buckingham, who, because of his volatile and indiscreet behaviour, was the least useful of the Ministry, received no honour; but then one could not rise higher than being a duke.

Charles had taken precautions to secure his position in Scotland and Ireland. The Scots tended to be pro-Dutch because they enjoyed an active trade with them across the North Sea. But Lauderdale had so manipulated matters that the Scottish Parliament was entirely under the influence of the Crown. In 1663 it had not only voted the King an annual revenue of £40,000 to be raised by customs and excise (which was a burden on a poor and sparsely populated kingdom) but it had undertaken to recruit a militia force of 20,000 infantry and 2,000 cavalry which became available to serve the King anywhere in his dominions. The King's supremacy in religious affairs had also been recognized. After the Restoration episcopacy had been re-established in Scotland. In June 1669 the King had issued a letter of indulgence which had to some extent benefited Scottish dissenting ministers. 'Never was a king so absolute', wrote a contemporary, 'as in poor old Scotland.'³

In Ireland the main danger was that an enemy might land troops there (as the Spaniards had done in the reign of Queen Elizabeth I). But in the Duke of Ormonde the King possessed a wise and considerate Lord Lieutenant who had promoted Irish industry (notably in linen and woollen textiles) and had pacified the Roman Catholics, who composed the bulk of the population. Following the fall of his friend Clarendon, Ormonde was re-called, but he continued to share the King's counsels and was in fact later to be reappointed. After Lord Robartes and Lord Berkeley of Stratton had proved failures as Lords Lieutenant, the King in February 1672 gave the post to Arthur Capel, Earl of Essex, who followed a positive policy of indulgence.

The King therefore had nothing to fear from the Scots or the Irish when he declared war on the Dutch. Clifford had undertaken to find the £800,000 that, it was estimated, was needed to put the fleet to sea during the year's campaign. It was also hoped that the war would yield rich prizes. Five hundred and twenty-two prizes had been seized during the previous Dutch war because the widely flung Dutch mercantile marine had been extremely vulnerable to capture by enemy warships. (In the war waged by the Commonwealth against the Dutch over a thousand prizes had been obtained.)⁴ The King's brother, James, as Lord High Admiral, was put in charge of the naval war against the Dutch, in which he had previous experience, and it had been agreed that the French admiral D'Estrées should obey his orders. The King's eldest son, the Duke of Monmouth, who was nearly twenty-three, was put in command of an English contingent to fight in the Netherlands under French orders. In Samuel Pepys (no longer the self-indulgent

Pepys of the diary), who had lost his French wife and never re-married, Charles had a devoted servant; although Pepys was the junior member of the Navy Board, he was obviously the ablest among its experts, and threw himself unstintingly into all the preparations for the naval war.

In his private as well as his public life Charles had reason to feel satisfied. Admittedly his Portuguese wife had failed to give him a legitimate heir, but there had been miscarriages and was still hope: Charles had rejected the advice of some of his Ministers, headed by Buckingham, to divorce her. On the other hand, he had acquired a new and desirable mistress, not a termagant like Barbara Palmer nor a vulgarian like Nell Gwyn: this was Louise-Renée de Penancoët de Kéroualle, a young Breton girl, who had first come to England as Maid of Honour to Charles's sister when she finalized the treaty of Dover. When Charles had loaded his sister with presents before her departure for France, she had sent Louise with her jewel case to ask him to select a jewel in return. Charles had replied that the only jewel he coveted was Louise. After the death of Henriette King Louis XIV had ordered Louise back to England in the autumn of 1670. John Evelyn when he saw her at the time thought she had 'a childish, simple and baby face'.[5] But she was no fool. Arlington had sent a yacht to fetch her. She held out for a time against the King's importunities, but eventually at Arlington's country house of Euston near New-market in October 1671 she yielded to Charles's desires. Accord-ing to Evelyn, a mock wedding took place and 'the stocking flung after the manner of a married bride'. In July 1672 she bore the King a son and was created Duchess of Portsmouth. In the end she became not unlike a wife to the King; but she was also an unofficial French ambassador at the court.

There was only one cloud on Charles's horizon. He had deliber-ately refrained from calling Parliament to tell it about his reasons for again going to war with the Dutch or to ask it for supplies to support the war. Here Charles was taking a deliberate gamble. He reckoned that he had enough money for one campaign. He also believed that his Declaration of Indulgence would unite all his subjects behind him. As Arlington put it, the object of 'the late

Declaration His Majesty hath made in favour of the nonconformists was 'that we might keep all quiet at home whilst we are
busiest abroad'.[6] But in fact the Anglican pulpits soon echoed with
the cry: 'no popery!' and Charles had to instruct his Archbishop
of Canterbury, Gilbert Sheldon, to put a stop to preaching on
controversial subjects since, he said, it was clearly done to alienate
the hearts of his people from him and his government. But this
was not a good omen, for what would happen when he did recall
his Parliament, which had already, over a period of eleven years,
shown itself violently antagonistic to nonconformists and papists?
Moreover how would the House of Commons react is the way
in which it had flagrantly been deceived over money? Funds that
had been voted to sustain the Triple Alliance had in fact been
used in preparing for war against the Dutch. Charles put these
thoughts on one side. As to money, the Dutch war might yield
not only prizes but a large indemnity. Victory would assuage any
disloyal feelings in a Parliament which had voted five millions
for the first Dutch war. Surely the members of the House of
Commons would agree to pay off the government's debt to the
bankers when they learned what their King's foreign policy had
achieved?

The English government decided to jump the gun. The original
plan had been for the joint Anglo-French assault on the Dutch to
begin in May. Charles's view was that a pretext must be found
for making war on his associates in the Triple Alliance. Sir George
Downing, who was notoriously anti-Dutch, was sent to The
Hague to demand that Dutch sailors should lower their flag
whenever they encountered an English warship. Arlington
declared that a way must be found to break with them 'and yet
lay the breach at their door'.[7] At the beginning of March the
news was received that a Dutch convoy of merchant vessels
from Smyrna, escorted by eleven warships, was sailing up the
Channel. After two meetings of the foreign committee on 4
and 5 March, it was decided to order Sir Robert Holmes to
intercept them off the Isle of Wight. In this he was far from
successful (his fleet was not large enough for the purpose) and his
own ships were badly damaged. However the fight furnished the

needed excuse: and on 17 March war was declared on the Dutch. Louis XIV did not bother to declare war, but issued a proclamation to his subjects saying that he was going to chastise the Dutch because of the 'poor satisfaction' they had given him.[8] But it was not until May when he had assembled two armies at Charleroi and Sedan that the land campaign got under way. At the same time the British and French fleets joined up at Spithead. On 3 May Charles inspected the French contingent there. Altogether the Duke of York had ninety-eight warships under his command, a formidable force. But the Dutch admiral, de Ruyter, was aggressive and the first naval battle of the war was fought off Southwold bay in Suffolk. The battle was fiercely contested, with heavy casualties on both sides, including leading English and Dutch admirals. The French admiral, D'Estrées, failed for some reason to carry out the instructions of the Duke of York, which was unhelpful to Anglo-French relations. On balance the victory went to the Dutch, who had kept their fleet in being and asserted their authority in the North Sea.

Charles followed his brother's actions with the closest attention. On 2 June, four days after the battle, Charles advised James to leave Southwold bay and make for the Buoy of the Nore to refit. The French army had crossed the Rhine and was in occupation of three out of the seven Dutch provinces. But the two richest provinces, Holland and Zeeland, held out defiantly. Charles therefore planned an assault on them from the rear, though he realized that this was not feasible until the Dutch had been defeated. At the end of July he ordered his brother to detach fifteen ships to intercept the Dutch East Indian fleet, but promised to send him an equivalent number of ships to take their place so that he would still be strong enough to cover an amphibious assault. But the Dutch merchant ships reached home safely, the allied fleet being dispersed in a storm. Moreover there was hesitation in the foreign committee over attempting to face the Dutch navy again in battle. It was at first argued that not enough money was available to refit the British warships which had suffered damage both in the battle of Southwold bay and in the midsummer storms. On the other side, it was contended that every effort should be exerted to finish off the war in 1672 while the Dutch were being so hard pressed by Louis XIV's armies on land. The Duke of York was opposed to risking his ships off the Dutch coast in the autumn gales. Prince Rupert, an experienced seaman, did not agree, but Charles supported his brother and called off the naval war until the following year.

One reason why the King did not press on with the war aggressively was that he was hopeful that peace would be concluded before the year was out. The Dutch had as early as the beginning of June dispatched deputies both to France and to England to discuss peace terms, while towards the end of the month Louis XIV had suggested that Charles should send ambassadors to the French headquarters to treat for peace. Charles sent the two leading rivals in the 'Cabal', Buckingham and Arlington, with instructions that the Dutch must be obliged to honour the English flag at sea, that they must pay an annual tribute for the right to fish off British coasts, that they must pay a large indemnity, and that they must surrender three or four ports to Great Britain in full sovereignty. The French also demanded a huge indemnity, the surrender of a number of fortresses, and the dispatch to Paris every year of a Dutch delegation humbly thanking Louis XIV for the mercy he had shown them.

The Dutch who, before the outbreak of war, had appointed William of Orange as their captain-general, had placed the negotiations in his hands. William was ready to grant pretty considerable concessions to both his enemies and also hoped, knowing his uncle's financial difficulties, to achieve a separate peace with England. But though he was willing to offer the French the parts of Brabant and Flanders under Dutch control, including the fortress of Maastricht, he refused to give up any territory in the United Netherlands proper. The only result of the Buckingham–Arlington mission was that a new treaty was signed with the French at Heeswick promising that neither side would conclude a separate peace. But William still had hopes that he could come to terms with his uncle; for that purpose he sent over a series of emissaries to England including his own secretary, Frederick Van Reede and his physician, Dr Rumff. Charles, on

Arlington's advice, no longer asked for Dutch towns in full sovereignty but only for 'cautionary towns' to be held for a ten-year period while the rest of the terms of the treaty were carried out. Dr Rumff was empowered conditionally to offer Sluys. Charles, however, was angry that his nephew refused bigger concessions. He said that he would be 'a beast or a fool' if he were disloyal to the French.[9] But he decided to postpone the next meeting of Parliament from October 1672 to February 1673, hoping that in the meantime a general peace congress, meeting in some neutral town under Swedish mediation, would bring the war to an end on satisfactory terms.

Such were Charles's hopes. But he feared from the temper of his young nephew, who was now supreme in the United Nether-lands (John de Witt, the architect of the Franco-Dutch alliance, had in August been murdered by an angry mob in the streets of The Hague), that the war might have to continue for another year, which would involve the recall of Parliament to obtain money. Charles took steps to strengthen and unify his administration. Political parties had not yet come into being, but there were fluctuating cliques in the House of Commons who often looked to leadership in the House of Lords. The members of the 'Cabal' had been united only in overthrowing Clarendon and later in signing the bogus French treaty. The Duke of Buckingham, evidently the heir of his father's immense charm, headed one political group, which included the Duke of Lauderdale and Sir Thomas Osborne, who since September 1671 occupied the key position of sole Treasurer of the Navy. The Earl of Arlington, who was generally at daggers drawn with Buckingham, had as his chief protégé, Lord Clifford, but he also relied on Sir Joseph Williamson, who was later to succeed him as Secretary of State. Anthony Ashley Cooper, now Earl of Shaftesbury, the fifth and perhaps the most brilliant member of the 'Cabal', stood in a some-what independent position but inclined towards the Buckingham group: he had, for example, acted as godfather to Buckingham's son by his mistress, the Countess of Shrewsbury. In the middle was a third group, headed by the Duke of York, which included the old Clarendonians and the Duke of Ormonde and Sir William

Coventry, able statesmen who had lost their offices through the machinations of Buckingham.

Even though he tended to play off one group against another, Charles did not care for these divisions among his advisers in time of war. As early as the autumn of 1671 he had given a solemn warning to Buckingham, Lauderdale and Ashley that if any quarrels among his Ministers hampered his Great Design the person responsible would suffer.[10] Charles was a pretty shrewd judge of ability and willingness to co-operate. In May 1672 he had appointed Shaftesbury's brother-in-law, Henry Coventry, to succeed Sir John Trevor, who had died, as Secretary of State for the North. Soon after that he invited Osborne to become a member of the Privy Council. Then in November he replaced the Lord Keeper, Sir Orlando Bridgeman, who had proved unco-operative by refusing to attach the Great Seal to the Declaration of Indulgence and was critical on constitutional grounds of others of Charles's measures, by the Earl of Shaftesbury, who was given, like Clarendon, the post of Lord Chancellor. Shaftesbury was not a lawyer by training and his appointment was therefore a tribute to Charles's admiration for the work he had done in the other offices he held, including that of Chancellor of the Exchequer. In the same month – November – Lord Clifford was appointed Lord Treasurer, thus becoming solely responsible for the King's finances, a responsibility hitherto divided among Treasury Commissioners. Arlington was naturally disappointed that neither of these important offices was offered to him; and he broke with Clifford who, he thought, owed his rise to power to him. Charles was well aware of Arlington's disappointment. He considered that he lacked the experience and qualifications to be Treasurer, while he valued his loyal assiduity as his effective foreign minister. Charles asked the Duke of York to soothe Arlington, but did not offer him the dukedom which he craved. The one man who received no promotion was Buckingham, whose spasmodic attention to public business and complete unreliability was at last clear to Charles. It was notorious that rich as he was Buckingham was now deeply in debt because of his absurd extravagances. He did manage later to wangle a commission as lieutenant-general

King Charles I and Queen Henrietta Maria, the parents of King Charles II

Charles II as a boy by Van Dyck (*left*): this portrait shows a resemblance between the young prince and his son by Lucy Walter, James Scott, Duke of Monmouth and Buccleuch (*right*)

RICHMOND.

Richmond palace, where Charles held court as a boy and received his early education

Charles II, portrait (*left*) by an unidentified artist and (*right*) Henri Gascar. The King was not vain about his looks, once remarking 'Odd's fish, I am an ugly fellow!'

Ralph, Lord Hopton,
Royalist general and Charles's
military adviser during the
first civil war

Below Charles (*right*) disguised
as a servant of Jane Lane
during his escape after the
battle of Worcester

Charles's sister Mary, widow
of William II, Prince of Orange

Charles dancing with his sister Mary at The
Hague on the eve of the Restoration.
Seated on a bench at the back are Queen
Henrietta Maria and Queen Elizabeth
of Bohemia. The child standing in front
of the two queens is William III of Orange

George Monck, Duke of
Albemarle

James, Duke of York, Charles's
brother and heir presumptive

The coronation procession of Charles II from the Tower of London to
Whitehall on 22 April 1661. He was crowned on the following day.

Above Queen Catherine of
Braganza

Right Henriette Anne,
Duchess of Orleans, favourite
sister of Charles II

Opposite Charles II by Kneller

Barbara Palmer (*née* Villiers)
Duchess of Cleveland and
Countess of Castlemaine

Frances Stuart, Duchess of
Richmond

Nell Gwyn

Louise de Kéroualle, Duchess of Portsmouth

Hortense Mancini, Duchess of Mazarin, niece of Cardinal Mazarin

Pheasant Hawking, etching by Hollar. Hawking was a favourite pastime of the ladies at Charles's court

Incidents during the Great Plague, 1665

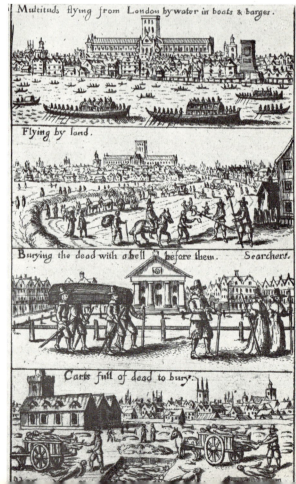

Multituds flying from London by water in boats & barges.

Flying by land.

Burying the dead with a bell before them.   Searchers.

Carts full of dead to bury.

The Great Fire of London, 1666 by Jan Wyck. 'The pains the King had taken day and night during the fire', recounted Clarendon, 'and the dangers he had exposed himself to, even for the saving of the citizens' goods had been very notorious.'

Edward Hyde, first Earl of Clarendon

'The Cabal': Lord Clifford (*left*), the Earl of Arlington (*below, left*), the second Duke of Buckingham (*below, right*), Lord Ashley (afterwards Earl of Shaftesbury) (*opposite, top*) and the Duke of Lauderdale (*opposite, below*)

Whitehall seen from the river Thames, etching by Hollar. On occasion Charles addressed members of his Houses of Parliament in the Banqueting House (*centre*)

Windsor castle, etching by Hollar

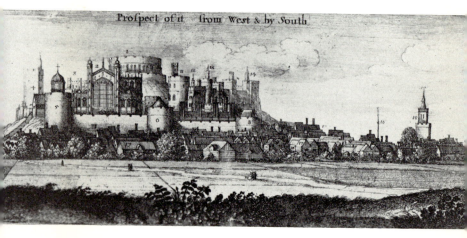

Prospect of it   from West & by South

Thomas Osborne, first Earl of
Danby

Samuel Pepys, the most active
member of Charles's Navy
Board and from 1673 Secretary
to the Admiralty

Tangier, seen from the land, etching by Hollar. Tangier came to England as part of Catherine of Braganza's dowry, but it was given up when the garrison was withdrawn from it in 1683

The 'Pineapple Picture': Mr Rose, the royal gardener, presenting King Charles II with the first pineapple grown in England

under the Duke of York. But before the end of 1672 it was commonly said that Buckingham was 'out with the King and everybody else'.[11] Thus the most mischievous and least useful member of the 'Cabal' was put on one side.

In February 1673 Charles had to meet his Parliament, adjourned since the spring of 1671, to ask it for money to continue the war. He was well aware that it would be in a critical mood, first because it had not been informed at the time of the reasons for fighting the Dutch, secondly because it was widely believed that the Declaration of Indulgence, published by royal prerogative, was aimed at giving encouragement to papists. Indeed as early as the summer of 1672 the French ambassador was reporting to Louis XIV that this Declaration, 'plus signs or rather almost certain proofs that the Duke of York has given of his conversion – and the suspicions which are also entertained of the conversion of the King himself – had so strongly irritated all other religions against the Government that one sees nothing but libels and seditious writings'.[12] The court had done its best to prepare the ground adequately. It had tried to select a congenial Speaker, but had failed. Shaftesbury, the new Lord Chancellor, had issued writs to fill thirty-six seats that had fallen vacant during the long adjournment and a substantial number of members friendly to the government had been elected. Shaftesbury had also drafted a strong speech, which was approved by his fellow members of the foreign committee, in defence of the war and pleading for money. Charles himself had published a declaration reaffirming his devotion to the Church of England.

On the very first day of the meeting of Parliament, 4 February, members of the Commons protested that the issue of writs for by-elections by the Lord Chancellor was unconstitutional: that was the duty of the Speaker. The newly elected members were required to leave the House. On the following day the King addressed the two Houses. He told them how he had 'been forced to a most important, necessary and expensive war' and asked for supplies. Charles then referred to the Declaration of Indulgence which he insisted was less beneficial to the papists than to other dissenters and was necessary to secure peace at home.

He said: 'I will deal plainly with you: I am resolved to stick by my Declaration.' He ended with an assurance that he would 'preserve the Church as now established in the kingdom and would invade no man's property'.[13] This was followed by Shaftesbury's speech in which he compared the relations between the English and the Dutch to those between the Romans and the Carthaginians, using the phrase *Delenda est Carthago*.

The Commons debated the King's speech for three days. It was agreed in principle that the King should be voted a supply of £1,260,000 (an assessment of £70,000 a month for eighteen months) and the House then turned to the other part of the speech dealing with the Declaration of Indulgence. A proposal that the King should simply be asked to withdraw the Declaration was defeated and it was then voted *nem. con.* that 'penal statutes in matters ecclesiastical cannot be suspended but by an act of Parliament' and that an address to the King should be drawn up accordingly. A speech by Sir Thomas Lee was typical of the tone of the debate:[14]

What [he said] is the use of his great Council of Parliament but to inform the King he has been misled and mistaken by his Privy Council? It is our duty to the people, and the King calls you to declare your opinion. It plainly appears to be a mistake in the Crown, and you must inform him of it.

On 14 February the terms of the address were agreed and it was also decided to bring in a bill for the ease of Protestant dissenters, thus excluding the Roman Catholics from any form of toleration.

The King's advisers in the foreign committee were divided on how he should answer the address. Only Shaftesbury urged that he should stand on his prerogative and refer the question, if necessary, to the House of Lords. Charles's own view, as reported, was 'that upon the whole matter let the Money Bill come first. What is the discretion for a man to be angry with his own hurt? And have a care not to be left without a fleet this spring.'[15] The French King, through his ambassador, also pressed Charles to put the question of supply first. On 24 February the King answered the address of the Commons in somewhat ambiguous terms. He said that he did not pretend to the right of suspending any laws which concerned the property rights or liberties of his subjects. His only design had been to take off the penalties which the statutes inflicted on dissenters, for that was necessary to the quiet of his kingdom. He added that if any bill were offered to him to achieve the same ends, he would speedily concur in it. But the Commons were adamant and reaffirmed their position. Sir Thomas Meres had said bluntly that only a gracious answer from the King would smooth the passage of the money bill, and the whole House was aware that once the money bill was passed Parliament would be adjourned.

The King wriggled in vain. The Commons insisted that he had been misinformed about his powers and sought a 'full and satisfactory answer'. Whilst they awaited his reply they proceeded to draw up a bill aimed against the Roman Catholics, which laid down that anyone who refused to take the oaths of allegiance and supremacy and to receive the sacrament according to the rites of the Church of England should be excluded from public office. This Test Bill was rushed through both Houses of Parliament. In the House of Lords it was violently opposed by Lord Clifford, the Lord Treasurer, and defended by the Earl of Shaftesbury, the Lord Chancellor. Later the bill for the ease of Protestant dissenters also went up to the Lords where a clause was added giving the King power to issue proclamations on religious matters if he thought fit. But that did not please the House of Commons who were now mounted on their constitutional high horse. The King was tired of the whole argument and yielded. On 8 March, in the words of Sir Edward Dering, 'the King in a short but very gracious speech said he would issue a proclamation in accordance with the address the day before presented to him by the two Houses, desired that they would consider the time of the year, the necessity for setting forth the fleet very speedily and proceed with the bill for supply. The answer exceeding pleasing to the House.'[16] The proclamation that had been asked for was a new one against Roman Catholic priests and Jesuits. The Declaration of Indulgence was withdrawn and the Great Seal, which Shaftesbury had attached to it, was removed. The King got his money bill and assented to the Test Act; but, owing to differences of opinion between the two Houses, the bill for the ease of Protestant dissenters was not passed when, on the day before Easter, Parliament stood adjourned.

The Test Act was a blow to the unity of Charles's government, while the restive temper displayed in the House of Commons augured ill for the war against the Dutch. It was noted that the Duke of York did not attend Easter communion and that Lord Clifford, who allowed it to be understood that he would take the sacrament in church on Whit Sunday, failed to do so. As James and Clifford had both fought against the Test Act in the House of Lords, the inference was obvious. On 15 June James resigned all his offices and on 19 June Clifford handed back his white staff of office to the King. Osborne was at once appointed Lord Treasurer. Thus Arlington was again dissatisfied, and Buckingham was far from pleased when Prince Rupert replaced James in the supreme command against the Dutch and the French Huguenot, Frederick, Count of Schomberg, was called over to take charge of the English land forces. Though Charles was hopeful of some good coming out of a peace congress, which met at the neutral city of Cologne in April, public affairs seemed to be at a standstill. James ceased to attend the Privy Council, engaged in hunting or was seen walking with a melancholy face through St James's park. The King was more happily employed with the Duchess of Portsmouth. On 29 July Sir Thomas Player wrote to Sir Joseph Williamson, who was one of the two English representatives at Cologne:

The truth is this year the Government begins to thrive marvellous well, for it eats and drinks and sleeps as heartily as I have known it, nor doth it vex and disquiet itself with that foolish, idle and impertinent thing called business . . . the people cry out for peace.[17]

William of Orange, through the agency of Peter du Moulin, a Huguenot who had formerly been employed by the British government, launched a highly successful propaganda campaign against France in England: du Moulin's pamphlet entitled *England's Appeal from the Privy Council at Whitehall to the Great Council of the Nation the Lords and Commons in Parliament assembled* made a particularly telling impression. Nothing emerged from the congress of Cologne: both the French and the Dutch positions had hardened, the French because their troops took the fortress of Maastricht in June, the Dutch because they were acquiring allies in Germany and Spain. On 11 August the superior Anglo-French fleet, commanded by Prince Rupert, again failed to defeat de Ruyter at the battle of the Texel. Once more the French admiral proved incapable of playing the part assigned to him and acted indeed as a motionless spectator of the struggle (Rupert made no bones about that); and French popularity with the English public sank low. The news that the melancholy James, no longer at sea, had cheered himself by completing a marriage contract with a young and pretty Italian wife, Mary of Modena (his first wife had died in March 1671) further exacerbated anti-papist feelings. When Parliament reassembled on 20 October 1673 – it was recalled because the King needed money – the predominant tone was not only anti-Catholic but anti-French.

Charles had decided that as soon as Parliament met it should be prorogued for a week. This would scotch the argument that two money bills could not be passed in one session and it might also enable Mary of Modena to arrive in the country. But this plan was bungled, and before Black Rod knocked at the door the Commons had already passed a resolution asking that James's marriage should not be consummated. During the week's recess Shaftesbury suggested that the King should divorce his wife and marry some Protestant princess who could bear him heirs and thus exclude his Roman Catholic brother from the succession. Among other things Shaftesbury also proposed that James should be sent away from London. Charles did not reject either idea outright, but he evidently still hoped that his once loyal Cavalier Parliament could be placated.

On 27 October the King addressed both Houses. He said that he had hoped to welcome them with the news of an honourable peace, 'but the Dutch have disappointed me in that expectation and have treated my ambassadors at Cologne with the contempt of conquerors, and not as might be expected from men in their condition. They have other thoughts than peace'.[18] Charles therefore asked for supplies adequate for him to resume the war in the following spring. He also commended to their care the debt he owed the bankers. In return he promised to fulfil the undertakings he had already given about religion and property 'and', he added, 'I shall be ready to give you fresh instances of my zeal for preserving the established religion and laws, as often as any occasion shall require'. The Commons naturally retorted by repeating their address against his brother's Roman Catholic marriage. But the Secretary of State, Henry Coventry, merely brought them the reply that the Duke's marriage had been completed (a proxy wedding had taken place on 30 September) and that the King could not comply with the desires of Parliament.

The Commons then turned to other grievances. Spain had entered into an alliance with the Dutch, and earlier in the month the French had declared war on Spain. The Commons did not want to be dragged into another war. One member said: 'Giving of money is certain to ruin the King and kingdom. . . . By falling out with Spain we spoil the best trade we have.'[19] Some members attacked the French, who had let down the British navy at sea, while other members expressed opposition to the whole idea of the war on the Dutch. The House of Commons then voted that no further supply should be granted to the King until the eighteen-month tax had expired, unless the Dutch proved obstinate about making peace. On 3 November the Commons decided to draw up a petition against the standing army, although Coventry pointed out that there was a basic difference between an army raised to fight in time of war and a standing army. Writing that day to Williamson, Sir Christopher Musgrave MP said: 'some apprehend a prorogation. Pray God direct His Majesty, for, to my poor reason, things never looked with a more dreadful aspect. If the session continue, I believe particular persons will be brought upon the stage.'[20] The first victim, he believed (rightly) would be the Duke of Lauderdale. Two days later another of Williamson's correspondents informed him that 'there was brought into the House an account of £400,000 given away since last session, of which the Duchesses of Cleveland and Portsmouth had the greatest share'.[21] With the Commons in this temper there was nothing more that Charles could do. Black Rod again knocked at the door. The King, addressing both Houses, said that the differences between him and his Parliament would only encourage his enemies at home and abroad. He therefore ordered a short recess so that 'all good men may recollect themselves against the next meeting' and meanwhile he promised that 'no care' could be greater than his own 'in the effectual suppressing of Popery'.[22]

Behind the scenes the King's Ministers were divided among themselves. Buckingham was pressing his sovereign to repudiate the French alliance and 'accept the good terms offered by Holland'; Arlington told the French ambassador that it was impossible for the King to continue the war; Osborne, who had not been involved in the original negotiations, was strongly anti-French; and Shaftesbury had his knife into both James and Lauderdale. Charles suspected, rightly or wrongly, that Shaftesbury was responsible for stirring up trouble for him in Parliament, and that he was intriguing with Dutch agents in England. On 9 November the King sent Henry Coventry to demand the seals of office from his brother-in-law. Shaftesbury answered defiantly, 'It is only laying down my gown and girding on my sword.'

The Venetian Secretary in London reported home at this time that 'the King calls a cabinet council for the purpose of not listening to it, and the Ministers hold forth in it so as not to be understood'.[23] It was certain that Charles now had to make up his mind about war or peace. In December 1673 the Spanish ambassador, the Marquis del Fresno, gave him the opportunity by presenting him with some peace proposals from the Dutch. Both Spain and England were interested in avoiding another war with each other, which would be difficult if England were still in alliance with France against the United Netherlands. Charles hesitated and referred the proposals back to the congress of Cologne. Meanwhile the French ambassador in London did all he could to keep Charles true to the alliance. The ambassador asked the French King to authorize him to offer a subsidy of £500,000 to Charles. Bribes were also offered to Ministers and Members of Parliament so as to induce them to uphold the French alliance. It was suggested to Charles that he should publish the 'bogus' treaty of December 1670 to show that he was in honour bound to continue to fight alongside the French.

The English King had still not made up his mind what to do when Parliament met again on 7 January 1674. Charles tried to propitiate the two Houses by saying that he was ready to undertake anything that they thought was necessary to secure religion and property. But, he added, he could not procure a good peace without a supply of money. 'No proposals of peace have yet been offered', he said, 'which can be imagined with intent to conclude, but only to amuse.' Therefore 'the way to a good peace is to set out a fleet'. Finally he offered to reveal the terms of the treaty with France to a small committee of both Houses, 'and I assure you', he added, 'there is no other treaty with France, either before or since, not already printed, which shall not be made known'. As he told this deliberate lie, Charles was seen to fumble with his notes.[24]

Parliament was not impressed. The members of the House of Commons, over whom there now hovered the ghosts of their predecessors a generation earlier, turned to discuss their grievances and to attack the King's evil counsellors. An address was passed unanimously for the removal from office of the Duke of Lauderdale, who was accused of raising an army in Scotland for the purpose of altering the English constitution. Buckingham tried to anticipate trouble by asking permission to address the House of Commons, although he failed to inform either the King or the House of Lords of his intention. But his speech was incoherent and carried little conviction. Next day he again appeared before the Commons and answered prepared questions. He tried to lay the blame for all that had gone wrong on the Earl of Arlington and on Lord Clifford, who was now dead. Two days later Arlington himself appeared before the Commons to maintain that he had always favoured moderate courses and that all decisions on foreign policy had been collective. He also assured them that he had made no large sums of money out of his office. The Commons decided to ask the King to dismiss Buckingham, but rejected by 166 votes to 127 an address for Arlington's removal. Thus the 'Cabal' broke up.

Charles had still to make his own peace with the Commons. He did not repeat his father's mistake by peremptorily dissolving Parliament or attempting to arrest the leaders of the Commons. On the contrary, with the approval of Arlington and his council, the King on 24 January took the unprecedented step of submitting the latest Dutch peace proposals, conveyed to him by the Spanish ambassador, to the two Houses of Parliament. He told them that he desired their speedy advice: 'for (he said) if you shall find the terms such as may be embraced, your advice will have great weight with me; and if you find them defective, I hope you will give me your advice and assistance how to get better terms'.[25] The House of Commons debated the question for two days and finally both Houses agreed to advise the King to make 'a speedy peace'. They carefully refrained from asking that it should be an honourable peace, for the Commons had no intention of voting further supplies. The House then turned to other questions including the dangers of popery and the threat of a standing army.

On 5 February the Dutch gave full powers to the Spanish ambassador to conclude peace in London. Sir William Temple and del Fresno worked out its terms. The Dutch agreed to concede the honour of the flag to British ships in British waters; to allow British colonists peacefully to leave Surinam; to refer disputes in the East Indies to arbitration; and to negotiate a commercial treaty. Overseas conquests made by either side were to be restored. The Dutch were to pay an indemnity of £200,000. Nothing was said about fishing rights or the position of William of Orange. A secret article provided that neither side should give assistance to each other's enemies. By giving way over the honorific question of the flag and conceding an indemnity the Dutch allowed Charles to save his face. But the terms were small beer compared with the grandiose ambitions with which the King had entered the war in alliance with France. Charles also tried to save his face with the French by leaving his delegates at Cologne and by not recalling his troops which were serving as paid auxiliaries with the French army. He had in fact been compelled by Parliament to conclude peace: the price he received was that he had saved his throne.

On 11 February Charles gave the news of the treaty (which had been signed at Westminster two days earlier) to the two Houses of Parliament. He claimed that he had made 'a speedy, honourable, and, I hope, lasting peace'. He assured them that he would at once set about disbanding his land forces, though he added wistfully that 'it will be necessary to build more great ships; for we shall not be safe, unless we equal the strength of our neighbours at sea'.[26] The Commons then turned back with zest to the consideration of a number of bills aimed at preserving liberty, property and the Anglican establishment. But Charles had had more than enough. Without consulting his Ministers, on 24 February the King adjourned Parliament until the autumn. Thus not a single bill was passed.

Charles ignored Parliament's request to him to dismiss Lauderdale, who continued to rule in Scotland. But Buckingham was removed from all his offices and dismissed from the Privy Council. The most valuable of Buckingham's offices, that of Master of the Horse, for which he had paid £20,000, was bought by the King for his son, the Duke of Monmouth. He also gave a pension to Buckingham's mistress, the Countess of Shrewsbury: the subject of the liaison had been debated in the House of Lords where the parties concerned were asked to give security for their good behaviour. The Countess retired to a nunnery in France, and Buckingham went to Yorkshire to hunt foxes. Arlington lingered on in his office of Secretary of State, which he had held for twelve years, until September, when he resigned it to Sir Joseph Williamson and acquired instead the post of Lord Chamberlain of the Household. Charles, who had found Arlington so valuable both in making war and making peace, continued to use him and seek his advice. But 1674 was to be a year of new men and new policies. Charles's principal adviser was to be his Lord Treasurer, Osborne, who in June of that year was created Earl of Danby.

12

Charles the Mediator 1674–7

Charles had been obliged to withdraw from the Dutch war because the House of Commons had refused to give him supplies on the scale that had been voted in the previous war. The comparative failure of the British navy, which was largely blamed on lack of cooperation by the French, and the overrunning of the Spanish Netherlands by Louis XIV's armies, had contributed to increasing hostility against France in the English Parliament. Moreover the Duke of York's marriage to a Roman Catholic princess and James's own conversion, which had become common knowledge, had aroused fears and suspicions about the heir presumptive to the throne. A bill for securing the Protestant religion, which contained a clause to prevent any future Stuart prince from marrying a Roman Catholic without the consent of Parliament, had been debated in both Houses. The atmosphere was such that even though Charles had submitted to the pressure it had put upon him to get out of the war, he felt he could no longer tolerate his restive Parliament. He is reputed to have said that 'he had rather be a poor King than no King'.[1] He prorogued Parliament and relied on his Lord Treasurer to restore his finances to order.

There was thus a close relationship between domestic and foreign affairs. Charles had hoped that through his alliance with the most powerful monarch in Europe he would strengthen his own position and authority. But this very alliance had brought upon him the distrust of his own subjects, which had been fanned by clever Dutch propaganda. Nevertheless he had at the outset of 1674 no intention of changing his own policy. He would continue, if he could, to remain on friendly terms with France; and by ruling without Parliament and giving at least lip service to anti-Catholic measures in England he hoped to create a calmer atmosphere at home.

At first Charles was nervous that he had given offence to the French King by his precipitate withdrawal from the war. He explained to the French ambassador that it was impossible for him to carry on the war without fresh parliamentary supplies of which he had no hopes. Ruvigny told him what was done could not be helped. He asked Charles to try to arrange an armistice at sea, to allow the hired English troops to continue in French service, and to join with the Swedes as a mediator between Louis XIV and his enemies.[2] For the Dutch had now raised a coalition against France, which included not only Spain, whose territories had been violated, but also the Holy Roman Emperor, the Elector of Brandenburg, and other German princes. Charles expressed his delight at the French reaction, although he was fully aware that the Dutch, Spaniards and Germans would think twice about accepting the mediation of a ruler who had only just ceased to be the ally of France.

Thus Charles determined for the time being to take things easily and to avoid giving provocation either at home or abroad. Dr Burnet wrote that 'the King and his brother were now at their ease . . . and the Court delivered itself up to its ordinary course of sloth and luxury'.[3] The Venetian representative in England, Alberti, put it less harshly:

The King lives from day to day [he reported at the end of February] and makes peace with the Dutch and a truce with parliament to live quiet. But this knot will again return to the teeth of the comb and never disentangle itself unless the King take courage to combat the licence of parliament; but others will do this as the King is intent on enjoying life, has no heirs and always hesitates to raise a finger for fear of a relapse into the miseries and perplexities of his youth.[4]

Yet it was not mere laziness that induced Charles for the time being to let sleeping dogs lie. It was plain enough that the coalition against France was not going to agree to his mediation until they saw the results of the coming military campaign. If Charles put

forward peace terms which could be interpreted as unduly favourable to France he would arouse what Alberti called 'the irrecon-
cileable antipathy' of his own people;[5] on the other hand, the
French were not going to accept peace terms which they thought
unsatisfactory unless Charles were ready, in the last resort, to
engage in 'armed mediation', in other words to put his own
forces at the disposal of the coalition. Charles's advisers were
divided among themselves. Arlington pressed the King to promote the marriage of his niece, Mary, to Prince William of
Orange. Danby was opposed to any active policy which would
interfere with the kingdom's economic recovery. For it was
obvious that while the French and Dutch were intensely occupied
in war, British trade and shipping would benefit substantially.
Danby was able to negotiate better terms from the farmers of the
excise and to improve the management of the customs. Although
much of the money which the Dutch had agreed to pay as an
indemnity in the treaty of Westminster went to meeting an old
debt to the House of Orange, Danby was successful in reaching a
temporary settlement with the bankers and threw himself into
negotiating commercial treaties with France and Sweden. Charles
contented himself with issuing proclamations to restrain the
spreading of false news and licentious talking on matters of state;
with ordering the judges to enforce the existing laws against
Roman Catholics; and with turning a deaf ear to Swedish pleas
that he should intervene jointly with them to procure peace. In
April he gave himself a fortnight's hunting at Newmarket and
then spent most of the summer in Windsor, leaving the Queen
at Hampton Court. But he paid a visit to Portsmouth to inspect
the building of the *Royal James*, a warship of one hundred guns;
and each week he went to Hampton Court to preside over meetings of his council. A majority of the councillors was in favour
of the dissolution of Parliament. But Danby was against it and
the King feared that elections would go unfavourably for his
government.

It was not until June that Charles made up his mind to take a
modest step towards mediation. He then decided to send Sir
William Temple, who had previously served at both Brussels

and The Hague and had been an architect of both the Triple Alliance and the treaty of Westminster, to sound the Dutch and the Spaniards about whether they would now accept Charles's mediation. Before he left Temple had an interview with the King to whom he gave a long lecture on the differences between the conditions in France and in England. According to Temple, Charles defended his previous policy of alliance with the French against the Dutch. The King observed: 'It was true that he had succeeded ill; but, if he had been well served, he might have made a good business enough of it; and so went on a good deal to justify what was past.' But Temple insisted that the King could not carry out a policy that 'the people hated and feared'. For, unlike Louis xiv, he could never obtain the supplies to raise a large army, while the Roman Catholics in England were not a hundredth part of the nation and in Scotland not a two-hundredth part. The King was rather impatient with this lecture. But when Temple quoted a saying of a Frenchman 'that a King of England, who will be the man of his people, is the greatest king in the world; but if he will be something more, by God he is nothing at all', Charles laid his hand upon the ambassador and declared, 'I will be the man of my people'.[6] About the same time Charles had an interview with the French ambassador and assured him that he would keep his people in good order and that, whether he decided to prorogue or dissolve his Parliament in the autumn, his aim would be to please the French King. A month earlier he had told him with tears in his eyes that he was in despair because he was unable to give Louis xiv more help against his enemies.[7] Thus Charles tried to make everybody happy and when by the middle of June he realized that Danby (who was then awarded his earldom) had made a good job of reorganizing the royal finances, he let it be known that he would prorogue Parliament again until the spring of the following year; for this decision he extorted from the French the modest sum of £145,000.

Temple did not find his mission an easy one. Not only had he to overcome the allies' suspicions of Charles ii's impartiality as a mediator, but he had been ordered to protest against the way in which Dutch agents had stirred up trouble for the King in

England and Scotland. Moreover when he arrived on the continental mainland no one had time to talk peace, for the campaign of 1674 was in full swing. Neither side was notably successful. Marshal Vauban took Besançon in Franche-Comté; Turenne won some minor victories over the Imperialists in Alsace; and the Prince de Condé fought his last set battle and William of Orange his first at Seneffe in Flanders. This was one of the bloodiest battles of the century, but it was not decisive. The French might claim to have won because they captured some of the Dutch baggage. On the other hand, the Imperial army had ravaged Alsace before they were driven out. The French lost Huy and Dinant in the Spanish Netherlands during late October and by his own exertions William of Orange recaptured Grave, the only town in the United Netherlands still held by the French.

When William did see Temple he was in a mood to discuss peace-making. He made it clear that he would not conclude a separate treaty with the French, but said that he had persuaded his Dutch and German allies to accept in principle King Charles's mediation. As to Dutch propaganda in England he admitted freely that he had used his influence to help force Charles to withdraw from the war; but he refused to betray his agents or friends.

Meanwhile in England Charles continued to play his cards calmly. He had to contend with rival groups of advisers. Arlington, although he had ceased to be Secretary of State in September, was still actively concerned with foreign affairs; he carried on a correspondence with William of Orange and he became a friend of Charles's Protestant son, the Duke of Monmouth. Opposed to them were the Duke of York, the Earl of Danby and the Duke of Lauderdale. But these latter were somewhat uneasy allies. Nobody knew exactly where the King stood. The French ambassador was reporting home that the 'cabals against France' were very fierce and that Members of Parliament were violently opposed to the French domination of Flanders; at the same time other observers thought that the court was still secretly partial to Catholicism and France.[8] At the beginning of October Charles returned to Newmarket for a month and, according to Alberti, the City of London was deeply resentful at the protracted sojourn of the King and his court in the country. But Charles was keeping his eyes on public affairs. When he learned from Temple that his mediation was now acceptable to the allies, he discussed with the French ambassador where the venue of a general peace conference should be and even hoped that it might meet in London. At the beginning of November the King surprised the entire political world by sending a special mission to Holland, headed by the Earl of Arlington. Even the French ambassador, to whom Charles had been complaining of the conduct of the Prince of Orange a month before, was not informed about the mission until after it had set out.

Arlington was assisted on this diplomatic mission by the Earl of Ossory, the eldest son of the Duke of Ormonde. Both of them had Dutch wives. Arlington was accompanied by his wife, his brother-in-law and his young daughter; and Ossory also took his wife. The mission had all the atmosphere of a pleasant family outing. But Arlington's rivals, Danby and Lauderdale, were so indignant that in order to soothe them Charles agreed to send Danby's son, Lord Latimer, to join the party. His function seems to have been to spy on his colleagues; but even they were given no detailed instructions.

William of Orange received the envoys graciously, but he did not conceal from Arlington the resentment he still felt over the part played by England in the assault of 1672 which had almost destroyed the Dutch republic. The first time they dined together Arlington observed that the English had got out of the war 'very cavalierly'. 'You went into it very cavalierly too,' retorted William.[9] In general, William reacted violently against Arlington's dictatorial attitude. But his mission – in view of his lack of instructions – was not altogether fruitless; for he returned with an outline of the terms on which the Dutch were willing to discuss peace and with the draft of a defensive and offensive alliance between the United Netherlands and Great Britain, given to him by the Grand Pensionary of Holland, Caspar Fagel, which he proposed should be concluded after the French war ended. The Earl of Ossory, who was no diplomatist, blurted out the suggestion that William should marry Princess Mary. He received the reply that the Prince would be willing enough to come to England to meet the lady after peace had been made, but meanwhile 'his fortunes were in no condition for him to think of a wife'.[10] Such was the information that Charles received when the envoys returned home in January 1675. Although all parties were willing to accept him as mediator (without the Swedes who were now committed to the French side) it was plain enough that the peace aims of the contestants in the war still lay far apart. Charles himself was unlikely to cut a figure in Europe unless he could produce a strong navy to back him. The King therefore turned his attention to the recall of Parliament, hoping that it might prove to be in a more amicable frame of mind than when it last met at the end of the previous year.

Danby, who was now the King's chief Minister, was anxious to effect a reconciliation between Charles and his Parliament. He himself, when he was Thomas Osborne, had been a Member of Parliament and he had good reason to feel that the majority of the members were basically loyal Cavaliers, though suspicious of Catholicism and of France. Danby's policy was twofold: first, he aimed to persuade Parliament that the King was a good Anglican at heart and that, in spite of the two Declarations of Indulgence, he was ready to enforce the laws against the Roman Catholics and dissenters. Secondly, he hoped by a modest distribution of patronage, either by the conferring of offices, grants of land or titles or, above all, the provision of regular pensions charged to the excise, to create a solid core of government supporters in the House of Commons. This was not as easy to achieve as it might have appeared, for Danby did not have large sums of money at his disposal, not all office-holders were willing to vote as the court wished, and other bribes were forthcoming from foreign ambassadors in London, who aspired to sway members to support their national interests. Moreover members of the House of Lords, like Shaftesbury, who had finally been expelled from the Privy Council in May 1674, the Duke of Buckingham, whose life had been one long intrigue, and the Earl of Arlington, whose political stock had fallen after his mission to Holland, had their own followings in the House of Commons and were all hostile to Danby.

Under the impulse of Danby conferences of bishops were held at the end of 1674 to consider how the Church of England might be invigorated and how papists and nonconformists might be repressed. They informed the King that the existing laws were sufficient for the purpose, provided that they were rigorously applied. On 3 February 1675 therefore an Order in Council was issued to enforce the penal laws against Roman Catholics, to suppress Catholic worship except in the chapels of the Queen and foreign ambassadors, which Englishmen were forbidden to attend, and to banish priests from England and Catholic laymen from the court. At the same time the Conventicle Act was to be put in force against the Puritans. Finally it was proposed to erect a brass statue of King Charles I at Charing Cross to remind people that it was in the Anglican cause that Charles's father had been martyred. Writing to the Earl of Essex in Ireland during April, Lord Conway said that Danby had told him 'that all their measures were altered since I last saw him, that the King and the Duke were resolved to keep up Parliament, to raise the old Cavaliers and the Church party and to sacrifice Papists and Presbyterians'.[11] The King, being volatile, was willing to give his Minister his head for the time being; it was more of a strain on the Duke of York to see his fellow religionists being persecuted, but he recognized that Danby was a determined champion of the interests of the monarchy.

When Parliament reassembled on 13 April 1675 the King said: 'The principal end of my calling you now is to know what you think may yet be wanting to the securing of religion and property, and to give myself the satisfaction of having used the uttermost of my endeavours to procure and settle a right and lasting understanding between us.' He concluded with his usual appeal for supplies for the navy.[12] Two days later Danby's brother-in-law introduced into the House of Lords a bill which required all Members of Parliament and all office-holders to declare that in no circumstances was it lawful to take up arms against the Crown and to swear that they would uphold the existing government in Church and State. If by this non-resisting test Danby hoped to make the two Houses more amenable to the government, he was sadly mistaken. For one of the first motions in the Commons was for an address to the King to remove the Duke of Lauderdale from his service and for an impeachment to be brought forward against Danby himself.

Although nothing came of these motions – the reasons given for impeaching Danby were feeble in the extreme – the Commons also demonstrated its anti-French feelings and its distrust of the way in which the finances of the navy were handled. On 19 April Sir Thomas Littleton moved for the recall of English forces in the service of the French King 'that the French may no farther be encouraged to ruin us and the rest of our neighbours'.[13] The Commons agreed to an address to the King on this subject and on 8 May the King replied that though he could not in honour recall the troops that had been sent to France before the treaty of Westminster, he would recall his subjects who had entered the service since then and would forbid any further recruiting. A proclamation to this effect was issued on 19 May, but in fact, with Charles's connivance, the recruiting continued. As to the navy, although Samuel Pepys assured the Commons that the King had spent £400,000 a year upon it and had built more ships than all his ancestors before him, the House merely voted that £450,000 should be appropriated to the navy out of the customs, which did not improve the King's finances one iota. Rumour had it that the King blamed Danby for this failure: Charles wondered why his Lord Treasurer was able to get so many votes for himself (when his proposed impeachment was rejected) yet 'none for the King'.[14] Charles gloomily informed the French ambassador that he was finding it more and more difficult to resist the violent demands of 'all his people' who were extremely jealous of the power of France on land and sea.[15] Nor were the feelings of the Commons assuaged by a proclamation against Roman Catholics. For, as Sir Thomas Meres observed, 'Our jealousies of Popery or arbitrary government are not for a few inconsiderable Papists here, but from the ill example we have got from France'.[16]

The bill for the non-resistance test got bogged down for a long time in the House of Lords, Shaftesbury and others arguing vehemently that it was an infringement of the privileges of their

House. On 31 May, however, the bill, heavily amended, was passed in the House of Lords, the King himself following the proceedings until twelve o'clock at night. But now a quarrel developed between the two Houses which was deliberately exploited by Shaftesbury and prevented the measure getting through the Commons. A certain Dr Shirley had brought a case against Sir John Fagg, a member of the Commons, in the Court of Chancery. On appeal this was referred to the House of Lords and Fagg was ordered to appear there to answer Shirley's petition. The Commons voted that this was a breach of their privileges, and after much coming and going between the two Houses the quarrel brought parliamentary business to a standstill. In a desperate effort to save something from the wreck the King on 5 June summoned the members of both Houses before him in the Banqueting House and the Lord Keeper, Sir Heneage Finch, accused 'ill men' of wanting to procure a dissolution of Parliament. But this did no good. Four days later Charles threw in the sponge. 'I must confess,' he told his Parliament, 'the ill designs of our enemies have been too prevalent against those good ones I had proposed in behalf of my people; and those unhappy differences between my two Houses are grown to such a height, that I find no possible means of putting an end to them but by a prorogation.'[17]

As in the previous year, Charles went back to Windsor to enjoy himself and left it to Danby to try to arrange a more agreeable meeting of Parliament in the autumn. But Danby's position was to some extent weakened by the failures of his policies, and neither Charles nor James was any longer willing to give him full support. James had always been restive about a programme which involved enforcing the laws against Roman Catholics, and he entered into negotiations with those who favoured indulgence towards the nonconformists including the statesman who was later to be his arch-enemy, the Earl of Shaftesbury. On 19 June William Harbord wrote to the Earl of Essex: 'the Treasurer has lost ground with the King and the Duke is trying to bring in Shaftesbury'.[18] On 13 June Shaftesbury, who had not been near the court for a year, had been admitted to kiss the King's hand. However a week later Danby had a three-hour interview with Charles and four days after that Shaftesbury received orders from the King to stay away from court in the future. Possibly Charles had been persuaded that Danby could secure a majority in the House of Commons which would vote him money to get out of his financial difficulties. For it was estimated that in spite of the improvements that Danby had contrived the King was a million pounds in debt and needed a further half-million to fulfil his naval programme.

Danby certainly did everything he could to obtain a favourable reception for the King when Parliament reassembled. He increased the number of excise pensioners, while the Secretaries of State wrote personal letters to more than a hundred members of the Commons, who they hoped would support the government, asking them to be sure to be in London in time for the opening of Parliament. Meanwhile Charles tried to reinsure himself through the French ambassador. The French campaign of 1675 had not been victorious: Marshal Turenne had been killed in battle, while the new French allies, the Swedes, had been surprisingly defeated in Germany. Louis XIV was anxious to avoid an anti-French Parliament at Westminster pushing Charles on to the side of his enemies and voting him money for that purpose. It was therefore agreed that if Parliament failed to vote supplies or proved hostile to France, Charles would dissolve it altogether and receive an annual subsidy of about £100,000. Danby's biographer is of the opinion that he cannot have been unaware of this bargain, but even if he did know of it, he must have regarded £100,000 a year as little more than chicken-feed and must still have hoped that his master would secure what he needed from Parliament.

When Parliament met in October 1675 Charles was extremely frank. He said that he hoped they would postpone the resumption of the constitutional debates between the two Houses that had broken up the previous session, and give their first attention to public bills. He desired them, above all, to furnish him with supplies 'as well to take off the anticipations which are upon my revenue as for building of ships'. He admitted that he had not been 'altogether so good a husband' as he might have been, but promised that he would behave himself better in the future. At the same time he assured Parliament that he had been 'far from such extravagancy in my own expense as some would have the world believe'.[19] But in spite of all Danby's efforts the Commons were now about equally divided between the court party and the 'country party' which was critical of the King and his Ministers. Although on 4 November a Grand Committee of the whole House voted £300,000 for the building of twenty warships (the King had wanted £500,000 and thirty ships) a week later this Bill was tacked on to another one appropriating the customs to the use of the navy. The court party's attempt to modify this decision was defeated by fourteen votes.

Meanwhile in the House of Lords Shaftesbury had again raised the bogy of Shirley v. Fagg with a view to provoking a crisis which would compel the King to dissolve Parliament. Shaftesbury believed that if elections were held for a new House of Commons the anti-French and anti-Catholic elements would be enormously strengthened. On 19 November a conference was held between the two Houses which ended in deadlock. On 20 November a motion was introduced into the Lords to address the King in favour of the dissolution of Parliament. Surprisingly the Duke of York supported this motion: this was possibly because he believed that a new Parliament would prove more tolerant towards the Roman Catholics. By a supreme effort Danby managed to defeat it by 50 votes to 48. But Charles considered that this was the end of the line. He felt he could not dissolve Parliament, for that would have been tantamount to a confession that he had surrendered to his enemies: instead he ordered the prorogation of Parliament for the unprecedented period of fifteen months and turned to the French King for consolation.

The year 1676 was a peaceable one for Charles II. In his capacity as a mediator he had been able to fix on the town of Nymegen as the site of a peace congress. Thither he sent Sir William Temple as his chief ambassador, and during the summer the diplomatic representatives of the warring nations gathered there in leisurely fashion and awaited the result of the season's campaign, which proved to be largely one of stalemate. At home Charles was not troubled by pressures from Parliament, while he left it to Danby to manage his finances as best he could and to try his hand once again at making the House of Commons more amenable to his wishes when it eventually had to be recalled. Charles himself concentrated on keeping on friendly terms with the French King and watching the contest of two French mistresses for his own favours.

But as Danby still stuck to a policy of rallying Parliament with a battle-cry of 'Church and King' and was aware that the bulk of the ruling classes were violently anti-French and anti-Catholic, he and his master did not always see eye to eye. As Professor Andrew Browning wrote, 'for more than a year two distinct and even contradictory lines of policy were pursued by the Government, one favoured by Charles and the Duke of York, the other by Danby and his immediate associates, each line of policy being in the most curious way tolerated and even connived at by the supporters of the other'.[20] Charles was at first faced by a rebuff from Louis XIV. The French King had promised him £100,000 a year if he would dissolve his Parliament; but as Parliament had been prorogued and not dissolved, Louis XIV did not see why he should pay the money. While the Duke of York was urging on Ruvigny, the French ambassador, that the spirit, if not the letter of the agreement had been honoured, Danby tried to persuade the King that he should conclude an alliance with the Dutch, lest the French should make a separate peace with the Dutch and thus put England at a disadvantage at sea and in commerce. But Charles was not convinced: for if the object of his foreign policy was to keep the United Netherlands and France apart, why should he not ally himself with France?

By the middle of January 1676 Louis XIV had given way over the subsidy, which he agreed to pay in quarterly instalments, and even before that Charles was begging Ruvigny to go over to France with proposals for a new secret Anglo-French treaty. At the same time he was careful to warn the French King that he could not hope to make peace with the Dutch unless he guaranteed the security of their frontier in Flanders. In Charles's view it was better and more honourable to conclude a treaty with the French, whose ally he had once been, than with the Dutch who had twice been his enemies. Louis XIV was delighted with Charles's proposal, which Danby resisted in vain. But Charles recognized that the new treaty (like the treaty of Dover) must be kept a close secret, 'as he being a mediator, people would not like him to sign a treaty with France'.[21] Danby and Lauderdale, to whom Charles confided the details of the transaction, refused to be directly concerned in it. But Charles was adamant. By this treaty the two Kings bound themselves to give no aid to the enemies of the other nor to make any treaty without the consent of the other: the States-General of the United Netherlands were specifically named as the government with which neither party would treat separately. Charles wrote out the treaty in his own hand and sealed it himself. Ruvigny signed the treaty on behalf of the French King on 11 February and Lauderdale changed his mind and witnessed Charles's signature. Not long after this treaty was signed Ruvigny was recalled to France and was replaced by Honoré de Courtin, who was a man of the world and was given specific instructions to cultivate and report upon Charles's mistresses. Once he had settled down in his new post, Courtin wrote to Louvois, the French War Minister, 'One must either be a man of pleasure in England or not come here at all'.[22]

While Charles had thus tied himself again to France and was enjoying his three-monthly *pourboire*, Danby was engaged in putting the royal finances in order, drawing up a scheme of economies which would limit the annual expenditure to under £1,200,000, in crushing political opposition inside and outside the government, and in preparing the way for the ultimate recall of Parliament; for he argued strongly, as against the Duke of York, the Earl of Arlington, the Duke of Ormonde and others, that it would be dangerous to dissolve Parliament, especially in view of the anti-papist feeling in the kingdom, which had been reinforced when it became known that the Duke of York had ceased even to accompany the King to the royal chapel during Holy Week.

Danby tried to hamstring the manœuvres of the political opposition first by persuading Charles to agree to a proclamation closing all the coffee-houses in London, where opposition leaders were accustomed to meet and where anti-government pamphlets were circulated and read; and secondly to compel the Earl of Shaftesbury, now the acknowledged leader of the opposition to the government, whose favourite resort was John's coffee house, to leave the capital altogether. The proclamation raised a storm of protest; it was questioned whether it was legal for the government to withdraw coffee-house licences; and a petition was presented to the Privy Council asserting that coffee-sellers would be ruined if they were left with unsold stocks on their hands. A compromise was reached which allowed the coffee-houses to keep open provided that the owners did not allow scandalous books or libels to be circulated there and tried to put a stop to anti-government agitation.

As to Shaftesbury, the King sent him a message 'that he had information that he was very busy here in town in matters that he ought not, and that His Majesty thought it were much better that he was at home in the country. . . .'[23] But Shaftesbury defied the King and explained he was occupied only in private business, though in fact he used his town house as a meeting-place for those who were to be known later as Whigs. It was easier for Charles to deal with men who were still in his employment: something of a purge was carried out; those like the Earl of Halifax and Lord Holles, who had championed the cause of the coffee-sellers, were excluded from the Privy Council; and Sir John Duncombe, who had presented their petition, was removed from his post as Chancellor of the Exchequer. Even Sir Stephen Fox, who had been so useful to Charles when he was in exile, lost his lucrative post of Paymaster of the Forces, because he was not a follower of Danby.

The King, as usual, divided his time between Newmarket, Windsor and London. Here he found a new interest. In January Hortense Mancini, Duchess of Mazarin, had arrived in England, dressed as a man, to stay with the Duchess of York who was a kinswoman of hers. When Hortense was in her teens and Charles was a penniless exile, he had offered her his hand in marriage. Though she was now nearly thirty, she was dark, flamboyant and by general consent still very beautiful. The King visited her first at his brother's house and then at a house in St James's Square, which the Duke of York had put at her disposal, and finally at the house of the Countess of Sussex, Charles's daughter by the Countess of Castlemaine. The latter, now Duchess of Cleveland, had retired to France, while Louise de Kéroualle, Duchess of Portsmouth, was the acknowledged *maîtresse-en-titre*. But the Duchess of Portsmouth was in a weak state of health; the King is said to have infected her with a venereal disease. In June she gave birth to a premature child and retired to Bath to recover. Courtin filled his dispatches with news of the rivalry between these French ladies: Hortense was believed to have a grudge against Louis XIV because he had failed to extract for her a larger pension from the eccentric husband whom she had understandably deserted. It was feared that she might be used by the anti-French party in England, so much so that it was thought advisable to let the delegates at the Congress of Nymegen know that the Duchess of Portsmouth was in the best of health and that her relations with Charles were unchanged. Courtin reported to Louis XIV in late July that the King went nearly every day to visit his daughter (who was with child) whom Hortense was nursing. But when he called on the Duchess of Portsmouth, which he did every day, a good many people went with him and remained in the room with him. What Charles did with his nights seemed of more importance. When he did not arrive home until five in the morning, the question was whether he had been with Hortense or with Nell Gwyn. Nell Gwyn had no political influence. But Hortense might have. Courtin reported that she was indignant because she had heard that the French King joked about her in public. 'We have the whole kingdom and the chief Minister against us here,' Courtin told the French Foreign Minister in July; 'if we are to have the mistress too, I leave you to judge of the future.'[24]

But Courtin need not have worried. If, as was generally believed, Hortense became the King's mistress towards the end of 1676, she had no interest in politics and remained a good Frenchwoman. Moreover she was inconstant in her love. When an old acquaintance of hers, the Prince of Monaco, arrived in England, she preferred this handsome young man to the middle-aged monarch, and the Duchess of Portsmouth, who was more politically-minded, soon resumed her sway over Charles. Thus Danby, who had always been careful to keep on the right side of Louise (over a period of two years he is known to have paid her £55,000) was not affected by the temporary success of her rival; and Arlington, who had backed Hortense, was unable to regain his influence.

The truth is that Charles's foreign policy was not materially influenced by his mistresses. He had in fact committed himself to France. Louis XIV was in a position to blackmail him either by letting leak the secrets of the treaty of Dover, in which Charles had promised to declare himself a Roman Catholic, or of the treaty of February 1676, in which Charles had bound himself to France although he had been constituted the official mediator between France and its enemies. Moreover Charles had seen from the changed temper of his Parliament in 1675 that his seat on the throne was precarious and that he might need to invoke the help of Louis XIV against his own subjects. He was only too anxious to bring about a peace that would satisfy the French and, in spite of everything, he still feared that the French and Dutch might conclude a separate treaty which would mean the loss to Great Britain of the command of the sea.

At the end of 1676 Charles refused to permit Prince William of Orange to come to England until peace had been settled, and he also rejected a renewed offer from the Dutch of a defensive treaty (although he did not turn down the idea of such a treaty once the war was over). He fell in with Danby's wish to conclude a maritime treaty with France, which was chiefly concerned with French seizures of neutral English mercantile marine, and he informed Courtin in confidence that he believed he had it in his hands to arrange a general peace. No progress had been achieved at Nymegen, where Temple had constituted himself a post office for the exchange of proposals between the various sides. But after Temple had interviewed William at Dieren, the Prince's country seat, when on his way back from The Hague to Nymegen, Charles though that he was in a position to put forward specific proposals for peace. His idea was that the French should give up Franche-Comté and in return obtain Cambrai, Aire and St Omer, towns which would create a viable frontier in Flanders.[25] But the French thought that these proposals were incompatible with the military situation, and they were flatly rejected by William. Thus Charles now had reluctantly to face his Parliament again, where he knew that pressure would be brought to bear on him to abandon his role as mediator and join the enemies of his secret ally, France.

13

Charles II and the Treaty of Nymegen

When Parliament reassembled after an interval of fifteen months on 15 February 1677 Charles had good reason to hope that it would be in a co-operative frame of mind, which would enable him to put his finances in order and, by allowing him to build new warships, to strengthen his position as a mediator in the European war. During the long recess Danby had improved the arrangements for farming the excise and had reached a settlement with the bankers. Moreover he had done everything he could to secure a majority favourable to the Crown in both Houses of Parliament. He had pressed the King to declare his emphatic support for the Church of England so as to offset the suspicions aroused by his brother's known conversion; and, by taking an active interest in the results of by-elections as well as by nobbling existing members (such as Sir John Reresby, M.P. for Aldborough in Yorkshire), he hoped that there would be a majority in the Commons sympathetic to the King. He also collected proxy votes in the House of Lords. But Danby was not alone in exerting influence on Members of Parliament. The Dutch, Spanish and Imperial ambassadors in London spent time and money on propagating their point of view, especially at dinner parties, aiming indirectly to shape Charles's foreign policy, while the Earl of Shaftesbury and the Duke of Buckingham planned to stir up an agitation for the dissolution of the existing Parliament in the hope that a general election would bring about the downfall of Danby.

Charles had no intention of being forced into dissolving Parliament or being jockeyed out of his position as a neutral mediator. He was well aware of the opposition's plans. The argument was that according to two statutes of the reign of Edward III Parliament had to be called once every year and therefore the present Parliament had ceased to exist. But a valid objection to this argument was that the Edwardian statutes had been superseded by the Triennial Act of 1664 which laid it down that parliaments should be held 'once in three years at least', and this was buttressed by the more practical objection that the members of the Commons had for the most part no wish to face an election and run the risk of losing their seats.

In his opening speech Charles said: 'I have called you together, after a long prorogation, that you might have an opportunity to repair the misfortunes of the last session, and to recover and restore the right use of parliaments.' He promised to give members every security for the Protestant religion, as established in the Church of England, and observed, apropos the quarrel between the two Houses over the case of Shirley *v.* Fagg, 'let all men judge who is most for arbitrary government, they that foment such differences as tend to dissolve all parliaments or I that would preserve this and all parliaments from being made useless by such dissensions'. He then asked them for a supply with which to build new ships and for a renewal of the additional excise of 1671 which was about to expire.[1]

The government got off to an excellent start. When Buckingham and Shaftesbury put forward their constitutional arguments in the House of Lords, they were ordered to be called to the bar of the House and ask pardon on their knees for showing contempt of the King and the House of Lords. After they had refused to do so they and two of their supporters were separately imprisoned in the Tower of London. The same arguments, put forward more mildly in the House of Commons, equally proved damp squibs. Four days later, following a persuasive speech by Samuel Pepys, who said that the King spent £400,000 a year on the navy but needed thirty more ships for the national safety, the Commons voted a supply of £600,000; and on 12 March it agreed to the renewal of the additional excise for three years.

Charles's main difficulty with the House of Commons was not over domestic questions but over foreign policy. The French army, though long driven out of the United Netherlands, was now occupied in building a fortified line beyond the existing frontiers of France which would enable it to dominate Spanish Flanders. The campaign opened exceptionally early and the French swiftly captured Valenciennes, Cambrai and St Omer. When William of Orange with some difficulty collected an àrmy to relieve St Omer he was defeated by Louis xiv's brother at the battle of Cassel fought at the beginning of April. The House of Commons at once expressed its alarm. As early as 6 March Sir William Coventry had said that all were agreed on the danger from the growing greatness of France.[2] Ten days later, after consultation between the two Houses, Charles was petitioned by Parliament to take measures for the preservation of Flanders. Charles was annoyed. He gave a colourless reply saying that he would use all measures for the preservation of Flanders that could 'possibly consist with the peace and safety of the kingdom'.[3] Privately he complained that the address was the work of 'but three or four rascals that would engage him in a war and then leave him in the lurch',[4] while he sent Louis xiv his congratulations on the capture of Valenciennes. In the House of Commons Sir Joseph Williamson, the Secretary of State for the North, said that of the £600,000 that they had voted £500,000 had already been laid out, 'yet the King is in no condition to declare war'.[5] But the Commons were by no means satisfied and on 30 March, without bothering to consult the Lords, they presented another address promising the King 'aids and supplies' if action taken for the preservation of Flanders should lead to war.

The King was thus driven into a corner and he took some time to consider his reply. Meanwhile the battle of Cassel had been fought and on 4 April his own chief Minister, Danby, drew up a long memorandum urging him to take a stand against France. Danby urged Charles to do this largely for domestic reasons, observing that 'when men's fears are grown both so general and so great as now they are by the successes of France, neither His Majesty nor any of his Ministers shall have any longer credit if acts do not speedily appear some way or other to their satisfaction'.[6] After taking thought, Charles on 11 April sent a message to the Commons saying that the only way to prevent dangers must be by putting him in a position to plan suitable preparations for war. At the same time he told the French ambassador, Courtin: 'You see how I suffer. I put myself in trouble with my subjects for love of the French King. I am resolved to keep my promises to him; but I beg him to help me a little and make peace before winter.'[7]

But the Commons, though eager for war, were reluctant to vote money. Charles himself had no wish to antagonize the French, and used lack of sufficient supplies as an excuse for doing nothing. On 12 April the Commons gave the King permission to borrow £200,000 at seven per cent on the security of the additional excise, and on the following day presented him with yet another address promising to provide him with supplies for whatever arrangements he might find necessary to undertake. The King retorted three days later that what he needed was £600,000 of 'new money', adjourned Parliament for Easter, and himself retired to Newmarket. But he still refused to be pushed by his Parliament with paltry sums and empty promises into preparing for the major operation of a war against France. In fact, ignoring a bill for recalling all English forces in the service of the French King, which the Commons had read for a second time at the beginning of the session, and a resolution, which had been passed on 16 March, that 'persons who have compelled, assisted or encouraged the raising of His Majesty's subjects into the military service of the French King since the proclamation of 19 May 1675 be deemed enemies to the peace and safety of the kingdom', Charles told the French ambassador that he would facilitate further recruiting for the regiments in French service. The Commons remained equally firm. When they met again on 23 May, although it was pointed out that the King had said it would be their fault and not his if 'our security be not sufficiently provided for',[8] a fourth address was drawn up asking the King point blank 'to enter into a league, offensive and defensive, with the States-General of the United Provinces ... and to make such other alliances' as he should think useful, but not committing themselves to providing any further supplies until he had done so. The Commons aimed to dictate foreign policy, which was a recognized royal prerogative; for that reason the address was approved by only 182 votes to 142 with a considerable number of abstentions. On 28 May Charles summoned the Commons to meet him in the Banqueting House in Whitehall and rebuked them for their audacity. The King said that not only were they invading his prerogative of making peace and war, but they were presuming to dictate the alliances that he must conclude.[9] He then adjourned Parliament until 16 July.

Neither Charles nor Danby thought that the session had been a failure from his point of view. A large sum of money had been voted to the King and on the whole the court party had prevailed in the House of Commons. But both of them appreciated the depth of the anti-French feeling among the ruling classes in the kingdom and perceived that a new effort must be exerted to mediate in the war even before the campaigning season was over. Danby again argued the case on grounds of domestic policy. In a memorandum, written during June, he said that 'nothing can spoil the King's affairs at home but unsteadiness of resolution in those steps he has begun. . . . Till he can fall into the humour of the people he can never be great nor rich, and while differences continue, prerogative must suffer, unless he can live without Parliament.' But, he added, the condition of his revenue would not permit that. He therefore urged that an alliance must be concluded with the Prince of Orange that would lead to peace.[10]

That same month Charles was able to learn almost at first hand something of William's point of view. The Prince sent over to England his most intimate confident, William Bentinck, who was soon to marry an English wife, to meet the King and his Ministers. Bentinck suggested the names of towns in the Spanish Netherlands that the French might be allowed to keep, and he sought permission for William himself to come to England after the campaign was over, if peace had not been achieved by then. While Bentinck was still in London Charles held a conference with his brother James, Danby and the French ambassador, Courtin. He pointed out that he had no wish to summon his warlike Parliament again until peace had been concluded, and proposed that the French should provide him with enough money to avoid the necessity of his doing so. He then advocated a separate peace between France and the United Netherlands, and went on to outline specific terms on which such a peace could be made. He suggested that the French should retain the towns of Cambrai, Aire, St Omer, Bouchain and Valenciennes, all of which they had captured during the war, but in return should give up certain other towns farther from the French borders, which they had possessed before the war began. Charles believed, after his conversations with Bentinck, that he would be able to persuade his nephew to agree to such terms; and in order to expedite matters he was willing to recall Sir William Temple from Nymegen, where no progress had been achieved at the conference, and send him over to help negotiate peace with William. He also expressed his willingness to do what Danby wanted, which was to conclude a defensive alliance with the Dutch as soon as the war was over.

This was one of the few occasions in Charles's life in which he showed he had the makings of a statesman. However vociferous public opinion might be, as expressed in Parliament, he did not intend to be rushed into a war which he did not believe could be won and for which he thought it was highly unlikely he would be granted the necessary supplies. On the other hand, he was convinced that the differences between the Dutch and the French were not so wide that a compromise could not be reached. If he could contrive a peaceful settlement, he might become, in Danby's words, the 'redeemer of all Christendom from an universal calamity or thraldom'.[11] And, in more practical terms, the Dutch, who had suffered so many defeats at the hands of the French armies, might show their gratitude to him by conceding to Great Britain reasonable advantages in terms of trade.

But Charles found the task of a peace-maker far from easy. Before the end of June Louis XIV rejected Charles's tentative proposals and put forward much larger demands. The French view was that if their armies could maintain pressure upon the Spanish Netherlands and in Germany they could extract profitable peace terms from their enemies. Little importance was attached to Charles as a mediator; but what concerned the French was the danger that Charles should be forced by his Parliament into active military and naval co-operation with the Dutch and their allies. As early as 25 March Ralph Montagu, the English ambassador in Paris, who was an unprincipled figure in the pay of France and on close terms with the Duchess of Portsmouth, suggested through Danby that in view of the bellicose attitude of Parliament Charles was in a position to extract big subsidies from France merely as payment for his continued neutrality. It was about the same time that Louis XIV's rejection of Charles's peace proposals arrived that the King, through the mediation of Nell Gwyn, gave permission for his evil genius, the Duke of Buckingham, to come out of the Tower; while Montagu, who rightly suspected that Danby had suppressed his earlier letter, wrote at length directly to the King advising him that the time was ripe to ask Louis XIV for a substantial sum of money. Charles was growing restless under the tutelage of Danby, as previously he had been with Clarendon. Charles instructed Danby to write a letter to Paris asking Louis XIV to pay him 1,000,000 livres a year as long as the war continued and 4,000,000 livres after peace was concluded. Danby wrote much against his will and did what he could to sabotage the subsidy negotiations. This haggling over money went on for several months. Charles's main purpose in asking for the money was to enable him again to adjourn Parliament, which was due to meet on 16 July. He had no wish, at this delicate stage in negotiations, to be again subjected to parliamentary pressure to go to war.

When Sir William Temple arrived in London, Charles vainly tried to persuade him to go and see William of Orange and induce him to grant further concessions to the French. Charles explained to Temple that 'his Parliament would never be quiet nor easy to him while the war lasted abroad'. He knew that 'factious leaders' wanted to draw him into it so that they might have him completely at their mercy. He added that the longer the war continued the worse it would be for the allies. More of Flanders would be lost every day: the conduct of Spain 'must certainly ruin all in time'; therefore he was sure it was best for William of Orange to compel the Spaniards to conclude peace. But Temple, though pressed by the Duke of York and Danby as well as by the King, refused the mission because he had found William unmovable. He suggested that Laurence Hyde, the Duke of York's brother-in-law, should try his luck instead.[12]

There Charles left the matter for the time being because William of Orange was now laying siege to Charleroi in the Spanish Netherlands and, if he were successful, Charles hoped Louis might become more amenable to making peace. Indeed, though Charles may not have known this, the French themselves were tiring of the war and suffering from an economic recession. That no doubt was why French money was not offered to Charles so lavishly as Montagu had forecast. Behind Danby's back the King accepted the promise of the modest sum of £145,000[13] for an undertaking that he would again adjourn Parliament, and then went off for a fortnight's inspection of his navy in the southern ports, returning on 21 August to be entertained by the Duke of Buckingham and Nell Gwyn. But when he learned that William had been compelled to abandon the siege of Charleroi without even fighting a battle, Charles took up Temple's suggestion that he should send Hyde to Holland with instructions to inform the Prince that Charles himself did not mean to enter the war and that William would be well advised to conclude peace on the best terms he could get. Hyde was instructed to suggest the names of towns that the French should be allowed to retain in the Spanish Netherlands, and Charles offered to guarantee the new frontier. William replied that he would not accept a 'ruinous peace' and left it till the time of his own projected visit to England to resume the discussions. Meanwhile from London Courtin tried to persuade his master to increase his subsidies to Charles, saying, 'Your Majesty hazards nothing, whereas the King of England hazarded his Crown by opposing, as he did, the universal desire of his subjects [for war against France].'[14] The haggling for money continued even after Courtin had handed over his embassy to his successor, Paul Barrillon, and returned home. In the end Charles received no French money at all as the price for his prorogation of Parliament.

It has sometimes been argued that Charles II cleverly fooled the

French King by getting money out of him and giving nothing in return. But the question needs to be put in perspective. Charles, it is true, was probably not influenced in his role as a mediator by the small sums of French money that were promised; but, on the other hand, it was obvious from Parliament's attitude during the early months of 1677 that it was rabid for war against France. If Charles had been obliged to summon it to meet in the summer or autumn of that year after the Dutch defeats in Flanders, almost irresistible pressure would have been put upon him to enter into an alliance against France. As it was, this is what happened before the year was out.

William of Orange landed at Harwich on 9 October and immediately went to join his uncles at Newmarket. Charles had already told the new French ambassador, Barrillon, that Louis XIV could trust him not to break their old friendship. William refused to enter into detailed political discussions until he had met his cousin, Princess Mary; but he and Charles talked in general terms. Charles insisted that he could not ally himself with the enemies of Louis XIV, while William said that he would like to know on what terms Louis would be ready to make peace and how the security of what remained of the Spanish Netherlands could be guaranteed. After a few days at Newmarket William was taken to London and there introduced to Mary, who was now a pretty girl of fifteen. William, who was short, dark and asthmatic and spoke English with a foreign accent, was hardly a prepossessing suitor. He promptly asked for Mary's hand in marriage; the answer was delayed because Charles wanted to discuss other matters first. William threatened to return home if he did not receive the King's consent. Charles gave way. On 20 October he told Temple, who acted as an intermediary: 'If I am not deceived in the Prince's face, he is the honestest man in the world, and I will trust him, and he shall have his wife, and you shall go immediately and tell my brother so, and that it is a thing I am resolved upon.'[15]

When Mary heard the news, she 'wept all that afternoon and the following day'.[16] Charles hastened to justify the engagement to Barrillon. He said that it would put an end to the suspicions of his subjects that the friendship he had with France had no other foundation than a change of religion. He added that the whole country was afraid that he would take measures to change the religion of his kingdom and that the Duke of York's behaviour had given rise to such suspicions.

The wedding, which took place on William's birthday, 4 November, was not exactly a splendid one. Neither the Queen nor the Duke of York's second wife, who was with child, was present; the jewels, which the groom had intended to present to his bride, arrived a day too late; and Charles with avuncular jocularity pulled the curtains across the bed, saying to William: 'Now, nephew, to your work! Hey! St George for England!'[17]

As soon as the marriage was completed, Charles and William got down to hard bargaining. Eventually William conceded that his allies could not expect to keep their gains from France's ally Sweden and that the Spaniards could not expect to regain Franche-Comté; the Duke of Lorraine was to be restored to his duchy, which had been lost to France, while Philippsburg was to be exchanged for Maastricht. The difficulties arose over which towns Louis XIV was to retain in Flanders, but finally these were whittled down to Cambrai, Aire, St Omer and Bouchain and in return for them the French were to be asked to hand back not only Valenciennes and Condé, conquered during the war, but also five other towns which they had obtained by the treaty of Aix-la-Chapelle. Charles was optimistic that a peace settlement could be reached on the basis of one town more or less. On 19 November William and Mary left England and about the same time Louis Duras, Earl of Feversham, a French Huguenot in English employment, arrived in Paris carrying the proposed peace terms.

When Louis XIV learned of the marriage of William and Mary he had given orders that the latest subsidy promised to Charles II should be stopped.[18] While William had been absent in England, the French army had been besieging another Flemish town, St Ghislain, and the French King promptly rejected the peace proposals brought to him by Feversham. Although Parliament was not sitting (it had again been adjourned from 3 December 1677 to 4 April 1678) this was a grievous blow for Charles.

Barrillon reported home at the beginning of December that Charles had said to him that the siege of St Ghislain had alarmed even the moderates in England and that he was being pressed on all sides to declare war on France. Though, he said, he would rather lose his head than do this, even his own servants would abandon him if he did not conform to the sentiments of the entire nation. Laurence Hyde, who had remained at Nymegen since his abortive mission of September, had been given permission as the uncle of the bride to visit the newly-weds in Holland. He was now selected as the bearer of a proposal to William that if the United Netherlands would exert pressure on Spain to agree to the proposed peace terms, England would join with the allies to enforce them on France. Though Barrillon made a last-moment offer to Charles that England should be given some place in Flanders, if peace were not concluded, on the last day of the year Laurence Hyde signed an offensive treaty with the Dutch to compel the French to accept the agreed peace terms. Charles had already announced that Parliament would be asked to meet again not in April but on 15 January 1678. Thus, virtually against his will, Charles had been driven to the verge of war with France.

Two factors stand out in the complicated diplomatic manœuvres that filled the first three-quarters of 1678. One was that Charles II, though willing to wound, was not ready to strike. Under compulsion from the majority of his subjects assembled in Parliament and to some extent that of Danby and James, Duke of York, who was now seized with martial ambitions, Charles had at least to go through the motions of threatening France if she would not conclude peace. The second factor was that the Dutch people were tiring of a war which they had carried on for over six years and which had damaged their economic prosperity. Magnificent gestures were assumed on all sides, but very little was actually done. Only the French, who by starting the campaign early quickly captured the important towns of Ghent and Ypres, strengthened their bargaining power and by subsequently insisting on being loyal to their Swedish ally followed a realistic and consistent policy.

To begin with, Charles and his committee on foreign affairs

rejected the Anglo-Dutch treaty that had been signed by Laurence Hyde and required that it should be re-negotiated. This involved the postponement of the meeting of Parliament from 15 to 28 January 1678. When Parliament met Charles was able to announce that he had 'made such alliances with Holland as are for the preservation of Flanders'. He went on to say that he had used all the fair means in his power to procure an honourable and safe peace for Christendom, 'but finding it no longer to be hoped for by fair means, it shall not be my fault if that be not obtained by force which cannot be otherwise'. He said that he had recalled his troops from France, but required 'ninety sail of capital ships' and thirty or forty thousand soldiers. As he had been obliged to bear the charge of suppressing a rebellion in Virginia and fighting a new war with Algiers as well as finding a dowry for Princess Mary, he required 'a plentiful supply'.[19] A few days earlier he had assured the French ambassador that he would not recall the British troops in haste and that he intended no war.[20]

The House of Commons responded more than enthusiastically to Charles's speech. It did not wish merely to enforce the terms of peace put forward by Lord Feversham in November but resolved on 30 January that all trade with France should be cut off and no peace be made until France was reduced to the boundaries laid down in the treaty of the Pyrenees of 1659. On 18 February the Commons voted that a million pounds should be provided for the purpose of waging war on France. On 8 March it passed a Poll Bill which would have raised at most £300,000; and on 15 March, after the news of the fall of Ghent had been received, an address was presented to the King desiring him at once to declare war on France, recall the English representatives from Paris and Nymegen, and dismiss the French ambassador from London. In the House of Lords however Danby argued successfully that the King had not the means to go to war immediately and on 26 March, after a deadlock had developed between the two Houses, Parliament was adjourned.

Meanwhile what was Charles doing? He was hovering uncertainly between the two sides. The only positive action he had taken was to dispatch a contingent of 800 men to Ostend. But on

25 March he had instructed Danby to write a dispatch to the English ambassador in Paris outlining peace terms and adding that if these conditions were accepted, he would expect the French King to supply him with 6,000,000 livres a year for three years 'since it will probably be two or three years before Parliament will be in a humour to give him any supplies after making any peace with France'.[21] This letter was remarkable because it did not contain terms that the French King was likely to accept and it asked for a subsidy that was more than he could be expected to furnish. Possibly Danby knew this and deliberately sabotaged a policy which he feared might lead to revolution. At any rate Louis XIV rejected the proposals and Charles was driven back to use the threat of force. He tried to build up a quadruple alliance between England, the United Netherlands, Spain and the Empire but, owing to Dutch obstinacy, little progress was achieved.

When Parliament met again, it was far from satisfied with a speech by the Lord Chancellor who outlined the negotiations to date and asked Parliament's advice. Sir Thomas Clarges complained that all the addresses they had made to the King had been in favour of war, while in the Chancellor's speech they heard of nothing but peace.[22] On 4 May the Commons resolved that the treaty that had been signed with the Dutch was not pursuant to the addresses of the House nor consistent with the good and safety of the kingdom. It proceeded to vote that the King be asked to conclude alliances to carry on war against France and that the importation of French goods should be prohibited. Three days later the King was requested to remove the counsellors who had advised his answer to the last address of the Commons. In the course of the debate Sir John Berkenhead, who had once been the publicity officer of Charles I, said, 'this very 7th day of May the Rump Parliament had revived'.[23]

But the bellicosity of the Commons was now out of date, for the Dutch were engaged in negotiating a separate treaty with France and an armistice was agreed upon. Only William of Orange favoured the continuation of the war, though both his uncles wrote to him urging him to give way. On 17 May Charles agreed to the French peace terms and personally signed a treaty with the

French ambassador by which he was promised a single payment of 6,000,000 livres. Parliament had been adjourned, much against its will, on 13 May. When it met again ten days later Charles informed the members that since he had asked their advice 'the conjunctures abroad and our distempers (which influenced them so much) had driven things violently towards a peace'.[24] He thought, however, that he must keep his army and navy in being until peace was concluded. The majority in the Commons were disappointed that England had not gone to war with France and thought that the terms of the peace would be repugnant to them; but they decided that none the less peace was certain and they had no wish to leave Charles with a standing army that might even be used against them to impose arbitrary government on the kingdom. On 30 May the Commons voted a supply appropriated to pay for the disbandment of the army and to meet the additional expenditure that had been required for the navy. They also agreed to repay the £200,000 that the King had been authorized to borrow on the security of the additional excise and to accept the cost of Princess Mary's dowry.

But Charles was still not satisfied and on 18 June asked for a further £300,000 a year to guarantee peace. The Commons, partly because they feared that if they gave him this money the King might in future be able to rule without parliament, refused the request. There was good reason for their fears. For, as Danby's biographer wrote, 'there is little doubt that at this stage Danby considered the possibility of maintaining the royal authority and his own supremacy by means of the army' and that the Duke of York supported the scheme. The suspicions of Danby's motives were so wide and deep in Parliament that, according to Gilbert Burnet, he 'became the most hated Minister that had even been about the King'.[25] But at this very time Charles's attention was again directed back to foreign affairs. Louis XIV had dropped a bombshell. He had let it be known that he would refuse to conclude peace or remove his troops from any of the places which they occupied in the Spanish Netherlands until his ally, Sweden, was restored to all the possessions it had lost during the war.

The sudden introduction of this condition at the last stage of the peace negotiations galvanized the allies into action. The States-General refused to finalize the treaty while French soldiers occupied much of Spanish Flanders. In England the disbandment of the army was halted, more troops were got ready to be sent to Flanders, and Sir William Temple was dispatched to Holland to conclude a fresh treaty with the Dutch. Barrillon warned Louis XIV that Charles would not in the changed circumstances remain loyal to the Anglo-French agreement of 17 May. Thus another promised French subsidy went down the drain.

Yet the whole affair was more or less a storm in a tea-cup. After Temple had with considerable difficulty concluded a treaty with the Dutch by which the French were given a fortnight to withdraw their Swedish condition and make peace, and Charles had dispatched more troops to Flanders, Louis XIV realized that he had gone too far. A diplomatic formula was found which protected the Swedish position. Temple's bellicose treaty was repudiated in London on the ground that he had exceeded his instructions. On 21/31 July the French and Dutch signed a separate treaty at Nymegen which purchased peace at the expense of the Spaniards. France gained Franche-Comté and a rational frontier in Spanish Flanders. The French also obtained Freiburg in Breisgau and French soldiers continued to occupy Lorraine. Louis XIV considered that the war had ended gloriously for him and advantageously for his kingdom; he said that he had fought it with 'both pleasure and success'. His subjects greeted him as Louis the Great.[26] On 7/17 September the treaty was ratified with the agreement of Spain.

How far can it be claimed that Charles had contributed to the conclusion of the long war which he had helped to begin when he signed the treaty of Dover? If he had been left to himself, he would undoubtedly have continued to assist the French cause and it was not until the last moment that he showed alarm about the French overrunning Flanders. On two occasions he had overruled his Ministers in order to conclude secret pacts with France. No real effort had been exerted to come to any complete agreement with the Dutch and two out of the three Anglo-Dutch treaties were in effect repudiated. Charles had asserted in his discussions with the French ambassadors in London and also in conversations with

Danby that he had only made the gestures of preparing to ally himself with the enemies of France in order to assuage the warlike attitude of his Parliament and to extract supplies from it for his army and navy. As Courtin had written to Louis xiv on one occasion, 'I can answer for it to Your Majesty that there are none of his own subjects who wish you better success in all your undertakings than these two Princes [Charles and James] do. But it is also true that you cannot count on any except these two friends in all England.'[27] Charles had perceived in the attitude of his 'Long Parliament', which had been so enthusiastically loyal when it was first elected in 1661, a willingness to defy his prerogatives and beat him into submission to its wishes about foreign policy as well as about religion – two subjects which the last of the Tudors would never have permitted her parliaments to decide. At times Charles had allowed his own wishes on foreign policy to be subjected to the needs of his domestic policy, for he had no wish to be sent on his travels again. Nevertheless suspicion had been created between him and his Parliament which had constantly criticized his leading Ministers, as the Parliament of 1640 had attacked the Earl of Strafford. When Parliament met again, this suspicion was to be converted into such a state of frenzy that Charles had to battle for his life to preserve the continuity of the Stuart dynasty.

14

The Popish Plot and the Fall of Danby

During the early summer of 1678 the suspicions engendered between a substantial part of the House of Commons and the Court had become deep. A 'country opposition' – although not a party in any modern sense – had grown up and was held together by hostility to Charles II's principal Ministers. The dismissal of the Duke of Lauderdale, whose conduct in Scotland had been cruel and despotic, was demanded and those who advised the King in his foreign policy, the chief of whom was (wrongly) believed to be Danby, were condemned. Charles's foreign policy had obviously been a failure; in both the Dutch wars England had in effect been defeated. After his withdrawal from the second Dutch war Charles's attempt to mediate in Europe had been ignored by both sides, while he had resisted the attempt by the Commons to thrust him into the war against his former ally, France. If he was not going to fight the French, the opposition in the Commons did not understand why he needed an army. In three divisions during May the court was narrowly defeated. When on 18 June Charles had asked for an additional supply of £300,000 a year, his request was unanimously rejected. There was a widespread fear that if that had been granted, the King would have retained his army and governed without parliament. Such was the atmosphere of doubt and dissension when Charles's Long Parliament finally adjourned on 15 July.

In the dead political season of the year there began a train of events which led to the dissolution of this Long Parliament and to the overthrow of Danby, although Charles II, unlike his father, managed after a manner to remain above, if not outside, the battle: indeed the preservation of Charles's own life came to be generally regarded as a safeguard against worse things to come. On 13 August Christopher Kirkby, a chemist who was employed in the royal laboratory and was therefore known to the King, accosted Charles as he was strolling through St James's park and told him that he had learned of a Jesuit conspiracy against his life. Charles, who was aware that Kirkby was an anti-papist fanatic, referred him to his secretary, William Chiffinch, and walked on.

When Kirkby approached Chiffinch, he was refused admittance to the royal apartments in Whitehall, but Kirkby lingered in the gallery and after the King returned, he being nothing if not affable to his subjects, allowed Kirkby to speak to him and asked him how he had acquired his information about a plot. Kirkby answered that he had it from Dr Israel Tonge, a pig-head Church of England rector, who regularly preached against the papists and also dabbled in botany and alchemy. That evening Kirkby returned with Tonge, who presented the King with an indictment of forty-three articles outlining the nature of the conspiracy in general terms: the Pope had commissioned the Jesuits to overthrow the King and his government so that they might be replaced by a Roman Catholic administration under the Duke of York. Charles was either to be shot, stabbed or poisoned, whichever proved the most convenient method of dispatch. Charles, who was going to Windsor on the following day, was not impressed by this rigmarole and referred the matter to Danby. But when Danby examined Tonge, it turned out that he was not himself the author of the forty-three articles; he had only found them, but he thought he knew their author. Meanwhile he offered to discover the lodging of two of the would-be murderers who, he said, had been waiting their chance to assassinate the King in St James's park. Danby thought it his duty to go to Windsor and notify the King of these revelations. The Lord Treasurer was not without hopes that the uncovering of a conspiracy against the monarch might enable him to extract money and arms from Parliament during the next session. Nevertheless Charles was unmoved. He refused to allow Danby to take any immediate action and even forbade him to tell the story to the Duke of York.

Dr Tonge had not yet reached the end of his revelations. He asserted that the papist assassins had actually attempted to kill the King in London, but that their pistols had failed to go off; then they had decided to make a new attempt in Windsor, but their horses had gone lame. Finally it was reported to Danby that five letters from Jesuits expounding treasonable designs had been dispatched to the Duke of York's confessor, Father Bedingfield, care of the post office in Windsor. Yet when Danby himself arrived in Windsor post-haste carrying this news, he found that Bedingfield had already collected these letters and had taken them to the Duke of York, who had shown them to the King. They were obvious forgeries. Yet they made the name of Titus Oates, who was the true manufacturer of the plot and had duped Dr Tonge into being his agent.

Titus, who was now about thirty, had already enjoyed an adventurous career. His father was Samuel Oates, who, after being an active Anabaptist during the Interregnum, had become rector of a church in Hastings after the Restoration; Titus himself had been expelled both from school and college but nevertheless acquired for a time a vicarage in Kent. A homosexual, who mixed with homosexuals, he joined the Roman Catholic Church in 1677 and went for a time to an English Jesuit seminary in Spain. Later he claimed to have been awarded the degree of Doctor of Divinity at Salamanca university, but this was entirely fictitious. After his return from abroad in June 1678 he obtained or renewed an acquaintanceship with Dr Tonge. Oates was the brains of the popish plot. He was quick in repartee and impressive in manner. Roger North wrote that he was 'a low man of an ill-cut very short neck and his visage and features were most particular. His mouth was the centre of his face, and a compass that would sweep his nose, forehead and chin within a perimeter.' His chin was long and his eyes were shifty and he wore his ill-gotten doctor's robes with an air.

How did it come about that Charles met Oates and listened to his stories? After the squib of the Bedingfield letters had been exploded, Dr Tonge, as a last resort, disclosed that Oates was the author of the forty-three articles. The King was still uninterested, but in his usual lackadaisical way allowed himself to be pushed by Danby and James into agreeing to invite Tonge and Oates to appear before a committee of the Privy Council. Danby, as has been said, had his own motives for further investigation of the alleged conspiracy. James thought that, because the Bedingfield letters were so plainly fakes, the allegations of disloyalty and treachery commonly bandied about by the enemies of his fellow Roman Catholics could be easily and completely exposed. Thus the Bedingfield letters were sent to members of the council preparatory to their interview with Tonge and Oates. Oates without hesitation named the supposed authors of the letters; as he had probably written them himself, this was not so remarkable. But he created a profound impression. Yet, as Sir Robert Southwell, the clerk of the Council, wrote afterwards, 'the five letters that made his [Oates's] fame were never from that time forward produced in evidence. Oates never so much as called them to his aid from that moment.'[1]

Before he appeared at the meeting of the council Oates had on 6 September sworn to the truth of his statements (there were now eighty-three of them) before a London magistrate of repute, Sir Edmund Godfrey; and on 27 September he had left a copy of his depositions with Godfrey. The Council Board, which met on 28 September, was at first inclined to incredulity. But after Tonge had introduced Oates and Oates had done his performance with the Bedingfield letters as well as glibly outlining the meetings, consultations, contrivances and ways of proceeding of the Jesuit conspirators 'their Lordships were strangely perplexed, and generally fell into the belief that there was something formidable in this matter'.[2] They were fascinated by Oates's prodigious memory, confidence and unexpected answers. Henry Coventry, the Secretary of State, observed: 'If he be a liar, he is the greatest and adroitest I ever saw.'[3] Warrants were therefore issued for the arrest that night of six Jesuits named by Oates; one of them who, according to Oates, had been engaged to stab the King with a dagger, escaped, but the other five were clapped into Newgate prison. On the following day, which was a Sunday and Michael-mas day, Charles himself attended the council and questioned Oates. He exposed him as a liar on two points: first, Oates claimed to have seen Don Juan of Austria who, he said, was aware of the plot. Charles asked Oates what Don Juan looked like. He was tall with fair hair, answered Oates; Charles, who had seen Don Juan, knew that he was short and dark. The King also asked about a Jesuit house in Paris where Oates had asserted he had seen Père de la Chaise, one of Louis xiv's confessors, paying out £10,000 to be used as a reward for the murder of the English King. Charles happened to know that no such house stood where Oates said it did. The King concluded that Oates was a rascal and was believed, as Southwell wrote to the Duke of Ormonde two days later, 'to undervalue all this business and think it but a contrivance'.[4]

But Oates struck luckily. Among the conspirators he named in the course of his examination on 29 September was Edward Coleman, an ardent Catholic convert with a gift for languages, who had at one time been secretary to the Duke of York and subsequently secretary to the Duchess. The Council issued a warrant for his arrest and Danby gave orders that his papers should be seized. Coleman duly gave himself up after a number of letters, which he had written during the years 1674–6 to Père de la Chaise and other French Jesuits, were discovered: these letters were indiscreet in the extreme. They envisaged the ultimate ascendancy of Roman Catholicism in England, established with the aid of French money, and glorious days for the true religion when James succeeded his brother upon the throne. There was nothing in them about murder or insurrection, but then the later letters were missing and had presumably been destroyed. When Coleman's correspondence with the French Jesuits and the Papal Nuncio at Brussels was read out in Council the Lords 'were all amazed' and realized that the whole affair had become too big for them or for the judges and would have to be referred to Parliament.

The second stroke of luck for Oates was the disappearance of Sir Edmund Godfrey with whom he had left a copy of his deposi-tions. Godfrey was reported missing from his home on 12 October. Five days later his dead body was discovered in a ditch at the foot of Primrose hill. His body was transfixed with his sword. But the medical evidence indicated that he had been strangled or hanged and the sword inserted after death. As his shoes were found to be polished and the autopsy showed that he had not eaten for two days, it came to be generally accepted that he had died elsewhere earlier and his body carried to Primrose hill. Since his money was intact, it was clearly no ordinary crime. Could he have been murdered by Jesuits to stop his mouth or might he have committed suicide, Oates and his confederates afterwards getting hold of the corpse and dressing it up to look like murder?

Two conclusions about the death of Godfrey appear to be well established. The first is that he was on friendly terms with Coleman and had actually warned him after he had read Oates's depositions. The second is that he could hardly have been murdered because he had been the recipient of a copy of the depositions, since a duplicate copy had been made available to the Lords of the Privy Council before he died. Godfrey was a bachelor who was known to suffer from hereditary melancholia, and he was a highly conscientious magistrate. It has been argued that the decision he took to warn Coleman may have preyed on his mind and that he might have hanged himself. Charles II, when he heard the story, certainly believed that Godfrey had committed suicide.[5] But the coroner's jury brought in a verdict of murder and most people thought that the murderers were Jesuits. Thus 'the plot' proved 'the murder' and 'the murder' proved 'the plot'.[6] Later, generous rewards having been offered, two different informers came forward to swear that they had seen Godfrey's dead body in Somerset house, the residence of Charles's Queen. And although their stories completely contradicted each other, three servants in Somerset house were ultimately convicted of the murder and hanged at Tyburn, protesting their innocence to the last.

After his exposure of Oates as a liar on 29 September Charles had gone, as usual, to Newmarket and he did not return to London until the day before the discovery of Godfrey's body. The King had not been in the least convinced by Oates's stories nor by the forged letters to Bedingfield found at Windsor. He therefore did his best to protect the Jesuits named by Oates. He gave orders that the Attorney General should refer the evidence to the judges, for he 'was not willing to have these men hurried off or their blood taken in a case so improbable, and because, if without more circumstance they were left to the mercy of a jury, he foresaw what must happen'.[7] But he was incensed against Coleman to the last degree. He fully realized that the publication of the impounded letters would set Parliament aflame; and he also expressed 'much displeasure against the sect of Jesuits, of whom there being a list of nearly three hundred in England, incorporated and working by steady rules to disquiet the peace and religion of others'. The King was determined 'to send them packing'.[8] In general Charles tried to cool the atmosphere in Whitehall after he came back from Newmarket, but the indignation aroused over Godfrey was such that it was clear that there would be an uproar as soon as Parliament met and any neglect by the Government to investigate the full story of the alleged plot against the King would provoke censure.

So far as his own personal safety was concerned Charles had good reason to keep calm. He had ample cause to believe that Titus Oates was a professional perjurer and he discounted stories of plots against his own life. He had faced much more dangerous situations when he had been fighting at and escaping from Worcester or when he had battled with the Earl of Warwick on the high seas. It was hard for him to appreciate that the mysterious death of a London magistrate or the obscurities of Coleman's letters (which had not yet been published) would endanger his throne. It was not until he perceived the attitude of Parliament that he began to scent the possibility of a rebellion against his government.

When Parliament first met on 21 October the attendance was sparse, possibly because the news of the sensational events in London had not yet penetrated to the provinces. In his opening speech Charles defended his decision not to disband the army. He had kept it in being 'for the well securing of what was left of Flanders and for keeping his neighbours from despair'. He argued that the money voted for disbandment was not ill employed in contributing to the peaceful settlement that was now being completed in Europe. Nevertheless he was out of pocket and the revenue was 'under great anticipations'. All he had to say about the popish plot was that he had been informed of a design against his person, 'but forebore to give his own opinions lest he should seem to say too much or too little'; he would leave the matter to the law.[9] In private he told Sir John Reresby two days later he did not believe one word of the plot.

But the country opposition, headed by Shaftesbury and Buckingham, still smarting over their earlier imprisonment in the Tower, was not to be fobbed off. Its objective was to break up the triumvirate of Charles, James and Danby and to destroy the existing House of Commons by raising a hue-and-cry against the papists. Shaftesbury, now a sick, ageing and bitter man, had not been behind Oates's revelations (he had been at his home in Dorset since Parliament rose). As he observed later, 'I will not say who started the Game, but I am sure I had the full hunting of it.'[10] Charles himself nevertheless believed that the Earl had been concerned from the beginning. Both Houses of Parliament proceeded to set up secret committees to inquire into the plot. On 28 October Oates gave information to the House of Commons, particularly against Hortense Mancini, who had recently arrived in England, maintaining that all agents resorted to her.[11] Charles might well have reflected that as his wife and principal mistresses were Roman Catholics (Nell Gwyn always boasted that she was 'the Protestant whore'), and that as he had committed himself to declaring himself a Roman Catholic eight years before, it was hardly likely that Roman Catholic agents would scheme to take his life.

But Members of Parliament were moved by the assumption that the King was the destined victim of a widespread Catholic conspiracy. On 26 October the Commons asked that all papist recusants should be expelled from the royal palaces and on 2 November Shaftesbury proposed that the House of Lords should agree with a unanimous resolution of the Commons 'that this House is of opinion, that there hath been and still is, a damnable and hellish plot contrived and carried on by Popish Recusants for the assassinating and murdering of the King, and for subverting the Government and rooting out and destroying the Protestant religion'.[12] The Earl went on to propose that James, Duke of York, as an acknowledged Catholic, should be expelled from the King's council. Two days later Lord Russell moved the same resolution in the House of Commons and on that day James himself (under pressure from his brother) declared in the House of Lords that for the present he would take no further part in public business.

But the House of Commons was by no means satisfied. It had learned about Coleman's correspondence and assumed that it had been started with the Duke's approval. At the same time one of the informers who asserted that Godfrey had been murdered in Somerset house, by name William Bedloe, a disreputable rogue from Bristol, appeared on the London scene and was taken up by Shaftesbury. The Commons quickly passed a new Test Bill excluding all Roman Catholics from membership of either House of Parliament (this was sent up to the Lords on 28 October) and the idea was even mooted for the first time of excluding James from the succession to the throne.

Charles did his utmost to assuage the tense feelings in Parliament. On 9 November he summoned the two Houses to meet him, thanked them for their care of his person and government, and declared that he would be ready to give his consent to such reasonable bills as should be presented to him to make them safe in the reign of any successor, provided that they did not tend to impeach the right of succession nor the descent of the Crown in the true line. Five days later the King agreed to tender oaths of allegiance and supremacy to all except his menial servants. But though Charles tried to be conciliatory, he refused to allow what he regarded as his own rights to be infringed. Thus he would not require all the Queen's servants, most of whom were Roman Catholics, to be put on oath. When on 18 November the House of Commons ordered the Secretary of State, Sir Joseph Williamson, to be sent to the Tower on the ground that he had given commissions to Roman Catholic officers, Charles at once ordered his release; and when Oates and Bedloe accused Queen Catherine of complicity in the plots against her husband, he told Dr Burnet that 'though she was a weak woman and had some disagreeable humours', she was 'not capable of a wicked thing: and considering his faultiness towards her in other things, he thought it a horrid thing to abandon her'.[13]

Neither the opposition's plan to force Charles to divorce his Queen (and by marrying again provide a Protestant heir) nor its attempt to separate James and Danby worked. A proposed address to exclude the Queen from court was easily defeated in the House of Lords. It is true that when the question of removing the Duke from the King's presence and counsels had been discussed Danby and his friends put up a rather tepid defence. But when the Test Bill proposing the exclusion of Roman Catholics from Parliament was debated, Danby, by exerting all his influence, managed to carry an amendment excepting the Duke of York from its provisions. Four days after this success of the court party, Charles tried to induce Parliament to turn its attention to foreign affairs. He asked permission to keep his army in Flanders, as the Spaniards wished him to do so. But the Commons immediately voted the disbandment of all forces raised since 29 September 1677 and instead introduced a bill to raise a militia. The King, remembering what had happened to his father, refused to give his assent to the bill to raise a militia on the ground that it was an infringement of his prerogative. The opposition, having thus been thwarted in different ways by the firmness of the King, now resumed its attack on Danby.

During the month of December 1678, when Charles rejected the militia bill and when the movement against Danby was gathering momentum, Dr Gilbert Burnet, that indefatigable and (on the whole) accurate chronicler of his times, often saw the monarch and to him is owed an insight into Charles's opinions.[14] The King insisted that the whole story of the popish plot, though now heightened and deepened by many new informers, was 'a contrivance', which he thought had been designed by Shaftesbury. Burnet pointed out that although he had accused nearly everyone else, Oates had not named the Duke of York, who was the main objective of Shaftesbury's manœuvres. Charles said he thought there was 'a design of rebellion on foot' aimed against the monarchy. Burnet did not believe this, but asked him if he intended to legitimize his eldest bastard, the Duke of Monmouth, thus providing a Protestant alternative to James as his successor. Charles 'answered quick that, as well as he loved him, he had rather see him hanged'. Burnet then suggested that Charles should bring pressure to bear on James to change his religion again. After all, Charles's grandfather, Henri IV of France, had thought that the throne was worth a Mass. But Charles answered 'that his brother had neither Henry IV's understanding nor his conscience; for he believed that King was always indifferent as to those matters'. Burnet thought that Charles had promised not to speak to his brother about religion. The Doctor then went on to tell the King how odious the Earl of Danby was. Charles said that he realized that the removal of Danby 'lay at the bottom' of the present movement in Parliament. Thus what emerged from these conversations was Charles's determination to preserve James's right of succession and to protect his chief Minister.

It was not until the middle of December that Charles had reason to grow alarmed over the behaviour of Parliament. He had acquiesced in the execution of Coleman, against whom the only solid evidence of a popish plot had been produced and who, he thought, deserved his fate. He had given his assent to the second Test Act. On the other hand, the accusations against the Queen, brought forward by Oates, had been rejected. James had been excluded from the scope of the Test and although he had ceased to attend meetings of the Cabinet Council, he was still by the King's side in Whitehall. Though three Jesuits, accused by Oates and Bedloe, had been convicted and five Roman Catholic peers, who had been named by Oates as potential members of a papist administration, were imprisoned in the Tower, no more blood had yet been shed. Moreover Charles had successfully defended his prerogatives, notably in regard to the control of the militia. So far an attack on Danby had not developed. But now it was to come.

Ralph Montagu, a known enemy of Danby, had been the English ambassador in Paris during the Franco-Dutch war and the recipient of letters from Danby, written at the King's command, asking for a subsidy from Louis XIV as the price for England remaining neutral in the war. In the summer Danby snubbed Montagu by refusing to allow him to buy the office of Secretary of State from Henry Coventry. Moreover the Duchess of Cleveland (formerly Charles's mistress, Barbara, Countess of Castlemaine), now enjoying the late summer of her life in Paris, had written a spiteful letter to the King reporting opprobrious remarks made by Montagu, that 'most abominable man', about Charles, his brother and his government.[15] Montagu had come over without permission from Paris to London to defend himself against these accusations; but Charles had dismissed him from his embassy and struck his name off the Privy Council. Montagu determined to revenge himself, and having been elected a Member of Parliament at a by-election he awaited his opportunity. Both Charles and Danby were aware of the danger that Montagu might disclose their secret correspondence in the House of Commons, but hoped that he would not do so because he would thereby incriminate himself. As a precaution, however, after the receipt of evidence that Montagu, when in Paris, had been engaged in intrigues with the Papal Nuncio there, Charles had on 19 December summoned an extraordinary meeting of the Cabinet Council where it had been decided to surround Montagu's house with King's messengers and impound all Montagu's papers. Charles then informed the Commons of Montagu's disloyalty and disobedience. But Montagu had protected himself from arrest by his membership of the Commons and taken care to hide some of the most damaging of his papers. On 20 December Montagu gave to the Speaker a letter written by Danby on 25 March asking Louis XIV for six million livres a year for three years after the conclusion of peace on the ground that if such a peace were made, he could not expect Parliament to grant the King any further supplies. The House was shocked by this revelation. Danby vainly tried to counter-attack by maintaining that members of the House of Commons, including Lord Russell, had actually been in receipt of French money. This was true enough, though Russell and his friends flatly denied it. On 21 December articles of impeachment were drawn up by the Commons against Danby accusing him of planning to overthrow the constitution with the aid of a standing army and French money.

On 23 December the articles of impeachment were presented to the House of Lords. Danby defended himself with spirit. After all, the King himself had written on the draft of the damaging dispatch, 'I approve this letter'.[16] Whether or not these words were written at the time has been debated by historians, but it was obvious enough to the House of Lords that Danby, who was known to have favoured an anti-French policy, had sent this dispatch on the King's orders. The majority in the House therefore refused to commit Danby to the Tower and gave him time to draw up a detailed reply to the articles of impeachment. On 30 December Charles suddenly prorogued Parliament, telling the two Houses that he had 'not been well used by them' and that he intended to get to 'the bottom of the Plot'. On the following morning he declared in Council that he would set up a committee to sit from day to day to inquire into the plot and the murder; he said that he would hasten the disbandment of the army, being 'resolved to restrict expenses and rather live as a private man than compass that work'; and he ordered Danby to stop 'all manner of payments'.[17] Afterwards Charles saw the Lord Mayor and Aldermen of the City of London and assured them, as he had assured the Houses of Parliament, that he would 'preserve peace, the Protestant religion and trade and would presently pay off the army to show the world he intended not to rule that way'.[18]

During the first two and a half months of 1679 Charles worked with unaccustomed energy to strengthen his government. It has sometimes been assumed that his decision to put an end to Parliament at the close of 1678 was taken in order to save Danby. That was not the case; as Danby's biographer has pointed out, the Lord Treasurer was satisfied with the way that things were going, and had a deadlock developed between the two Houses over his fate he might well hope to re-establish his position.[19] After all, the House of Commons, which had originally been elected in 1661, although its membership had been changed by hundreds of by-elections, had until the emergence of Oates never been consistently hostile to the court. To begin with, it had been exceptionally loyal. In turn the Earl of Clarendon, the Earl of Arlington (assisted by Thomas Clifford) and Danby himself had shown themselves capable of managing the House, relying especially on large numbers of placemen and pensioners, even though some of them had not always been docile. Danby had created a clientele of members under obligation to him for pensions paid indirectly by the excise farmers. Danby thought that he could still keep the Commons under control by punishing members who had voted against the government through withdrawing their pensions or dismissing them from their offices.

But Charles himself did not share the optimistic view of his chief Minister. He could remember only too clearly the events of 1641 which had led to Parliament taking up arms against his father. As he told Burnet, he genuinely feared a rebellion against him. He was also haunted by another memory. He was unhappy about the fate of the Jesuit priests and Roman Catholic peers whose lives Oates was busily trying to swear away. Finally, what might happen to his faithful servant, Danby, who had been accused by Shaftesbury and his followers of high treason merely for obeying his master's wishes? No wonder Charles was heard to say that 'he remembered what his father had suffered from consenting to the Earl of Strafford's death'.[20] Shaftesbury, as his latest biographer admits, was using every episode and every perjured informer who came his way to procure his political aims.[21]

About the middle of January, with the permission of the King, Danby entered into negotiations with some of the members of the 'country party'. These included the aged Lord Holles who, under the name of Denzil Holles, had been the inveterate foe of Oliver Cromwell, and Richard Hampden, who was the son of John Hampden of ship money fame. The proposal was that Charles should undertake to disband his army and summon a freely elected Parliament; in return for this Holles and his friends promised to raise funds necessary for the disbandment and also to grant the King an additional supply of money. They were not prepared to entrust the Lord Treasurer with the money, but offered to let him off lightly if he resigned his office. It does not seem that these moderates carried any decisive weight in the House of Commons and they certainly had no right to speak for Shaftesbury, who was the real leader of the country opposition.[22] Charles accepted these undertakings seriously. One advantage of the arrangement, it has been suggested, was that the King was thereby relieved of any anxieties over revelations that might be forthcoming about his own dealings with the French Court if Danby were subjected to impeachment proceedings. The Duke of York also favoured the calling of a new Parliament, according to Burnet, because 'he thought a new parliament would act in a milder strain and would not fly so high'.[23]

In the end Charles, having assimilated the advice that he had been given, made up his own mind and, without consulting his council, announced on 24 January 1679 the dissolution of the Parliament that had sat for nearly eighteen years. Certain changes were made in his government. Sir Joseph Williamson, the unpopular Secretary of State for the North, was replaced by the ambitious and clever Robert Spencer, second Earl of Sunderland, and the other Secretaryship was again offered to Sir William Temple, who had acquired a reputation as the friend of the Dutch. The Solicitor General, who had been active in forwarding Danby's impeachment, was replaced. After a vain attempt had been made by the Archbishop of Canterbury to convert the Duke of York back to the Church of England, Charles signed an order instructing his brother to go abroad. He told him that if he did not return to the Church of England he must for some time remain beyond sea or else Parliament would be incensed.[24] To ensure that Monmouth should not be taken up as the Protestant heir to the throne, the King formally declared in Council that he had never been married to any woman but the Queen. Danby carried out his purge of former Members of Parliament who had held offices and yet voted against the court. Finally, as to Danby himself, Charles insisted upon his accepting a free pardon under the Great Seal for all offences he had committed before 27 February 1679. Seven days after the new Parliament met the King asked Danby for his resignation and offered him a pension of £5,000 a year for life and the rank of Marquis.

The elections, as was customary in the seventeenth century, were largely determined by local factors and influences and not by party organization: in fact parties did not yet exist. But the Crown was able to exert influence and patronage, notably in ports where the Admiralty provided employment; and some of the Lords Lieutenant did what they could for the Court. On the other side, Shaftesbury issued propaganda literature from his headquarters in the City of London which was distributed in some of the larger towns. 'The number of contested elections in 1679', writes Professor J. R. Jones, who has investigated the question thoroughly, 'was an indication of the intense passions aroused and the violence of partisan feeling.'[25] On the whole it is safe to say that the opposition to the court won considerable successes in London, many of the counties and most of the bigger boroughs. When Shaftesbury came to analyse the results, he concluded that 302 opposition members had been elected as againt 158 courtiers.[26] This was at least better for Charles than the gloomy estimate of the French ambassador in London that the court could only count on forty votes. As 245 new members were elected, nobody could be absolutely certain how the new House of Commons would behave. Charles even persuaded himself that it might be more moderate than the last one. But the fact remains that even in its last year Charles II's Cavalier Parliament sometimes divided in favour of the court and that, on the whole, court and country were pretty evenly balanced. Though some historians have maintained that the dissolution was 'inevitable', from his own point of view Charles seems to have made a mistake of judgment. For would not the conciliatory steps he had taken at the beginning of 1679 have made more of an impression on the preceding parliament?

When Charles II opened Parliament on 6 March he put forward a plea for national unity. 'I meet you with the most earnest desire that man can have to unite the minds of my subjects both to me, and to one another. And I resolve it shall be your faults, if the success be not suitable to my desires.'[27] He drew the attention of the two Houses to what had been done to put an end to the popish plot: the exclusion of the popish lords from their seats in Parliament and 'the execution of several ill men upon the score of the plot and the murder of Godfrey'; the execution of Coleman in December, of two of the three Jesuits named by Oates in January (Charles vainly tried to reprieve the third of them) and of the alleged murderers of Godfrey in February. He said that he had disbanded as much of the army as he could with the money available to him. Above all, he emphasized that he had sent his brother away from him. He then asked for a supply to pay off the rest of the army, to maintain the fleet, and to meet his debts. In particular he mentioned the loss in customs revenue that he had suffered by the embargo imposed on the importation of French wines and brandy. He promised to continue to investigate the plot and the murder. But he pleaded with the two Houses to employ their time upon the concerns of the nation and not to be drawn into private animosities. He hoped that they would 'curb the motions of unruly spirits'; for 'there can be no man that must not see how fatal differences amongst ourselves are like to be at this time both at home and abroad'. In order to exercise some control over the Commons Charles tried to obtain a congenial Speaker. Sir Edward Seymour (the former Speaker), though in his later years he was to acquire the reputation of being an out-and-out Tory, was unfriendly to Danby and the court put forward the name of Sir Thomas Meres, although he had been a member of the opposition. Eventually a compromise candidate was found in a colourless lawyer named William Gregory. This episode only succeeded in irritating the House against the government. Moreover in refusing to accept Seymour Charles had committed a mistake; for Seymour was soon to reveal himself an opponent of the exclusion of James from the throne.

The new Parliament at once showed that it was not going to be diverted from its investigations into the popish plot or the impeachment of Danby. The House of Commons established a new secret committee of inquiry and concerned itself with the fate of the five peers in the Tower. Moreover the resignation of Danby on 13 March did not appease Parliament, for it had leaked out not only that he had been given a pardon by the King and rewards for his services on laying down his office, but that two of the members of the Treasury Commission which was to take over his duties were his personal friends. On 20 March the Commons reminded the Lords that the impeachment proceedings against Danby as against the five peers still stood, and asked that, like them, he should be taken into custody. Charles did his utmost for Danby. On 22 March he summoned the two Houses before him and assured them that Danby was innocent of the charges laid against him, that the letters to Montagu had been written at his command, and that he had given him a full pardon, which, if it were defective, he would repeat if necessary ten times over.[28] Nevertheless on the following day Charles ordered Danby to go into hiding and on the day after that he advised him to flee abroad. Charles had recognized the temper of Parliament; for on 24 March he had received an address from the Commons about the irregularity of Danby's pardon, and Black Rod had been ordered by the Lords to place him under arrest. One of the absurd accusations made against Danby in the Commons was that the army that had been raised was 'a limb of popery' set up by him to destroy Parliament.[29]

The two Houses now proceeded to disagree about how Danby should be punished. The Lords favoured an act of banishment, the Commons an act of attainder. Eventually a compromise was reached; it was decided that if Danby did not give himself up by a specified date, a bill of attainder should be submitted to the King. Charles still wanted Danby to go into exile abroad, as the Earl of Clarendon had done, thus preserving his life. But Danby was a younger and tougher statesman than Clarendon; he was not conscious of having committed any crime; he had merely obeyed the King's orders; he did not regard his political career at an end; nor in fact was it. He therefore asked the King's permission to surrender to Black Rod; on 16 April he appeared at the bar of the House of Lords who committed him to the Tower.

The fall of Danby marks the close of a stage in the career of Charles II as a statesman. Except possibly for a few months at the beginning of his reign he had in effect always been his own Prime Minister. It must be remembered that in those days before political inform and social welfare became the principal concern of governments, the main duty of the executive was to look after foreign affairs and defence. Even today this is a major function of great powers. But in those days when war was endemic, the King's working hours were largely devoted to questions of war and peace. Charles took his own decisions on these matters (although he had to some extent been pushed into his first Dutch war and pushed out of his second one). His leading Ministers were expected to supervise the day-to-day affairs of the kingdom and, above all, to handle Parliament – a problem virtually unknown to other European kings. Thus in turn Clarendon, Arlington and Danby had done their best to keep the Parliament, which first met in 1661, friendly to the King. But unlike Robert Walpole or Henry Pelham, who in the eighteenth century acted as intermediaries between the monarch and Parliament, none of these statesmen were members of the House of Commons and had to rely on colleagues or agents. None of them was successful for long: Clarendon went into banishment abroad; Arlington was 'kicked upstairs'; Danby was committed to the Tower. And in fact the House of Commons took long constitutional strides forward. The Commons's right to appropriate supply was firmly established; the King's right to employ non-Anglicans in his service was denied by statute; and his attempts to confer a degree of religious toleration on his subjects by declarations of indulgence were firmly resisted. The Commons had tried, sometimes with success, to use the power of the purse, finally won in the reign of Charles I, to dictate to the King on questions of foreign policy and defence. Only Charles's own determination had prevented Parliament asserting control over the militia, a demand which, when denied by his father, had led directly to the first civil war.

But Charles had of course been able, to some extent, to shelter behind his Ministers from parliamentary onslaughts on his powers and prerogatives. Like his father, he was said to have been badly advised. Moreover the fact that the inventors of the popish plot had insisted that the main design of the conspiracy was to murder him invoked a sense of loyalty to his person: there was virtually no republican movement in the first twenty years of his reign.[30] But after the attempt to attaint Danby, Charles realized that if he were to preserve the Stuart dynasty and the authority of the monarchy he could no longer rely on anyone but himself. If, as was commonly said, a triumvirate of the King, Duke of York and Earl of Danby had ruled the country in the middle seventies, it had now been completely shattered. Charles had from henceforward to employ his own abilities, if not as a statesman, at least as a consummate politician, to rescue 'the royal authority from the dangers which beset it amid the strife of warring factions'.[31]

15

Exclusion–1

Charles was at a loss without his Lord Treasurer, Danby. But he was a good judge of able politicians and competent administrators. He persuaded the Earl of Essex, an upright member of the country opposition, to head the new Treasury Commission and Sidney Godolphin, who was to disclose his brilliance as a financier in Queen Anne's reign, to become a Lord of the Treasury. The secretary of the Commission, Henry Guy, was also a man of first-rate capacity. The Earl of Sunderland, the new Secretary of State for the North, though still an apprentice politician, was soon to master the arts of administration and was particularly valuable to Charles as an intermediary between the leaders of the court and the opposition: he was on equally friendly terms with the Duchess of Portsmouth and the Earl of Shaftesbury. For a third time the King offered the other Secretaryship of State to Sir William Temple after his return from the peace conference at Nymegen. Temple tendered his humble excuses 'for not putting His Majesty upon the use of an old beaten horse in which hard service as I took that station to be';[1] but he was willing to serve in the Privy Council and give Charles his confidential advice. Temple wrote in his memoirs: 'I never saw any man more sensible of the miserable condition of his affairs than I found His Majesty upon many discussions with him. . . . But nothing he said to me moved me more than when he told me he had none left with whom he could so much as speak to them in confidence since my Lord Treasurer's being gone.'[2]

In fact Danby continued to give Charles advice from the Tower of London. But it was of a violent character. He pressed Charles to take control of the army, navy and garrisons and secure the

Tower so as to deal with a possible insurrection. The King, he thought, should appeal to the nation at large against the unreasonable conduct of the House of Commons and then dissolve and summon a new one to meet outside London.

Charles wisely considered that the time was not yet ripe for any such extreme measures. Instead he accepted a suggestion from Temple that he should form a new Privy Council in order that, as he told Parliament, he might be guided by it on 'weighty and important affairs' next to the advice of Parliament itself. Sir William, who was an honest man, if somewhat naïve, recorded that 'the whole matter was consulted and deduced upon paper, only between the King and me, and lasted in debate and digestion about a month'.[3] There is little doubt that the King's principal mistress and his son, the Duke of Monmouth, were consulted and approved. Earlier the King had settled his affairs in his foreign committee or committee of foreign affairs, the precursors of the modern Cabinet, while the Privy Council had become a largely formal body. The new council was to consist of thirty-three members including a Lord President, the princes of the blood, fifteen official members and ten lords and five commoners in effect drawn from the opposition. The remodelled council had two purposes: to bring the leaders of the country party into the royal counsels; and to enable the King to govern by the constant advice of his council. The King was at first reluctant to include a rising statesman, George Savile, Lord Halifax, who had been a prominent believer in the popish plot and the enemy of the Queen. After he was persuaded to do so, Charles said that in that case he might as well enlist the Earl of Shaftesbury too, who, if he were left out, 'might do as much mischief as any'. And since Charles feared Shaftesbury would not be content with an ordinary councillor's place, he revived for his benefit the office of Lord President. Charles obviously hoped that once Shaftesbury obtained office again he would become more friendly to the court.

The new council, whose formation was announced to Parliament the day after Easter, was not optimistically received, although the Lord Mayor of London was instructed to light bonfires in its honour. How genuine were Charles's intentions? According to the memoirs of the Earl of Ailesbury, published many years later, Charles said that the new council should sit only for form's sake and was not to be let into any secret of State. 'God's fish!' he added, 'they have put a set of men about me but they shall know nothing.'[4] It is true that to a man of so much political experience as the King the number of thirty-three must plainly have been unwieldy. On the other hand, the council was immediately (on 22 April) divided into four committees, for Intelligence, Ireland, Tangier, and Trade and Plantations. The first committee, consisting of nine members, was the most important and of this Shaftesbury was a member. So too were Halifax, Essex and Russell. One should not therefore too lightly assume, on the basis of Ailesbury's memoirs, that the King was insincere in his intentions. He wanted to prove to Parliament that he had broken completely with Danby and Danby's 'creatures', and may well have experienced a hope that these rich and powerful magnates would offset the passions of the House of Commons and also create divisions between the opposition and its leaders. As Burnet wrote, 'the King was weary of the vexation he had been long in, and desired to be set at ease'.[5]

On 27 April 1679 the Commons voted unanimously that the Duke of York, being a papist, encouraged conspiracies against the King and the Protestant religion. Two days later Charles summoned an extraordinary meeting of his new Privy Council and it was there agreed that specific constitutional limitations should be imposed on the monarchy if a papist king succeeded to the throne. Such a king should be allowed no control over ecclesiastical or judicial appointments, and a Parliament should immediately reassemble on his succession. Only the Earl of Shaftesbury opposed this proposal in council; Halifax (who was Shaftesbury's nephew by marriage) strongly favoured it and indeed the idea may have originated with him.

Next day, after Charles had asked the House of Commons to be put in mind of three particulars: the prosecution of the plot, the disbanding of the army, and the provision of the fleet, the scheme for limiting the authority of a popish successor was outlined to Parliament by the Lord Chancellor, Lord Finch, on behalf of the King. The initial reception of the proposal in the House of Commons was enthusiastic.[6] But by the time the debate was resumed on Sunday, 11 May the mood had changed, and while the new councillors still supported the scheme of limitations Shaftesbury's followers, such as Thomas Bennett, were rabid for James's exclusion from the succession. By the time that the candles were lit that Sunday evening it was obvious that the court had lost ground. The argument was used that no laws could be devised which would actually be effective in binding a popish king. Four days later the Exclusion Bill received its first reading.

A day earlier the King send an urgent message to the Commons about the need for having a fleet at sea during the summer, in the hope that the necessary supplies would be voted. Most leading politicians still feared the power of France after Louis XIV's success at the conference of Nymegen, and were anxious to build up an alliance in case Flanders should again be subjected to French attack. The British contribution to such an alliance would be the fleet, and Charles's new councillors favoured the provision of a supply for the purpose. Those councillors who were members of the House of Commons therefore put the case for immediately having a fleet at sea. But the majority of the members were now determined on exclusion and nothing but exclusion. They regarded questions of foreign policy or defence as mere diversions on the part of the King. It is reasonable to assume that Charles himself was becoming disillusioned about his new Privy Council since its members had failed either to push through the policy of limitations or to obtain money for the navy. On 21 May the second reading of the Exclusion Bill was carried in the Commons by 207 votes to 128. The Commons did not hurry over a third reading, however, because they were rightly afraid that the House of Lords would reject the bill. Complicated disputes had developed between the two Houses over the trial of Danby and of the five Roman Catholic peers accused by Titus Oates. Charles regarded this quarrel as his opportunity. Taking the advice of Halifax, Essex and Sunderland, but without bothering to consult the whole Privy Council, the King prorogued Parliament on 27 May until 14 August. Before he did so, he gave his assent to the Habeas

Corpus Amendment Act, the only bill passed in this session by the two Houses of Parliament.

Although the prorogation of Parliament gave Charles some respite from his difficulties, the popish plot was still in full swing: on 20 June five Jesuits were executed; in the following month the Queen's physician, Sir George Wakeman, was put on trial for his life; and in the autumn a new informer named Willoughby or Dangerfield came forward and, after he had tried to sell the idea of a Presbyterian plot to the King and his brother, changed his story and asserted that he had been hired by papists to bring false charges. In the second place, the King had to contend with a rebellion in Scotland. That country had been badly treated since the Restoration. Bishops had been imposed on an unwilling Presbyterian Kirk; the Dutch wars had damaged the Scottish export trade; and the Duke of Lauderdale had upon a trifling excuse quartered a 'highland host' upon the Covenanters of the western lowlands and subjected them to six weeks of plunder. Provoked by this and by the penal laws fastened upon the exercise of their religion – services were defiantly held in open-air conventicles – the Archbishop of St Andrews was murdered and a small band of insurgents gathered near Glasgow. On 7 June a meeting of the Privy Council was summoned to discuss the rebellion and Shaftesbury and Russell blamed it on Lauderdale, the King's Commissioner in Scotland, who was present. But Charles defended his Commissioner, who had extracted money from the Scots and raised an army for him there, and he dispatched the Duke of Monmouth with ample forces to put down the rebellion. Shaftesbury seems to have hoped that the rebellion would compel the King to seek help from Parliament, as Charles I had been obliged to do forty years earlier. But Charles II was firmer and better prepared than his father had been. Monmouth's easy victory at Bothwell Bridge and his merciful treatment of the rebels raised him in the public esteem and frustrated Shaftesbury's attempt to force the King to recall the English Parliament.

Nevertheless Charles's principal advisers – Essex, Halifax and Sunderland, known as the Triumvirate – were afraid that Monmouth's popularity would induce Shaftesbury to sponsor him as a Protestant successor to the throne and thus give a focus to the exclusionist movement in the House of Commons when it met again. (In this they were wrong, for Monmouth was certainly not at this stage Shaftesbury's candidate for the throne.) They therefore urged Charles to dissolve the existing Parliament. On 3 July Charles raised the question in his Privy Council where the majority spoke against the proposal. A week later the King made up his own mind. He told the council on 10 July that he was determined to dissolve Parliament immediately and he asked for no opinions. Shaftesbury vainly tried to protest. But the King said that he was fully convinced of the necessity of a dissolution and that he was not compelled to adhere to the majority view of the council: the calling and dissolving of parliaments was a royal prerogative. That was in effect the end of Temple's constitutional experiment.

Charles, ever resilient, had evidently decided that the policy of trying to reconcile his political opponents was useless, though he recognized that his own position was precarious. Indeed in the previous May a Member of Parliament, Sir Hugh Cholmley, had insisted that 'if maxims etc are not changed, it is to no purpose to remove Ministers'. He was obliged to apologize for this remark, but it was plain to the King that he could no longer shelter behind the backs of his Ministers, but must fight his own battles. He had overruled his Privy Council on the question of dissolution even though only four members of the board agreed with him. He hoped that the new House of Commons, which was to be elected in August and September, would be more favourable to him; he relied on Sunderland and other courtiers to use their influence on his behalf; and instructions were sent to Lords Lieutenant to do what they could to help. In the second place, Charles approached the French ambassador, Barrillon, to see whether the French King would help him out with a grant of money; he excused the persecution of English Roman Catholics as best he could and hinted that if such assistance were not forthcoming he might be forcibly drawn into an alliance against France. Lastly he was cheered by the acquittal of Sir George Wakeman at his trial on 18 July. He had been afraid that if Wakeman had been convicted the Queen would be 'injuriously reflected upon'. It has been suggested that Lord Chief Justice Scroggs, who had presided over the trial and summed up in the prisoner's favour, though he was no friend to Catholics, had been influenced by the King; but there is no clear evidence of that. When at the beginning of August the last meeting of the Privy Council was held until October and Shaftesbury protested at Scroggs's behaviour, Charles retorted that 'if men proceeded according to their consciences he knew no fault they had done'.[7]

On 19 August Charles played a game of tennis; and after he had been in bed and rubbed he walked for a long time by the river at Windsor. Next day he fell ill and on the following day he developed a heavy chill. Now the doctors played their characteristic part: first they purged him sixteen or seventeen times, and two days later he was blooded sixteen ounces and again was purged and vomited. No wonder that the courtiers thought the King was dying. His brother James was sent for from his exile in Brussels. Here then was a political crisis not of the King's making. What if James should succeed to the throne with full authority, no exclusion bill having been passed, while the popish plot agitation had still not subsided? Even if Charles recovered from the attentions of his doctors – as soon he did – James was stiff and obstinate; and if he had been allowed to stay by his brother's side he might have persuaded him to embark on drastic or despotic courses. James remained in England for a month and during this time it became evident that the elections were going against the government. Another exclusionist House of Commons was likely to assemble, if Parliament met, as Charles had promised, at the beginning of October.

But Charles played it cool. Taking advice from Halifax and Essex, he told his brother that he must again leave England, but instead of returning him to his exile in Brussels he allowed him to fetch his wife and go with her to Edinburgh to act as the Royal Commissioner in Scotland. At the same time, lest he should be accused of favouritism, he also asked the Duke of Monmouth to leave the country and deprived him of his commissions. On 4 October it was reported from Newmarket that 'His Majesty is in good health and in very good humour, that they have every day the divertisement of the comedy and at night dancing and merriment'.[8] Sir Robert Southwell, who sent this information, thought that a stranger finding himself in Newmarket and hearing about the loud alarms of treason would conclude himself in two very different regions. Three days later the Earl of Shaftesbury, still Lord President of the Council, who had returned to London from his home in Dorset in expectation of the assembly of a new Parliament, summoned of his own volition a meeting of the Privy Council to discuss the rumour that he had heard about James's going to Scotland, purporting that he assumed that James was doing so without the King's permission. He remarked that 'the Mass and Presbytery would make but a mad medley together', and thought that it were 'fit to advise His Majesty thereof in case the Duke had undertaken such a thing of himself'. Later he said 'that it was the worst counsel that was ever given to the King and [that] the Council ought to have been consulted'.[9] That was the end of the road for Shaftesbury as a Minister. For Charles had now decided that he did not intend to meet his new Parliament that year. On 14 October Shaftesbury was dismissed, and on the following day Charles told the Privy Council that he was proroguing Parliament until 26 January 1680. He sent a message to his nephew, William of Orange, that there was no other remedy, 'that they would have his Crown' and the Commons were likely to be so violent that they would impeach the Duke of York and the Queen.[10] The King also expressed to his Council his scepticism about the latest popish plot invented by the criminal, Thomas Dangerfield. In private he remarked that 'he loved to discover plots but not to create any'.[11] Although tremendous pressure was brought to bear on him, Charles remained unmovable in his refusal to meet Parliament. After his favourite son, Monmouth, had come back from abroad without permission, Charles was extremely angry and dismissed him from all his offices. Even the intercession of Nell Gwyn was unavailing. When a number of peers presented him with a petition asking him to meet Parliament on 26 January, the King said calmly he wished that everyone took as great a care of the nation as he did.

Three days later, on 10 December, in defiance of the objections of most of his Privy Council, he declared that he would not allow Parliament to meet until the following November. He then went on a milk diet 'to abate the sharpness of some humours'.[12]

Although one last attempt was made by the court to come to terms with Shaftesbury after his dismissal from the office of Lord President of the Council, the line of battle had been clearly drawn between Charles and those who, led by Shaftesbury and soon to be known as Whigs, were determined to exclude the King's brother from the succession to the throne and to force Charles to get rid of his Roman Catholic Queen. Charles had appointed his brother-in-law, the industrious Laurence Hyde, as First Lord of the Treasury in place of the Earl of Essex, who had resigned in the middle of November after Charles had rebuked him in council for proposing the recall of Parliament to deal with the plot. Hyde, together with the Earl of Sunderland and Sidney Godolphin, became the King's principal advisers. They were known as the second Triumvirate or, since all of them were under forty, as the Chits. In May 1680 Sir Leoline Jenkins, a protégé of Sir William Temple, a high churchman and former Principal of Jesus College, Oxford, replaced Henry Coventry as Secretary of State; and the Earl of Sunderland became the senior of the two secretaries, Secretary of State for the South. After the King had prorogued his new Parliament on 26 January (although Charles had let it be known that he did not intend to call this Parliament until November, he made a number of short prorogations, thus enabling him to summon it earlier in case the state of his affairs abroad required it) he recalled his brother from exile in Edinburgh, though he wisely forbade any special rejoicings in London when James arrived. It was even said that if the Duke of Monmouth had left London again, James would not have been sent for. The two leading moderates, Halifax and Temple, withdrew to their country homes and took little active part in politics for the time being. And at the end of January Shaftesbury's four friends in the Privy Council, Russell, Cavendish, Capel and Powle, resigned. Charles let them go with considerable relish. He wanted, if possible, to have a year in which political tempers might subside after the agitation of the popish plot. He desired neither an acrimonious Cabinet nor an uncontrollable Parliament.

Although tumultuous petitioning had been made illegal by an Act of 1661, which had been reinforced by a royal declaration of December 1679, the first of a number of monster petitions, for which signatures had been collected in the London taverns, demanding that the King should meet his Parliament at once, was presented to Charles on 13 January 1680. 'His Majesty,' reported Sir Robert Southwell on the same day, 'manifested his displeasure. He said that he saw no names of remark in the bundle except that of Major-General Desborough [Oliver Cromwell's brother-in-law] and added that he knew better than anyone else what concerned the government of the kingdom and would take therein all the care that was fit'.[13] Nine days later a petition purporting to carry the names of 30,000 Wiltshiremen was handed in by Thomas Thynne, to whom Charles said 'he did not think a gentleman of fortune and estate would have concerned himself in anything that looked like rebellion'.[14] When the Lord Mayor of London was asked to hold a meeting of the Common Council that January in the same cause the King asserted that if the Common Council petitioned for Parliament to meet 'he would next day dissolve it and if a war ensued he would declare that they had begun it'.[15] By the time James arrived back in London the Lord Mayor and the majority of the Aldermen of the City had decided that discretion was the better part of valour and entertained the royal brothers to a lavish supper. The Dowager Lady Sunderland wrote to Henry Sidney, who was the English ambassador to the United Netherlands, that 'the people showed as much affection and duty as the expressions at such a time could be'. Afterwards the Aldermen attended the King to Whitehall at two in the morning and 'all went merry out of the King's cellar'.[16]

It has sometimes been suggested that by the spring Charles had more or less washed his hands of politics, had withdrawn into seclusion and left the government of his kingdom to the Chits. It is true that after the Lord Mayor's supper (on 8 March) Charles had left Whitehall, as his custom was, for Newmarket and stayed there for the rest of the month. But he kept a close watch on public affairs and approved an attempt sponsored by Sunderland to inaugurate an active and popular foreign policy, the fruits of which might be shown to Parliament when it eventually met.

Louis XIV had been far from satisfied with the gains he had achieved by the treaty of Nymegen. After he had dismissed his comparatively mild Foreign Minister, Arnaud de Pomponne, he had, with the support of Pomponne's successor, Colbert de Croissy, and his War Minister, Louvois, embarked upon an aggressive foreign policy aimed at extending his hold over the Spanish Netherlands, Alsace and Franche-Comté. Charles had at first attempted to follow his previous policy of buying help from the French King as the price of English neutrality. But Louis could see from the reports of his ambassadors that the divided domestic situation in England was such that he had little to fear and that it was more to his advantage to obtain an alliance with the Dutch, who were weary of war and wanted to revive their commerce in peace. Charles protested indignantly about the proposed Franco-Dutch treaty, but he was astute enough to realize that he had little to offer and said to the French ambassador, Barrillon, at the end of January: 'Let us not talk about the past but think about the future. I beg the King my brother to make up his mind and not be restrained by the fact of my not being able at present to be very useful to him. But if he will put me in a state of showing my gratitude to him, no one will be more attached to his interests.'[17]

Neither Barrillon nor Louis XIV was impressed by this attitude, whereas Charles continued to be alarmed by rumours of a Franco-Dutch agreement. The King therefore gave Sunderland a free hand to try to build up a coalition against France. The Dutch had already rejected an English proposal for a treaty guaranteeing the *status quo* as established by the peace of Nymegen. William, who was in close touch with Sunderland through Henry Sidney (Sunderland's uncle), advised him to try to negotiate a triple alliance with the United Netherlands and Spain. After the Dutch had repulsed the French advances, Sunderland therefore attempted to construct a wide system of alliances against France; special envoys were dispatched to negotiate treaties with the northern Protestant states (except Sweden); Spain and the Holy Roman

Empire were approached; and it was hoped that finally 'a firm alliance between England and Holland . . . would lock the whole structure together'.[18] But the scheme was overambitious. Charles did not even have the navy to back it; and it was largely a façade to impress domestic opinion. As Laurence Hyde wrote to Henry Sidney on 16 March: 'If we can make good alliances abroad everything at home will do very well.'[19] Charles permitted joint Anglo-Dutch representations to be made at the French Court. The only positive result that finally emerged was a treaty of mutual guarantee concluded with Spain, by now one of the weakest military powers in Europe. Charles himself gave the show away when he said to Barrillon at the very time the treaty was being concluded, early in June: 'I know very well what the condition of the Spaniards is. What I do is not out of love for them: I act out of necessity. I must pacify the English and do my best to prevent the outbreak of war. That is my only aim.'[20]

Yet Sunderland was not without his aspirations. He fully realized that the only sound basis for a viable foreign policy was an alliance not with the Spanish but with the Dutch. Although he had to contend with Charles's intimate conversations with Barrillon in the Duchess of Portsmouth's boudoir, he assured Sidney that the King realized he was not going to get anything worth while out of the French at this stage. Sunderland's hopes centred on William of Orange, and both he and Godolphin believed that if William could be persuaded to visit London at the right time his influence could be brought to bear on the King, to wean him from his never-abandoned hankerings after a French alliance. What Sunderland and Godolphin presumably did not know was about the secret treaty of Dover, a copy of which was in the French archives. In the last resort Charles could be blackmailed, and 'once in the summer of 1680' Louis authorized 'his ambassador in London to drop hints about a certain secret which his master possessed, and which, if revealed, could ruin Charles'.[21]

Meanwhile Charles's affairs at home were not going too badly. Shaftesbury attempted to heap fresh coals on the now dying fires of the popish plot. He had found informers in Ireland to bring over evidence of a plan for a Catholic revolt there aimed at exter-

minating the Duke of Ormonde and massacring all the Protestants. In the King's absence the Privy Council had taken these
revelations seriously. But the King hurried up to London, showed
his scepticism about the new plot, and took precautions to ensure
that the Irish witnesses were not suborned. By May the excitement
had died down and when on 11 June the informer Dangerfield
was exposed as the criminal he was and a popish midwife, against
whom he had levelled accusations of high treason, was acquitted,
the popish plots had almost burned themselves out. Charles was
also helped that summer by the production of addresses 'abhorring'
the petitioners who had been trying to oblige him to call Parliament. These abhorrers acquired the nickname of Tories and the
petitioners that of Whigs. And a veritable shower of books and
pamphlets written by both sides (their publication was simplified
because the licensing laws of 1662 had been allowed to fall into
abeyance in January 1679) kept the political pot boiling throughout the summer of 1680.

After the interruption of his holiday in Newmarket by the
Irish plot, the King had stayed for a time in Whitehall frustrating
the mischief-making of Shaftesbury, trying to scotch the ever-
growing rumours that he had been married to Monmouth's
mother and that Monmouth (not James) was the legitimate heir
to the throne, and approving the addresses from abhorrers vouch-
safing their loyalty to the monarchy. On 27 April Sir William
Temple wrote that 'the King looks better in health than I have
known him since his sickness last year. And since I have known
Whitehall I never saw such a Court as at the Duke's levee'.[22] But
in May Charles moved to Windsor. There he was visited by the
Yorkshire Tory, Sir John Reresby, bringing him once more the
story about the Duke of Monmouth's mother. 'The King,'
Reresby recorded in his memoirs, 'lived there very privately at
this time. There was little resort to him, and he passed the day in
fishing and walking in the park, which indeed he naturally loved
more than in a crowd or in business.'[23] But five days later, owing
it was said either to his early morning walks in the river mists
or to his habit of fishing in all weathers, Charles was again taken
ill. Freed perhaps from the attentions of his London doctors, he

soon recovered his health, but the episode was enough to arouse the anxieties of Shaftesbury and the exclusionists who knew that James was with him at Windsor and ready to step into his shoes. They had suffered the political setbacks of the failure of the Irish plot, the signature of the Spanish treaty, the exposure of the criminal Dangerfield, and the issue on 2 June of a public declaration by the King that he was never contracted or married to the Duke of Monmouth's mother. They now took a daring step. They induced a Grand Jury of Middlesex to present bills of indictment against James as a popish recusant and the Duchess of Portsmouth as a common whore. The Grand Jury had been packed and the leading Whigs crowded into the court room. But the Lord Chief Justice Scroggs had been forewarned by the King, who rushed up to London for the purpose, and the jury was discharged before it could make its presentments.

Although this Whig attempt to indict the King's brother and mistress was quashed, it caused a sensation in Europe and dismay among the royal Ministers. The evident weakness of the monarchy suggested that England would hardly be an attractive ally in a new war against France, while Shaftesbury's boldness was a clear indication that when Parliament met again the hereditary monarchy would be fiercely attacked. In June after the Anglo-Spanish treaty had been concluded the Earl of Sunderland had held a conference at his house of Althorp, which had been attended by the Earl of Halifax, in which a policy had been agreed, subject to the King's approval. To pacify Parliament the King would ask for no more money unless his foreign policy required it, and he would offer every possible security against popery short of an alteration in the succession. William of Orange was to be invited to come to England in the hope that an Anglo-Dutch alliance would be facilitated and his presence as a Protestant statesman married to James's elder daughter would provide an assurance of the future safety of the Anglican religion.

But Shaftesbury's *coup* had unnerved the King's entourage. The Duchess of Portsmouth, frightened by the public attack upon her, was now willing to exert her influence on the side of exclusion; indeed there was even a possibility that her own son by the

King, the Duke of Richmond, might become a candidate for the throne when Charles died. The Earl of Sunderland was also shaken and some time during the summer or early autumn – it is not clear when – decided that he himself must enter the exclusionist camp. The King, after all, might be induced to fear that a civil war was in the offing and be compelled to bow to opinion inside and outside Parliament.

Comparatively little is known about Charles's own attitude at this time. Except for one or two short visits to London he spent the entire summer at Windsor, where he supervised the rebuilding of a large part of the castle and was presented with a statue of himself on horseback which was decorated with sculpture by the distinguished carver, Grinling Gibbons, and placed in the castle grounds. Charles was aware that there were two possible candidates for his throne if James was excluded: Monmouth, 'the Protestant Duke', and Princess Mary, who was married and devoted to William of Orange. But the King was reluctant to give encouragement to either of them. In July a pamphlet was published entitled *A Letter to a Person of Quality concerning the King's Disavowing the having been married to the Duke of Monmouth's mother*. In August Monmouth made a tour or 'progress' in the west of England, where he was warmly received, although Charles had instructed the local authorities that no special notice was to be taken of him. After his return it was rumoured that Monmouth had secret meetings with the King, although what was said is not known. While William intimated that he was willing to visit England in October, he insisted that he would not come without an invitation from Charles; and Sunderland hesitated to press the King to issue such an invitation.

On 20 July Charles came up to London to attend a supper given to the sheriffs in Fishmongers hall. Charles had endeavoured to prevent the election of two new sheriffs for Middlesex who were reputed to be of a republican turn of mind, but in fact they were elected. This showed the strength of the Whigs in London and was likely to have political consequences since the sheriffs selected the juries. But Charles was more concerned over foreign policy. Tangier, the prize which had formed part of Queen Catherine's dowry, though its strategic value as a naval base and port of call was unquestionable, had never proved to be of much economic importance to England. It had been under constant attack by the Moors from 1678 when Lord Inchiquin was governor. The isolated garrison had since March 1680 been subjected to siege and its outer forts captured; and Charles was so angry with Inchiquin's neglectful conduct that he refused to let him kiss his hand when he had been recalled home. Inchiquin was replaced by the Earl of Ossory, the Duke of Ormonde's son and a devoted subject of the King. But the reinforcements allocated to him were, in his opinion, inadequate and in any case before he could take up his post he died. The Duke of York asserted that the Moors had a force of 15,000 infantry and 1,500 cavalry engaged in the attack on Tangier, whereas the garrison was under 2,000.[24] Charles hurried out reinforcements. He decided to ratify the treaty with Spain, and to appeal to Parliament for its support over his foreign policy and over the relief of Tangier. On 18 August Charles came up to London and on 26 August a proclamation was published announcing that Parliament was at last to meet on 21 October.

Meanwhile the King's Ministers were growing more gloomy. The States-General had again rejected the proposed Anglo-Dutch treaty of guarantee; this put paid to the idea of a defensive triple alliance against France, and William of Orange was reduced to making a personal visit to Germany to see if he could rally some of the German princes to resist French aggression: the earlier efforts of the English envoys had come to nothing. Sunderland sent for Henry Sidney, the English ambassador to the United Netherlands, to consult him about the situation and at the same time Halifax came up to London. Conferences were then held with some of the more moderate Whigs in the hope of reaching a *modus vivendi* between the King and the House of Commons. One suggestion was that James should be sent out of London, the Commons be given a free hand to secure the Protestant religion, and in return money voted for the fleet. A report reached the French ambassador of an even more far-reaching proposal: that Charles should be granted £600,000 and the right to nominate his own successor, if Sunderland and the Duchess of Portsmouth could persuade him to accept exclusion.

All this was discussed without consulting the King. Charles had finally left Windsor on 9 September, and after spending a week in Whitehall had removed himself to Newmarket for three weeks. When he again returned to London on 9 October great pressures were brought to bear on him. Four days earlier Halifax had noted that 'The Town sayeth as confidently the King will quit his brother, as those of his party say the contrary'.[25] Sunderland was one of those who believed that Charles would desert his brother; and Monmouth and the Duchess of Portsmouth both used their personal influence with the King to persuade him to do so. But all that Charles could be induced to do – and that with some reluctance – was to send James back to Scotland before Parliament met. The Privy Council was divided on the question. Seven members favoured James staying by the King's side. It was the fact that James was shown to have a group of influential supporters that prompted Charles to send him away; for he feared that the Duke's continued presence in London when Parliament met might lead to civil war. There was also the possibility that he would be impeached. James himself was for staying and fighting it out; he blamed the 'atheist' Halifax and the feline Duchess of Portsmouth, but he obeyed the King's orders and departed.[26] Charles still hoped that the House of Commons would help him solve his foreign affairs problems, if he agreed to drastic limitations on the rights of a popish successor. Farther than that he would not go. He refuted all the rumours that he could be bribed or bullied into abandoning his brother. For he believed that if he did so the monarchy itself would be destroyed.

16

Exclusion – II

After Charles II's fourth Parliament had been in session for five weeks the opinion was expressed in Oxford and elsewhere that it ought to be called 'the Tangier Parliament' just as the last one had been called 'the Danby Parliament'.[1] Perhaps that was meant in a negative sense; for just as the previous Parliament had failed to impeach Danby, so the new Parliament proved unwilling to provide any assistance for Tangier. The correspondent who reported this opinion added that 'the neglect of Tangier is as bad or worse than the Jesuit fury', and 'the strengthening of Tangier is one of our best helps to keep off Popery'.

It was primarily to invite help for Tangier that Charles had summoned Parliament, and when it met on 21 October 1680 he was in no apologetic mood.[2] 'The several prorogations I have made,' he said, 'have been very advantageous to our neighbours and very useful to me.' After referring to his alliance with Spain and, in somewhat ambiguous terms, to his relations with the United Netherlands, he insisted that they were 'the best measures that could be taken for the safety of England and the repose of Christendom'. He added that these measures could not fail to attain their end, 'if our divisions at home do not render our friendship less considerable abroad'. To prevent such divisions he promised to give the fullest attention the hearts of his hearers could wish for to the security of the Protestant religion so long as it was consistent with 'the succession of the Crown in its due and legal course of descent'. He then went on to ask for the advice of Parliament and to invoke its assistance on the question of Tangier. He concluded by asserting that 'all Europe have their eyes on this assembly' and that upon the efforts of the Members of Parliament depended the happiness or misery of their European allies as well their own.

But the members of the House of Commons who had been elected more than a year earlier were neither to be flattered nor soothed. They were still under the influence of the agitation provoked by the popish plot and still determined to exclude the Duke of York from succession to the throne: indeed a substantial number of members who had voted against exclusion in the previous Parliament had now changed their minds. The Earl of Longford noted that the King's gracious speech did not please them 'because there is a limitation from meddling with the succession'.[3] Thus this Parliament was to be known not as the Tangier Parliament but as the second Exclusionist Parliament, and the great majority of its members were more aggressive and more anti-papist than those in its predecessor.

Five days after Parliament met, the already discredited criminal Dangerfield appeared at the bar of the House of Commons and accused the Duke of York of having given him twenty guineas to invent his story of a sham plot manufactured by the Presbyterians. Although Dangerfield spoke 'with great ease, clearness and presence of mind', wrote Secretary Jenkins to the Vice-Chancellor of Oxford, 'I cannot believe anyone believed a word he said'. The Commons may not have been as impressed by Dangerfield as they had been by Titus Oates, but they immediately embarked on a warm debate on the subject of suppressing popery and preventing the enthronement of a popish successor; and they decided to draw up an address to King Charles II emphasizing their determination to preserve and support his government and the Protestant religion at home and abroad. On the following day the Commons insisted that the subjects of the King had been within their rights in petitioning him to call Parliament, and in order to underline their words two 'abhorrers' of these petitions were expelled from the House. Other 'abhorrers' or Tories were unseated by the committee of privileges and, ignoring other questions, the considerable Whig majority turned its attention to bringing in a new Exclusion Bill on the ground that the Duke of York's religion had given encouragement to popish plots.

Charles was furious. When Henry Sidney, who had been brought over from Holland by his nephew Sunderland to help to bring pressure on the King in favour of exclusion, asked the King for his commands on 28 October Charles 'immediately fell upon the proceedings in Parliament with great heart' and showed his displeasure at Sidney's attitude.[4] On the other hand, when Sir John Reresby, the former MP for Aldborough, had supper with the King ten days later and told him that he too might be called to account as an abhorrent, Charles answered: 'Do not trouble yourself, I will stick by you and my old friends, for if I do not, I shall have nobody to stick by me.'[5] Thus Charles constituted himself the leader of the Tories.

The only difference among the Whigs was whether they were Williamites or Monmouthians. If an Exclusion Bill were to be passed simply banning James from the succession, then (provided that James had no son by his second wife) his elder daughter Mary, a convinced Protestant and obedient to her husband, Prince William of Orange, would succeed to the throne. But Prince William was little known in England and was reputed to have absolutist tendencies. The Duke of Monmouth, for his part, was a popular figure with influential backing and a high reputation as 'the Protestant Duke'. Though Charles twice denied that he had been married to Monmouth's mother, might he not be persuaded to legitimize his favourite son? The debate on the Exclusion Bill in the Commons began on 2 November and by 11 November had received its third reading. On 8 November it had been amended in a Williamite sense, possibly through the influence of Sunderland, who earlier in the year had persuaded Charles to agree to a visit from his nephew. Sunderland, Temple, Sidney and others imagined that if William came over to England at this stage, his presence might swing the King in favour of exclusion. But William was too canny to commit himself against his father-in-law and Charles gave no sign that he intended to change his mind about exclusion.

On the contrary, on 7 November Charles had sent through Jenkins a message to the Commons, drawn up with the approval of Halifax and Hyde, assuring them that he would accept any remedies they decided upon in relation to popery and the plot, providing that they were consistent with preserving the hereditary succession. The Commons retorted by proceeding with the impeachment of the Roman Catholic Lords in the Tower, starting with the aged Lord Stafford, by drawing up a long answer to the King's message, and by giving the Exclusion Bill an unopposed second reading. A few days' interval then elapsed in the hope that Charles might be pressured or persuaded into changing his mind. On 12 November the Common Council of the City of London presented a petition to the King asking him to be advised by his Parliament. Possibly it was hoped by the exclusionists that Charles would be intimidated by the London mob, as his father had been. But Charles told the London petitioners not to meddle with what did not concern them 'and that he understood his own business better than they'.[6]

When on 15 November the Commons sent their Exclusion Bill up to the House of Lords, the King, having strengthened his guards in the City, spent the entire day in the Upper Chamber following the debate, which lasted from eleven in the morning until nine at night, and only retiring briefly to a neighbouring room to have his meals. The Earl of Halifax, who had become the King's principal adviser now that Sunderland had deserted to the exclusionists, crossed swords with the Earl of Shaftesbury in a prolonged oratorical debate which has unfortunately not been preserved in full for the edification of posterity; but it is now generally accepted that it was the King's influence and the King's presence that determined the result. Most of the peers whom Charles himself had created, the royal officers of state (except Sunderland), the courtiers and the bishops voted against the Bill, which was defeated by sixty-three votes to thirty. There were no riots in the streets and the House of Commons was left speechless.

Next day an animated but inconclusive debate took place in the House of Lords, now that the Exclusion Bill had been thrown out there, on other ways of securing the Protestant religion in the kingdom. Halifax, following the line approved by Charles the year before, proposed strict limitations on the power of the Crown in the event of there being a popish King, and the banishment of James for five years or the duration of Charles's life to a spot 500 miles from England. Shaftesbury proposed that the King should immediately procure a divorce on the ground of his wife being barren and should marry a queen capable of producing a Protestant heir. The Earl of Essex wanted a Bill of Association drawn up, similar to that passed in the reign of Queen Elizabeth I, to protect the King against assassination by Roman Catholics. When the House met again Shaftesbury ceased to press for the divorce, probably because he was convinced that Charles could still be compelled to agree to exclusion.

Certainly the Lower House believed this. Charles himself, thinking the question settled for the time being, sent a message to the Commons reminding them of the needs of Tangier. For he did not yet know that, thanks to the reinforcements he had sent out, the Moors had been decisively defeated in battle. The subject was brushed aside: Colonel Titus said that 'to talk of the condition of Tangier now is like Nero, when Rome was on fire, to fiddle'.[7] It was agreed that an address should be presented to the King not only about the fears of popery and a popish succession but asking that the Earl of Halifax should be removed from his counsels on account of the pernicious advice that he had given about dissolving the last Parliament and proroguing this one. After the address asking for the removal of Halifax had been presented on 22 November, Halifax offered to resign; but Charles refused to accept his resignation and sent a message to the Commons saying that 'my Lord Halifax was of his counsel and he did know no reason why he should not be'.[8] If they did, the law was open and the Parliament sitting and they might proceed to impeach Halifax for any crime he had committed. The Commons were now out of hand and went on to attack other 'evil Ministers' and some of the judges; and during the first week of December they engaged in the impeachment of Lord Stafford for treason before the House of Lords in order to remind the kingdom of the reality of the popish plot. On 7 December Stafford, who had defended himself feebly against the lies of the perjurers, was found guilty by a majority of the House of Lords. The King said that he would not have hanged a dog on the evidence of these witnesses and asked the Earl of Anglesey why he had voted Stafford guilty. Anglesey retorted boldly that he had done so for the same reason that Charles had accepted the verdict and agreed to the execution.[9]

On 15 December Charles delivered a speech to the two Houses of Parliament reminding them once more that he had called them together in the first instance to seek their help over foreign affairs and the condition of Tangier. He repeated that he had promised in return to agree to any remedies for the security of the Protestant religion consistent with the preservation of the succession to the Crown 'in its due and legal course of descent'.[10] He expressed his fear that their behaviour had damaged the reputation of the kingdom with its allies. In fact only ten days earlier Charles had received from Henry Sidney in Holland a memorial from the States-General urging him to come to terms with his Parliament for the sake not only of England but of Europe. The King was very angry about this interference in his domestic affairs and suspected it was a put-up job by Sidney and Sunderland, both of whom had voted in favour of exclusion.

The Commons's answer to the King's latest appeal given on 20 December was to the effect that they saw no safety without the exclusion of the Duke of York and an Association to guarantee it and they demanded the expulsion from their offices of all who favoured the succession of Prince James; if that were granted, then they would supply money to defend Tangier and support alliances with foreign countries. At the same time the Commons asked the King in future to appoint judges of known affection to the Protestant religion who should hold office during good behaviour and not, as lately, be appointed 'at the King's pleasure'. Some of the more ambitious Whigs, headed by Ralph Montagu, attempted to come to a specific and secret arrangement with the King, promising him that if he agreed to exclusion and to their entry, or in the case of Sunderland retention, in office, they would undertake to procure for him a generous supply of money.[11] But when the majority of the Commons got wind of these intrigues, they promptly passed a vote on 30 December that no

Member of Parliament might accept an office or place of profit under the Crown without the leave of the House.

During these winter months of 1680–1 therefore no Whig politician or hanger-on seems to have believed that Charles would remain firm on the question of exclusion. The Whigs thought that if his Ministers and advisers were attacked – and the House of Commons named not only Halifax, but Laurence Hyde, his brother, the second Earl of Clarendon, the Marquis of Worcester and Lord Feversham (all of whom were Protestants) – Charles would fear a civil war and the danger of being sent on his travels again. But Charles never flinched. On 4 January 1681 he sent a message to the Commons in reply to their address of 20 December 1680 reiterating his determination not to agree to exclusion and saying that the vote against it in the House of Lords confirmed him in his opinion. He ignored the address about the judges.

On 10 January Charles prorogued Parliament for ten days; and before that time was up, on 18 January, he dissolved it. On that same day the Countess of Sunderland wrote to Henry Sidney (now back in Holland) that the King's idea was to clear the court of factions;[12] 'but, after all,' she added optimistically, 'I daresay the King will never be brought up to it, for you and I know what a spark he is at going through with anything; but he treateth me and my lord [the Earl of Sunderland] at such a rate that he has asked to sell his place.' But, like the rest, she was living in a dream world. On 24 January Charles ordered Sunderland to surrender the seals of office to Lord Conway, whom he had called over from Ireland for the purpose, and refused to allow Conway to reimburse the purchase price of £6,000 which Sunderland had originally paid for the office. The King also dismissed other exclusionist members of his Privy Council. Finally, he strengthened his troops so as to prevent any armed rising in the City of London.

Charles had not consulted his Council about the dissolution of Parliament. He gave orders for the proclamation to be made, but at the same time he appointed a new parliament to meet in Oxford on 21 March. The original suggestion for holding a meeting of Parliament outside Westminster seems to have come from the imprisoned Earl of Danby, and the King assured himself that there were precedents – for example during the plague in the reign of James I – for summoning it in Oxford. Charles sprang his decision on his council on the morning of 18 January. The third Earl of Salisbury, a Whig peer who was on friendly terms with Shaftesbury, tried to argue against the decision but was silenced by the King. Salisbury then desired to withdraw from the Council. Charles answered sharply that 'he could not make any request that would more easily be granted and ordered his Lordship's name to be struck out of the Council book'.[13] The Earl of Halifax also argued strongly against this step, and in private 'complained of the unsteadiness of the King's temper' and said that 'whilst he seemed to approve the counsel given him, he hearkened to other counsels at a back door';[14] but Charles was grateful to Halifax for his fight against exclusion and said that he did not doubt that, despite rumours to the contrary, the Earl would behave in the same way at Oxford as he had done in Westminster.

Why did Charles immediately call another Parliament in Oxford? He can hardly have expected that the general election would materially alter the complexion of the House of Commons. It is true that he discouraged Temple, an exclusionist, from standing and advised Reresby, a Tory, to stand. In fact the opinion of modern historians who have examined this election – and the contemporary opinion of the French ambassador – was that there was some slight setback to the supremacy of the Whigs. On the other hand it was a highly organized election, and addresses of instructions were drawn up by Whig supporters both for the benefit of new members and others, urging them to push through an Exclusion Bill, to prosecute the plot, to punish abhorrers and (in the case of an address drawn up by John Locke) to press for annual parliaments. Thus although Charles did what he could by dismissing known Whigs from such local offices as the deputy lieutenantships and the commissions of peace, the pressure of the Whig organization was so powerful that in some parts of the country Tories were afraid to stand.

The real reason why Charles called this Parliament seems to have been that he was genuinely afraid that unless he were able to come to terms with the Whig leaders a civil war, similar to that of 1642, might ensue. The intransigent behaviour of the last House of Commons, the conduct of the Common Council of the City of London, the trial and execution of Lord Stafford, the attacks on the Earl of Halifax and other Privy Councillors, the proliferation of addresses, petitions and pamphlets critical of the government all contributed to Charles's fear that it was not merely his brother's succession that was at stake but that there was a genuine danger to the Crown itself. Halifax wrote on 9 March that 'this meeting at Oxford is very critical; there may be short turns and sharp changes'.[15] A month earlier Secretary Jenkins had in a letter written from London observed: 'Here is a wonderful deal of art and industry to stir up the seamen, the watermen, the hackney coachmen, the suburbs men, to petition that the Parliament may sit here and not in Oxford.'[16] Sir William Temple wrote that 'the nation [is] divided into two strong factions with the greatest heats and animosities, and ready to break into violence on the first occasion'.[17] Nobody expected that the Oxford Parliament would sit for long. But Charles hoped that, away from the perfervid atmosphere in London, tempers would be calmer and an opportunity for conciliation be created.

Charles in fact acted in a highly intelligent way from his own point of view. While he was ready to grant concessions, he was determined not to show any sign of weakness that might encourage his enemies or open the road to armed insurrection. Before he departed for Oxford he appointed the Earl of Craven, a veteran Royalist, commander-in-chief of all the troops left in London with orders to secure quiet in the City and in Westminster, to suppress tumultuous meetings and disorders, and if necessary to kill or destroy those who disturbed the public peace. The road from Windsor to Oxford was lined with soldiers, and guards were sent to Oxford. Household troops were also distributed in the villages round Oxford. Some of the Whigs brought armed retinues to Oxford, but this was more out of fear than because they themselves planned a military *coup*. The undergraduates were dismissed from Oxford; the King commandeered Christ Church, Merton and Corpus Christi for his court (the King himself staying in Christ Church), while the Whigs fixed their headquarters in Balliol. The Commons met in Convocation house and the Lords in the Geometry School. When Charles first arrived in Oxford, 'a bold old fellow accosted him and said "Remember your royal father and keep the staff in your own hands." The King retorted: "Ay, by God, I will and the sword too." '[18] The King was accompanied to Oxford by the Queen, the Duchess of Portsmouth and Nell Gwyn and he spent a day at the Burford races before making ready to meet his Parliament.

In opening the session on 21 March Charles spoke for longer than he usually did. His tone was firm, even severe.[19] He said that 'the unwarrantable proceedings of the last House of Commons were the occasion of my parting with my last Parliament. For I, who will never use arbitrary government myself, am resolved not to suffer it in others.' Nevertheless he had let them see, 'by my calling this Parliament so soon, that no irregularities in parliaments shall make me out of love with them'. He reiterated his opposition to exclusion but promised 'to remove all reasonable fears that may arise from the possibility of a popish successor's coming to the Crown', and added that 'if means can be found that in such a case the administration of the government may remain in Protestant hands, I shall be ready to harken to any such expedient, by which the religion might be preserved and the monarchy not destroyed'. What Charles had in mind was a suggestion, probably emanating from the fertile mind of Halifax, that on the King's death, while James should have the title and honours of kingship, the administration should be placed in the hands of his Protestant daughter, Mary of Orange, with the name of Protector or Regent. On the face of it this was not a very plausible scheme and Charles preferred to hint at it rather than put it forward himself. But most Whigs were committed by their election addresses to exclusion (though still without any agreement about who Charles's successor would be). It was felt by many that Charles's speech was 'an excellent gracious one', though the rest thought it 'a subtle crafty one'.[20] It was certainly a disingenuous one, for Charles had by now fallen out of love with parliaments and did not intend to convene another one after this unless he were forced into it.

The first thing that happened in this Parliament was that Shaftesbury raised in the House of Lords the question what had happened to a bill passed by both Houses in the previous Parliament to give relief to dissenters by repealing an Act of 1593. This bill, though it would have been of benefit to Protestant nonconformists, would not have been of any advantage to Roman Catholics, and Charles, in his anger at the behaviour of the last Parliament, had ordered the clerk not to present it to him. That had now to be admitted. But it was not a matter of major consequence. In the Commons the question of exclusion was soon revived, but it was decided not to debate the matter until 26 March, thus opening an opportunity for a compromise to be reached. In the course of the week there were informal conversations or negotiations between the King and the Whig leader, Shaftesbury. The contemporary sources are contradictory about the precise course of events. But it appears to have been on 24 March that Charles, being in the House of Lords 'to entertain himself', asked Shaftesbury whether no expedient could be found for exclusion.[21] According to one account Shaftesbury answered no and added that the whole nation appeared to be of that opinion. But according to another account, two days later Shaftesbury asked the Marquis of Worcester to hand an anonymous note to the King containing an 'expedient' that might meet with Charles's wishes. When the King opened this note, he found that it stated that if he would declare the Duke of Monmouth to be his successor the whole matter could be settled in a day. Thus Shaftesbury at last – and in contradiction to other exclusionists such as Sunderland and Sidney – had committed himself to the cause of the King's eldest illegitimate son. Charles answered that such a solution was contrary both to the existing laws and to divine justice. Shaftesbury, who had personally followed up this devious approach, replied that Parliament could pass a bill to legitimize Monmouth. But Charles would not be moved.

My Lord [he is reported to have said], let there be no self-delusion. I will never yield and will not let myself be intimidated. Men ordinarily become more timid as they grow old; as for me, I shall be, on the contrary, bolder and firmer and I will not stain my life and reputation in the little time that perhaps remains for me to live. I do not fear the dangers and calamities which people try to frighten me with. I have the law and reason on my side. There is the Church (pointing to the bishops) which will remain united with me.[22]

In fact this was not a certain expedient from the Whig point of view. For the Williamites were against it. They had good reason to doubt if the weak-willed Monmouth would make an effective king. His enthronement might only lead to another civil war.

Meanwhile, at about the same time that these conversations were taking place, the House of Commons had been examining the case of a member of the Titus Oates tribe, named Edward Fitzharris, the son of an Irish Roman Catholic baronet, who on 27 February had been arrested in bed by a London magistrate, Sir William Waller, on the basis of information received. Waller had found on Fitzharris the draft of a pamphlet asserting that the King was as much a papist as his brother and ought equally to be put out of the way. Although Fitzharris was in the Tower of London awaiting his trial the Whigs in the Commons, having heard a report from Waller and others suggesting that Fitzharris had promised some juicy revelations about a plot to kill the King with the connivance of the Duke of York, voted that he should not be left to the ordinary courts of law but should be impeached for high treason before the House of Lords. Much against his will, Sir Leoline Jenkins took a message to the House of Lords accordingly. New evidence about such a plot would obviously be a fillip to exclusion. Moreover the Whigs believed that once impeachment proceedings were started, Charles would not dare to dissolve Parliament.

Saturday 26 March was a busy day in the House of Commons. First of all Sir Thomas Littleton, acting on behalf of the Earl of Halifax, put forward the idea of establishing a regency if a Roman Catholic king succeeded to the throne, and proposed that the Regents should be William and Mary. The proposal had the approval of the King. But many objections were put forward against this solution on the ground that it was impractical and that James would never agree to it. The House then read the Exclusion Bill for the first time. The members were annoyed, however, to receive a message from the House of Lords refusing to agree to the impeachment of Fitzharris. Thus once again the two Houses were at loggerheads. This was the same excuse that Charles had used before to put an end to a sitting. It was now obvious to him that no compromise with the Whigs was possible, and he prepared with extreme cunning for a dissolution. The Commons had been complaining about their cramped quarters in the Convocation house. Charles therefore said that they should be removed on the Monday to the Sheldonian theatre, the masterpiece built by Sir Christopher Wren. Workmen were sent to make the necessary arrangements. When Monday came Charles went into the House of Lords in his ordinary clothes, as his custom was. But his robes had been brought in separately. He sent for the Commons, put on his crown and ordered the Lord Chancellor to dissolve Parliament. 'My Lords and Gentlemen,' the King said, 'that all the world may see to what a point we are come, that we are not like to have a good end, when the divisions at the beginning are such: therefore, my Lord Chancellor, do as I have commanded you.'[23] So ended Charles II's last parliament.

There were no demonstrations or armed risings after the dissolution of the Oxford Parliament. Both in this and the previous Parliament the Whigs had imagined that they held the King in the hollow of their hands and that they could compel him to agree to exclusion. Charles, for his part, had combined conciliation with firmness: he had offered the alternatives of limitations or a regency and both had been rejected. Aware of his father's fate at the time of the Long Parliament, he had protected himself and his court with armed guards and he had taken care to see that the men who commanded authority in the counties, the Lords Lieutenant, the deputy lieutenants, the officers of the militia and the justices of the peace, were not men who were likely to be disloyal to the Crown.

Sir Leoline Jenkins expressed the official point of view when he wrote, a week after the dissolution, to Henry Sidney, now again back in Holland: 'Though all is quiet in the City and for aught I know everywhere else, yet we must reckon the dissolving of the Parliament a misfortune: the heats growing between the two Houses about Fitzharris made it necessary to part them. Besides nothing but the exclusion of the Duke would serve their turn.'[24] Charles himself made these points at much greater length in a declaration which he published on 8 April and ordered the Archbishops of Canterbury and York to have read in all churches during service time on Sunday. He began by saying: 'It was exceeding great trouble that we were brought to the dissolving of the two last Parliaments without more benefit to our people by the calling of them.' After outlining the course of events from his own point of view and repeating that out of 'honour, justice and conscience' he could never consent to exclusion, he ended with the assertion that he did not intend to lay aside the use of parliaments and that no irregularities should ever make him out of love with them. Halifax is believed to have had a hand in the composition of this declaration, which was certainly drawn up with the co-operation of the council. By the dubious promises given Charles hoped to allay 'the restless malice of ill men who are labouring to poison our people, some out of fondness for their old Commonwealth principles'.[25] It was reported to Secretary Jenkins that 'all good churchmen were doubtless well pleased with his Majesty's speech and resolution since this makes them brisk and the fanatics dejected'.[26]

Some historians have argued that the summoning of the Oxford Parliament was a farce put on by the King because he already knew that Louis XIV was going to grant him a subsidy on condition that England remained neutral in Europe, and that no further parliaments, which might show themselves anti-French, were called. But in fact the subsidy was a small one amounting to 2,000,000 écus (about £480,000) for one year and 500,000 écus (£120,000) for two succeeding years; and the three exclusionist Parliaments had shown themselves completely indifferent to foreign affairs. The negotiations secretly conducted through the French ambassador Barrillon had been going on for a long time, and at first the French King had been little concerned over them because he thought that the English government was powerless and that he could keep the kingdom impotent just as easily by handing out a few small bribes to members of parliament.

The negotiations had been conducted first by the aged Earl of St Albans (once the reputed lover of Charles's mother), and later by Laurence Hyde. Charles himself had been careful not to be seen with Barrillon because he feared that direct dealings with France might cause an explosion and endanger his throne. What Charles wanted was not so much money as an undertaking that the French King would lend him his support in the event of a civil war. The agreement finally reached was of a somewhat nebulous character. Louis asked for no specific undertakings from Charles whom (in the light of the events of 1674 and 1677-8) he certainly did not trust. Hyde assured Barrillon that Charles would conduct himself in a way compatible with his obligations and would disengage himself gradually (*peu à peu*) from alliances opposed to French interests, including specifically the treaty concluded with Spain. On the other hand he sought assurances from the French King that he would not again attack either the Spanish Netherlands or the United Provinces. But what Hyde told Barrillon at Oxford on 24 March (after Parliament had met there) was that the importance of the agreement was 'the certainty of the French King's friendship', which meant that Charles 'could not be despoiled (*dépouillé*) of his legitimate authority'.[27] Nothing was committed to paper. Even the Duchess of Portsmouth was not let into the secret; and Charles said that he would be chased out of his kingdom if these dealings with Louis XIV were suspected. But he promised Barrillon that he would never forget the help that had been given him.

Charles had committed himself to very little except the threat of blackmail, and this, after all, had hung over his head ever since the treaty of Dover had been signed more than ten years earlier. And when later in the same year Louis XIV in fact menaced the security of the Low Countries by aggressive action, first in the county of Chiny and later against the town of Luxembourg, Charles had no hesitation in strongly pressing the French King to avoid an open rupture of the peace and gave a warning that he would be obliged to call parliament if Louis continued to pursue his aims by force.[28]

It is therefore wrong to say that the calling of the Oxford Parliament was a mockery because of the promise of French subsidies which were but a fraction of the royal budget. Charles was determined at all costs to preserve his throne and avert civil war which, granted the temper of the House of Commons, seemed to him to constitute a genuine danger. He therefore reinsured himself. He tried to negotiate terms with Shaftesbury. He allowed the regency proposal to be put before the Commons. But he was relieved by the promise of the French King (not given until after the Oxford Parliament was in session), who had previously been indifferent to his fate, that he would give Charles his moral and material backing in the event of civil war. Moreover Charles again tried to open a line of communication with the Whigs when his nephew, William of Orange, paid a visit to England at the end of July. He ignored the blusterings of James, still marooned in Scotland: Charles would compromise but he would not be bullied.

The Whigs, again thwarted in their demand for exclusion, tried to blow fresh life into the story of the popish plot, which was the original impulse behind it. Some extremists may even have been turning against the King himself. One informer claimed in April that Major John Wildman, an erstwhile Leveller and a consistent republican, had said that 'We had enough of a king and such a one as this is and it was no sin to cut him off.'[29] The same informer also averred that Lord Howard of Escrick, another extremist, had asserted that the King was the real head of the plot.[30] In *The True Englishman speaking Plain English*, the draft pamphlet found on Fitzharris when he was arrested in February, it had been argued that since Charles was as guilty as James he should be deposed.

The case of Fitzharris was as much a *cause célèbre* in 1681 as the revelations of Titus Oates had been three years earlier. Fitzharris was related to Mrs Wall, a maid of the Duchess of Portsmouth. After he had lost his commission in the army because of the Test

Act, having a wife and several children to support, he haunted the Duchess of Portsmouth's lodgings and obtained small sums of money from her and the King, though for exactly what services is not clear. Fitzharris was such an incorrigible liar and told so many contradictory stories that it is difficult to attach importance to anything he said. One of his stories was that he was paid to plant his libellous pamphlet on various Whigs so that they could be arrested and accused of treason. Whatever the truth about the pamphlet may have been, he soon changed his tack after he had been caught red-handed, and he told the Lord Mayor, the Recorder of London and Sir Robert Clayton, an ex-Lord Mayor of Whig persuasions, when they examined him in Newgate prison on 10 March, that he had revelations to make about the Queen, the Duke of York, the Earl of Danby and the part they had played in Godfrey's murder. But when the King interviewed him in the presence of the Privy Council on the following day he refused to give any details about the plot unless he were assured of a pardon. Charles then said that he would give him no pardon 'though twenty parliaments should address him for it' and ordered him to be sent to the Tower.[31] When the House of Commons had attempted to impeach him (Shaftesbury and eighteen other peers also supporting the proposed impeachment) the Whig hope had been that Fitzharris might prove himself another and more valuable Titus Oates; for Oates had never actually framed accusations against the Duke of York.

But Charles was not going to be caught napping twice. He was steadfast in his refusal to grant a pardon to Fitzharris or any other informer. He showed an intense interest in the trial of Fitzharris and said that he wanted to make the most of it to re-establish his own authority; and he admitted that he was anxious to see Fitzharris hanged. The Whigs were equally determined that Fitzharris should be given the fullest opportunity to implicate the Queen and the Duke of York in the popish plot, and in fact four months elapsed between the time of the Irishman's arrest and his ultimate execution. Shaftesbury and the Whigs tried to argue that he could not be tried before the ordinary courts of law when the Commons had sought his impeachment; for the Commons had declared that any procedure against Fitzharris would be 'a high breach of the privilege of parliament'. But Lord Chief Justice Pemberton (whom Charles had recently appointed in place of the unreliable Scroggs) successfully resisted this argument; a true bill was found against Fitzharris by the the grand jury of Middlesex and at the end of April he was brought before the King's Bench and arraigned. On 7 May Fitzharris asked that he should be allowed to disclose in a private interview with the Lord Chief Justice, the Lord Mayor of London, Sir Robert Clayton, the Earl of Essex and the Earl of Salisbury the details of the evidence he had against the Queen, the Duke of York and the Earl of Danby for their participation in the murder of Godfrey. But the Lord Chief Justice not unnaturally ruled that he could say what he had to say in open court. In fact he did assert that the murder of Godfrey had been contrived at Windsor, and he was also willing (according to Shaftesbury) to reveal the part played by the papists in the Great Fire of London. But no witness was able to corroborate these stories and when Shaftesbury tried to secure a pardon for an unknown person who had 'a great discovery' to make, Charles refused to sanction it.

Fitzharris now shifted his ground and claimed that the Duchess of Portsmouth and Mrs Wall could bear witness that he had performed secret services for the King and done nothing without his participation. The Duchess and her maid duly appeared at the trial and denied his story. Any money that had been given him was out of charity to a ne'er-do-well hanger-on about the court. After his inevitable trial and sentence to be hanged, drawn and quartered, he changed his line again and offered to reveal to the King who had suborned him to accuse the Queen, the Duke and Danby, provided his own life was spared. Before he died he deposited a confession with the prison chaplain that it had been the Whig sheriffs who had suborned him and, to balance things out, he left letters for his wife saying that this was untrue. In his speech before his execution he declared that he had been employed by the King to give him notice what libels and other accusations were being made against him.[32] The execution on 1 July of this pathetic informer, caught in the trammels of his own super-ingenuity and exploited alike by Tories and Whigs, merely cast retrospective doubt on the whole of the popish plot. Yet on the same day that he was executed Oliver Plunkett, the Roman Catholic Archbishop of Armagh, was also executed on the testimony of Titus Oates and a host of lying Irish witnesses (brought over and sustained in London by Shaftesbury and the Whigs) for his alleged part in the popish plot.

1 July 1681 is a significant date in the reign of Charles II. In the first place, it marked a turning point in the struggle between the King and the Whig leaders, the aftermath of the dissolution of the Oxford Parliament, which had ended so surprisingly peacefully: for just as the Whigs had failed to force Charles to agree to exclusion in Oxford, so in Westminster they had been unable to reinvigorate the popish plot or to prove the Duke of York's part in it through the agency of Fitzharris. Secondly, whatever the truth might be about Fitzharris's activities, the impression could not be erased that he was but one in a long line of perjurers whose stories had been exploited to damage or destroy the Stuart monarchy. Lastly, the martyrdom of the Irish Archbishop made sensible men sick of the spilling of innocent blood. The King was now in a position to counter-attack and a Tory reaction began.

17

The King Hits Back

The quiet that followed the dissolution of the Oxford Parliament
and the conviction and execution of Fitzharris encouraged Charles
II to hit back against his enemies. It appeared as if the immediate
danger of civil war had passed. All the evidence goes to show that
Charles himself directed the operations against the Whigs. His
programme consisted of three parts. First, he was determined not
to call another Parliament unless he was driven into it by a war
in the Netherlands. Secondly, he decided to use every resource
to put Tories into positions of authority and influence both in
London and the provinces. Early in June, for example, an Order in
Council was issued that persons left out of the Commission of
Peace should be excluded from all public employments. Lords
Lieutenant and Deputy Lieutenants were changed. Recorders and
town clerks were dismissed. Orders were given that penal laws
against dissenters were to be enforced. On one excuse or another
corporations were pressed to surrender their royal charters for revision and, where this was refused, the more complicated procedure
of issuing a *quo warranto* writ for their forfeiture was employed.

London, hitherto a Whig stronghold, was harder to subdue.
But on Michaelmas day 1681 Sir John Moore, a Lord Mayor
sympathetic to the court, was elected because the Whig votes
were split. The King had made it clear that he would not confirm
the new Lord Mayor if the election were irregular or contrary to
the customs of the City. Sir John Moore's election turned out to
be the beginning of a difficult but ultimately successful campaign
launched against the City Whigs. Thirdly, it was decided to
enlist the help of the legion of informers which had been conjured into existence after the initial successes of Titus Oates,

including the poverty-stricken group of perjurers who had been brought over from Ireland by the Whigs, to change sides and act as witnesses in the law courts against their former employers. Charles himself had no misgivings about their character; he told Mr Justice Warcup later (in December 1682) that informers were all knaves.[1] It is possible, as has been seen, that the Irishman Fitzharris, aware of this policy, had been attempting to help the Tory cause by concocting evidence against the Whigs. But he had lost his nerve and in trying to play the game both ways had lost his life as well.

In June 1681 two minor Whig minions, John Rouse, a servant of Sir Thomas Player, a member of the London Common Council, and Stephen College, known as 'the Protestant joiner', who was alleged to have plotted an armed rebellion against the King at the time of the Oxford Parliament, were placed under arrest. But on 2 July the government flew at higher game. The Earl of Shaftesbury was woken at his London house early in the morning and taken into custody. He was brought before the King (who had ridden up from Windsor for the purpose) and the Privy Council, over which Shaftesbury himself had once presided, and accused of treason. He denied his guilt and asked who the witnesses against him might be. But his defence was ignored. Charles stood firm and insisted that seventeen members of the council (three had already withdrawn from the meeting) should sign a warrant committing Shaftesbury to the Tower. Lord Howard of Escrick, another leading Whig of dubious character, whom Fitzharris had tried to bring over to the King's side, was already in the Tower. So too were the Earl of Danby and three of the five Roman Catholic Lords originally accused of treason by Titus Oates (one having died and another, Lord Stafford, having been executed). Shaftesbury's house was searched for incriminating documents, but the only thing of moment that was found was a draft Bill of Association, anonymous and undated, whose signatories were invited to protect the King and prevent a Roman Catholic succession.

Before Shaftesbury could be put on trial before a commission of his fellow peers (who would be nominated by the King) a true bill had to be found against him, accepting that there was a case to be answered, by a grand jury chosen in Middlesex, the county where the alleged crimes had been committed. The grand juries were packed with their own adherents by Whig sheriffs, and a true bill was found against neither Rouse nor College: the juries returned the verdict *ignoramus*. But in the case of College the government found an ingenious if mean solution. The case was retried in Oxford on the ground that the treasonable deeds had been done there. College was quickly indicted and subsequently arraigned before the Assizes and found guilty. On 22 August Secretary Jenkins wrote to the Sheriff of Oxfordshire that the King was 'abundantly satisfied with his conduct'. He added that Charles thought 31 August a proper day for the execution and ordered that the traitor's head should be sent up to London and set up on Temple Bar.[2] On the other hand, Charles was infuriated by the behaviour of the London juries. Reresby related how in October both when walking in St James's park and when seated in the Duchess of Portsmouth's lodgings Charles had talked at length of the unjust verdicts and said: 'It is a hard case that I am the last man to have law and justice in the whole nation.'[3]

But with these verdicts as precedents it never seemed likely that a true bill would be found against Shaftesbury. Nevertheless it was possible: for had not a true bill been found against Fitzharris and might not Shaftesbury also be brought before a grand jury not in London but in Oxford? Shaftesbury, who was sixty and a sick man, had suffered discomfort in the Tower and had petitioned the King to be released on the grounds of health. Charles allowed him only to take coach drives with his wife. He was kept there for nearly nine months on the ground that it was too late to try him before the next law term. Shaftesbury had consequently attempted to strike a bargain with the King. Approaching Charles through his old colleague in 'the Cabal', the Earl of Arlington, who still held office as Lord Chamberlain, Shaftesbury offered to leave the country and retire to the colony of Carolina, of which he was one of the proprietors, provided that he was given a pardon together with the sum of £3,000, which he said was owing to him. But Charles was not to be moved. He said: 'If it were anybody else, though he knew he were guilty and could prove it upon him, he would grant what he desires; but to him he knew that if he should do this he would say the condition was exacted from him and that it was a force put upon him.'4

So Shaftesbury's case had to be heard before the grand jury. It was a struggle between the Tories and the Whigs. Leading Whig magnates and 'a great rabble', favourable to the accused, crowded into the court room at the Old Bailey. The new Lord Chief Justice of the King's Bench, Sir Francis Pemberton presided over the proceedings and attempted to impress upon the jury that it was their patrotic duty to find a true bill if the King's witnesses showed there was any kind of a case to answer. But the grand jury was not to be intimidated. It consisted of wealthy Whigs, the foreman being a successful East Indian merchant who had formerly been an exclusionist Member of Parliament. The foreman and jury had no difficulty in exposing the credibility of the witnesses. The only solid piece of evidence produced was the draft Association discovered among Shaftesbury's papers; but it could be seen that this Association was similar to one passed by Parliament during the reign of Queen Elizabeth 1 and another discussed in the House of Commons in 1680. There was no question that the verdict of *ignoramus* given on 24 November was a fair one, though it is true that the grand jury would, even had the evidence been more convincing, have done the same.

Four days later Shaftesbury appeared before the Court of King's Bench and asked for bail. The King's own son, the Duke of Monmouth, offered to stand surety. Shaftesbury was released on his own recognizances and lived for another year to direct the machinations of the Whigs. But in the absence of a Parliament there was little that the Whigs could do to forward the cause of exclusion except publish pamphlets and fight what proved to be a losing battle for the control of the City government. Even before Shaftesbury's trial it was reported to Jenkins that the 'fanatic party' are 'in very great readiness for rebellion'.5 John Locke, the philosopher who was Shaftesbury's secretary and confident, had already written most of his treatises on government in which he argued in favour of the right of rebellion against a government that had betrayed its trust. And there is little doubt that the thoughts of the Whig grandees were turning towards a conspiracy against the throne. Charles II still had a stiff struggle ahead of him. He openly complained to the foreign ambassadors in London 'of the hard measure done him by Lord Shaftesbury's jury'.[6] And his path was not eased because during that time he was under constant pressure both from the Dutch and Spanish ambassadors and from some of his own council to summon another Parliament in order that measures might be taken against the continuing aggressions of the King of France in Europe.

Since the conclusion of the treaty of Nymegen Louis XIV had done everything in his power by what his latest biographer calls 'a policy of violence and terror'[7] to extend and strengthen the eastern frontier of France. Taking advantage of the complicated territorial structure that had survived from the Middle Ages, claims, many of which had lain dormant, were revived for French sovereignty over districts that might be called dependencies or appendages to areas acquired by France. Invoking the services of tribunals known as Chambers of Reunion, which were under French influence, many claims were put forward and these were backed by an army of some 150,000 men that the French King had kept in being. In midsummer 1681 the Chamber of Reunion at Metz had discovered that the country of Chiny, a fief of Luxembourg, belonging to the King of Spain, really ought to be French. It was promptly occupied by French troops, and clearly the fortified town of Luxembourg itself would soon be threatened. By August a blockade of the town was quickly being established. At the end of September the Free City of Strasbourg in Alsace was subjected to a military *coup* on the ground that it had been assigned to France by the treaty of Westphalia. At the same time the strategic city of Casale on the river Po in northern Italy was purchased from the Duke of Mantua.

All France's neighbours were in a state of consternation. When William of Orange had visited England after the dissolution of the Oxford Parliament, he had vainly tried to interest Charles in the situation. Charles was too absorbed in his own internal difficulties to offer any help. Moreover the secret subsidy agreement concluded with the French ambassador in March, though its terms were not very specific, had to some extent made him the clandestine ally of the King of France. On the other hand Charles hoped and believed he was in a position to influence and perhaps restrain his royal brother. As early as April Hyde, who alone of the King's councillors was aware of the secret agreement, told Barrillon that the King would be embarrassed if the French moved in the Low Countries or Alsace, and Charles himself expressed his hope that there would be no 'open rupture'.[8] In fact Charles was principally worried about the French provoking the Dutch or the Spaniards into declaring war; for if the Dutch were engaged, Spanish Flanders would again be the centre of the fighting, while the Spaniards might feel obliged to make war in defence of Luxembourg. In either case the King of Spain would have the right to invoke English help under the terms of the Anglo-Spanish treaty of June 1680, while the Dutch might demand English intervention on the ground that Charles had guaranteed the terms of the treaty of Nymegen.

In the autumn of 1681 Charles agreed, on the advice of Halifax, that his ambassador in Paris should undertake a joint representation with the Dutch to the French King begging him to refrain from *voyes de fait* (acts of aggression)[9] and asking him to refer all matters in dispute to a frontier conference which had been sitting at Courtrai since the ratification of the treaty of Nymegen. At the same time Charles personally pressed the French King not to carry out fresh conquests of the Low Countries. While Charles assured Barrillon of his continuing friendship, he said he would be 'lost' if this happened and that he might be compelled to call a Parliament.[10] In October London was thick with rumours that a new Parliament was going to be summoned. Halifax informed William of Orange that while Charles was in no position to go to war, if the French King violated the peace in the Spanish Netherlands, he would join with the Dutch in 'taking measures' and would call a Parliament.[11] Charles himself told the Dutch ambassador in London that because he was reluctant to call a Parliament, which was certain to be factious, he could not declare war on France, but that if the Dutch declared war, he would be loyal to his obligations as a guarantor of the treaty of Nymegen and would furnish what assistance he could. At the same time Charles repeatedly warned Barrillon that he might be compelled to call a Parliament; and while the Duchess of Portsmouth expressed the opinion to the French ambassador that Charles dared not do so, Hyde told Barrillon that if the blockade of Luxembourg were not lifted Charles would be forced into it.

Louis XIV rejected the joint Anglo-Dutch representations in Paris. Charles had never expected that much good would come from them, and he was in fact pushed into agreeing to them by his advisers. He preferred to rely on his own influence with Louis XIV and himself suggested an 'expedient' or compromise. In December he told Barrillon frankly that he had no intention of calling a Parliament: 'they are devils,' he said, 'who want my ruin'. But, he went on, 'in the name of God please tell the King my brother to relieve me of my embarrassment, for despite what I say, I shall have to call parliament if an expedient is not found over the Luxembourg affair'.[12] Charles's own suggested expedient was that he himself should try to persuade the Spaniards to yield Luxembourg provided that its fortifications were destroyed and provided that he himself were given four months in which to make the effort. In return for the surrender of Luxembourg and its surrounding villages, the French King was asked to agree to withdraw his troops from Alost, Ghent and other places in Spanish Flanders within three months.

Louis XIV refused to accept Charles's secret proposal and also publicly snubbed the English and Dutch ambassadors in Paris. Nevertheless he began to back-pedal over Luxembourg. At the beginning of 1682 he allowed food into the town, and in March he suddenly lifted the blockade and at the same time announced that he would refer disputed questions in the Low Countries to the arbitration of the King of England. Charles was delighted and took the credit to himself. He had, after all, made plain the lines on which he would arbitrate. He did venture to suggest, however, that the Dutch should be joined with him as arbitrators, but this was refused by France. Nevertheless he thought he was now in a strong enough position to warn the Spanish ambassador that if the Spaniards were to renew war against France he would not help them.

Historians have disputed why Louis XIV in fact raised the blockade of Luxembourg in March 1682. One historian has argued that it had nothing to do with Charles but was because the Dutch were making overt preparations to assist Spain. Louis XIV's latest biographer claims that Louis was concerned over the assault that the Turks were now known to be preparing against Vienna. As Most Christian King, Louis did not want to be accused of indirectly facilitating the Turkish offensive by starting a war in the Netherlands. It is nevertheless reasonable to assume that Louis also did not want to drive Charles to desperate measures. Certainly Halifax, who was at the centre of affairs, thought so. If a Parliament had then been called in England, a triple alliance might have been formed against Louis XIV, as it had been in 1668. Although an additional million *livres* had been offered to Charles as the price of his neutrality, there is no reason to suppose that Louis entirely trusted the English King's constant professions of friendship or ignored the gist of the lengthy dispatches from his ambassador in London who reiterated that Charles might be compelled to call a Parliament if Luxembourg had been occupied.

Thus during 1682 Charles was mainly occupied with foreign affairs. He was determined to avoid calling a Parliament and being pushed into a war from which he had nothing to gain. The year was also one of success for the King in his domestic affairs. As Dr Burnet wrote, 'the Court was everywhere triumphant'.[13] Why was this? The decline of Shaftesbury and the Whigs has recently been subjected to close analysis. The answer appears to be that the Whigs had been able to frustrate the King's Government only so long as they met together in Parliament and refused to discuss any other question but the exclusion of the Duke of York from succession to the throne. But once they had rejected any kind of compromise over exclusion and Charles had decided to try to govern without calling a Parliament, the Whigs lost their forum and rallying ground; the struggle between the Whigs and Tories had then been transferred from Parliament to the law courts: and there the only advantage that the Whigs possessed was their ability, through the power of the London sheriffs to nominate juries, to protect their adherents and particularly their leader, Shaftesbury, from condemnation for treason.

So during 1682 Charles also intensified the policy of obtaining Tory control over local government and especially of winning Tory supremacy in London. The struggle was long and complicated. It began the previous December when, after Shaftesbury had been released on bail, the Treasury solicitor, Richard Graham, delivered a *quo warranto* writ to one of the Whig sheriffs. But this writ was bound to be resisted and would involve long-drawn-out proceedings in the law courts. Meanwhile the complexion of the City government might be changed. Advantage was taken of the fact that the Lord Mayor, Sir John Moore, favoured the court and so did many of the Aldermen, although the Common Council had a Whig majority. Elaborate manœuvres and counter-manœuvres went on throughout the summer, in which the Tories had the active assistance of the King. He personally encouraged Sir John Moore to stand firm, and at one stage tried to help by ordering the arrest of the Whig sheriffs. Finally by Michaelmas both a new Tory Lord Mayor, Sir William Pritchard by name, and two Tory sheriffs had been elected. There was also a small Tory majority in the Common Council. It was then said that 'the King has mastered this great beast, the City'.[14] But it was not until nine months later that the validity of the *quo warranto* writ was upheld by the judges. When the news was received by the King at Windsor in June 1683 Charles was 'very well pleased with it'. Within a week regulations were issued to which the City had to submit. Among other things these regulations gave Charles a complete veto over the choice of the Lord Mayor and sheriffs.[15]

Charles had now grouped round him loyal and efficient servants: Laurence Hyde, who in due course was created Earl of Rochester, was at the head of the Treasury; Halifax, who was promoted to be a Marquis and in October became Lord Privy Seal; Sir Leoline Jenkins, Secretary of State for the South, a Cavalier of the old school, who had fought for Charles I in the civil war, and proved himself exceptionally industrious and a peace-maker between Rochester and Halifax; and finally the Earl of Sunderland, whom

Charles restored to his favour during the summer and in January 1683 appointed Secretary of State for the North in place of the ineffective Conway: he was invaluable for his knowledge of foreign affairs. Of these Ministers the most independent-minded was Halifax. He wanted Charles to be reconciled to Shaftesbury and to call another Parliament. On the other hand, he recognized the gulf that existed between the King and the exclusionists and he warned William of Orange to remove the impression that 'anyone known to be contrary to the King's interests in London can have any credit or influence with him [William]'.[16] Many of the surrendered or forfeited charters passed through Halifax's office as Lord Privy Seal. Thus he was, as he himself later boasted, a 'trimmer' in politics. In foreign affairs he was anti-French. But Barrillon told Louis XIV that there was no need to worry over Halifax's influence with the King; for, he wrote, 'When one of his Ministers was of an opinion opposed to his, Charles would know how to act as a master and to make decisions independently of their advice.'[17]

In the summer Charles recalled his brother James from Scotland. At the same time Charles's son, Monmouth, attempted to obtain a reconciliation with his father, but added that he would not on any account be reconciled to his uncle, the Duke of York. Monmouth also threatened to fight a duel with the Marquis of Halifax, whom he accused of influencing his father against him. Charles was furious: he refused to see his son and completely exonerated Halifax. He also gave orders that none of his courtiers was to have anything to do with Monmouth. The result was that Monmouth drew closer to Shaftesbury. The two of them hoped to compel the King to call another exclusionist Parliament, and even talked about the possibility of an armed rising. Early in September Monmouth set out on a 'progress' in the north of England, hoping to whip up the same kind of public acclaim as he had achieved during his tour of the west in 1680. But on 20 September Monmouth was arrested for disturbing the public peace at Stafford and was brought back to London; though he was allowed bail, he was forbidden to appear at court. Shaftesbury is alleged to have said: 'the Duke of Monmouth was an unfortunate man, for God had thrice put it in his power to save England, and make himself the greatest man in Europe; but he had neglected the use of all those opportunities'.[18] Yet after the final election of the Tory sheriffs in London on 28 September, Shaftesbury himself lost his nerve and, fearing that he might again be put under arrest, hid himself in London for eight weeks; then he fled to Holland where, on 21 January 1683, he died.

During this year of political triumph Charles was a little lonely. The days of his complete sexual promiscuity were over. 'The King', wrote Dr Burnet, 'divided himself between Louise de Kéroualle and mistress Gwyn: and he had no other avowed amour.' But the vulgar vitality of Nell Gwyn was no real substitute for the gracious charm of the Frenchwoman who 'studied to please him and observe him in everything'.[19] Louise was expensive and demanding. Her son, the Duke of Richmond, was appointed the King's Master of the Horse at a precocious age in place of the disgraced Duke of Monmouth. When in the following year the connoisseur, John Evelyn, visited the Duchess of Portsmouth's dressing room in the company of the King, he noted 'the rich and splendid furniture of this woman's apartment, now twice or thrice pulled down and rebuilt to satisfy her prodigal and expensive pleasures'. There he saw 'the new fabric of French tapestry, for design, tenderness of work and incomparable imitation of the best paintings beyond anything I had ever beheld . . . then for Japan cabinets, screens, pendulum clocks, huge vases of wrought plate, tables, stands, chimney furniture, sconces, *braseros* . . . all of massive silver without number'.[20] The Moroccan ambassador when he was shown round these apartments by the King was surprised 'at the fine glass room', 'where he at once saw himself a thousand times all at once'.[21] The King's affair, if such it was, with the other Frenchwoman, Hortense Mancini, Duchess of Mazarin, was now over, but in February 1682 he begged Louis XIV to induce her husband to resume the payment of her pension, which had been discontinued for two years. For Louise he sought a French title. In the end the French King thought it advisable to grant both these requests.

Towards the close of February 1683 the Duchess of Portsmouth left England with her son for a holiday in France. Charles became lonelier still; it was reported on 7 March that 'at Newmarket His Majesty is so alone that he is forced to play at basset [a card game]'.[22] When Louise returned in July the King went to the Downs to meet her and was delighted when she told him of the excellent treatment she had received in France. Although it was said that Cabinet councils used to meet in her apartments, it is perfectly clear from Barrillon's dispatches that she had nothing like the political influence or information possessed by Louis XIV's morganatic wife, Madame de Maintenon. She was not let into the secret of the agreement of March 1681, and Charles does not appear to have consulted her about any of his major decisions. It is true that she helped to facilitate James's recall to London and that she was also helpful in the Earl of Sunderland's restoration to royal favour. But the King might well have done these things of his own accord. At most her political influence was marginal. But the affair lasted fifteen years and she became more like a wife than a mistress. On the whole, she was faithful to the King. But it was widely rumoured after her return to England that she bestowed her favours on a young Frenchman, Philippe de Vendôme, Grand Prior of France, the younger son of the Duc de Vendôme and Laura Mancini, sister to Hortense. The King had shown little jealousy over his other mistresses. But in November 1683 he ordered the Grand Prior to leave the country; and when he showed himself reluctant to do so, Charles said that if he did not depart within a few days he would send his guards to conduct him to the packet boat. Alternatively Charles requested Barrillon to provide his fellow countryman with a yacht. Charles was not easy to arouse and was quick to forgive. But that episode was a measure of his dependence on Louise de Kéroualle.

While Louis XIV was preparing to gratify Charles by granting the concessions he sought for his French mistress and ex-mistress, and was paying the remainder of the agreed subsidy in driblets of 50,000 *livres* (under £4,000) at a time,[23] almost the whole of the continental mainland of Europe was menaced by war. In March 1683 it was commonly said in London that though at the moment peace still prevailed, there was war in the offing. It was known that the Turks were assembling a huge army in preparation for an attack on the Habsburg Empire from the east in co-operation with dissident Hungarians. The aggressive policy of the French King was provoking the proud Spaniards beyond endurance, while the Prince of Orange feared for the security of the United Netherlands. Some German princes, including the Great Elector of Brandenburg, who were jealous of the Emperor Leopold I, were selling themselves to the French. Finally there was a strong possibility of a war in the Baltic between the Swedes (now allied to the Dutch) and the Danes (now allied to the French).

Charles's consistent policy was to keep out of war: apart from the fact that he had not the resources to pay for it without parliamentary help, he was afraid that if he sent troops to fight in northern Europe there might be a Whig revival or even a Whig rebellion against his government at home. To cut down his expenses on foreign affairs the decision was taken at the end of 1682 to abandon Tangier – for whose succour Charles had vainly pleaded with the House of Commons in 1680. In the summer of 1683 the Earl of Dartmouth was commissioned to go to Tangier with a fleet, destroy the fortifications and the mole, and bring back the garrison. This task he completed by March 1684. Meanwhile the Spanish and Dutch ambassadors in London continued to press Charles to act as an arbitrator or general mediator in the disputes between France and Spain. In May they presented him with a memorial inviting him to send a representative to a conference which was being held between the Dutch and their allies at The Hague. Charles refused to participate in this conference or to act as a general mediator. Equally he rejected a suggestion from William of Orange that he should take action to prevent a war in the Baltic; and at about the same time he protested to the Dutch over their behaviour at Bantam in Java where the merchants of the English East India company had been driven from their factory. In desperation the King of Spain offered Charles money for his help: it seems by then to have been commonly suspected that the King of England was receiving a subsidy from France. But Charles spurned this offer as well.

One thing was clear, as Charles realized. The Spanish Habsburgs were not going to receive any assistance from the Austrian Habsburgs. By the middle of July the Turks had encamped outside the walls of Vienna and the Emperor had fled from his capital. Taking advantage of this distraction in eastern Europe, Louis xiv renewed the blockade of Luxembourg. The Spaniards thereupon declared war on France in the evident hope that the Dutch and English would be obliged to come to their assistance. Ronquillo, the Spanish ambassador in London, promptly demanded English aid in accordance with the terms of the treaty of 1680. Charles decided to give no reply in writing and laughed at the offer of Spanish money. Though his Ministers were divided over what reason the King should give for refusing to fulfil his treaty obligations, Charles himself told the Spanish ambassador that he was unable to do so for internal reasons and advised him to urge his King to raze the fortifications of Luxembourg and hand it over to the French.

Louis xiv replied to the Spanish declaration of war with a *Blitzkrieg*. In September 1683 a French army invaded the Spanish Netherlands: the frontier towns of Courtrai and Dixmude were bombarded into submission; the countryside was systematically ravaged. Louis xiv then demanded that the Spaniards should give up Luxembourg and fourteen or fifteen surrounding villages; that they should hand over Courtrai and Dixmude, whose fortifications he agreed to destroy; and for the return of Chimay to Spain he should be granted an 'equivalent' in Catalonia or Navarre.[24] Spain was given until the end of the year to accept these conditions. Charles thought that they were reasonable and ordered that they should be translated into English and printed. The King and his Ministers did venture to suggest to the French that, upon the conclusion of peace, they should offer some sort of guarantee of the neutrality of the Low Countries. For they were aware of the sensitivity of English public opinion to French aggression in this area.

During the winter of 1683–4 Charles concentrated his diplomatic efforts on pressing the Spaniards to conclude peace on the French terms. He thought that the Spaniards had been foolish in making war in the first place; he was convinced that William of Orange was mistaken in imagining that the States-General of the United Provinces would be willing to intervene; and he was aware that the Holy Roman Emperor, whose troops, assisted by a Polish army, had defeated the Turks at Vienna after a two-month siege in the previous autumn, was now absorbed in a great counteroffensive in Hungary. Charles was also opposed to offering Anglo-Dutch arbitration and throughout the spring of 1684 he continued to press the Dutch and the Spaniards to agree to peace. He even refused to allow the Spaniards to recruit soldiers in England. And when he and his Ministers learned that Luxembourg had fallen, they were delighted because they were now convinced that peace would be re-established.

The secret agreement between Charles II and Louis XIV expired in April 1684 (although it was calculated that 770,000 *livres* of the subsidy were still owing). But this made no difference to Charles's foreign policy, which remained pro-French. After the fall of Luxembourg Louis XIV offered to conclude a twenty-year truce with the Spaniards, the Dutch and the Holy Roman Emperor of the German nation. This was accepted by the Diet of Ratisbon and much more reluctantly by the United Netherlands and Spain. Charles 'liked it well', arguing that it would bring a settled peace on reasonable terms and that the whole of Christian Europe could now turn against the Turks.[25] William of Orange thought the peace infamous, but the Regents of Amsterdam, who held the purse-strings, had all along been opposed to another war with France. Charles said that William was pig-headed. At the end of June Barrillon reported his opinion that 'the King of England feels pleased with his conduct up to the present and recognizes more and more every day that his understanding with Your Majesty is very advantageous to the good of his affairs'.[26] In August Charles told Barrillon that he had taken the side of Louis XIV for all his life; that this inclination and esteem for him had begun at the time when he was in France and since then he had always aimed to enjoy Louis XIV's friendship.[27]

It would be a mistake however to take Charles's sycophancy at its face value. In the first place, Charles's observations to Barrillon were a prelude to the expression of a hope that the truce would not mean that the French government was going to grant trading concessions to the Dutch which would be detrimental to England. At the same time the Duchess of Portsmouth, evidently speaking under Charles's prompting, said that she trusted 'there was no substance in the belief that Louis XIV always preferred the friendship of the States-General to that of the King of England'.[28] When the news of the signature of the peace treaty between France and Spain was confirmed in London later in the month, Charles once more talked to Barrillon in the Duchess's apartments and begged him to persuade Louis XIV not to grant commercial concessions to the Dutch.

Charles was undoubtedly extremely anti-Dutch at this time. He was furious about the expulsion of the English merchants from Bantam; he was annoyed with William of Orange for trying to involve him in war; and he feared that the United Netherlands would give underhand assistance to his political enemies in England. It was to Holland that the Earl of Shaftesbury had fled after the City of London had turned against the Whigs, and several of Shaftesbury's friends and supporters had also gone there (including John Locke). So too had the ninth Earl of Argyll, who in 1681 had been condemned to death for treason in Scotland and had escaped from imprisonment in Edinburgh castle. Finally the Duke of Monmouth, who had to some extent taken Shaftesbury's place as the Whig leader, had recently visited Holland and received a warm welcome from William of Orange. Charles was annoyed about this and also about a report that William was putting the command of British troops in Dutch service into the hands of officers recommended to him by Monmouth. But, on the whole, Charles reckoned that his foreign policy had been a success. He believed that 'factious people' in his kingdom might have engaged in rebellion against him if war had set the whole of Europe on fire.[29] He had indeed been supplied with information that such a rebellion had been in contemplation from the time when Shaftesbury went into hiding. To these discoveries and their consequences for the remainder of Charles's life we shall revert in the next chapter.

18

The Last Years

The firm policy adopted by the King during the two years following the dissolution of the Oxford Parliament threw the Whigs
into a state of confusion. When Charles was away from his capital
in Windsor or Newmarket he ordered the Earl of Craven, who
was in command of his troops in London, to prevent and disperse
all dangerous meetings. The Lord Mayor and Aldermen of the
City were instructed to see that 'conventicles and unlawful
assemblies were not held in the common halls of the City companies',[1] and they were warned on no account to entertain the
Whig leaders. Titus Oates was turned out of his lodgings in
Whitehall and his brother, Samuel Oates, offered to go over to
Holland and 'smoke out the designs' of those Whigs, headed by
Shaftesbury, who had fled there after the election of the Tory
sheriffs. Before Shaftesbury's flight and death the King had
declared that he would have nothing more to do with him, 'the
noble patriot of his country, the Protestant Lord',[2] and although
Charles was prepared to forgive his son the Duke of Monmouth
on terms, a careful watch was kept on all his movements; and in
view of his friendship with Shaftesbury the King declared that
he was 'very angry with him [Monmouth] and resolved to take
every way to undeceive the world that he is not'.[3] In the autumn
of 1681 the great poet, John Dryden, had published the first part of
his satire *Absalom and Achitophel*, holding up Monmouth and
Shaftesbury to ridicule, and had followed this up with another
satire on Shaftesbury and the Whigs, the theme of which had
been suggested to him by Charles himself. Charles had said to
Dryden that if he were a poet – and he was poor enough to be a
poet – this was the kind of poem he would have written. When

Dryden finished *The Medal* in March 1682, the King gave him a hundred broad pieces.

The Whigs, after their defeat in London, had embarked on a pamphlet war. Booklets with such titles as *A Defence of the Charter and the Municipal Rights of the City of London*, *The Irregular Account of the Swearing the Two Pretended Sheriffs*, *The Growth of Popery*, *The Raree Show*, *The Perplext Prince* and *The Whore's Rhetoric* were published. In spite of his arrest at Stafford and subsequent release on bail, Monmouth continued to court popularity in different parts of the kingdom. In February 1683 he was presented with a purse of gold and a barrel of ale by the city of Hull, of which he had formerly been the Governor, and thence he went to Chichester in Sussex where he was reported 'to have animated the factious very much'.[4] The Bishop of Chichester sent news of 'three young men who drank a health to the Duke of Monmouth and confusion and damnation to the King and Duke of York and withal swore they would set the Crown on the Duke of Monmouth's head in spite of all the Tory soldiers'.[5] In this same month Sir Robert Vyner, a former Lord Mayor of London, gave information that 'fanatics' were 'consulting to disturb the Government and were lurking about the City with fire-arms and battle-axes'.[6] In April a riot took place in Oxford, the townsmen crying 'A Monmouth, A Monmouth'.[7] News of similar unrest reached the King from Taunton. The question was whether the opposition to Charles and his brother James, manifested in the distribution of libels and isolated riots and demonstrations, went further: whether there had in fact been, since the election of the Tory sheriffs, a concerted plan for rebellion and for the murder of the King and Duke of York. In June 1683 informers came forward and swore that this was indeed so.

The first informer to appear was a negligible figure, Josiah Keeling by name, a bankrupt Anabaptist 'oil-man' or dyer, who had been haunting the London taverns in search of money. His story was that a one-eyed maltster, Captain Rumbold, owned a house, called the Rye after a nearby meadow, situated in Hertfordshire some eighteen miles from London. This house looked down on a side road which the King and Duke of York sometimes used when travelling by coach from Newmarket to London. A plan had been concocted, it was said, in the previous March, for which recruiting took place in the London taverns, to attack the coach and murder its occupants. Some of the murder party were to assault the coachman, some the guards, and the others to kill the King and the Duke. Blunderbusses were to be provided for the purpose and it was estimated that forty or fifty men were required to complete the job. If the horses did not drop, two men, disguised as labourers, were to pull an empty cart across the lane to block the coach. Unfortunately there was a severe fire at New-market that March, which burnt down half the town, and the King decided to return to London earlier than had been an-ticipated. Thus his life was miraculously saved. Keeling's story was subsequently confirmed by two other informers, who them-selves were knee-deep in the plot but, like Keeling had been promised pardons. These were Robert West, a barrister of the Middle Temple, reputed to be a determined atheist and a student of Machiavelli, and Colonel John Romsey, a former Crom-wellian officer and tax collector at Bristol, who himself had volunteered to kill the King. As these three and another man named Nehemiah Bourne were all pardoned and Rumbold, the owner of Rye House, was frightened into fleeing the country, not many of the alleged conspirators were left to be tried and punished. Among these was Captain Thomas Walcot, who was alleged by the informers to have been willing to kill the King's coachman but not to kill the King, a nice distinction which, as Walcot said at his trial, he failed to understand; a half-witted joiner named William Hone; and two sea captains, John Rouse and William Blague. Walcot, who was put on trial first, insisted that he had been framed; and though he admitted on the scaffold to having listened to some treasonable talk, he denied that he was involved in any murder plot. The idea of killing the King on his way to or from Newmarket had been floating about in London alehouses and coffee houses ever since 1678: it originated perhaps in the fertile mind of Major John Wildman, a professional plotter and double spy since the days of the Commonwealth, but little evidence exists that it ever approached the realms of reality. It is probable that it was as much a myth as the popish plot and that Robert West, the most voluble informer, who frequently contradicted himself, was as big a liar as Titus Oates.[8]

But from the government's point of view the story had rich possibilities. In the first place, news of 'a horrid plot' to assassinate the King was at this stage well calculated to inspire patriotic loyalty. In the second place some of the informers, notably West and Romsey, in order to give verisimilitude to their stories, alleged that there had been in existence at least since the autumn of 1682 a council of leading Whigs, comprising the Duke of Monmouth, Lord Russell, the Earl of Essex, Algernon Sidney (Henry's brother), John Hampden (grandson of the hero of Charles I's reign), and Lord Howard of Escrick, who had been planning an insurrection on a national scale. When orders were given for the arrest of these men, Howard, who was found hiding in a chimney, offered to turn King's evidence. It was on the basis of his testimony that Russell and Sidney were condemned to death. Essex killed himself with a borrowed razor in prison. Hampden (against whom two witnesses could not be found) was subjected to a crippling fine. Monmouth, after being promised a pardon by his father if he would confirm the complicity of his fellow conspirators, fled abroad, where he remained for almost the whole of the rest of the reign. Thus the Whig party, with its leaders dead or in exile, was shattered.

What is the truth of the matter and how far was Charles himhimself responsible for the judicial murder of his enemies? The stories of the informers and particularly of Thomas Shepherd, a wine merchant, at whose house Monmouth, Russell and others met at least once in the autumn of 1682, when considered in conjunction with the narratives written in Holland by Ford, Lord Grey, a boon companion of Monmouth, and Robert Ferguson, another friend or servant of the Duke, during the reign of James II, seem to show that conspiratorial talk had taken place and tentative plans examined. The suicide of Essex was suspicious, for though he had 'protested that "he knew nothing of any design to murder the King," he said nothing to vindicate himself from being in other designs against the Government'.[9]

Russell, in a letter to the King to be delivered after his death, did not deny that he had 'heard many things and said some things contrary to my duty',[10] though at his trial he maintained that this was not treason but no more than 'misprision of treason'. Monmouth declared to the King at the end of the year that Russell, Essex and the Earl of Salisbury (all of whom, admittedly, were then dead) had been concerned in a conspiracy. It seems likely enough that Shaftesbury, when he was hiding in London during October 1682, had turned his thoughts towards rebellion. The story was frequently repeated that Shaftesbury had claimed to have 'ten thousand brisk boys' in Wapping ready to do his will. The talk was then said to have been of organizing a concerted rising in London, Taunton and Cheshire – all three places which were known by the government to have been disaffected. No doubt it was little more than talk, for the Duke of Monmouth, the only experienced soldier among the alleged conspirators, thought Shaftesbury had 'too hot a brain', had 'leaped out of the frying pan into the fire', and that his 'brisk boys' were non-existent.[11] So in the end nothing came of the proposed rebellion, which the informants called 'the general point', and it was left to them to invent and reveal 'the lopping point', the proposed assassination of the King.

Charles himself, with his long memory stretching back to the civil wars, had no reason to doubt that his enemy, Shaftesbury, who in his youth had served in Oliver Cromwell's Council of State, when thrice defeated on exclusion in Parliament, might in the last months of his life have been plotting a rebellion against the throne; and assassination is an occupational hazard of kingship. Charles was not a vindictive man. He was ready to forgive Monmouth, who had to some extent taken Shaftesbury's place as the Whig leader. He would have spared the life of Russell, had he not allowed his brother to dissuade him against it. In the opinion of a modern lawyer, the conduct of Lord Chief Justice Pemberton, who presided over Russell's case, was 'exemplary', though it is admitted that the conviction of Algernon Sidney was 'a gross miscarriage of justice'.[12] George Jeffreys, whom another modern lawyer has attempted to whitewash,[13] and was appointed by

Charles Lord Chief Justice of the King's Bench in July 1683, once opined that the judges were all rogues. And after 1680 it has been concluded by an impartial student that 'by free use of the power of appointment and removal and by the power of persuasion which comes from royal prestige, Charles gradually moulded the judges into an instrument of personal power'.[14] To that extent Charles contributed unfairly to the destruction of his domestic enemies.

Some of those who were implicated in the so-called Rye House plot managed to flee the country including Ford, Lord Grey, Robert Ferguson, James Holloway and Sir Thomas Armstrong, while Major John Wildman (together with two others), who first dreamt up the murder plot, was released for lack of evidence. Holloway was later recaptured in the West Indies and was executed after he confessed what little he knew, and Armstrong was also captured and put to death as an outlaw. But the most important character to escape was the Duke of Monmouth, of whom Lord Bruce, then a Gentleman of the King's Bedchamber, wrote in his memoirs that 'he was a fine courtier, but of a most poor understanding as to cabinet and politics and gave himself wholly up to flatterers and knaves by consequence'.[15] Monmouth, in the end, had been Shaftesbury's candidate for the succession to the throne if James had been excluded. Thus James naturally feared and disliked him; on the other hand, Monmouth was Charles's eldest and favourite son and so his position was unique.

On 12 July 1683 a grand jury had found a true bill against Monmouth and a reward of £500 was offered for his capture. But he managed to make his way by stealth from London to Toddington in Bedfordshire. This was the home of his mistress, Henrietta, Lady Wentworth. Her mother welcomed the distinguished visitor as a guest and there he lay concealed for five months. Meanwhile his father resumed his usual activities. Difficulties with the City, which had not welcomed its new charter, and the importunities of the Spanish ambassador had kept Charles in London longer than he usually cared for. It was not until the beginning of October that he went back to Newmarket, and then he was unable to take the ladies with him, because owing to the fire in March insufficient lodgings were available and the town was still in the process of being rebuilt. But Charles had discovered another town which he liked, Winchester. There he could indulge his love of hawking, a sport which was also agreeable to the ladies. Being charmed with the beautiful country around Winchester, he ordered that the ruins of the old castle there should be pulled down and bought up many of the houses around it and sufficient ground to lay out a palace, a garden and a park. It was estimated that the cost of the new palace would be £40,000. At Newmarket and Winchester Charles meditated on what he should do about his son. He knew quite well where Monmouth was hiding and so did one of his principal Ministers, the Marquis of Halifax. On 13 October Halifax went to Toddington to give Monmouth a message from his father. Halifax told him that Charles 'would never be brought to believe that he knew anything of that part of the plot that concerned Rye House, but, as things went, he must behave himself as if he did believe it'.[16] Halifax therefore suggested that Monmouth should write his father a contrite letter (which Halifax himself appears to have drafted). In the letter Monmouth assured the King that he never had any intention of murdering him or the Duke of York. But, in order to be forgiven and to be restored to royal favour, Monmouth had not only to persuade his father of his innocence and sorrow but also his uncle James. Thus a second and even more abject letter was drafted and signed, and this did the trick.

Monmouth first met his father secretly at the lodgings of the Duke's old governess in Whitehall: then on 25 November he officially surrendered and his confession was published in the *London Gazette*. Legal proceedings against him were stopped, but it was immediately rumoured that he had confirmed the reality of the entire plot. Charles now himself drafted a letter for his son to sign in which he was made to say: 'Your Majesty and the Duke know how ingenuously I have owned the late conspiracy; and though I was not conscious of any designs against Your Majesty's life, yet I lament the having had so great a hand in that other part of the said conspiracy.'[17] Monmouth signed the letter, but then asked to withdraw it under pressure from friends, such as John Hampden, who urged that it could be used as evidence against them at their trials. Charles was naturally furious; he ordered Halifax to return the letter and to tell Monmouth to go to hell. Excluded from the court, Monmouth retired to his estate at Moor Park and then left the country for the Spanish Netherlands, where he was joined by his mistress, Lady Henrietta. Later they went to Holland where they were hospitably entertained by William of Orange. The Duke of York was understandably angry with both his nephews; and the episode did Charles no good. On 21 January 1684 Barrillon reported to Louis XIV: 'The King is informed that in most parts of England people are beginning to doubt the conspiracy and the King's friends are astonished at the impunity enjoyed by Monmouth.'[18]

Nevertheless in 1684 Charles was at peace with himself. Once the truce of Ratisbon had been generally accepted there was no danger of his kingdom being involved in another war. With Shaftesbury dead, Monmouth in exile and parliament in abeyance, the succession question at last appeared to be settled. He had enough money; and, as Lord Bruce noted, 'a good Ministry'.

He was [Bruce added] out of intrigues with France and to my know-ledge, although a French lady and the ambassador at that Court were seemingly well . . . he gave no countenance to loose and buffooning persons that flourished so and no one else in former years. In fine his heart was set to live at ease and [he wished] that his subjects might live under their own vine and fig tree.[19]

From the time when Sunderland was restored to favour as Secretary of State the King had a strong government. It was said that 'Ministers communicated their thoughts freely and with little difference in their opinions'.[20] But Halifax, who was an ambitious if pusillanimous statesman, with few duties of his own, was critical of the handling of the finances by the Earl of Rochester, First Lord of the Treasury. Halifax asserted, on the basis of in-formation supplied to him, that the farmers of the hearth money or chimney tax had fraudulently obtained a far better contract than they should have done. Rochester was understandably annoyed at this interference with his office and the King sided with him: it appears that if any fraud had taken place, Rochester himself had not been involved in it. Lord Halifax also criticized a scheme put forward by the Duke of Ormonde, the Lord Lieutenant of Ireland, for a reform of the Irish revenue: this time he considered that the farmers had offered the Treasury advantageous terms, but again he was overruled and the management of the Irish revenues handed over to commissioners. Finally, Halifax himself was involved in a consortium for farming the English excise on more beneficial terms for the Crown. But once again the King was against him and Halifax hastily withdrew his offer. Nor was Charles any more receptive to his Lord Privy Seal's suggestion at the beginning of 1684 that it was time the King called another Parliament. Halifax thought that Charles ought to have summoned one after the exposure of the Rye House plot, though he was careful to add that even if one were not called now he would acquiesce in the King's wishes and not relinquish his office. Charles had no intention of resuming parliamentary government. On the contrary, he took advantage of the peaceful domestic situation to obtain the release of his former Minister, the Earl of Danby, on bail from the Tower of London after nearly five years imprisonment, though Charles hastened to assure the King of France that this would make no difference to his foreign policy.

It was said at this time that 'the Duke of York did now chiefly manage affairs but with great haughtiness'.[21] That appears to have been an exaggeration, but in May Charles informed his Cabinet Council that he intended to abolish the Commissioners for the Admiralty and to restore James in fact, if not in name, to his old position of Lord High Admiral, from which he had felt himself obliged to resign after the passing of the first Test Act. Furthermore Charles instructed his new Lord Chief Justice Jeffreys to investigate the question of the position of the Roman Catholics who were punished for breaches of the penal laws, and to arrange for the release of such as had been imprisoned for their alleged complicity in the popish plot. Titus Oates, the father of that plot, was further humiliated by being ordered to pay £100,000 in damages when James brought a suit against him for uttering scandalous words.

About the same time that James resumed his post as Lord High Admiral other ministerial changes were arranged. Sunderland was promoted to the senior post of Secretary of State for the South instead of Sir Leoline Jenkins, while Sidney Godolphin, another former exclusionist, became Secretary of State for the North. In July Charles appointed two new members of the Treasury Commission (one of them a relative of Halifax) without consulting Rochester as First Lord of the Treasury. Rochester was not pleased, especially as he thought that the post of Lord Treasurer ought to have been revived for his benefit. But instead of that Rochester was appointed Lord President of the Council (instead of Lord Radnor, who was seventy-eight) and Godolphin became First Lord of the Treasury. Godolphin's place as Secretary of State was given to Charles, second Earl of Middleton, who, after the death of Lauderdale in 1682, had served the King well in Scotland. Barrillon, reporting these changes to Louis XIV, reached the conclusion that Charles wanted to show people that he was not 'entirely governed by the Duke of York',[22] for Rochester was the Duke's brother-in-law and the French ambassador thought it certain that if James had been king Rochester would have obtained his desire of being appointed Lord Treasurer. It was later disclosed that Rochester was only to hold the position of Lord President temporarily: in the spring of the following year he was scheduled to replace the Duke of Ormonde as Lord Lieutenant of Ireland. But he was not to take up this post until the Duke of York had paid another visit to Scotland.

There is no reason to draw any elaborate political conclusions from these ministerial changes. Jenkins was ill, tired and over-worked and therefore glad to give up his onerous position as senior Secretary of State. Though it was observed that Rochester might prove more favourable to the Roman Catholics in Ireland than Ormonde had been, Rochester in fact was a strong Anglican and Ormonde was an old and faithful servant of the King whose retirement was overdue. Both Sunderland and Godolphin were highly efficient Ministers, while the King no doubt thought, in view of Halifax's persistent criticisms, that Rochester had not been a success as First Lord of the Treasury.

Charles was content with his position and was inclined to take things more easily after his exertions over domestic affairs in 1682 and 1683 and over foreign affairs in the earlier part of 1684. However he thought it worth his while to go and inspect a sizable army encamped at Blackheath, including sixty-eight companies of foot and over 1,500 horse, which ensured the security of London. When in September 1684 Rochester paid his master a visit at Winchester, whither the King had gone to examine the progress being made on his new palace, he found the time he was there 'fully taken up by the King's hunting and hawking and the French plays at night' so that he was unable to do any business. Charles, he said, was 'not much disposed to be drawn from his divertisements'.[23] He then went to Newmarket as usual. After the King returned to London in November, he once more had difficulties with Halifax. The charters of Massachusetts and other New England colonies had recently been forfeited or annulled, and the question at issue of a united dominion of New England was whether the Governors and Councils should be made absolute under the control of the Crown or whether they should be required to summon provincial assemblies to vote taxes and debate policies. When Halifax advocated that 'the same laws, which are in force in England, should also be established in a country inhabited by Englishmen',[24] he was once again overruled in the Cabinet Council. Indeed it was rumoured that he was now going to be dismissed. But Charles retained his services, possibly to demonstrate that he was not under the thumbs of the Duke of York and the Earl of Rochester.

On the whole, the trend of Charles's behaviour in the last years of his life was towards absolutism; and it is not impossible that if he had been succeeded by a Protestant prince as flexible as himself the English monarchy might have followed the road taken by most other European monarchies in the direction of more or less enlightened despotism. Charles had no thought of calling a Parliament, although the Triennial Act of 1664 had envisaged that one should meet every three years. The reorganization of the Treasury Commission with Godolphin at its head promised that sufficient funds would be forthcoming, especially from the customs and excise, which had been voted Charles for life for the needs of a kingdom at peace. The army encamped outside London was a sufficient menace to a revival of Whiggism in the City; in any case most of the Whig leaders were dead or in exile. The projected missions of the Duke of York to Scotland and the Earl of Rochester to Ireland were clearly intended to strengthen the position of the monarchy there. There was even talk of recruiting Roman Catholic officers in Ireland and of easing the situation of the Roman Catholics in England. On the other hand, many dissenters, particularly Quakers, were still imprisoned. The decision taken about the government of New England was a reflection of Charles's absolutist tendencies. His only fear was that the Prince of Orange and the Duke of Monmouth were engaged in Holland in plotting a rising against him in his three kingdoms. He therefore took all precautions and in October he assured Barrillon that 'the friendship of the King of France was more necessary to him than ever'.[25]

Three personal matters were settled by Charles during 1684. On 28 July he married his niece, Princess Anne, to Prince George, the younger brother of King Christian v of Denmark. For this he first obtained Louis XIV's approval, over which there was no difficulty as France was then allied to Denmark. James, Duke of York, the father of the bride, was satisfied too because he found the Whigs were 'as much troubled by it' as the Tories were pleased.[26] Prince George was to earn the nickname '*Est-il-possible?*' and King Charles said of him that he had tried him drunk and tried him sober and either way there was nothing in him. Secondly, Charles asked the French King for letters of naturalization for his youngest son, the Duke of Richmond: if he possessed these, he would be ensured of succeeding to the property of his mother, Louise de Kéroualle, Duchess of Portsmouth, in France. Louis XIV made no difficulty about acceding to this request. Lastly, again through the mediation of the Marquis of Halifax, he saw his eldest son, the errant Duke of Monmouth, for what proved to be the last time. Monmouth travelled over to England in extreme secrecy by a circuitous route from Dieren, the home of the Prince of Orange. Apparently he saw his father on 30

November, but what they said to each other is not known, and Monmouth immediately returned to Brussels and thence to The Hague. At the end of December 1684 Monmouth received a letter from Halifax saying that he would be allowed to return in the following February, but that he must come suddenly, for the secret of his projected return was being concealed from the Duke of York. But by the beginning of February Charles II was dead.

The last days on earth of Charles II are fully documented. During the winter of 1684–5 he suffered from prolonged attacks of gout and had been prevented from taking his usual exercise; instead he spent much time in his laboratory trying a process for the fixing of mercury;[27] but by the end of January 1685 he was walking twice a day in St James's park or in Arlington Garden nearby. Although in his later years he had no meals in private and 'drank only for his thirst', he often had a good supper.[28] On Sunday 1 February this included goose's eggs. After supper he visited the Duchess of Portsmouth's apartments, as was his custom, and appeared to be in the best of humour. On his return Thomas, Lord Bruce, the Gentleman of the Bedchamber on duty that week, lighted him to his bed.

Lord Bruce and Henry Killigrew, the Page of the Bedchamber on duty, slept that night, as was customary, in the same room as the King. Bruce has left a picture of the scene: 'the King slept in a room with a great grate filled with Scotch coal that burnt all night, a dozen dogs came to our bed and several pendulums that struck at the half quarter and all not going alike it was a continual chiming. The King being constantly used to it, it was habitual.' But 'the King turned himself contrary to his custom'.[29] Next morning when he was due to discuss the question of hearth money with the Marquis of Halifax, who was still pursuing his vendetta against the Earl of Rochester, the King got up after a restless night looking pale and ill. He spoke with difficulty and his mind was dazed. He dressed himself mechanically and sat down in a barber's chair to be shaved. Just after he did so, he had what was generally described as 'an apoplectic fit' and fell into Bruce's arms. Dr Edmund King, who happened to be in the room because he was waiting to treat a sore heel, of which Charles had complained, immediately bled him on Bruce's orders, forcing the clothes away from the King, taking out his lance, and tying up the arm with his handkerchief; later other physicians arrived and bled him again copiously, thrust emetics and purgatives down his throat and applied blisters to his body. Since what he was in fact suffering from was a kidney disease, this treatment was fatal: 'the extensive bleeding robbed the kidneys of their last vestige of functional activity'.[30]

In spite of this, on the following day Charles appeared to be better and lay on his bed while the doctors applied every remedy known to their limited repertoire. On Wednesday, after he had again been blooded, he went into a cold sweat and had further convulsions. Prayers for the King were published that day. Yet in the afternoon he recovered and was quite cheerful. Company was admitted to his bedroom and he talked for several hours. Next day the *London Gazette* stated that he was out of danger. But at four o'clock in the afternoon of that day, the Thursday, he had yet more convulsions and was again blooded ten ounces. The Archbishop of Canterbury and other bishops, who were standing by, moved into action to administer spiritual consolation and Bishop Ken read the prayers for the sick. Charles said he was sorry for his sins.

It was now obvious that the King was dying. The Duchess of Portsmouth asked the French ambassador, Barrillon, to tell the Duke of York that the King was a Roman Catholic and to think what could be done to save Charles's soul. James hesitated over the wisest course. Eventually he whispered to the King in the crowded bedroom, seeking his consent to bring him a Roman Catholic priest. Charles answered that he agreed with all his heart. To find such a priest was not easy, for most of the priests in the palace were those who served the Portuguese Queen and they spoke no English. But Father John Huddlestone, who had first met Charles during his escape after the battle of Worcester, now an old man, happened to be in the palace; when he was found, he was smuggled in disguise into the King's bedroom through a secret door. According to Lord Bruce, Charles called out to him:

'you that have saved my body, is now come to save my soul'. To Huddlestone Charles declared that he wished to die in the faith and communion of the Holy Roman Catholic Church; he confessed his sins and was given Extreme Unction. These rituals lasted three quarters of an hour and during that time only the Earl of Bath, who was Groom of the Stole, and Lord Feversham, Chamberlain to the Queen, were present.

Later that evening Charles, who was fully conscious, apologized to the crowd of functionaries and relatives who were gathered in his room for being such a long time dying. At midnight he saw the Queen who wept and fainted away. The Marquis of Halifax later brought him a message from Catherine asking him to forgive her if at any time she had offended him. To this he replied: 'Alas, poor woman! She ask my pardon? I beg hers with all my heart. Take back that answer.'[31] At two in the morning he began a long conversation with the Duke of York. Charles twice or more commended the Duchess of Portsmouth to James's care; he also said, 'Let not poor Nelly starve'. Then he blessed all his sons who were present, Southampton, Grafton, Northumberland (by the Duchess of Cleveland), St Albans (by Nell Gwyn) and Richmond (by the Duchess of Portsmouth): Monmouth, his eldest son, was not there and two of his other sons were dead. At six in the morning of Friday 6 February the physicians again blooded him of sixteen ounces in an attempt to relieve his pain. Charles asked that the curtains round his bed should be drawn and the windows opened. At 8.30 he began to lose his speech and between 11.30 and noon he died.

Eight days later in the evening of 14 February the funeral took place privately after dark. The new King, James II, himself a Roman Catholic, did not want his brother to be publicly subjected to Anglican rites. Prince George of Denmark was the chief mourner; James, as was the custom, took no part in the ceremonies. Charles's body was carried from the Painted Chamber in Westminster hall to the Abbey, where he was buried in the chapel of King Henry VII. 'Never', wrote one of his subjects, 'was a prince more entirely beloved nor more universally lamented for.'[32]

19

The Man and the Statesman

Two legends have persisted about the character of Charles II: the first, for which the evidence is more substantial, is that he was congenitally lazy; the second is that he was weak-willed. Edward Hyde, Edward Nicholas and the Marquis of Ormonde wrote to each other during the days of exile complaining that they had difficulty in inducing the King to attend to his affairs and even to write letters; Pepys and Evelyn, those famous diarists, thought during the course of his reign that he lacked the application to make a great king. Pepys once wrote that 'he hates the very sight or thought of business'. The Marquis of Halifax condemned in retrospect his 'immoderate love of ease', though he also wrote that Charles 'grew by age into a pretty exact distribution of his hours both for his business, pleasures and the exercise of his health'.[1] But when one studies Charles's life carefully, it is difficult to point clearly to any occasion when decision was needed or determination had to be shown that he failed to take the necessary action. His mind was quicker than that of most of his advisers, but he was one of those statesmen who are not addicted to paper work. He preferred to reach his conclusions through conversation rather than the study of documents; he loved talking and had an excellent memory; at the same time he was no orator and he kept his speeches, which were usually carefully prepared, short and to the point and thus avoided the blunders sometimes committed by his loquacious grandfather, King James I.

The idea that Charles was weak-willed also derives from several good contemporary sources. Sir William Temple suggested that he was liable to accept the opinion of the last person to whom he had spoken. Halifax complained that 'whilst he seemed to approve the counsel given him, he hearkened to other counsels at a back door'. The Countess of Sunderland, wife of one of Charles's Ministers, wrote to Henry Sidney that 'you and I know what a spark he is at going through with anything'; and on two occasions it had been thought desirable to assure Louis XIV that Charles was not a puppet who could be manipulated by his counsellors. Yet at almost every political crisis of his reign Charles, once he had made up his mind, could not be shaken from his decision. This was particularly true in his relations with the House of Commons. Though constantly pressed to do so, he refused to dismiss the Duke of Lauderdale, who did not give up office until his health broke down. He prevented the Earl of Danby, who had served him loyally, from being impeached for treason and eventually secured his release from imprisonment in the Tower. Unlike his father, Charles was unyielding in upholding his inherited prerogatives: he insisted that it was his sole right to summon, prorogue and dissolve Parliaments; that he alone was entitled to take final decisions on foreign policy; and that he was the authority who directed the movements of the army and navy and controlled the use of the militia. As he himself justly boasted, the older he grew, the firmer he became.

Charles never at any time lacked courage either as a boy when he was fighting to rescue his father or as a young king in exile, who stood ready to lead the Scots or English into battle to regain his lost thrones; and he died bravely and without complaint. This courage was manifested most clearly during the prolonged exclusion crisis. His brother James was frightened by the thought of civil war and even Danby urged forcible measures upon the King. The rest of his entourage took it for granted that he would sacrifice his brother's right to the succession rather than en- danger his own position. But though Charles sought for expedients, he never budged for one moment from the attitude he had taken up. He was at once tough and resilient. He exerted himself to destroy the Whig leadership; he used every possible resource; and in the end he won through. No one could accuse him either of laziness or lack of will power at this time of supreme political testing.

Charles's earlier biographers stressed his personal immorality and suggested that this weakened his capacity to govern. By 'immorality' of course is meant his sexual behaviour. It is not supposed that he drank to excess. Indeed he was often sparse both over food and alcohol, though he enjoyed a good meal and could be mellowed by wine. But nobody has ever been able to make a complete count of his mistresses. He is said to have had seventeen during his exile alone; and he acknowledged fourteen illegitimate children. In our own times, in what is called the permissive society, the point of view of historians has shifted, as it is always doing. One generation approves the behaviour of King Edward VII; yet in the next, King Edward VIII's love affair cost him his throne. But the only question of real importance is whether such a way of private life damages a statesman's political ability or conduct. King Henry VIII is often hailed as a great monarch; so is King Henri IV of France, Charles II's own grandfather. Disraeli's love of feminine society did not affect his prestige in the Victorian era; David Lloyd George has been accepted as one of the outstanding statesmen of the first half of the present century.

There is no evidence that any of Charles's mistresses when he was a reigning monarch had real influence over his policies. The most they could ever do was to reconcile the King to an erring courtier, as Nell Gwyn did for the Duke of Buckingham. Although Louise de Kéroualle, Charles's most enduring mistress, was first sent to him by Louis XIV of France, she was not even let into all the secrets of Anglo-French relations. Her temporary entry into the camp of the exclusionists did not impress Charles II in the least. It is true that the King sometimes held long conversations with the French ambassador in her apartments, but this was a mere convenience. And if one is to believe, as Charles himself once averred, that he was always fundamentally pro-French at heart, he had attained that attitude of mind long before he ever met the young girl from Brittany. Even when she was firmly established as Duchess of Portsmouth, Louise was never consulted as Louis XIV consulted Madame de Maintenon.

To talk of the debauchery of Charles II's court is to exaggerate. Gramont, when he came to London, thought that it compared favourably with the court of Louis XIV where social etiquette was prescribed with courtesy, elegance and good taste as its guide-lines. And compared with the ribald and drunken court of Charles II's paternal grandfather Charles II's Court was a model of propriety. But two things may fairly be pointed out about Charles II and his harem. The first is that it constituted an expensive hobby. It has sometimes been argued that Charles's expenditure on his mistresses and their children was a drop in the ocean in relation to the over-all costs of monarchical government. But recent research shows that substantial sums were indeed paid not merely from the King's privy purse but also out of other revenues, such as naval prize money;[2] and this must have been known or suspected at the time. Charles, as has been seen, had been obliged to undergo the humiliation of promising the House of Commons that if it voted him money it would not be spent on his own self-indulgences; and there is no doubt that the reluctance of the House at times to vote him additional supplies was partly motivated by a belief in the extent of his personal extravagances. It was one of the reasons why money was appropriated to specific purposes.

Secondly, Charles's escapades with women did in fact shock members of the older generation, like the first Earl of Clarendon and John Evelyn, even if it did not undermine their loyalty, and can scarcely have endeared the King to the persecuted puritans. But it can have hardly offended Samuel Pepys, whose diary is a well-worn source for criticisms of Charles's weakness (if that is the right word) for women. Pepys had his own enjoyable in-fidelities. Even John Evelyn had a sanctimonious and repressed love affair with Margaret Blagge, a young Maid of Honour, whose secret marriage to Sidney Godolphin he resented almost as much as Charles II resented the marriage of Frances Stuart.[3] Only a psycho-analyst can measure the unconscious hypocrisies of the human mind.

If Charles II's mistresses were of relatively small and indirect political importance, Charles's loyalty to his own kindred was immense and significant. His father had built up a happy family life when the civil war came to disrupt it. On the only occasion when Oliver Cromwell met him, he had been moved by Charles i's devotion to his children. His eldest son had been prepared to undergo any hardship and undertake any risk to save his father's life and, after Charles i's public execution, his eighteen-year-old heir swore to be avenged on his murderers. But he had learned much from his father's mistakes. Watching the development of both the English and French civil wars, Charles ii had come to realize that a king needed to be resolute and unscrupulous if he were to retain his authority and that he must act quickly and decisively whenever danger threatened. If, owing to the position which his mother enjoyed of right in the court of Paris, Charles had come to admire French methods of government and French tastes, including music and the theatre, he acquired a dislike for the Dutch because of the manner in which the Regent class had treated his widowed sister, Princess Mary of Orange, and her posthumous son. Mary was barely thirty when she died suddenly in England; Charles could never forget her devotion, generosity and self-sacrifice when he was a penniless exile.

If for family reasons Charles was antipathetic towards the Dutch burghers and approved of the French aristocracy, his inclination towards France was further enhanced by his intimate relationship with his youngest sister, Henriette. Some biographers have believed that she was the only woman whom Charles ever really loved. She certainly played a large part in framing the secret treaty of Dover, the signature of which was one of the most remarkable events in Charles's political career. It is possible that the second clause of the treaty in which he promised to 'reconcile himself with the Church of Rome as soon as the welfare of the kingdom will permit' was first included in order to please her as a convinced Catholic and that the postponement of its implementation was then accepted by him in order to meet her wishes. The spirit of Henriette – the third of Charles's sisters to die young – lived on in Louise de Kéroualle, who had been her Maid of Honour.

But the most important instance of Charles's family loyalty related to his brother, James. He and Charles had been brought up together and, after hearing the clash of arms on Edgehill, had shared the perils and deprivations of war-time Oxford. Though as a young officer James was much commended for his gallantry, Charles can scarcely have found his brother's unyielding temper and lack of humour at all congenial. He was fully aware of James's shortcomings and later blamed him for the troubles brought about by his bigotry. Nevertheless Charles would not buy his own comfort and convenience at the price of James's exclusion from the succession, even when the Earl of Shaftesbury offered to substitute for it the succession of Charles's eldest and favourite son, the Duke of Monmouth. It is probable that Charles's attitude to his brother was ambivalent. Danby said that while the King 'denied almost nothing to the Duke, he did not really love him', and Halifax thought that he 'had his jealousies of him'. But in public he embraced him and swore that those who sought their separation were rebels.[4] He could have had few illusions about James's character: indeed Charles doubted whether anyone would attempt to kill him to hand over the government to the '*sottise de mon frère*'. But when Charles died he left a rich political inheritance, free from any new constitutional limitations, to a man whose ability to rule he clearly mistrusted.

One thing that the two brothers had in common was their religion. It is facile to say that Charles had no religion, and he was certainly too astute to endanger his Crown by making such a public demonstration of it as James did when he threw up the office of Lord High Admiral after the first Test Act had been passed. But the evidence is really almost conclusive that Charles was always at heart in sympathy with the Church of Rome. Cardinal de Retz believed that his inclinations lay that way when he was in exile: Halifax thought that to say that Charles 'had not religion enough to have conviction' was 'a vulgar error' and that he was certainly a Roman Catholic when he returned to England. Halifax also wrote that 'some pretend to be very precise in the time of his reconciling', namely at the date when he entered into negotiations with Cardinal de Retz,[5] that is to say in 1658-9. It is notable that Sir Richard Bellings, the Roman Catholic gentleman who acted in a secretarial capacity in the correspondence with De Retz, was also concerned in much the same way with the negotiations for the secret treaty of Dover and was in fact one of its signatories. James's account of how Charles had declared on 25 January 1669 that he found it 'uneasy' not to be able to profess publicly the faith in which he believed is at least circumstantial; and the second clause of the treaty of Dover, after all, stated in black and white that he 'was convinced of the truth of the Catholic religion'.

There are at least three pieces of evidence that Charles was always persuaded by the argument from the apostolic succession: his discussion with Father Huddlestone after the battle of Worcester in 1651, his conversation with Sir Robert Moray in December 1672, and the two papers written by him in 1686 which were published on King James II's orders after Charles's death. James II assured Samuel Pepys that Charles 'both was and died a Roman Catholic' and showed him the originals of the two papers written in the King's own handwriting.[6] No one has ever proved that they were forgeries. Finally, the Duchess of Portsmouth, who was surely in as good a position to know as anyone, declared to Barrillon that 'at the bottom of his heart the King is a Catholic', and Barrillon himself heard Charles say 'aloud from time to time' on his death-bed that he would welcome 'with all my heart' the presence of a Roman Catholic priest to administer the last rites. Roman Catholicism, Charles believed, upheld the authority of kings; it could also wash away, after confession and repentance, those sins which Charles himself regarded as venial.

To conclude these reflections on Charles as a man, it must be said that he was a habitual liar. Three factors contributed to this unpleasing characteristic. The first is that he was a professional charmer and genuinely disliked hurting the feelings of other people. Clarendon remarked on this propensity of his, noting for example that when he was at Breda before his return to England he 'expressed himself with more condescension than was necessary' and gave such answers to those who came as suitors for his favour 'as for the present seemed full of grace'. Secondly, it was a trait that he inherited from his father. Once Charles I had become a prisoner, he regarded it as legitimate to give every kind of promise which might contribute to his restoration to the throne. He had tried to play off the English Independents against the

Scottish Presbyterians, making diametrically opposite promises to the two sides.[7] To regain power he regarded it as justifiable to give undertakings which he intended to break. Even in his younger days he consented to the Petition of Right and then, once Parliament was dissolved, broke both its letter and spirit. For much the same reasons as his father Charles II set no store by the word of a king. Thirdly, Charles II, when he was twenty, had felt obliged, in order to buy his acceptance as King in Scotland, to accuse his father of being a criminal and his mother an idolatress. He had also been compelled to sign and swear to a Covenant which 'he hated in his heart'. Like his father, he made one set of promises to the Scots and completely opposite ones to the Irish. This started him along the road of lying for political ends. After he returned to England, he constantly told his parliaments how much he loved them; but in private he admitted that they were burdensome and, in the end, he deliberately did without them.

Voltaire made Moses say, 'It is not the business of a ruler to be truthful but to be politic.' Certainly statesmen do not always care to tell the whole truth to the public or to each other. But with Charles lying was deliberate and constant. Those historians who, relying on Barrillon's dispatches, have condemned Charles II for being habitually pro-French tend to overlook the fact that the King's reiterated assertions that he was an unswervingly faithful friend of France must not be taken at their face value. Louis XIV learned by experience that Charles was not to be trusted and depended less on his word than on the hold that the French government had over him, once he had signed the secret treaty of Dover. And when Charles addressed his Parliament about his obligations to France, he deliberately lied when he said that he had given no other undertakings than that which he was prepared to show it.

Such were some of Charles's personal characteristics and such was their impact on his political behaviour. What can be said of his statesmanship? First, it may be contended that he had the knack of selecting able Ministers. There were of course one or two failures: the Earl of Southampton was not an ideal Lord Treasurer; nor apparently was the Earl of Rochester, and Charles came to recognize that. But during the twenty-five years of his reign he employed many highly capable men: Clarendon, Arlington, Shaftesbury and Danby were all first-class administrators. Men like Sir William Coventry and Sir Leoline Jenkins were industrious and devoted servants of the Crown. Charles may have been entertained by characters like the second Duke of Buckingham or Charles Berkeley, Lord Falmouth, but he never employed them in really key positions. On the other hand, he came to recognize the conspicious abilities of Samuel Pepys, who rose from a relatively humble position to become the linchpin of the Admiralty. In General Monck and Prince Rupert he found admirals who served him well within the limits placed upon them. The Earl of Craven proved a trustworthy commander of his small army. Arlington and Sunderland were excellent foreign ministers; Danby and Godolphin were brilliant financiers.

But all these men were his servants. None of them – not even Clarendon – was a Richelieu or a Mazarin. Charles, for better or worse, determined his own policies and took every critical decision during his reign. Time and again one is impressed by the strength of his character and his cleverness in getting out of difficulties. Like other statesmen, he was not always able to achieve what he wanted. He was compelled to abandon his policy of religious toleration owing to the intransigence of his Long Parliament; he had to permit some of the judicial murders committed after the discovery of the popish plot because of the wave of mass hysteria throughout his kingdom. But he never showed the weakness or fear displayed by his father. He saved the lives of both Clarendon and Danby from the fury of parliaments. He outmanœuvred the Whigs. He preserved his throne and his dynasty.

What must be said about Charles II's foreign policy? On the whole, it was a failure. It is true that through the King's marriage Great Britain gained Bombay, which was to become an important part of British India, and that Charles retained Cromwell's conquest, Jamaica, which was developed as a prosperous island in the British West Indies. On the other hand, Dunkirk and Tangier were given up, though it is likely that, for military reasons, they could not have been kept for long. Great Britain was in effect defeated in both the wars against the Dutch and made no significant gains from the peace treaties. Afterwards Charles committed himself to a more or less permanent alliance with France, though from time to time he tried to restrain Louis XIV's aggressions. He also insisted on British naval supremacy over the French and attempted to sustain it.

Why did Charles become so pro-French? Fundamentally it was neither because he admired the French King nor because he was related to him through his mother. It used once to be argued that Charles was driven into accepting French subsidies because his parliaments failed to vote him sufficient supplies for the needs of his government. This view can no longer be sustained. It has been calculated that the total value of the subsidies which Charles received from France was no more than £1,200,000, which was equivalent to less than a single year's expenditure at the beginning of his reign.[8] The precise amount depends on how many *livres tournois* one allows to the English pound at the time – say, thirteen, fourteen or fifteen. As has been pointed out, some earlier historians were misled by the fact that the subsidies were doled out in *livres tournois* and not in *livres*, meaning pounds sterling.[9] Charles's real financial difficulties were probably greatest during the early years of his reign when he was pocketing none of these subsidies.[10] But in ten of the last fourteen years of his reign he received an average of over £160,000 a year more from his customs revenue than had been calculated by the Commons when they voted him the receipts of the Customs for life.[11] Equally it has been calculated that during the last ten years of his reign he received more from the excise than the Commons had originally estimated.[12] This probably reflected the increasing economic prosperity of the nation during the last eleven years of Charles's reign when the kingdom remained at peace. For the first part of this period Great Britain's principal rivals in commerce and shipping were still absorbed in expensive warfare on the European mainland.

Charles had been pushed into the first Dutch war, against the advice of his leading Minister, Clarendon, by his Parliament which had voted generous supplies for it; and he was understandably angry when the Dutch won, after holding up the British navy to ridicule. Charles then reached the conclusion that it was out of the question for him to maintain a war against the Dutch as well as against the French, who were then the Dutch allies. Since it was his belief, in which he was supported by Members of Parliament as well as merchants trading abroad, such as the merchants of the East India company and the Royal Africa company, that war against the Dutch was likely to prove more profitable than a war against France (although France was trying to become a maritime power) he decided to seek a French alliance and for the rest of his reign his objective was largely to detach the French from the Dutch and to obtain better trading terms from the French than they gave to the Dutch.

But during the last seven years of Charles's reign another factor came into play. When the popish plot was uncovered in 1678 it was difficult for Charles to foresee that a curious train of events was going to lead to the peril of civil war. But of course it was always possible that the terms of the secret treaty of Dover might be revealed in which he had declared himself a convert to Roman Catholicism. Certainly there were men who suspected that the court was deliberately encouraging the growth of popery – Andrew Marvell, for instance. There seemed both to Charles and James a genuine danger that the Whig parliamentary leaders might rally the English Protestants against them; and indeed it was obvious that thoughts of conspiracy and rebellion would enter the minds of Whig leaders when they realized that they could not push exclusion through Parliament nor compel Charles to acquiesce in it. Charles had only a small army, and many discontented Cromwellian officers and soldiers (though admittedly they were now ageing) were still alive. Charles therefore sought – in the last resort – for French military support if a rebellion broke out against him, the same kind of support that had been guaranteed in the secret treaty of Dover. It was not so much the subsidies from France that Charles needed during the last years of his reign in order to govern without a Parliament as the implication that a close relationship with the French King meant that Charles could depend on Louis's material and moral aid if the English throne were threatened.[13] Thus, as seldom has happened in British history, foreign policy was determined by domestic considerations instead of the other way about.

Charles II has often been commended for his care of the British navy, and there is no question that he and his brother took a personal interest and pride in it. Though it is difficult to undertake precise comparisons, it seems that the strength of the navy was maintained – at any rate on paper – during the first twenty years of the reign.[14] Charles inherited 156 or 157 warships from the Commonwealth when he came to the throne. Though by 1673, taking into account the losses in the two Dutch wars, Charles possessed only 148 ships, their total tonnage was slightly higher and their gunpower slightly lower. By 1684 Charles is estimated to have had 162 warships with a total tonnage well in excess of that of 1660. This was partly because in 1677 Samuel Pepys had persuaded Parliament to vote £600,000 for the building of thirty up-to-date vessels. Victualling was improved about this time, admirals received an increase in pay, and officers obtained pensions or superannuation. But though superficially this does not appear to have been a bad record, account had to be taken of the number of ships that were in need of repair or unseaworthy and of the quality of the sailors. Pepys said in 1675 that England had only ninety-two effective ships available, compared with ninety-six French and 136 Dutch. And it was estimated by him that a fleet of ninety effective warships was needed simply to protect British commerce. The navy was the most expensive item in the royal budget. It was said to cost £400,000–£500,000 a year in time of peace (and Pepys claimed that Charles always found that amount) but four times this sum in time of war. There was certainly maladministration and peculation before in the end Pepys took more or less complete control. But the late J. R. Tanner, who examined the question most thoroughly, wrote that 'the want of money was the root of all evil in the navy' and Charles never had the means to put it on a first-class footing. Only rigorous economies in other direc-directions would have permitted this. Two facts speak of Charles II's failure with his navy. The first was the disgrace of 1667 after the decision had been taken (with the King's approval) to lay up all the first and second rates, while the majority of the third-rates required repair. The second is that when, three and a half years after Charles's death, his brother, James II, needed a strong fleet to protect his kingdom from invasion by William of Orange, he could not put to sea a force capable of contending with the Dutch in the autumn of 1688 and was reduced to relying on his army to repulse invasion.[15]

In many ways the reign of Charles II, in David Ogg's words, could claim 'a record of achievement'.[16] After the ending of the wars, there was a trade boom (though real wages appear to have fallen).[17] It was, after all, the age of two great poets, Milton and Dryden, of a great composer, Purcell, and of a great scientist, Sir Isaac Newton. But only to a limited extent did Charles lend his patronage to either art or science: his taste in the arts was French, his interest in science was spasmodic, and even his special concern for navigation did not prevent naval defeats and naval inadequacies. It may be argued by those who look primarily to the structure of society to explain movements in history that there is little that any one man can do to affect their course. Charles was, on the whole, a successful politician, but he was certainly not a great statesman; and nearly everything he struggled for was destroyed during the reign of his successor.

Authorities and Notes

When Dr A. W. Ward (later Sir Adolphus Ward) contributed his article on King Charles II to the *Dictionary of National Biography* in 1887, he noted that no biography of Charles II 'of any pretensions exists except Dr William Harris's *Historical and Critical Account of the Life of Charles II* [two vols, 1766] written "after the manner of Mr Bayle" '. In 1901 Dr Osmund Airy wrote a biography for the Goupil series, which was published in an octavo edition in 1904. In 1931 Sir Arthur Bryant first published his best-selling biography, which has gone into many editions. Other biographies have been written by Sir Henry I. Terry, *A Misguided Monarch* (1917), John Drinkwater, *Mr Charles King of England* (1926), David G. Loth, *Royal Charles* (1931) and Hesketh Pearson, *Charles II: his life and likeness* (1960), but none of these appear to have been based on detailed research.

In 1930 Sir Keith Feiling published his book on *British Foreign Policy 1660–1672*, which was essentially a first-class analysis of Charles II's foreign policy, and in 1934 David Ogg (one of my two principal tutors at Oxford) published his wide-ranging *England in the Reign of Charles II*, which will not be superseded for a long time. David Ogg was critical of Sir Arthur Bryant's view of the King. Since those two books appeared by historians of outstanding ability a vast amount of research has gone into Charles II's reign. I list just a few of the books to which I am particularly indebted:

de Beer, E. S. (ed.), *The Diary of John Evelyn* (1955)
Bosher, R. S., *The Making of the Restoration Settlement* (1951)
Browning, Andrew, *Thomas Osborne, Earl of Danby and Duke of Leeds 1632–1714* (1944–51)
—— (ed.), *English Historical Documents 1660–1714* (1953)
Bryant, Arthur, *The Letters, Speeches and Declarations of King Charles II* (1935)
—— *Samuel Pepys* (1933–8)
Chapman, H. W., *The Tragedy of Charles II* (1964)
Clark, G. N., *The Later Stuarts*, 2nd ed. (1956)
Davies, Godfrey, *The Restoration of Charles II* (1955)

Edgar, F. T. R, *Sir Ralph Hopton: The King's Man in the West 1642-1652* (1968)

Foxcroft, H. C., *A Character of the Trimmer* (1946)

Haley, K. D. H., *The First Earl of Shaftesbury* (1968)

Hardacre, Paul H., *The Royalists during the Puritan Revolution* (1956)

Hartmann, C. H., *Clifford of the Cabal* (1937)

—— *The King My Brother* (1954)

Henning, B. D. (ed.), *Parliamentary Diary of Sir Edward Dering 1670-1673* (1940)

Jones, J. R., *The First Whigs* (1961)

Kenyon, J. P., *Robert Spencer, Earl of Sutherland* (1955)

—— *The Stuart Constitution* (1966)

—— *Halifax: Complete Works* (1969)

Lee, Maurice, *The Cabal* (1965)

Matthews, William, *Charles II's Escape from Worcester* (1967)

Nicholas, David, *Mr Secretary Nicholas 1597-1669* (1953)

Ollard, Richard, *The Escape of Charles II* (1966)

—— *Man of War: Sir Robert Holmes and the Restoration Navy* (1969)

Powell, J. R., *The Navy in the English Civil War* (1962)

Robbins, Caroline (ed.), *The Diary of John Milward Esq 1666-1668* (1938)

Roberts, Clayton, *The Growth of Responsible Government in Stuart England* (1966)

Rogers, P. G., *The Dutch in the Medway* (1970)

Routledge, F. J., *England and the Treaty of the Pyrenees* (1953)

Turner, F. C., *James II* (1948)

Underdown, David, *Royalist Conspiracy in England 1649-1660* (1960)

Wilson, Charles, *Profit and Power: A Study of England in the Dutch Wars* (1957)

Witcombe, D. T., *Charles II and the Cavalier House of Commons 1663-1674* (1966)

Wolf, J. B., *Louis XIV* (1968)

Wormald, B. H. G., *Clarendon Politics, History and Religion 1640-1660* (1951)

I hope that, if I have accidentally omitted any books by living historians from this selective list, I may be forgiven. I asked permission of Professor C. D. Chandaman to read his thesis on 'The English Public Revenue 1660-1688', but this was refused. Modern estimates of Charles II by distinguished historians include Godfrey Davies, 'Charles II in 1660' in *Huntington Library Quarterly* (1955-6), J. P. Kenyon, 'Charles II 1649-1685' in *The Stuarts* (1958), E. S. de Beer, 'King Charles II Fundator et Patronus 1630-1685' in *Notes and Records of the Royal Society of London*, vol. 15 (1960), and K. D. H. Haley, *Charles II* (Historical Association pamphlet, 1966). I have not attempted to list the innumerable articles on the reign of Charles II, but some of these will be found in the notes. Earlier books and articles will be found in the standard bibliographies such as *Bibliography of British History: Stuart Period 1603-1714* (edited by Godfrey Davies and revised by Mary Frear Keeler, 1970).

I hesitated for a long time before I decided whether to append (as is a modern fashion) a miniature bibliography for every statement in this book. I finally decided only to give references to verbatim quotations either from contemporary documents (printed or unprinted) or later historians. Experts will, I fancy, recognize the obvious sources; other readers can easily discover them if they wish. I have adapted a few paragraphs from my own earlier books which are now out of print.

The following abbreviations have been used in the references:

Baschet: Transcripts of the dispatches of French ambassadors in London in the Public Record Office: PRO 31/3

Browning, A.: Andrew Browning, *Thomas Osborne, Earl of Danby and Duke of Leeds 1632-1712, Life and Letters* (1944-51)

Burnet: *Gilbert Burnet, History of His Own Time* (edition of 1823)

Bryant, A.: *Arthur Bryant, The Letters, Speeches and Declarations of King Charles II* (1935)

CSP (Dom): *Calendar of State Papers (Domestic)*

CSP (Venetian): *Calendar of State Papers (Venetian)*

Clarendon: *The History of the Rebellion and Civil Wars in England*, ed. W. D. Macray (1888)

Grey, A.: Anchitel Grey, *Debates of the House of Commons from the year 1667 to the year 1694* (1769)

Haley, K. D. H.: *The First Earl of Shaftesbury* (1968)

Hartmann, C. H.: *The King My Brother* (1954)

HMC: *Reports of the Royal Historical Manuscripts Commission*

Pepys: *Samuel Pepys Diary,* ed. H. B. Wheatley (1893-9)

Additional Mss. and Lansdowne Mss. are in the British Museum; Carte Mss. and Clarendon Mss. are in the Bodleian Library at Oxford.

1 *The Prince 'Unboyed'* (pages 1 to 16)

1 Henrietta Maria to Madame St George, Sept. 1630: M. A. E. Green, *Letters of Queen Henrietta Maria* (1857), p. 17.

2 Green, *Letters of Queen Henrietta Maria*, p. 18.

3 Thomas Smith to Sir John Pennington, 12 April 1638: *CSP (Dom) 1637-8*, p. 361.

4 *Life of Newcastle*, ed. C. H. Firth (1886), pp. 9-10.

5 *Life of Newcastle*, ed. Firth, pp. 326-30.

6 Clarendon, IV, p. 296.

7 Clarendon, VI, p. 324 and *Dictionary of National Biography* sub 'Thomas Howard'.

8 *Life of Newcastle*, ed. Firth, p. 120.

9 *CSP (Venetian) 1640-2*, p. 151 and C. V. Wedgwood, *Thomas Wentworth* (1961), pp. 372 *et seq.*

10 Peter Young, *Edgehill 1642* (1967), p. 119.

11 E. Walker, *Historical Discourses* (1705), pp. 43-5, cit. C. V. Wedgwood, *The King's War* (1958), p. 354.

12 Cf. F. T. R. Edgar, *Sir Ralph Hopton: The King's Man in the West* (1968) and S. R. Gardiner, *The Great Civil War* (1889) II, chaps XXVIII and XXIX.

13 Clarendon, IX, p. 10 *et seq.*

14 *CSP (Dom) 1644-5*, p. 511, cit. F. T. R. Edgar, *Sir Ralph Hopton*, p. 177.

15 Clarendon, IX, pp. 133-6.

16 Charles I to the Prince of Wales, 7 Dec. 1645: Clarendon, IX, p. 114.

17 Edward Hyde to Goring 12 April 1645: Gardiner, *The Great Civil War*, II, p. 155.

18 E. B. G. Warburton, *Memoirs of Prince Rupert* (1849), III, p. 221.

2 *The Second Civil War* (pages 17 to 30)

1 *Memoirs of Lady Fanshawe*, ed. Beatrice Marshall (1893), p. 71.

2 S. E. Hoskins, *Charles the Second in the Channel Islands* (1854), I, p. 347.

3 *Memoirs of Lady Fanshawe*, ed. Marshall, p. 72.

4 Hoskins, *Charles II*, I, p. 349.

5 Clarendon, X, p. 44.

6 Clarendon, X, p. 58.

7 *Mémoires de Mlle de Montpensier*, ed. A. Chéruel (1889), I, p. 137

8 *Mémoires de Mlle de Montpensier*, ed. Chéruel, I, pp. 142-3.

9 Burnet, I, p. 172.

10 Clarendon, X, p. 160.

11 J. R. Powell, *The Navy in the English Civil War* (1962), p. 155.

12 Powell, *The Navy*, p. 172.

13 Powell, *The Navy*, p. 172.

14 Lord George Scott, *Lucy Walter: Wife or Mistress* (1947), p. 128.

15 Cf. Clarendon, XI, p. 131.

16 Charles I to the Prince of Wales, 25 Nov. 1648: Clarendon, XI, p. 193.

17 Prince Charles to Fairfax, 13 Jan. 1649: A. Bryant, p. 7. Dame Veronica Wedgwood has shown that the often repeated story that Charles sent a blank

sheet of paper, signed and sealed, on which terms could be written to pre-serve his father's life is not authentic: *The Trial of Charles I*, pp. 170, 239.

3 *In the Arms of the Scots* (pages 31 to 48)

1 Green, *Letters of Queen Henrietta Maria*, I, pp. 350–7.
2 *Mémoires*, I, p. 219.
3 Cit. O. Airy, *Charles II*, p. 74.
4 Charles II to Montrose, 12/22 Jan. 1650: Mark Napier, *Memoirs of the Marquis of Montrose* (1856), II, p. 752.
5 Instructions for Sir William Fleming, 3/13 May 1650: Napier, *Memoirs of the Marquis of Montrose*, II, p. 757.
6 S. R. Gardiner, *Charles II and Scotland in 1650* (1894), p. 126.
7 S. R. Gardiner, *History of the Commonwealth and Protectorate, 1649–1651* (1894), pp. 258–9.
8 Diary of Alexander Jaffray, cit. John Willcock, *The Great Marquess* (1903), p. 241.
9 E. Walker, *Historical Discourses*, p. 170.
10 20 Aug. 1650: Gardiner, *Charles II and Scotland*, p.143.
11 20 May 1650, letter from The Hague, in Gardiner, *Charles II and Scotland*, p. 114.
12 Cit. Eva Scott, *The King in Exile* (1905), p. 200.
13 Clarendon, XIII, p. 53.
14 Hamilton to Crofts, 8 Aug. 1651, cit. Gardiner, *History of the Commonwealth and Protectorate*, p. 431.
15 'Account of the battle of Worcester': Clarendon Mss. 42, f. 149 *et seq.*
16 Clarendon, XIII, p. 63.
17 Clarendon Mss. 42, f. 149.
18 Clarendon Mss. 42, f. 149 v.
19 Clarendon, XIII, p. 78.

4 *In the Arms of France* (pages 49 to 67)

1 *Charles II's Escape from Worcester*, ed. William Matthews (1967), p. 5.
2 Pepys's account is printed in *Charles II's Escape*, ed. Matthews, p. 38 *seq.* This is the account I have followed, checked against Richard Ollard, *The Escape of Charles II* (1966). There are many versions of the story.
3 *Mémoires*, I, p. 320 *et seq.*
4 A. Bryant, p. 26.
5 *Mémoires de Mlle de Montpensier*, I, p. 320.
6 Clarendon, V, p. 231; Hyde to Rochester, 5 Dec. 1653: *Calendar of Clarendon State Papers*, II, p. 281.

7 Hyde to Nicholas, 24 May 1652: *Clarendon State Papers*, III, p. 72.

8 Hyde to Nicholas, 9 Aug. 1652: *Clarendon State Papers*, III, p. 86.

9 Hyde to Nicholas, 11 July 1652: *Clarendon State Papers*, III, p. 82.

10 Clarendon, V, pp. 258-9.

11 Hyde to Nicholas, 21 Nov. 1653: *Calendar*, II, 275.

12 Hyde to Nicholas: *Clarendon State Papers*, III, p. 230.

13 A. Bryant, p. 27.

14 Charles II to the Earl of Balcarres, 22 Sept. 1653: A. Bryant, p. 27.

15 Hyde to Nicholas, 13 June 1653: *Clarendon State Papers*, III, p. 171.

16 Hyde to Rochester, 20 Oct. 1653: *Calendar*, II, p. 267.

17 Hyde to Nicholas, 6 Mar. 1654: *Clarendon State Papers*, III, p. 222.

18 Nicholas to Hyde, 6/16 May 1652: *Nicholas Papers*, ed. G. F. Warner (1886), I, p. 299.

19 *Clarendon State Papers*, III, p. 174: *Calendar*, II, pp. 261, 285.

20 Hyde to Nicholas, 6 June 1653: *Clarendon State Papers*, III, p. 170.

21 Hyde to Nicholas, 22 Nov. 1652: *Clarendon State Papers*, III, p. 117.

22 Hyde to Nicholas, 24 May 1652: *Clarendon State Papers*, III, p. 71.

23 Cf. Lord Gerard to Charles II, 23 Dec. 1653: *Calendar*, II, p. 285: Clarendon, V, p. 327.

24 *Calendar*, II, p. 277.

25 Hyde to Nicholas, 12 June 1654: *Clarendon State Papers*, III, p. 247.

26 Hyde to Nicholas, 13 Feb. 1654: *Clarendon State Papers*, III, p. 218.

5 *Towards the Restoration* (pages 68 to 90)

1 Clarendon, XIV, p. 82.

2 Letter of Intelligence from Spa, 31 July/10 Aug. 1654: *Thurloe State Papers*, II, p. 546.

3 8 July 1654: *Calendar*, II, p. 282.

4 *Thurloe State Papers*, II, p. 546.

5 Monck to Thurloe, 2 Dec. 1654: *Thurloe State Papers*, III, p. 3.

6 *Calendar*, II, p. 256, cit. David Underdown, *Royalist Conspiracy in England* (1960), p. 86. I have followed Professor Underdown's account of the Sealed Knot.

7 Charles II to Ormonde, 31 Jan. 1655: cit. Eva Scott, *The Travels of King Charles II 1654-1660* (1907), p. 65.

8 *Calendar*, III, p. 18.

9 Cit. Scott, *Travels of King Charles II*, pp. 57-8.

10 *Clarendon State Papers*, III, p. 256; Underdown, *Royalist Conspiracy*, p. 133; Scott, *Travels of King Charles II*, p. 69.

11 *Calendar*, III, p. 19.

12 Clarendon, XIV, p. 136.
13 Hyde to Nicholas, 21 April 1655; *Clarendon State Papers*, III, p. 268.
14 *Thurloe State Papers*, III, p. 429.
15 *Clarendon State Papers*, III, p. 275.
16 Hyde to Henry de Vic, 7 Dec. 1655: *Clarendon State Papers*, III, p. 280.
17 11 Feb. 1656, *Clarendon State Papers*, III, p. 286.
18 Charles II to Ormonde, 12 Mar. 1656: *Clarendon State Papers*, III, p. 288.
19 *Clarendon State Papers*, III, p. 296.
20 *Clarendon State Papers*, III, p. 299.
21 18 June 1657: *Clarendon State Papers*, III, p. 346.
22 *Clarendon State Papers*, III, p. 351.
23 Hyde to Mordaunt, 22 April 1658: *Clarendon State Papers*, III, p. 401.
24 Scott, *Travels of Charles II*, p. 367.
25 *Nicholas Papers*, IV, p. 73; *Clarendon State Papers*, III, p. 410.
26 Hyde to Howard, 22 Jan. 1659: *Clarendon State Papers*, III, p. 422.
27 Underdown, *Royalist Conspiracy*, chap XI.
28 Hyde to Baron, 10 May 1659: *Clarendon State Papers*, III, p. 268.
29 Charles is said to have had seventeen mistresses in exile: *A Panegyric to Charles II* (1661), p.7.
30 Airy, *Charles II*, p. 127.
31 Ormonde to Hyde, 27 Jan. 1658: *Clarendon State Papers*, III, p. 387.
32 F. J. Routledge, 'Charles II and Cardinal de Retz', *Transactions of the Royal Historical Society*, 5th series, vol. VI (1956), p. 55.

6 *The Restoration* (pages 91 to 103)

1 Clarendon Mss. 63, ff. 237-8.
2 25 Oct./4 Nov. 1659, *Clarendon State Papers*, III, p. 597.
3 Culpeper to Nicholas, 13/23 Oct. 1659, cit. F. J. Routledge, *England and the Treaty of the Pyrenees* (1953), p. 75.
4 Bristol to Hyde, 18 Nov. 1659: *Clarendon State Papers*, III, p. 607.
5 O'Neill to Hyde, 25 Oct./4 Nov. 1659: *Clarendon State Papers*, III, p. 607.
6 *Clarendon State Papers*, III, p. 611.
7 Hyde to Willoughby, 21/31 Jan. 1660: *Calendar*, IV, p. 500.
8 *Clarendon State Papers*, III, p. 417.
9 *Clarendon State Papers*, III, p. 651.
10 *Clarendon State Papers*, III, p. 642.
11 *Calendar*, IV, p. 620.
12 Cf. Godfrey Davies, *The Restoration of Charles II* (1955), pp. 312-13.
13 Clarendon, XVI, pp. 173-9.
14 *Calendar*, IV, p. 528.

15 To Charles Howard, 20 Feb. 1660: *Calendar*, IV, p. 552.

16 Clarendon Mss. 72, f. 72.

17 23 May 1660: *Diary*, ed. H. B. Wheatley (1893-9), I, p. 157.

18 *CSP (Venetian)*, 1/11 June 1660.

19 *The Diary of John Evelyn*, ed. E. S. de Beer (1955), III, p. 246.

7 *The Settlement* (pages 104 to 124)

1 Samuel Tuke, *A Character of Charles II* (April 1660).

2 Burnet, I, p. 159.

3 'A Character of Charles II', H. C. Foxcroft, *The Life and Letters of Sir George Savile, Bart* (1898), II, p. 345.

4 Foxcroft, *Life and Letters of Sir George Savile*, II, p. 344.

5 Burnet, I, p. 158.

6 K. D. H. Haley, *The First Earl of Shaftesbury* (1968), p. 328.

7 Clarendon, *Life* (1827), I, pp. 362-3.

8 *The Diary of John Evelyn*, III, p. 284.

9 Clarendon, *Life*, I, pp. 380-1.

10 Clarendon, *Life*, I, p. 363.

11 Clarendon, *Life*, I, p. 370.

12 27 July 1661: Pepys, I, p. 328.

13 J. S. Clarke, *The Life of James II* (1816), p. 387.

14 Maurice Ashley, *John Wildman Plotter and Postmaster* (1947), p. 164.

15 Charles II to Clarendon, 7 June 1662: Lansdowne Mss. 1236, f. 132. Cf. Violet A. Rowe, *Sir Henry Vane the Younger* (1970), p. 232 et seq.

16 *Notes which Passed at Meetings of the Privy Council between Charles II and the Earl of Clarendon 1660-1667*, ed. W. D. Macray (1896), p. 29.

17 Mordaunt to Hyde, 31 Oct. 1659: *Calendar*, IV, p. 429.

18 Printed in J. P. Kenyon, *The Stuart Constitution* (1966), p. 358.

19 Cf. David Ogg, *England in the Reign of Charles II*, I, p. 165.

20 Anne Whiteman, 'The Restoration of the Church of England' in Geoffrey F. Nuttall and Owen Chadwick, *From Uniformity to Unity 1662-1962* (1962), p. 80.

21 D. T. Witcombe, *Charles II and the Cavalier House of Commons 1663-1674* (1966), p. 2.

22 Mordaunt to Nicholas, Feb. 1660: *Calendar*, IV, p. 552.

23 Cf. Joan Thirsk, 'Sale of Royalist Lands during the Interregnum', *Economic History Review*, 2nd series, V, and 'The Restoration Land Settlement', *Journal of Modern History*, XXVI.

24 *Diary*, III, pp. 280-1.

25 Keith Feiling, *British Foreign Policy 1660-1672* (1930), p. 38.

26 A. Bryant, p. 104.

27 Lansdowne Mss. 1236, f. 124 and v.

28 Lansdowne Mss. 1236, f. 128 and v.

29 Ogg, *England in the Reign of Charles II*, I, p. 128.

8 *Charles and Clarendon* (pages 125 to 143)

1 C. H. Hartmann, p. 155.

2 A. Bryant, p. 111.

3 David Ogg, *England in the Reign of Charles II* (1934), II, p. 197.

4 A. Bryant, p. 115.

5 A. Bryant, pp. 139-40.

6 Speech of 16 May 1664: A. Bryant, p. 165.

7 Cf. Lydia M. Marshall, 'The Levying of the Hearth Tax 1662-1688', *English Historical Review* (1936).

8 Clarendon Mss. 78, f. 58.

9 Speech of 4 Nov. 1664: A. Bryant, p. 172.

10 V. Barbour, *Henry Bennet, Earl of Arlington* (1914), pp. 46-7.

11 Clarendon, *Life*, II, p. 210.

12 Clarendon to Ormonde, 25 Oct. 1662: Clarendon Mss. 78, f. 48.

13 C. H. Hartmann, p. 95.

14 Charles II to Madame, 24 Oct. 1664: Hartmann, p. 115; Feiling, *British Foreign Policy*, p. 125.

15 Charles II to Madame, 15 Dec. 1664: C. H. Hartmann, p. 134.

16 K. D. H. Haley, *The First Earl of Shaftesbury*, p. 187.

17 Clarendon, *Life*, p. 35.

18 Diary, 2 Sept. 1666: Pepys, V, p. 419.

19 Clarendon, *Life*, III, pp. 101-2.

20 A. Bryant, p. 199.

21 Clarendon, *Life*, III, p. 199.

22 Clarendon, *Life*, III, p. 194.

23 Pepys, VI, p. 177.

24 Arlington to Lords Lieutenant, 29 May 1667: PRO Entry Book 20, ff. 145-6.

25 Pepys, 14 June 1667: VI, p. 368.

26 T. H. Lister, *Life and Administration of Edward, First Earl of Clarendon* (1838), II, pp. 402, 421.

27 Lister, *Life and Administration*, p. 424.

28 A. Bryant, p. 204.

29 Clarendon, *Life*, III, p. 283 *et seq.*

30 *Charles II*, p. 223.

9 *The Private Life of Charles II* (pages 144 to 153)

1 Pepys, 8 Sept. 1667: VII, p. 103.
2 Pepys, 11 Nov. 1667: VII, p. 191.
3 Anthony Hamilton, *Count Gramont at the Court of Charles II*, ed. and trans. Nicholas Deakin (1965), p. 5.
4 H. C. Foxcroft, *A Supplement to Burnet's History of My Own Time* (1912), pp. 48-50.
5 William Temple, *Works* (1814), II, pp. 419-20.
6 Charles II to Madame, 7 Feb. 1660: C. H. Hartmann, p. 10.
7 1 Oct. 1661: *Diary*, III, pp. 296-7.
8 July 1666: *Diary*, V, p. 359.
9 *Reresby Memoirs*, ed. A. Browning (1936), p. 259.
10 C. H. Hartmann, pp. 88-9.
11 Pepys, July 1666: V, p. 383.
12 July 1666: IV, p. 373.
13 20 June 1667: VI, p. 381.
14 20 June 1667: VI, p. 381.
15 Pepys, 12 July 1667: VII, p. 17.
16 Hamilton, *Count Gramont*, ed. Deakin, pp. 22-3.
17 *Count Gramont*, ed. Deakin, p. 55.
18 April 1666: V, p. 270.
19 C. H. Hartmann, p. 201.
20 I, p. 160.
21 C. H. Hartmann, *La Belle Stuart* (1924), p. 72 *et seq.*
22 Pepys, 26 Sept. 1666: V, p. 447.
23 C. H. Hartmann, p. 94.
24 Hamilton, *Count Gramont*, ed. Deakin, p. 138.
25 A list is printed in vol. VI of the *Complete Peerage*, but it is almost certain that the father of Lady Castlemaine's daughter, Barbara, was John Churchill. I have reduced the number from fourteen to thirteen.

10 *The Foreign Policy of Charles II 1667–72* (pages 154 to 173)

1 *Négotiations rélatives à la succession d'Espagne sous Louis XIV*, ed. F. A. Mignet (1835), II, p. 43.
2 *Négotiations*, ed. Mignet, II, p. 514.
3 *Négotiations*, ed. Mignet, II, pp. 521-2.
4 C. H. Hartmann, p. 209.
5 Maurice Lee, *The Cabal* (1965), p. 95.

6 John B. Wolf, *Louis XIV* (1968), p. 213.

7 A. Bryant, pp. 214-15.

8 C. H. Hartmann, p. 214.

9 *The Diary of John Milward*, ed. C. Robbins (1938), p. 252.

10 Barbour, *Henry Bennett*, p. 142.

11 C. H. Hartmann, p. 223.

12 J. S. Clarke, *The Life of King James II* (1816), p. 442.

13 C. H. Hartmann, p. 250.

14 Keith Feiling, *British Foreign Policy*, p. 268.

15 Maurice Lee, *The Cabal*, p. 103.

16 John B. Wolf, *Louis XIV*, p. 215.

17 C. H. Hartmann, p. 233.

18 C. H. Hartmann, p. 265.

19 C. H. Hartmann, p. 284.

20 Keith Feiling, *British Foreign Policy*, p. 305.

21 Text in *English Historical Documents 1660-1714*, ed. A. Browning (1953), p. 863 *et seq.*

22 C. H. Hartmann, p. 321.

23 Maurice Lee, *The Cabal*, p. 30.

24 *Memoirs of Thomas, Earl of Ailesbury* (1890), I, p. 104.

25 D. T. Witcombe, *Charles II and the Cavalier House of Commons*, p. 104.

11 *The Break-up of 'the Cabal'* (pages 174 to 192)

1 Ralph Davis, 'Merchant Shipping in the Economy of the Late Seventeenth Century', *Economic History Review*, series 2, no. 9, p. 71.

2 Charles II to William of Orange, 22 April 1672: A. Bryant, p. 249.

3 Cit. D. Ogg, *England in the Reign of Charles II*, II, p. 413.

4 Cf. Ralph Davis, 'English Foreign Trade 1660-1700', *Economic History Review*, series 2, no. 7 (1954).

5 Nov. 4 1670, *The Diary of John Evelyn*, III, p. 564.

6 Arlington to Sir Bernard Gascoigne, *Miscellania Anglicana* (1702), p. 66.

7 Foreign Entry Book 177, 8 March 1672, cit. Barbour, *Henry Bennet*, p. 182.

8 Pierre Goubert, *Louis XIV et vingt millions de Français* (1966), p. 96.

9 Keith Feiling, *British Foreign Policy*, p. 349.

10 Colbert de Croissy to Louis XIV, 9 Nov. 1671, cit. Barbour, *Henry Bennet*, p. 182.

11 Keith Feiling, *History of the Tory Party 1640-1714* (1924), p. 139.

12 Colbert de Croissy to Louis XIV, 7 June 1672, cit. F. Bate, *The Declaration of Indulgence 1672* (1908), p. 89.

13 Speech of 5 Feb. 1673, A. Bryant, p. 260, misdated 4 Feb.

14 A. Grey, II, p. 25.

15 16 Feb. 1673: Foreign Entry Book 177, cit. Barbour, *Henry Bennet*, p. 208.

16 8 March 1673: *The Parliamentary Diary of Sir Edward Dering 1670-1673*, ed. B. D. Henning (1940), p. 134.

17 *Letters addressed from London to Sir Joseph Williamson*, ed. W. D. Christie (1874), I, p. 133.

18 A. Bryant, pp. 270-1; *Parliamentary Diary of Sir E. Dering*, ed. Henning, p. 51.

19 Sir E. Harvey, 31 Oct. 1673: A. Grey, II, p. 202.

20 *Letters to Sir Joseph Williamson*, ed. Christie, II, p. 60.

21 *Letters to Sir Joseph Williamson*, ed. Christie, II, p. 62.

22 Speech of 4 Nov. 1673: A. Bryant, pp. 271-2, misdated 3 Nov.

23 10 Dec. 1673, *CSP (Venetian) 1673-1675*.

24 A. Bryant, pp. 273-4.

25 A. Bryant, pp. 275-6.

26 A. Bryant, p. 276.

12 *Charles the Mediator 1674–7* (pages 193 to 210)

1 Conway to Essex, 28 Feb. 1674: *Essex Papers 1673-1675*, ed. O. Airy (1890), I, p. 181.

2 Ruvigny to Louis XIV, 19 Feb. 1674: *Négotiations*, ed. F. Mignet, IV, p. 268.

3 *History of His Own Time* (1823), II, p. 42.

4 Alberti to the Doge, 9 Mar. 1674: *CSP (Venetian) 1673-1675*, p. 233.

5 Alberti to the Doge, 9 Mar. 1674: *CSP (Venetian) 1673-1675*, p. 234.

6 *The Works of Sir William Temple, Bart* (1814), II, p. 269.

7 Ruvigny to Louis XIV, 18 June and 14 May 1674: Baschet.

8 Ruvigny to Pomponne, 18 June 1674: Baschet.

9 A. de Wicquefort, *Histoire des Provinces Unies des Pais-Bas* (1874), IV, p. 735.

10 Nesca Robb, *William of Orange* (1966), II, p. 28.

11 Conway to Essex, 27 April 1675: *Essex Papers 1675-1677*, II, p. 1.

12 A. Bryant, pp. 280-1.

13 A. Grey, III, p. 3.

14 William Harbord to Essex, 4 May 1675: *Essex Papers*, II, p. 7.

15 Ruvigny to Louis XIV, 2 May 1675: *Négotiations*, ed. Mignet, VI, p. 347.

16 A. Grey, III, p. 136.

17 A. Bryant, p. 282.

18 *Essex Papers*, II, p. 32.

19 A. Bryant, p. 282.

20 *Thomas, Earl of Danby* (1951), I, p. 185.

21 Ruvigny to Louis XIV, 27 Feb. 1676: Dalrymple, *Memoirs* (1790), III, p. 107.

22 Courtin to Louvois, 24 Sept. 1676, cit. C. H. Hartmann, *The Vagabond Duchess* (1926), p. 194.

23 K. D. H. Haley, p. 404.

24 Courtin to Pomponne, 16 July 1676, cit. C. H. Hartmann, *Vagabond Duchess*, p. 184.

25 K. H. D. Haley, 'The Anglo-Dutch Rapprochement of 1677', *English Historical Review*, LXXIII (1958), pp. 623-4.

13 Charles II and the Treaty of Nymegen (pages 211 to 226)

1 A. Bryant, pp. 286-7.

2 A. Grey, IV, p. 201.

3 A. Grey, IV, p. 268.

4 K. D. H. Haley, 'The Anglo-Dutch Rapprochement of 1677', *English Historical Review*, LXXIII (1958), p. 626.

5 A. Grey, V, p. 260.

6 A. Browning, II, p. 67.

7 Courtin to Louis XIV, 12/22 April 1677, cit. *Négotiations*, ed. F. Mignet, IV, p. 445.

8 A. Grey, IV, p. 362.

9 *Commons Journals*, IX, p. 426: cf. *Transactions of the Royal Historical Society*, fourth series, XXX, p. 21.

10 A. Browning, II, p. 70.

11 A. Browning, II, p. 67.

12 W. Temple, *Works* (1814), II, pp. 421-2.

13 Grose says that the sum agreed was 700,000 *écus*; Browning says 2,000,000 *livres tournois*. £145,000 is Ralph Montagu's estimate of the net amount that might have been received in London: A. Browning, II, p. 291.

14 Dalrymple, *Memoirs*, III, p. 113.

15 Temple, *Works*, II, pp. 432-3.

16 *Diary of Dr Edward Lake* (Camden Society, 1846), p. 5.

17 *Diary of Dr Edward Lake*, VI.

18 Dalrymple, *Memoirs*, III, p. 127.

19 A. Bryant, pp. 288-90.

20 Barrillon to Louis XIV, 24 Jan./3 Feb. 1678: Dalrymple, *Memoirs*, III, p. 127.

21 A. Browning, II, pp. 346-9.

22 A. Grey, V, pp. 277-9.

23 A. Grey, V, p. 355; cf. P. W. Thomas, *Sir John Berkenhead 1617-1679* (1969), p. 231.

24 A. Bryant, p. 295.

25 A. Browning, I, p. 282; Burnet, II, p. 140.

26 J. B. Wolf, *Louis XIV*, p. 265.

27 Courtin to Louis XIV, 28 Jan. 1677: Dalrymple, *Memoirs*, III, p. 117.

14 *The Popish Plot and the Fall of Danby* (pages 227 to 246)

1 Add. Mss. 38015, f. 278.

2 Sir Robert Southwell to the Duke of Ormonde, 1 Oct. 1678: *H. M. C. Ormonde*, IV, p. 454.

3 *H. M. C. Ormonde*, IV, p. 207.

4 *H. M. C. Ormonde*, IV, p. 457.

5 Barrillon to Louis XIV, 21 Oct. 1678, cit. John Pollock, *The Popish Plot* (1903), p. 103 n. 2.

6 Roger L'Estrange, *Brief History of the Times* (1688), III, p. 10, cit. K. D. H. Haley, p. 459.

7 Southwell to Ormonde, 19 Oct. 1678: *H. M. C. Ormonde*, IV, p. 459.

8 *H. M. C. Ormonde*, IV, p. 460.

9 *Lords Journals*, XIII, p. 293.

10 L. Echard, *History of England* (1718), III, p. 460, cit. J. R. Jones, *The First Whigs* (1961), p. 23.

11 A. Grey, VI, p. 116.

12 K. D. H. Haley, p. 471.

13 Burnet, II, p. 169.

14 Burnett, II, pp. 168-70.

15 Duchess of Cleveland to Charles II, 18/28 June 1678, cit. P. W. Sergeant, *My Lady Castlemaine*, p. 221.

16 Danby to Montagu, 25 March 1678: A. Browning, II, pp. 346-9.

17 A. Grey, VI, pp. 400-1; *H. M. C. Ormonde*, IV, p. 495.

18 *H. M. C. Ormonde*, IV, p. 495.

19 A. Browning, I, p. 310.

20 *H. M. C. Ormonde*, IV, p. 495.

21 K. D. H. Haley, chaps XX and XXI; cf. David Ogg, *England in the Reign of Charles II*, II, p. 570: 'Shaftesbury, one of the most assiduous coadjutors of Oates, solemnly recorded on paper statements made by boys of 15 and 17 of what had been said to them by a child of 6.'

22 Burnet, II, p. 177; Haley, p. 496.

23 Burnet, II, p. 177.

24 *Hatton Correspondence*, I, p. 177.

25 *The First Whigs*, p. 43.

26 K. D. H. Haley, p. 500; J. R. Jones, 'Shaftesbury's "Worthy Men"',
   Bulletin of the Institute of Historical Research (1957), pp. 232-41.
27 *Lords Journals*, XIII, p. 449.
28 A. Browning, I, p. 322.
29 This is what Mr Bennett (Thomas Bennett?) said in the Commons on
   29 Mar. 1679.
30 Cf. Maurice Ashley, *John Wildman: Plotter and Postmaster* (1947), chaps
   XIV-XVI.
31 D. L. Keir, *The Constitutional History of Modern Britain* (1960), p. 257.

15 *Exclusion – I* (pages 247 to 263)

1 *Works* (1814), II, p. 503.
2 *Works*, pp. 506-7.
3 *Works*, p. 508.
4 *Memoirs of Thomas Bruce, 2nd Earl of Ailesbury* (1890), I, pp. 34-5. For this
   Council see E. R. Turner, 'The Privy Council of 1679', *English Historical
   Review* (1915) and G. Davies, 'Council and Cabinet 1679-1688', *English
   Historical Review* (1922).
5 Burnet, II, p. 199.
6 A. Grey, *Debates*, VI, p. 191, 6 May 1679.
7 Southwell to Ormonde, 9 Aug. 1679, *H. M. C. Ormonde*, IV, 533.
8 *H. M. C. Ormonde*, IV, p. 539.
9 *H. M. C. Ormonde*, pp. 540-1.
10 Sidney, diary 15 Nov. 1679: *Diary of the Times of Charles II*, ed. R. W.
   Blencowe (1843), I, p. 187.
11 'The Journals of Edmund Warcup', *English Historical Review*, XL (1952), p. 245.
12 Southwell to Ormonde, 13 Dec. 1679: *H. M. C. Ormonde*, IV, p. 568.
13 *H. M. C. Ormonde*, IV, p. 574.
14 Cit. K. D. H. Haley, p. 563.
15 K. D. H. Haley, p. 564.
16 12 Mar. 1680: *Diary of the Times of Charles II*, ed. Blencowe, I, p. 301.
17 Barrillon to Louis XIV, 2/12 1680: Baschet.
18 J. P. Kenyon, *Sunderland*, p. 42.
19 16 Mar. 1680: *Diary of the Times of Charles II*, ed. Blencowe, II, p. 7; *CSP
   (Dom.) 1679-1680*, p. 469.
20 Barrillon to Louis XIV, 7/17 June 1680: Baschet.
21 K. D. H. Haley, *Charles II* (1966), p. 19.
22 Temple to Sidney, 27 April 1680: *Diary of the Times of Charles II*, ed. Blencowe, II, pp. 53-4.

23 *Memoirs*, ed. A. Browning, p. 194.

24 E. M. G. Routh, *Tangier* (1912), chap. XVI; P.R.O. 31/3/145, f. 216.

25 Halifax to Sir Thomas Thynne, 5 Oct. 1680: H. Foxcroft, *A Character of the Trimmer* (1946), p. 113.

26 *Life of James II*, I, pp. 596–600.

16 *Exclusion – II* (pages 264 to 282)

1 28 Nov. 1680: *CSP (Dom) 1680*, p. 92.

2 A. Bryant, p. 314.

3 23 Oct. 1680: *H. M. C. Ormonde*, V, p. 456.

4 Sidney diary: *Diary of the Times of Charles II*, ed. Blencowe, II, p. 116.

5 7 Nov. 1680: *Reresby Memoirs*, p. 202.

6 13 Nov. 1680: letter to John Ellis, Add. Mss. 28930 f. 201 v.

7 17 Nov. 1680: A. Grey, VIII, p. 11.

8 25 Nov. 1680: *Diary of the Times of Charles II*, ed. Blencowe, II, p. 134.

9 Cit. J. R. Jones, *The First Whigs*, p. 144.

10 A. Bryant, p. 316.

11 Francis Gwyn to Ormonde, 1 Jan. 1681: *H. M. C. Ormonde*, V, p. 541.

12 *Diary of the Times of Charles II*, ed. Blencowe, II, p. 159.

13 Francis Gwyn to Ormonde: *H. M. C. Ormonde*, V, 555.

14 10 Jan. 1681: *Reresby Memoirs*, p. 210.

15 H. Foxcroft, *Character of the Trimmer*, p. 132.

16 1 Feb. 1681: *H. M. C. Ormonde*, V, p. 570.

17 *Works*, II, pp. 566–7.

18 19 Mar. 1681: *CSP (Dom) 1680–1681*, p. 226.

19 A. Bryant, p. 317, misdated 20 Mar. 1681.

20 Col. Edward Cooke to Ormonde, 24 Mar. 1681: *H. M. C. Ormonde*, V, p. 619.

21 Cooke to Ormonde, 25 Mar. 1681: *H. M. C. Ormonde*, VI, p. 7.

22 Barrillon to Louis XIV, 28 Mar. 1681: Baschet. The dates of these conversations are confusing: see K. D. H. Haley, pp. 634–5 and notes 1 and 2. Cooke appears to suggest that one conversation took place on 24 or 25 March and Barrillon that the other took place on 26 March. My guess is that it was all the same conversation.

23 A. Bryant, p. 319.

24 *Diary of the Times of Charles II*, ed. Blencowe, II, p. 186.

25 A. Bryant, p. 319 *et seq.*, 8 April 1681.

26 11 April 1681: *CSP (Dom) 1680–1681*, p. 236.

27 24 Mar./3 April 1681: P.R.O. 31/3/148 f. 93 v.

28 9/19 June 1681: P.R.O. 31/3/148 f. 159.

29 Information of Charles Rea, 7 April 1681: *CSP (Dom) 1680-1681*, p. 232.

30 *CSP (Dom) 1680-1681*, p. 254.

31 Arran to Ormonde, 12 Mar. 1681: *H. M. C. Ormonde*, v, p. 609.

32 *State Trials* (ed. W. Cobbett, 1809-28), VIII, p. 426.

17 *The King Hits Back* (pages 283 to 298)

1 15 Dec. 1682, *English Historical Review* (1925), XL, p. 258.

2 L. Jenkins to the Sheriff of Oxfordshire, 22 Aug. 1681: *CSP (Dom) 1680-1681*, p. 412.

3 19 Oct. 1681: *Reresby Memoirs*, p. 234.

4 Sir Charles Lyttleton to Lord Hatton, 11 Oct. 1681: *Hatton Correspondence* ed. E. M. Thompson (1878), II, p. 8.

5 to L. Jenkins, 27 Sep. 1681: *CSP (Dom) 1680-1681*, p. 472.

6 29 Nov. 1681: *Reresby Memoirs*, p. 238.

7 J. B. Wolf, *Louis XIV*, chap. 25.

8 18/28 April: Baschet.

9 L. Hyde to William of Orange, 24 May 1681: G. Groen van Prinsterer, Archives (1862), v, p. 501.

10 25 Sep./5 Oct. 1681: Baschet.

11 11 Oct. 1681: Halifax to William: Prinsterer, *Archives*, v, p. 527.

12 12/22 Dec. 1681: Baschet.

13 Burnet, II, p. 323.

14 Cit. K. D. H. Haley, p. 704.

15 12 June 1683, Sunderland to Jenkins: *CSP (Dom) 1683*, p. 311; *State Trials*, VIII, p. 1281.

16 2 June 1682, Halifax to William: Prinsterer, *Archives*, v, p. 552.

17 10/20 Aug. 1682: Baschet.

18 Ford Grey, *Secret History of the Rye House Plot* (1754), pp. 19-20.

19 Burnet, I, p. 586.

20 4 Oct. 1683, *Diary of John Evelyn*, ed. de Beer, IV, p. 343.

21 26 Jan. 1682: *Diary of John Evelyn*, ed. de Beer, IV, p. 120.

22 26 Jan. 1682: *CSP (Dom) 1682*, p. 43.

23 21 Mar./1 April 1684: Baschet.

24 Carte Mss. 216, f. 371 *et seq*.

25 Charles liked the proposed twenty-year truce when he first heard of it as early as February: Jenkins to Arran, Carte Mss. 216 f., 423.

26 30 June/10 July 1684: Baschet.

27 11/21 Aug. 1684: Baschet.

28 11/21 Aug 1684: Baschet.

29 18/28 Aug 1684: Baschet.

18 *The Last Years* (pages 299 to 313)

1 4 Jan. 1683: *CSP (Dom) 1683*, p. 3.

2 5 Sept. 1682: *Hatton Correspondence*, ed. Thompson, II, p. 19.

3 26 Sept. 1682: *Hatton Correspondence*, ed. Thompson, II, p. 20.

4 21 Feb. 1683: *Hatton Correspondence*, ed. Thompson, II, p. 70.

5 18 Feb. 1683: *Hatton Correspondence*, ed. Thompson, II, p. 61.

6 20 Feb. 1683: *Hatton Correspondence*, ed. Thompson, II, p. 66.

7 18 April 1683: *Hatton Correspondence*, ed. Thompson, II, p. 186.

8 See Maurice Ashley, *John Wildman*, chap. XVIII for the details of the argument that the idea of the murder plot stemmed from Wildman.

9 14 July 1683: *Hatton Correspondence*, ed. Thompson, II, p. 29.

10 19 July 1683: Russell to the King, *State Trials*, IX, p. 688.

11 *Ailesbury Memoirs*, I, pp. 66, 73; *Secret History of the Rye House Plot*, p. 30.

12 A. F. Havighurst, 'The Judiciary and Politicians in the Reign of Charles II', *Law Quarterly Review* (1950).

13 G. W. Keeton, *Lord Chancellor Jeffreys and the Stuart Cause* (1965).

14 A. F. Havighurst, in *LQR*, p. 249.

15 *Ailesbury Memoirs*, I, p. 83.

16 13 Oct. 1683: Monmouth's diary, cit. A. Fea, *King Monmouth* (1902), p. 171.

17 Fea, *King Monmouth*, p. 184.

18 P.R.O. 31/3/157, f. 143 and v.

19 *Ailesbury Memoirs*, I, pp. 23-4.

20 30 Mar. 1683: Ormonde to Arran: *H. M. C. Ormonde*, VII, p. 3.

21 30 Jan. 1684: *Reresby Memoirs*, p. 329.

22 21/31 July 1684: Baschet.

23 Rochester to Ormonde, 25 Sep. 1684: *H. M. C. Ormonde*, VII, p. 274.

24 H. Foxcroft, *A Character of the Trimmer*, pp. 204-5.

25 16/26 Oct. 1684: Baschet.

26 James to Queensberry, cit. F. C. Turner, *James II*, p. 224.

27 E. S. de Beer, 'King Charles II, Fundator et Patronus 1630-1685', *Notes and Records of the Royal Society of London*, vol. 15 (1960), p. 42. It has been argued that Charles died of mercury poisoning, but Dr Crawfurd's arguments (see note 30 below) that Charles died of chronic grandular kidney, a form of Bright's disease with uraemic convulsions, are persuasive.

28 *Ailesbury Memoirs*, I, p. 85.

29 *Ailesbury Memoirs*, I, p. 88.

30 Raymund Crawfurd, *The Last Days of Charles II* (1909), pp. 14-16.

31 H. Foxcroft, *Character of the Trimmer*, p. 210.

32 *H. M. C. Egmont*, II, p. 147.

19 *The Man and the Statesman* (pages 314 to 326)

1 'A Character of Charles II', *Halifax Complete Works*, ed. J. P. Kenyon (1969), p. 261.

2 K. D. H. Haley, pp. 173, 175; A. Browning, I, p. 236 note 4, quoting Add. Mss. 28094, f. 54.

3 Cf. W. G. Hiscock, *John Evelyn and Mrs Godolphin* (1951), especially chap. VIII.

4 I owe these quotations to F. C. Turner, *James II*, pp. 91-5.

5 *Complete Works*, p. 248.

6 *The Diary of John Evelyn*, IV, pp. 476-9 and 477 note 1.

7 Cf. Maurice Ashley, *The Greatness of Oliver Cromwell* (1966), p. 197.

8 C. L. Grose, 'Louis XIV's Financial Relations with Charles II and the English Parliament', *Journal of Modern History*, I (1929): I make the total 18,000,000 livres tournois between 1671 and 1684, but from one payment of 2,000,000 livres tournois sixteen per cent was deducted and some was still owing at the time of Charles II's death.

9 Professor J. P. Kenyon makes this point in his book, *The Stuarts* (1958), p. 149.

10 Cf. D. T. Witcombe, *Charles II and the Cavalier House of Commons*, p. 104 quoting Professor Chandaman.

11 W. A. Shaw, *Calendar of Treasury Books*, vii, *1680-1685* (1916), XVI.

12 Shaw, *Calender of Treasury Books*, XVIII.

13 Professor J. R. Jones has pointed out to me that this argument is supported by D'Avaux, the French ambassador to the United Netherlands, who 'assumed that loyalty of Englishmen was, in the last resort, assured by the reserve of French support'.

14 This paragraph is based on four articles by J. R. Tanner, 'The administration of the navy from the Restoration to the Revolution', *English Historical Review*, XII-XIV; cf. also David Ogg, *England in the Reign of Charles II*, chap. VII and A. Bryant, *Samuel Pepys*.

15 Cf. Maurice Ashley, *The Glorious Revolution of 1688* (1968), p. 181.

16 *England in the Reign of Charles II*, chap. XIX.

17 Christopher Hill, *The Century of Revolution 1603-1714* (1961), pp. 215, 318; R. Davis, 'English Foreign Trade 1660-1700', *Economic History Review*, series 2, no. 7 (1954).

Appendix

Charles II and the Mistresses by whom he had Children

LUCY WALTER or BARLOW (1630–58)
James Scott, Duke of Monmouth (1649–85).

ELIZABETH KILLIGREW, LADY SHANNON
Charlotte (born *c.* 1650).

CATHERINE PEGGE
Charles FitzCharles, Earl of Plymouth (*c.* 1650–80).

BARBARA VILLIERS or PALMER, COUNTESS OF CASTLEMAINE AND DUCHESS OF CLEVELAND (1641–1709)
Anne Fitzroy (born 1661) married Thomas Lennard, Earl of Sussex; Charles Fitzroy, first Duke of Cleveland (1662–1730); Henry Fitzroy, Duke of Grafton (1663–90); Charlotte Fitzroy (1664–1718) married first Earl of Lichfield and George Fitzroy, Duke of Northumberland (1665–1718).

NELL or ELEANOR GWYN (1650–87)
Charles Beauclerk, Duke of St Albans (1670–1726) and James Beauclerk (1671–80).

LOUISE-RENÉE DE PENANCOET DE KÉROUALLE, DUCHESS OF PORTSMOUTH (1649–1734)
Charles Lennox, Duke of Richmond (1672–1723).

MOLL or MARY DAVIS (fl. 1663–9)
Mary Tudor (1665–1705) married the Earl of Derwentwater.

Since this book went to press Stephen Parkes and Timothy Crist published in *The Times Literary Supplement* of 30 April 1971 extracts from some newly discovered letters of Charles II now deposited in Yale University. They are personal letters written by the King to Lord Taafe (later the Earl of Carlingford) and throw some light on Lucy Walter and Charles's personal life in 1655–1660. I quote from one of these letters on page 87.

Index